Palgrave Macmillan Series in Global
Public Diplomacy

Series Editors
Philip Seib
Annenberg School for Communication
and Journalism
University of Southern California
Pasadena, CA, USA

Kathy Fitzpatrick
Washington, USA

At no time in history has public diplomacy played a more significant role in world affairs and international relations. As a result, global interest in public diplomacy has escalated, creating a substantial academic and professional audience for new works in the field.

The *Global Public Diplomacy* Series examines theory and practice in public diplomacy from a global perspective, looking closely at public diplomacy concepts, policies, and practices in various regions of the world. The purpose is to enhance understanding of the importance of public diplomacy, to advance public diplomacy thinking, and to contribute to improved public diplomacy practices.

More information about this series at
http://www.palgrave.com/gp/series/14680

Ilan Manor

The Digitalization of Public Diplomacy

Ilan Manor
Department of International
Development
University of Oxford
Oxford, UK

Palgrave Macmillan Series in Global Public Diplomacy
ISBN 978-3-030-04404-6   ISBN 978-3-030-04405-3   (eBook)
https://doi.org/10.1007/978-3-030-04405-3

Library of Congress Control Number: 2018961425

This Palgrave Macmillan imprint is published by the registered company Springer Nature
Switzerland AG
The registered company address is: Gewerbestrasse 11, 6330 Cham, Switzerland

To the memories of First Lieutenant Lotan Slavin &
First Sergeant Ran Hendifer

ACKNOWLEDGEMENTS

In this book, I have relied on the support, insight and research of four public diplomacy scholars. Without them, this book would not have come to fruition. The first of these is Corneliu Bjola, whose mentorship has awarded me the skills and encouragement necessary to undertake academic research. The second is James Pamment. Our academic collaborations and conversations about diplomacy have substantially shaped my own research endeavors. The third is Jan Melissen, who first introduced me to the world of public diplomacy and has always been kind enough to review my work and offer much needed feedback. The fourth is Philip Seib, whose work on real-time diplomacy inspired this book. I am also indebted to five of my peers, who each reviewed a different section of this book and thus contributed to it immensely. Chief among these is Elad Segev. I consider myself a fortunate person to have met Elad and continue to learn from him daily. Additional reviewers have included my collaborator Efe Sevin, my friend Susan Jackson, and my visual guide Rhys Crilley. I would also like to thank Giles Strachan, whose passion for history, art, and the English language can be found on nearly every page of this book. I dare say that I would have never become interested in diplomacy had it not been for my father's decision to embark on a diplomatic career. He has taught me that in life wings are as important as roots. He has also remained my chief copy editor, soundboard, and source of diplomatic tales that can be found throughout this book's various chapters. I could not have conducted any of the quantitative analysis found in this book without the guiding hand of my chief statistician,

Orly Manor, who lovingly took with her my statistical data to Geneva, Greece, and beyond. I would also like to thank our family's resident author, Michael Karpin who not only helped edit this book but also supplied me with a steady stream of articles and video pertaining to the state of the world today. This book was written in Oxford during the summer and autumn of 2018. I would not have made it to Oxford, let alone to this book, had it not been for Amir Mandel, Yonatan Pesses, Yaara Rosolio and the Weidenfeld-Hoffmann Trust. And so this book is as much theirs as it is mine. I am also indebted to a group of diplomats who were kind enough to be interviewed for this book. These include Alexadra Lutyens, Elad Ratson, Graham Lampe, Laurens Soenen, and Rytis Paulauskas. Whenever the task of writing became too daunting, I could rely on the support of Patrick Thewlis of the University of Oxford and our fellow soccer team members. It was they who helped me move from one chapter to the next. I would also like to thank the editors of this series for allowing me to share my thoughts and research on public diplomacy. Above all, I am grateful to my family members, Oren, Shiri, Itay and Gilad, who have talked of nothing else but public diplomacy for three months, and of course to Amit, the joy of my life.

CONTENTS

LIST OF FIGURES

LIST OF TABLES

CHAPTER 1

Introduction

Diplomacy is, perhaps, one element of the U.S. government that should not be subject to the demands of 'open government'; whenever it works, it is usually because it is done behind closed doors. But this may be increasingly hard to achieve in the age of Twittering bureaucrats.

—Evgeny Morozov

INTRODUCTION

September of 1814 was the scene of unprecedented commotion, even by the standards of imperial Vienna. The city, adorned by the golden leaves of early autumn, was host to more than 200 diplomats who had assembled for the Congress of Vienna. These were accompanied by herds of assistants, chefs de cabinet, journalists, and intellectuals, resulting in a 33% increase in the city's inhabitants. Yet even this great clamor of Europe's elite was but the backdrop for the month's main attraction: the procession of allied sovereigns who descended upon Vienna with all their majesty.

The Imperial Palace, the Hofburg, was soon overrun with preparations for hosting the sovereigns of Europe. The Russian Tsar, as well as the Kings of Prussia, Denmark, and Bavaria, were to be the personal guests of the Austrian Emperor, and banquets held in their honor demanded no fewer than 300 carriages with 1400 horses. Other dignitaries, including 11 ruling princes, occupied whatever palaces and hotels

© The Author(s) 2019
I. Manor, *The Digitalization of Public Diplomacy*,
Palgrave Macmillan Series in Global Public Diplomacy,
https://doi.org/10.1007/978-3-030-04405-3_1

Vienna had to offer, bringing with them fleets of servants, ministers, and delegates (Jarrett, 2013).

The Congress of Vienna is an exemplar of traditional diplomacy. A group of like-minded, European, middle-aged male aristocrats convened in an imperial capital to decide the fate of some 23 million Europeans. Napoleon had already been defeated, peace had been negotiated, and the monarchy had been reinstated in France. The purpose of the Congress was thus not to negotiate peace, but to ensure its durability by balancing the respective power of European empires.

The flurry of social activities that accompanied the Congress offered diplomats ample time to coordinate their negotiating tactics. These included lavish banquets, a masquerade ball, a traditional joust, and a performance of the Seventh Symphony conducted by its composer, Ludwig van Beethoven (ibid.). Under the magnificent chandeliers of the Hofburg ballroom, or amid its inner sanctums where all noise was muffled by red velvet carpets, French and allied diplomats huddled in small groups to prepare for each day's deliberations. Yet even they were not privy to the secret negotiations in which European sovereigns carved up a continent, while in the background a string quartet made love to Mozart. This was the world of traditional diplomacy, one that ceased to exist in World War I, a world that Stefan Zweig referred to as the world of yesterday (Zweig, 1953).

Nearly two centuries later, diplomats from six modern powers descended upon Vienna to peacefully resolve the crisis surrounding Iran's nuclear weapons program. Vienna had markedly changed by then, as did the diplomats who now inhabited it. The negotiations no longer took place in the Hofburg (now one the of the world's most popular museums) but in the Coburg hotel. The negotiators were no longer like-minded, aristocratic, or even European, as they included the foreign ministers of the USA, China, and Iran. Europeans were not represented by a monarch anointed by God but by Mrs. Federica Mogherini, who was appointed by a European Parliament, and the lavish masquerade balls were replaced by the all too familiar salmon dinners.

Yet perhaps the greatest difference between the Iran negotiations and the Congress of Vienna lies in the influence of digital technologies. World leaders did not attend these talks, but were kept abreast on their progress in real time via teleconferencing, Skype conversations, and text messages. Journalists sitting in hotel lobbies with laptops on their knees continuously published news stories describing the mood among key negotiators. These stories reached a global, digital, public brought together through a World Wide Web of connections. Even social media was employed during the negotiations, both to force one side to make concessions and announce major breakthroughs (Duncombe, 2017).

In fact, Twitter had accompanied the Iran negotiations from their humble beginnings. The journey to Vienna began two years earlier on Lake Geneva. Representatives of the five permanent members of the UN Security Council and Germany met opposite Iranian diplomats for the first direct talks regarding the Islamic Republic's nuclear ambitions. These intense negotiations ended with a preliminary agreement in which Iran agreed to partially halt advancement in its nuclear program in exchange for the lifting of certain economic sanctions. News that an interim agreement had been reached first broke when Iran's foreign minister, Javad Zarif, took to Twitter to publish the tweet in Fig. 1.1.

The Iranian foreign minister's tweet was meant to reach a diverse global audience consisting of diplomats and diplomatic institutions, journalists, newspaper editors, bloggers, Non-governmental organizations (NGOs) and connected individuals hoping to learn about events shaping their world. As this book will demonstrate, all these audiences now comprise the constituency of public diplomacy.

Zarif's tweet was thus not a faux pas or an act of mischief, but rather a well-timed announcement that enabled the foreign minister to determine how and when the world learned about the results of the negotiations. Even more importantly, the tweet enabled Zarif to control the

Fig. 1.1 Iranian foreign minister announces a deal has been struck (*Source* https://twitter.com/JZarif/status/404430013488852993)

media's coverage of the agreement as newspapers throughout the world announced that Iran's foreign minister, and not the US Secretary of State, confirmed that a deal had been struck. Zarif could therefore be depicted as the victor of the negotiations, and to the victor go the spoils.

By turning to Twitter, the Iranian diplomat was also forging a new image for his nation. In 2013, social media sites such as Facebook and Twitter were still regarded as positive forces in society and the weapon de jour of democratic revolutionaries. Facebook, it was argued, facilitated the mass protests in Egypt's Tahrir Square, while Twitter enabled the Green Revolution in Iran (Arsenault, 2013). By employing social media, Zarif associated Iran with democracy and the hopeful spirit of the Arab Spring, as opposed to religious zeal and weapons of mass destruction. Even Zarif's profile image on Twitter, showcasing the statesman looking hopefully to the future, was part of Iran's global rebranding attempt nicknamed "the Charm Offensive" (*The Economist*, 2013).

One can only imagine how the Kings of Denmark and Prussia would have reacted to a similar tweet published from within the Hofburg Palace. Would they have found it a vulgar display of populism? A vain attempt by an elder statesman to appear "folksy" by interacting with the common man? Or would they have viewed it as an outrageous breach of protocol? In 1814, official summaries of international summits were carefully drafted documents that had been read, edited, re-read, and approved by a series of civil servants and the various parties seated at the negotiation table. Zarif's tweet might have therefore been seen as an insult or a violation of trust. Perhaps the European sovereigns would have simply been petrified by this tweet, realizing that diplomacy was no longer secret, that diplomats were no longer hidden from the public's eye and that treaties would now have to be ratified in the court of public opinion. Not even the string quartet making love to Mozart could have eased the angst of an 1814 diplomat forced to practice twenty-first-century public diplomacy.

Selling the Iran Deal

Once a breakthrough had been reached at the 2015 Vienna nuclear talks, the foreign ministers of all seven nations took part in a time-honored diplomatic tradition: the photograph opportunity. Posing opposite their national flags, the architects of the agreement stood shoulder to shoulder on a large stage blinded by the flashing of cameras. This time, however, images of smiling diplomats were not disseminated solely by journalist and news agencies. The Ministries of Foreign Affairs (MFAs) of the EU, UK, USA, France, Germany, Russia and Iran all took to social media to announce that the Iranian crisis had been peacefully resolved. The EU's foreign service even live-tweeted the press conference held by Zarif and Federica Mogherini while updating followers in real-time on the terms of the agreement, the concessions made by each side and the new relationship envisioned between Iran and the world. By the end of the day, the EU's foreign service published the entire Iran agreement which could be read, debated, and shared by digital publics throughout the world (Fig. 1.2).

Fig. 1.2 Press conference announcing the Iran nuclear agreement (*Source* https://twitter.com/eu_eeas/status/620905968046604288)

However, the Vienna photograph opportunity was but a moment's distraction from the arduous task facing these diplomats: ratifying the Iranian agreement in their domestic parliaments. For the Obama administration, the ratification process would prove especially complicated given the need to gather support from Republican lawmakers and pacify the concerns of U.S. allies in the Middle East. The Republican-held Congress had voiced its opposition to the Iranian negotiations since their beginning in 2013. Some Congressmen argued that the "Iran Deal" was a betrayal of America's longstanding friends in the Middle East, namely Saudi Arabia and Israel. Other lawmakers likened the deal to Neville Chamberlain's appeasement of Hitler in the 1938 Munich Agreement (Bjola & Manor, 2018).

American legislators may have had genuine concerns about the Iran Deal and the concessions made to Iran. Others may have seen it as a springboard for launching the next phase of their political careers. Future presidential hopefuls Ted Cruz, Donald Trump and Marco Rubio were among the most ardent opponents of the Iran Deal, both offline and on Twitter (Fig. 1.3).

Fig. 1.3   Presidential hopefuls opposing Iran Deal on Twitter (*Source* https:// twitter.com/tedcruz/status/637244524352278529)

Domestic opposition was not the only hurdle facing the Obama White House. Throughout the Iran negotiations, Israel's Prime Minister, Benjamin Netanyahu, repeatedly told the media that Iran was an existential threat to Israel. He argued that Iran had deceived the international community in the past and would do so again in the future. Netanyahu also stated that no deal should be made with a nation that openly calls for the destruction of Israel or the Jewish State, as this would be tantamount to repeating the mistakes of the past.

If President Obama hoped he would have time to charm Prime Minister Netanyahu into acquiescence, be it through grand state dinners at the White House or new military aid packages, he was mistaken. Within hours of the announcement in Vienna, Netanyahu employed Twitter to criticize the deal, highlight the many compromises made to appease Iran, and lament the fact that Israel's security had once again been forsaken by world powers. The Israeli PM added that Israel retained the right to act militarily against any nation that posed a threat to its existence (Figs. 1.4 and 1.5).

The immediate response of world leaders to the Iran Deal announcement demonstrates the speed at which diplomacy is currently practiced. News of the 1814 Congress of Vienna took a few days to reach Berlin, while news of the 2015 Iran Deal took a few seconds to reach Jerusalem. Prime Minister Netanyahu's rebuke of the Iran Deal also demonstrates that digital platforms are now contested arenas in which different actors,

PM of Israel ✓
@IsraeliPM

☼ Following

PM: The leading international powers have bet our collective future on a deal with the foremost sponsor of international terrorism.»

RETWEETS   LIKES
219   121

6:19 PM - 14 Jul 2015

↰ 16   ⇄ 219   ♥ 121   •••

Fig. 1.4 Prime Minister Netanyahu denouncing the Iran Deal (1) (*Source* https://twitter.com/IsraeliPM/status/620975954291064833)

Israel is not bound by this deal with Iran
because Iran continues to seek our destruction.
We will always defend ourselves.

Fig. 1.5 Prime Minister Netanyahu denouncing the Iran Deal (2) (*Source* https://twitter.com/IsraeliPM/status/620976500158771200)

nations, and diplomats promote their narration of global events while vying over the attention and support of digital publics.

The Iran Deal proved a hard sell for the Obama administration, one that would require winning over both domestic and foreign publics. The communications strategy decided upon included the launching of a dedicated Twitter channel, @theIranDeal, that would explain to the American public and skeptical foreign populations the terms of the Iran agreement and portray it as a suitable alternative to war (Toosi, 2015). The use of Twitter to secure foreign policy achievements both at home and abroad is but one example of digital technologies' impact on public diplomacy. Social media sites such as Twitter blur the distinctions between the global and the local. This is because the same social media profile attracts domestic and foreign audiences and facilitates interactions with both domestic and foreign constituencies. This leads to a form of "glocalized" public diplomacy in which foreign policy practitioners target both local and global publics, as was the case with the Obama White House when it launched the @theIranDeal Twitter channel (Fig. 1.6).

On Tuesday, the 21st of July, at 2:30 in the afternoon the @theIranDeal Twitter channel was inaugurated in a social media blitz. In the days and weeks that followed, White House staffers continuously tweeted about the restrictions placed on Iran, the methods through which the world could verify that Iran had abandoned its nuclear

Fig. 1.6   The Iran Deal Twitter channel (The Iran Deal Twitter page. *Source* https://twitter.com/TheIranDeal)

ambitions, the ability of the USA to "snap" economic sanctions back into place if Iran violated the agreement, and even testimonials from Ernest Moniz, Secretary of Energy and nuclear physicist, who explained to audiences that hiding uranium from international inspectors was scientifically impossible (Bjola & Manor, 2018). Special infographics and images were designed in advance with the aim of winning public support, which would translate into congressional ratification of the agreement.

Moreover, the @theIranDeal account constantly rebuked arguments made by Republican lawmakers against the Iran agreement. These activities are also demonstrative of digital technologies' impact on public diplomacy, as digital publics now expect to learn about events as they occur. The digital age is, after all, the age of instant connectivity. As Philip Seib has argued, the need to immediately comment on world events and the actions of global actors has given rise to a form of real-time public diplomacy (Seib, 2012) (Fig. 1.7).

Notably, the Iran Deal was also promoted by the U.S. government in a global Twitter campaign that was intended to reach a host of constituencies, ranging from domestic media outlets to global media organizations, journalists, parliamentarians, other members of the diplomatic community, and digital publics assembled online, eager to make sense of their world. Tweets emphasizing the achievements of the Iran Deal and portraying it as a validation of President Obama's policy of engagement were published by the White House, Vice President Biden, Secretary of Energy Moniz, Secretary of State John Kerry, the State Department, the Under Secretary of State for Public Diplomacy, the National Security Advisor, the Deputy National Security Advisor, the U.S. Ambassador to the UN,

Fig. 1.7 Infographics prepared by @theIranDeal Twitter channel (*Source* https://twitter.com/TheIranDeal/status/624231943362748417)

the U.S. missions to the UN in New York and Geneva, and American embassies all over the world (Manor, 2015). These activities enabled the American government to promote a single narrative on a planetary scale, thus possibly shaping the opinions and attitudes of individuals all over the world. The blurring of domestic and foreign constituencies, the emergence of "glocalized" public diplomacy, the need to comment on events in near-real time, and the use of Twitter to announce breakthroughs in negotiations are all part of the digitalization of public diplomacy.

What Is the Digitalization of Public Diplomacy?

James Pamment has argued that for most of the twentieth century, the term "public diplomacy" was associated with the term "propaganda". As a communicative act, public diplomacy was the communication of an international actor's policies to the populations of foreign countries (Pamment, 2013). The intent of such communication, according to Gifford Malone (1988), was to influence the behavior of a foreign government by influencing the attitudes of its citizens (Spry, 2018). In the words of William Roberts (2007), public diplomacy included activities that aimed to create a positive climate among foreign publics to facilitate the acceptance of another nation's foreign policy.

Twentieth-century public diplomacy conceptualized influence in three ways. First, public diplomacy was predicated on the assumption that there were certain influential groups within society that should be targeted by public diplomacy actors, be they MFAs, embassies, or international broadcasters. Second, public diplomacy activities aimed to influence the opinions, beliefs, and behaviors of these elites. Third, these elites would, in turn, be expected to influence their governments' policies (Pamment, 2013, pp. 6–8).

Communication technologies such as radio and television were the mediums through which public diplomacy messages could be disseminated among foreign elites. As the medium is the message, twentieth-century public diplomacy consisted of one-way flows of information that saw limited interaction between messengers and recipients and allowed diplomats to tightly control their messages (ibid.). Radio broadcasts, posters, and other mass media did not offer foreign elites the opportunity to respond to or contest public diplomacy messages. Twentieth-century public diplomacy was thus a monologic one, or one that relied on monologue. Like Shakespeare's Hamlet, diplomats would pontificate the meaning of life, both asking "to be or not to be" and offering an answer to that question. The dawn of the twenty-first century, however, saw a conceptual shift among scholars and practitioners of public diplomacy referred to as the "new" public diplomacy. The instigators of the "new" public diplomacy were the 9/11 terror attacks, the emergence of a global media ecology, and the rise of the digital society.

In the wake of the 9/11 terror attacks, the Bush administration declared a War on Terror and a war over the hearts and minds of the Muslim world. America's need to create relationships with Muslim communities led to a global debate on the merits of traditional, monologic public diplomacy (Manor, 2016). Importantly, Muslim communities had, by now, migrated to digital platforms and were coming under the influence of Al-Qaeda's digital narrative of holy Jihad against Western imperialism. Already in 2008, it was estimated that 80% of youths recruited to jihadi groups were contacted on the Internet (Hallams, 2010).

Additionally, globalization created a new media landscape in which public diplomacy would be conducted. The planetary proliferation of Information and Communication Technologies (ICTs) and digital technologies gave rise to a global media ecology characterized by continuous flows of information within and between networks of connected individuals. Notably, these flows of information were not restricted by space, time, or national borders. This global media ecology posed three challenges to the practice of traditional public diplomacy. First, diplomats and MFAs lost their monopoly over diplomatic communication as NGOs, civil society organizations, activists, bloggers, and even terrorist groups could disseminate public diplomacy messages online (Pamment, 2013). Second, "new" public diplomacy actors, such as NGOs and bloggers, transformed the digital world into a competitive arena in which multiple actors vied for the attention of digital audiences while trying to influence their understanding of world events (Manor, 2016). Third, the globalized media ecology led to the fragmentation of the audiences of public diplomacy to "networks of selective exposure," as Craig Hayden has brilliantly argued (Hayden, 2012). While some people learned about the world through Facebook, others turned to bloggers or traditional news sites. Gone were the days when diplomats could communicate with large segments of a foreign population through a small number of newspapers or news shows.

Lastly, the digital society is predicated on dialogue and not monologue. As this book will demonstrate, members of the digital society do not merely absorb information; they comment on it, edit it, redistribute it, and engage with its authors (Spry, 2018). Content creation and dissemination lead to the formation of digital collaborations and relationships, be it in the form of individual ties, communities, or networks. Monologic public diplomacy is thus ill-suited for the task of communicating with digital publics. A diplomat tweeting "To be or not to be" would nowadays be flooded with responses and GIFs from digital publics.

The 9/11 terrorist attacks, the emergence of a global media ecology, and the rise of the digital society would all be manifest in the definitions of the "new" public diplomacy. Jan Melissen (2005) defined the "new" public diplomacy as one that centers on engaging with "connected" publics while transitioning from monologue toward dialogue, engagement, and long-term relationship building. Nicholas Cull (2008) defined the "new" public diplomacy as a process through which international actors seek to accomplish their foreign policy goals by engaging with foreign publics. James Pamment (2013) stated that two-way communication was the very essence of the "new" public diplomacy that was dialogical, collaborative, and inclusive as it no longer focused on elites, but rather on foreign citizens. Moreover, the "new" public diplomacy represented a clear break from twentieth-century broadcast models while taking advantage of new digital technologies such as social media sites (ibid.). Influence could now be obtained through tweets, posts, and engagement.

Importantly, Melissen (2005) and Seo (2013) argued that the intent of public diplomacy also changed at the turn of the century. While the "new" public diplomacy still aimed to persuade foreign publics, it hoped to do so through dialogue and acknowledging the importance of audiences' opinions, values, and beliefs. The focus of the "new" public diplomacy was thus on creating and leveraging relationships with foreign publics to create a receptive environment for another nation's foreign policy. Other scholars maintained that the "new" public diplomacy was relational in nature or focused on creating relationships, and as such, the goal of online dialogue was dialogue itself, not influence (Brown, 2013; Causey & Howard, 2013). Bruce Gregory amply summarized the logic of the "new" and relational approaches stating that "public diplomacy is now an instrument used by states, associations of states and non-state actors to understand cultures, attitudes and behaviors, to build and manage relationships and to mobilize actions that advance one's interests" (Gregory, 2011, p. 353).

Daryl Copeland (2013) has asserted that in a world prone to crises, reaching out to new partners is key to increasing stability. Thus, he views the "new" public diplomacy as one that reaches out to and engages with new stakeholders such as NGOs, civil society organizations, and networked individuals. However, Copeland has also argued that in a complex world, MFAs must explain to their citizens what is happening in the world and what their state is doing in return. The "new" public diplomacy might therefore focus on engaging with both domestic and foreign populations.

Public diplomacy scholars and practitioners soon came to regard digital platforms as the medium of the "new" public diplomacy as such platforms enable organizations to transition from broadcast to communicative paradigms which are centered on mutual interactions (McNutt, 2014). Moreover, relationships are the foundations of digital platforms, as is the case with social media sites (Waters, Burnett, Lamm, & Lucas, 2009) which also provide ideal conditions for two-way engagement as organizations, and publics can discuss issues of mutual concern (Bortree & Seltzer, 2009). The initial adoption of digital technologies by diplomatic institutions was thus intrinsically linked to the goals and logic of the "new" public diplomacy. Through social media sites, diplomats could foster relationships with connected publics, while virtual embassies could serve as platforms for debating issues of shared concern. It was thus in the realm of public diplomacy that twenty-first-century digital technologies debuted in international relations.

The emergence of the "new" public diplomacy has been accompanied by the rapid adoption of digital technologies by MFAs, embassies, and diplomats the world over. To date, scholars have offered a plethora of terms to conceptualize the utilization of digital technologies in the conduct of public diplomacy. These have included, among others, "public diplomacy 2.0" (Hallams, 2010), "virtual diplomacy," "net diplomacy" (Wehrenfennig, 2012) and "digital diplomacy" (Bjola & Holmes, 2015). It is the contention of this book that none of these terms amply captures the impact of digital technologies on the conduct of public diplomacy. This is because diplomatic institutions do not exist in a binary state of being (either digital or non-digital), nor can they be separated into those who have digitalized their public diplomacy activities and those that have not. Additionally, terms such as "public diplomacy 2.0" and "net diplomacy" relate to the utilization of specific digital technologies including Wikis, social media, and the Internet. Yet diplomatic institutions now employ a host of digital technologies ranging from smartphone applications such as WhatsApp to sentiment analysis tools and algorithms written by diplomats.

The term "digital diplomacy", which is often used as a synonym for "digitalized public diplomacy", also suggests that the use of digital tools is its own subset of diplomacy. Just as there is bilateral diplomacy and multilateral diplomacy, so diplomats practice digital diplomacy. However, digital tools are employed by MFAs and diplomats to obtain certain diplomatic goals, be they in the realm of public or multi-lateral diplomacy. Ambassadors to UN forums use WhatsApp groups to coordinate their votes on various resolutions while press attachés use Twitter direct messages to interact with journalists. Digital technologies are thus used to practice diplomacy and are not a form of diplomatic practice. Lastly, MFAs do not adopt digital tools in one fell swoop. Rather, digital technologies are introduced into diplomatic institutions through a slow process of trial and error.

It is therefore the contention of this book that none of the aforementioned terms amply describe the impact of digital technologies on the conduct of public diplomacy, nor do they offer an adequate conceptual prism through which this impact may be studied. Thus, this book introduces the term "the digitalization of public diplomacy" and argues that digitalization should be conceptualized as a long-term process in which digital technologies influence the norms, values, working routines and structures of diplomatic institutions, as well as the self-narratives or metaphors diplomats employ to conceptualize their craft.

The process of "the digitalization of public diplomacy" can best be exemplified through the activities of the State Department's Digital Outreach Team (DOT) in 2009. On June 4, President Obama delivered a speech at Cairo University calling for a new beginning in the relationship between Islam and the USA. Following the speech, DOT members visited popular websites in the Arab World to converse with Arab and Muslim Internet users and demonstrate America's newfound commitment to diplomatic engagement. Yet the DOT soon found itself unable to respond to audiences' questions and comments. In fact, it took DOT members more than two days to respond to questions and comments posted online. The reason was that each DOT response had to be researched for accuracy and approved in a meeting by all DOT members (Khatib, Dutton, & Thelwall, 2012).

These working routines prevented DOT members from conversing with Muslim Internet users in real-time. Moreover, they prevented the DOT from meeting the expectations of digital publics who have become accustomed to using the Internet as a medium for constant and instant communication. Following the DOT's experience, the State Department began to develop new working routines and adapt existing routines to the affordance of digital technologies. Interacting with digital publics in real-time required that diplomats be allowed to publish online messages based on their own judgment. This would necessitate digital training so that diplomats venturing online would be able to meet the needs, expectations, and demands of digital publics. Yet diplomats would also require training in dealing with trolls and the negative backlash that often accompanies digital communications. In addition, diplomats were in need of a set of best practices that could help them leverage each digital platform to the maximum; while Twitter can best be used to narrate a nation's foreign policy, Facebook can help foster relationships with digital publics. Diplomats would also need software and tools through which they could analyze their digital activities and augment them when necessary. Lastly, diplomats required guidelines stipulating what measures should be taken to overcome digital faux pas, of which there would be many. The DOTs' experience led the State Department to offer its diplomats digital training, while guidebooks and manuals were disseminated to embassies around the world. In other MFAs, similar experiences led to the formation of digital departments, which managed diplomats' training, offered feedback to embassies employing digital technologies, and supervised embassies' use of social media sites. Soon, different MFAs adopted different models of digital training and supervision. So, the process of digitalization began to influence the working routines, norms, and even structure of MFAs.

The DOT's example demonstrates that digital technologies are not adopted overnight, nor is the process of digitalization one of constant, tectonic shifts. Rather, digitalization is a slow process in which the adoption of digital technologies challenges well-entrenched working routines and norms, as well as accepted risks and rewards. As this book will demonstrate, throughout the process of digitalization, diplomats and their institutions have sought to mitigate the risks that are sown into the coattail of digital innovations. While the DOT's activities constituted a form of open communication in which Muslim Internet users set the agenda for their online discussions with diplomats, by 2013 MFAs frequently interacted with digital publics through Q&A sessions that were limited in scope and duration. Twitter Q&As enabled diplomats to meet the demands of digital publics for real-time interactions while at the same time ensuring that diplomats could set the agenda for online discussions and determine which issues to address and which to avoid, or which users to engage with and which to ignore. The somewhat risk-intolerant culture of MFAs thus adapted to the use of social media sites and the empowerment of digital publics.

Importantly, the digitalization of public diplomacy is not uniform across all MFAs. Rather, each MFA is amid its own unique process of digitalization. While some MFAs adopted digital technologies a decade ago, others are only now migrating online. As such, whereas some MFAs have become accustomed to communicating with a digital public that is erratic, unpredictable and yearning to be heard, others are still in the process of adapting their institutional communicative culture to the advantages and perils of digital platforms. Moreover, while some MFAs dedicate digital resources to cultivating relationships with journalists and diasporas, others focus on using social media to manage the national brand. Digital ends also shape an MFA's process of digitalization. Nation branding, for instance, requires that a ministry become proficient in the production and dissemination of multimedia content, while relationship building with diasporas requires constant two-way interactions on digital platforms.

The digitalization of public diplomacy in a certain MFA is also influenced by a myriad of organizational and national factors. These can include the number of embassies an MFA operates abroad, as digital technologies can be employed to extend the reach of one's public diplomacy activities and overcome limited physical representation. Additionally, the average age of diplomats may influence the process of digitalization as digital natives (those born into the digital society) may be more willing to experiment with innovative technologies, even at the cost of diplomatic blunders (Prensky, 2001). The digitalization of public diplomacy may also be influenced by the professional background of those managing digital departments within MFAs. While some departments are headed by branding and public relations specialists, others are led by seasoned diplomats. The former may utilize digital technologies toward communicating with elites such as journalists and media outlets, while the latter may strive to identify foreign policies that are viewed as contentious by digital publics. National factors such as government-wide adoption of digital technologies, foreign policy goals, and national narratives further shape the digitalization of public diplomacy. For instance, New Zealand's MFA first adopted digital technologies given the digitalization of other government ministries, the adoption of digital technologies by its allies, including the USA and the UK, and the foreign policy goal of monitoring digital conversations so as to anticipate shocks to the international system, such as popular uprisings. Conversely, the Polish MFA has increasingly used YouTube to distance Poland from Nazi atrocities in World War II and promote a national narrative that labels Poland as the first victim of Nazi Germany.

Yet as this book will show, the digitalization of public diplomacy is also shaped by the affordance of digital technologies and the logic and culture of the digital society. The infrastructure or design of digital technologies often shapes an MFA's public diplomacy activities. Social media sites such as Twitter, for example, transcend national borders and enable MFAs to interact with the populations of enemy states laying the foundation for future diplomatic breakthroughs. However, Twitter interactions are limited to 280 characters resulting in short bursts of public diplomacy (Sengupta, 2013) that may fail to cultivate relationships with intended audiences. Similarly, social media analytics may offer MFAs the ability to measure the impact of their digital activities. Yet as these analytics focus mostly on a user's digital reach, they lead diplomats to count shares and likes rather than assess the scope of interactions between embassies and digital publics.

Crucially, the digitalization of public diplomacy is influenced by the logic of the digital society and its culture, given that diplomats are not islands entirely of themselves. Rather, they are social beings, and as such, processes that take shape in society invariably influence diplomats. When societies adopt new norms and values, these are also likely to be adopted by diplomats who then introduce these norms and values into their MFAs. For instance, the digital society is one that celebrates the values of openness and authenticity. Openness relates to a willingness to lead a transparent life. Indeed, on social media sites, users are motivated to share their successes and failures, their triumphs and defeats, their weddings and their divorces. This motivation stems from the infrastructure of social media sites that include the "Like" and "It's Complicated" buttons. The more open a user is, the more likes he will receive and the more attention he will attract. Authenticity relates to a user's need to compete over the attention of digital publics with all other Facebook users. Such competitions are won by creating a unique online brand, or iBrand, that has its own appearance, tone, and areas of interest. These values, however, are inherently linked to the logic of the digital society, whose foundation is algorithms. It is the task of algorithms to amass data on digital publics and translate that data into knowledge that can be sold to the highest bidder. Facebook algorithms analyze every like, share, and comment and thus provide the company with a rich profile on each user, including his or her artistic taste, political ideology, spending habits, and favorite products. This knowledge is then used to tailor advertisements to a user's heart's delights. Openness and authenticity are celebrated by the digital society *because* they ensure that digital publics constantly supply algorithms with a stream of data that can be monetized.

Sociologist Manuel Castells (2006) has stated that the organizing structure of the digital society is that of the network. As such, the digital society is also the network society in which networks of individuals, states, and businesses coordinate action on a planetary scale thanks to digital technologies that transmit information instantaneously around the globe. According to Castells, the network structure has resulted in a society that constantly strives to annihilate time and space (Castells, 2013). Such is the case with digital technologies that enable individuals to converse and exchange information in real time, regardless of their physical distance. Other scholars, such as Zygmunt Bauman and David Lyon (2013), have argued that the digital society is one that operates at a distance. A student in Paris can attend a university course in New York, while drones in the skies of the Middle East can be operated from the American Midwest. What follows is that society becomes accustomed to operating at a distance or manipulating space.

The diffusion of the values, norms, and logic of the digital society into MFAs is already evident. Given that MFAs and embassies are now forced to compete over the attention of digital publics, they too must adopt the values of openness and authenticity. For if diplomats cannot attract digital publics, they cannot practice public diplomacy. The Russian embassy to the UK has thus adopted a unique tone on digital platforms, one that taunts and berates the UK government while spinning conspiracy theories. From the perspective of traditional public diplomacy scholarship, this tone may prevent the Russian embassy from creating a receptive environment for Russia's foreign policy. Yet from the perspective of the digital society, the Russian embassy has created a unique iBrand, one that separates it from other embassies and potentially increases its digital reach and ability to attract digital publics.

As is the case with the digital society, diplomatic institutions are also relentless in their efforts to render time and space meaningless. Such is the case with virtual embassies that enable diplomats to converse with distant populations in real-time regardless of the distance between them. Embassies in virtual worlds also occur in their own time zone, which is independent from the physical world. Similarly, the digitalization of public diplomacy has seen the manipulation of space as diplomats author selfies for their state on social media sites. When operating a social media profile for their nation state, diplomats individualize the nation as it acquires the traits of a digital self. On social media sites, the nation state can interact with other users, respond to their comments, and even like and share content. This reduces the distance between the citizen and his nation, which is no longer imagined, but rather favored into existence. Space is thus manipulated, and the nation state becomes a part of the citizen's everyday life.

To summarize, this book has three modest goals. The first is to offer a new conceptual framework for understanding and researching the influence of digital technologies on the conduct of public diplomacy. This framework is rooted in the term "the digitalization of public diplomacy", which relates to a long-term process in which digital technologies influence the norms, values, and working routines of diplomatic institutions, as well as the metaphors and self-narratives that diplomats employ to conceptualize their craft. Metaphors are crucial to the digitalization of public diplomacy, for as Manor (2016) has argued, before diplomacy can be practiced, it must be imagined. Moreover, this book argues that each diplomatic institution is undergoing its own unique process of digitalization, which is influenced by organizational, national and global factors.

The book's second goal is to demonstrate that one cannot understand the digitalization of public diplomacy without first characterizing the digital society. This is because public diplomacy is practiced by social beings who belong to societies that have been fundamentally reshaped by the advent of digital technologies. To understand the digitalization of public diplomacy is thus to understand the norms and values celebrated by the digital society, as well as its logic.

The book's third goal, which stems from the previous two, is to significantly diversify the public diplomacy research corpus by examining the digitalization of public diplomacy in numerous MFAs from numerous world regions. By analyzing MFAs from around the globe, this book can demonstrate that digitalization is a unique process that advances at different paces and in different directions in various MFAs. This diverse sample also demonstrates that while societies differ from one another, the norms, values, and logic of the digital society have begun to permeate MFAs irrespective of their geographic location. Lastly, this sample offers an important contribution to the study of public diplomacy, which tends to separate the "West from the rest" while paying attention mostly to the activities of the USA and Western European countries. This book therefore examines the digitalization of public diplomacy in the MFAs of Botswana, Canada, Denmark, Ethiopia, France, India, Iran, Israel, Kenya, Lithuania, Palestine, Poland, Russia, Rwanda, Sweden, Turkey, the EU, the Netherlands, the UK, Uganda, and New Zealand.

For the sake of clarity, this book adopts Melissen's (2005) definition of the "new" public diplomacy. Yet rather than emphasize the need to interact with connected individuals, this book focuses on attempts to foster relationships with members of digital societies, or societies that have been substantially reshaped by digital technologies. Thus, this book defines the "new" public diplomacy as one that centers on engaging with members of digital societies while transitioning from monologue toward dialogue, engagement, and long-term relationship building.

It should be noted that this book limits its analysis to MFAs, embassies, and diplomats. It does *not* analyze the activities of "new" public diplomacy actors such as NGOs and civil society organizations, nor does it explore the public diplomacy activities of connected individuals. This decision does not suggest that these actors are not relevant to the study of the digitalization of public diplomacy. On the contrary, it is the process of digitalization which has further empowered these actors and enables them to exert greater influence over diplomatic processes. Rather, this book focuses on the digitalization of diplomats and diplomatic institutions given the scarce attention that has been paid to them thus far. Indeed, few studies to date have investigated how digital technologies impact the working procedures, structure, norms, and values of MFAs and their embassies. This book aims to fill this important gap.

In line with Pamment's critique that scholars should map processes of change in MFAs rather than analyze their numbers of followers and the number of networks they belong to, this book employs traditional methodologies. These include in-depth interviews, content analysis, framing analysis, and thematic analysis. These methodologies are necessary as this book seeks to answer fundamental questions which have yet to be adequately addressed by scholars such as: How do MFAs define the term "engagement"? What type of content do ambassadors publish on Twitter? How do diplomats maintain contact with national diasporas? How do diplomats conceptualize the term listening? And how have new norms influenced the communicative culture of MFAs?

THE STRUCTURE OF THIS BOOK

Chapter 2 of this book introduces readers to the digital society. By building on the works of digital anthropologists, sociologists, and economists, it illustrates what it means to live in a digital society, or a society that has been fundamentally reshaped by digital technologies. To do so, the chapter explores the norms and values that are celebrated by the digital society and the behaviors that are expected from digital society members. The digital society is unraveled through the prisms of the network society, the information society, and the sharing society. This chapter also demonstrates how the digital society is manifest in the case studies that comprise this book. As such, this chapter serves as the book's theoretical foundation and roadmap. Readers who are interested in a specific chapter of this book are encouraged to first immerse themselves in the digital society, for without it, much of the book's insights may be lost.

Chapter 3 offers a decade-long review of digital interactions between MFAs, diplomats, and digital publics. The chapter contends that while diplomats sought to leverage digital technologies toward interacting with digital publics, they failed to account for the vocal, opinionated, and erratic nature of the public they would encounter online. Consequently, each act of digital interaction led diplomats to formulate new working routines, adopt new practices, and acquire new skills. The case studies explored in this chapter include Sweden's virtual embassy to Second Life, online Q&A sessions with Israeli and Hamas officials, EU social media campaigns in Israel, and U.S. framing activities on Twitter. The chapter is chronological so as to demonstrate that digitalization is a long-term process spanning nearly two decades.

Chapter 4 segments the process of public diplomacy's digitalization in two. The chapter argues that the Crimean crisis of 2014 was a watershed event that influenced the way MFAs and diplomats employ digital technologies to obtain public diplomacy goals. The transition between the first and second stages of digitalization also saw a transition from linear to algorithmic communications models, digital tactics to digital strategies, engagement with networks of influence to engagement with networked gatekeepers, argument-based diplomacy to narrative-based diplomacy and, most importantly, from targeted to tailored communication. Case studies reviewed in this chapter include Canada's consular diplomacy, the iBrand of the Russian embassy to London, Israel's algorithmic attempts to stem the flow of hate speech on social media sites, the use of Twitter by Iranian leaders to narrate their nation's foreign policy, and the smartphone applications and web-based platforms developed by India's Ministry of External Affairs.

Chapter 5 deals with the threats of filter bubbles, echo chambers, and digital influence campaigns that include disinformation or propaganda. The chapter begins by arguing that the current disinformation zeitgeist may be more myth than reality. Through a review of recent studies and a historical perspective, the chapter suggests that the specter of echo chambers is *not* haunting the skies of public diplomacy. The chapter then evaluates the goals and methods of delivery of Russian disinformation and propaganda and reviews the computational propaganda activities of other nations. Finally, the chapter analyzes two case studies of public diplomacy activities aimed at countering disinformation and propaganda: the UK Foreign and Commonwealth Office's blogosphere and Israel's new model of algorithmic diplomacy.

Chapter 6 asks whether the "new" public diplomacy is fact or fiction. To do so, the chapter first introduces a new model for measuring dialogic engagement between diplomatic institutions and digital publics. Next, the model is used to evaluate the dialogic activities of five African MFAs and four Lithuanian embassies. While the chapter finds little evidence of two-way interactions between diplomats and digital publics, its results do suggest that diplomats are progressing in their quest to adopt more interactive forms of communications with digital publics.

Chapter 7 demonstrates how the desire to overcome the limitations of traditional diplomacy has shaped the process of the digitalization of public diplomacy. This chapter analyzes four virtual embassies launched by Sweden, the USA, Israel, and Palestine all with the goals of overcoming traditional limitations such as lack of bilateral ties, hostile media landscapes, and limited diplomatic representation. The chapter also evaluates two global public diplomacy campaigns meant to influence the opinions and attitudes of digital publics. These include the State Department's promotion of the legalization of same-sex marriage in the USA and Turkey's use of Twitter to narrate the 2016 failed coup attempt.

Chapter 8 introduces the concept of selfie diplomacy, which relates to the use of social media to manage a national brand. These activities individualize the nation state, which has a profile page, a profile picture, and can like and share content. The chapter reviews America's selfie in the age of President Donald Trump, as well as Poland's attempt to refashion its historical selfie by distancing itself from World War II. This chapter ends by arguing that digitalization facilitates the presentation of the state in everyday life, to borrow Erving Goffman's terminology.

Chapter 9 analyzes the use of digital technologies by ambassadors. The chapter demonstrates that ambassadors now use social media to celebrate the values of openness and transparency, to curate information for their followers, and to create a distinct iBrand that sets them apart from their peers. As such, this chapter suggests that the digitalization of public diplomacy has impacted the higher ranks of MFAs and is in no way limited to junior diplomats who came of age in the digital society.

Chapter 10 summarizes this book's main findings and elucidates the relationship between digital technologies, the digital society, and the digitalization of public diplomacy. It serves to demonstrate that while all societies and MFAs differ from one another, they all share certain commonalities and are all experiencing a prolonged process of digitalization that challenges established working routines, procedures and structures. The chapter also identifies new avenues for public diplomacy research.

In conclusion, this book will demonstrate that MFAs and diplomats are not relics that need to be relegated to the dustbin of history. Previous scholars such as Daryl Copeland (2013) have characterized MFAs as disconnected, change-resistant organizations that are inadequately resourced and without a domestic constituency. In contrast, this book finds that MFAs and diplomats are flexible and agile and employ digital technologies in innovative ways. While their response to innovation may not be immediate, over time MFAs learn to balance the affordance of digital technologies, the demands of the digital society, and their own goals. At times, the adoption of digital technologies is a top-down process in which the MFA as a whole integrates new platforms or working procedures, while at other times, change is a bottom-up process in which diplomats' successful experiments with technologies are emulated across desks and departments. Change also comes about when diplomats and MFAs engage with their peers. The past decade has seen numerous digital conferences, workshops, camps, and retreats in which diplomats share case studies, insight, and lessons learned with one another, thus advancing their collective ability to leverage digital technologies.

Evgeny Morozov's quote at the beginning of this chapter suggests that digitalization is an either/or process. Either diplomats keep diplomacy discrete, or they will forfeit their ability to influence global events. This book argues that digitalization is a balancing act between diplomatic ends and digital affordance, an act that diplomats are increasingly mastering. As mentioned earlier, this book seeks to accomplish three goals. Whether it has been able to do so will be determined by the readers, who are now invited to turn the page and delve into the rabbit hole that is the digital society.

REFERENCES

Arsenault, A. (2013). Networks of freedom, networks of control: Internet policy as a platform for and an impediment to relational public diplomacy. In R. S. Zaharna, A. Arsenault, & A. Fisher (Eds.), *Relational, networked and collaborative approaches to public diplomacy* (pp. 192–208). New York, NY: Taylor & Francis.

Bauman, Z., & Lyon, D. (2013). *Liquid surveillance: A conversation.* Cambridge: Polity Press.

Bjola, C., & Holmes, M. (2015). *Digital diplomacy: Theory and practice.* Oxon: Routledge.

Bjola, C., & Manor, I. (2018). Revisiting Putnam's two-level game theory in the digital age: Domestic digital diplomacy and the Iran nuclear deal. *Cambridge Review of International Affairs, 31*, 1–30.

Bortree, D. S., & Seltzer, T. (2009). Dialogic strategies and outcomes: An analysis of environmental advocacy groups' Facebook profiles. *Public Relations Review, 35*(3), 317–319.

Brown, R. (2013). Taking diplomacy public: Science, technology and foreign ministries in a heteropolar world. In R. S. Zaharna, A. Arsenault & A. Fisher (Eds.), *Relational, networked and collaborative approaches to public diplomacy* (pp. 44–55). New York, NY: Taylor & Francis.

Castells, M. (2013). *Communication power.* Oxford: Oxford University Press.

Castells, M., & Cardoso, G. (Eds.). (2006). *The network society: From knowledge to policy* (pp. 3–23). Washington, DC: Johns Hopkins Center for Transatlantic Relations.

Causey, C., & Howard, P. N. (2013). Delivering digital public diplomacy. In R. S. Zaharna, A. Arsenault, & A. Fisher (Eds.), *Relational, networked and collaborative approaches to public diplomacy* (pp. 144–156). New York, NY: Taylor & Francis.

Copeland, D. (2013). Taking diplomacy public: Science, technology and foreign ministries in a heteropolar world. In R. S. Zaharna, A. Arsenault, & A. Fisher (Eds.), *Relational, networked and collaborative approaches to public diplomacy* (pp. 56–69). New York, NY: Taylor & Francis.

Cull, N. J. (2008). Public diplomacy: Taxonomies and histories. *The Annals of the American Academy of Political and Social Science, 616*(1), 31–54.

Duncombe, C. (2017). Twitter and transformative diplomacy: Social media and Iran–US relations. *International Affairs, 93*(3), 545–562.

Gregory, B. (2011). American public diplomacy: Enduring characteristics, elusive transformation. *The Hague Journal of Diplomacy, 6*(3–4), 351–372.

Hallams, E. (2010). Digital diplomacy: The internet, the battle for ideas & US foreign policy. *CEU Political Science Journal, 4*, 538–574.

Hayden, C. (2012). Social media at state: Power, practice, and conceptual limits for US public diplomacy. *Global Media Journal, 11*(21), 1–21.

Jarrett, M. (2013). *The Congress of Vienna and its legacy: War and great power diplomacy after Napoleon.* New York, NY: I.B. Tauris.

Khatib, L., Dutton, W., & Thelwall, M. (2012). Public diplomacy 2.0: A case study of the US digital outreach team. *The Middle East Journal, 66*(3), 453–472.

Malone, G. D. (1988). *Political advocacy and cultural communication: Organizing the nation's public diplomacy.* Lanham, MD: University Press of America.

Manor, I. (2015, July 14). *The framing of #IranDeal on digital diplomacy channels* [Blog]. Retrieved from https://digdipblog.com/2015/07/14/the-framing-of-irandeal-on-digital-diplomacy-channels/.

Manor, I. (2016). Are we there yet: Have MFAs realized the potential of digital diplomacy? *Brill Research Perspectives in Diplomacy and Foreign Policy, 1*(2), 1–110.

McNutt, K. (2014). Public engagement in the Web 2.0 era: Social collaborative technologies in a public sector context. *Canadian Public Administration, 57*(1), 49–70.

Melissen, J. (2005). The new public diplomacy: Between theory and practice. In J. Melissen (Ed.), *The new public diplomacy: Soft power in international relations* (pp. 3–27). New York: Palgrave Macmillan.

Pamment, J. (2013). *New public diplomacy in the 21st century: A comparative study of policy and practice.* Abingdon: Routledge.

Prensky, M. (2001). Digital natives, digital immigrants part 1. *On the Horizon, 9*(5), 1–6.

Roberts, W. R. (2007). What is public diplomacy? Past practices, present conduct, possible future. *Mediterranean Quarterly, 18*(4), 36–52.

Seib, P. (2012). *Real-time diplomacy: Politics and power in the social media era.* New York, NY: Palgrave Macmillan.

Sengupta, S. (2013, October). New diplomatic avenue emerges, in 140-character bursts. *The New York Times.* Retrieved from https://www.nytimes.com/2013/10/04/world/new-diplomatic-avenue-emerges-in-140-character-bursts.html.

Seo, H. (2013). The "virtual last three feet": Understanding relationship perspectives in network-based public diplomacy. In R. S. Zaharna, A. Arsenault, & A. Fisher (Eds.), *Relational, networked and collaborative approaches to public diplomacy* (pp. 157–169). New York, NY: Taylor & Francis.

Spry, D. (2018). Facebook diplomacy: A data-driven, user-focused approach to Facebook use by diplomatic missions. *Media International Australia, 168*(1), 62–80.

The Economist. (2013, September). His biggest smile. Retrieved from http://www.economist.com/middle-east-and-africa/2013/09/21/his-biggest-smile.

Toosi, N. (2015, July). White House to engage Iran critics through @TheIranDeal. *Politico.* Retrieved from https://www.politico.com/story/2015/07/white-house-to-engage-iran-critics-through-theirandeal-120408.

Waters, R. D., Burnett, E., Lamm, A., & Lucas, J. (2009). Engaging stakeholders through social networking: How nonprofit organizations are using Facebook. *Public relations review, 35*(2), 102–106.

Wehrenfennig, D. (2012). From an analog past to a digital future: Information and communication technology in. *Cyberspaces and global affairs, 23.*

Zweig, S. (1953). *The world of yesterday: 1943.* London: Cassell.

CHAPTER 2

Public Diplomacy and the Digital Society

I grew up in a physical world, and I speak English. The next generation is growing up in a digital world, and they speak social.
—Angela Ahrendts, Vice President of Apple Inc.

It began with war, rebellion, and romance. In May, French forces decisively defeated the combined armies of Britain, Hannover, and the Netherlands in the Battle of Fontenoy. In August, Bonnie Prince Charlie led the Jacobite Uprising in an attempt to seize the British throne. In September, Madame de Pompadour was first presented at the court of Louis XV in Versailles. In this way, 1745 was not so different from many other years in the eighteenth century. Amidst the violence, however, was the Enlightenment.

By the time Madame de Pompadour became the mistress of Louis XV, Versailles was no longer the shining jewel it once was. The great thinkers of the day did not gather in its halls or marvel at its beauty. They had returned to Paris, where the culture of the salon had taken root. French salons were never as ostentatious as those of Versailles, nor as rigid and overburdened with ceremony. The salons were simple parlor gatherings hosted by sophisticated women for the advancement of knowledge. Thought could roam freely in the salons. Ideas could be tested and new visions could be breathed to life. It is not surprising that the

© The Author(s) 2019
I. Manor, *The Digitalization of Public Diplomacy*,
Palgrave Macmillan Series in Global Public Diplomacy,
https://doi.org/10.1007/978-3-030-04405-3_2

Encyclopédie was first conceived of in the salons of 1745 (Clark, 1987, pp. 249–258).

The Encyclopédie was a collaborative endeavor meant to conquer ignorance. Its editor, Denis Diderot, intended to author the world's most extensive catalog of human knowledge, covering diverse fields such as religion, medicine, government, and the arts. Soon, a community of writers, or Encyclopédistes, gathered to undertake the monumental task set forth by the editor. While the Encyclopédistes worked to catalog human knowledge, their goal was to advance scientific thought, promote tolerance, reform government, free knowledge from the tyranny of religion, and be true to the spirit of Enlightenment (ibid.).

Published in France between 1751 and 1772, the Encyclopédie has been credited with instigating an intellectual revolution in Europe and stoking the fervor of the French Revolution (ibid.). It was also the very manifestation of Kant's later definition of Enlightenment as "man's emergence from his self-incurred immaturity" (Kant, 2013). Yet for all its scientific splendor, the Encyclopédie is now but a time capsule, a still portrait of eighteenth-century European society. It is therefore the very antithesis of the digital society in which knowledge is continuously created, contested, amended, and redistributed.

DIPLOMACY AND SOCIETY

When examining how digital technologies influence the conduct of public diplomacy, scholars and practitioners often begin their analysis with the activities associated with public diplomacy. Their goal is to understand how digital technologies facilitate public diplomacy activities. Scholars may therefore focus on social media's ability to connect diplomats with foreign populations (Bjola & Jiang, 2015), diplomats' use of virtual embassies to overcome the limitations of traditional diplomacy (Metzgar, 2012), and Ministries of Foreign Affairs (MFA) use of big data to gauge public opinion in a foreign nation. Such conceptualizations suggest that the practice of public diplomacy has remained similar in the digital age and all that has changed are the tools, methods, and strategies employed to obtain public diplomacy goals.

Other studies examine how digital technologies have disrupted public diplomacy. Such is the case with the use of web forums by diaspora populations to denounce their former governments (Bernal, 2014), citizen journalists' abilities to counter diplomatic narratives online (Causey &

Howard, 2013), and the ease with which online publics can reject public diplomacy messages (Manor, 2016). Such conceptualizations suggest that the digital age has complicated the conduct of public diplomacy. Some have even gone as far as asking if public diplomacy can survive the Internet, indicating that what has altered is the contentious digital environment in which public diplomacy is now practiced (Powers & Kounalakis, 2017).

Scholarly work has also investigated how digital technologies give rise to new diplomatic actors. These studies have explored how NGOs use digital networks to stimulate innovative solutions to global challenges (Slaughter, 2009, 2017) or to coordinate action on a global scale, aiming to influence diplomatic processes (Zaharan, 2013). Other studies focus on the emergence of a globally-connected public that is volatile, unpredictable, and yearning to be heard (Haynal, 2011). While these studies turn their attention to diplomatic actors rather than practices, they focus primarily on the affordances of digital technologies. Such conceptualizations suggest that public diplomacy has altered due to the transformative nature of digital technologies, which redistribute power among state and non-state actors.

This book offers a different departure point by arguing that one cannot understand the influence of digital technologies on public diplomacy without first characterizing the digital society. This is imperative for several reasons. Chief among these is that diplomats are social beings and MFAs are social institutions. As Jan Melissen (2005) has argued, while diplomats are "extraordinary and plenipotentiary," they are not islands unto themselves; rather, they are members of society. Societal processes influence both their private and professional lives. Diplomats are likely to adopt the values celebrated by their societies, whether these include a firm belief in freedom of speech, a celebration of personal entrepreneurship, or a commitment to gender equality. Moreover, diplomats are likely to adopt new norms and behaviors as a result of societal change. As a society transitions from applauding uniformity to accepting diversity, diplomats too may come to view immigration as a strength rather than a weakness. As this book will demonstrate, diplomats have already adopted many of the norms, values, and behaviors celebrated by the digital society, including the constant sharing of personal information on digital platforms and searching for a unique and authentic digital voice. Diplomats have also adopted the tools with which they can adhere to the norms of the digital society, including hardware, such as smartphones and tablets, and software, such as blogs and messaging applications.

Diplomats' personal use of digital technologies also influences their attitudes toward digital technologies and behaviors. Like other members of the digital society, diplomats may use social media sites to maintain close ties with physically distant friends and family (Broadbent, 2017). Such activities may lead diplomats to view the world as a connected village no longer bound by the physical constraints of time and space. In turn, diplomats may use social media sites to maintain ties with distant diaspora populations who suddenly appear much closer than they physically are. Similarly, diplomats may use Twitter to receive real-time information on breaking news, leading them to regard Twitter as a tool for real-time crisis management.

The pervasiveness of digital technologies in the family life of the digital society also impacts diplomats' processes of digitalization or adoption of and attitudes toward digital technologies. For instance, diplomats may use WhatsApp messaging groups to coordinate family holidays or communicate with other parents in their child's kindergarten class. In time, diplomats may create WhatsApp groups to coordinate the provision of emergency consular aid or to coordinate collective action in multilateral forums (Bjola, 2017). Alternatively, diplomats may sit down at the dinner table only to discover that each family member is immersed in a different digital device, leading them to regard digital technologies as invasive and isolating. Such diplomats may then accept the depiction of social media sites as creating filter bubbles that increase societal fragmentation and drive political extremism (Lesk, 2013).

Even the depiction of digital technologies in the cultural products of the digital society influences diplomats' adoption of digital tools. When social media sites are celebrated by the digital society for facilitating democracy, as was the case during the Arab Spring (Arsenault, 2013), diplomats may favor using such platforms to communicate with foreign populations. When social media sites are depicted by society as the undoing of democracy, as was the case following the 2016 US elections, diplomats may view these platforms as new battlegrounds over public opinion. In similar fashion, television shows such as *Mr. Robot* can promote fear of digital fragility or the ease with which the digital world may be brought to a halt by malicious hackers. Shows such as *Westworld*, on the other hand, can promote fear of fragile reality, or the loss of the ability to distinguish between the real and the fictitious, the human and the automated bot.

Upon adopting digital technologies, diplomats also embrace the norms and behaviors of the digital society and introduce these into their workplaces. Diplomats' acceptance of the maxim "sharing is caring" can lead to organizational change as MFAs abandon their risk-intolerant communication cultures in favor of risk-tolerant ones (Copeland, 2013; McNutt, 2014). Diplomats' search for an authentic digital voice can influence the type of content embassies share on social media sites, while the assumption that digital influence is determined by the size of one's Twitter following can lead to a focus on *counting* followers rather than *interacting* with followers. It is thus through diplomats that the digital culture (culture here defined by Manuel Castells (2000b) as a set of values, norms, and behaviors) permeates MFAs and constitutes MFAs as social institutions. It is also through diplomats that MFAs come to regard digital technologies as facilitating or disrupting public diplomacy.

MFAs also can be regarded as social institutions as they must meet the expectations of digital society members. For instance, the digital society is "timeless" insofar as its members have become accustomed to communicating with one another in real-time and across great distances. Members of the digital society therefore expect to learn about local and world events as they unfold. This expectation necessitates that MFAs narrate and comment on world events while they are still taking shape. Meeting this challenge and the expectations of digital society members require the establishment of new working routines, the creation of new departments and the adoption of new technologies for the rapid dissemination of information (Seib, 2012, 2016).

Lastly, MFAs are social institutions as they are part of governments, which govern the social behavior of individuals. Governments' approaches to and adoption of digital technologies also influence how MFAs utilize digital technologies in public diplomacy (Miller & Horst, 2017). Early e-government initiatives, for example, aimed to provide citizens with an array of services ranging from filing taxes online to purchasing public transportation loyalty cards. Following suit, MFAs also began to regard themselves as service providers, leading to the digitalization of consular services and the provision of digital consular aid (Israel MFA, 2017). More recently, governments have come to view big data as a potential asset that can inform policies in the fields of health, policing, and education (Lupton, 2015). Subsequently, some MFAs have begun incorporating big data into their public diplomacy activities, such as using sentiment analysis to evaluate how one nation is viewed by the population of another (E. Ratson, personal communication, May 15, 2018).

In summary, as a stepping stone toward understanding the digitalization of public diplomacy, this chapter explores the values, norms, and behaviors of the digital society. It is, of course, impossible to assert that the whole world is now part of a single digital society that shares one culture. Indeed, local norms influence how and which digital technologies are adopted. In addition, the spread of digital technologies across the globe is not uniform, nor is access to digital platforms universal (Van Dijk, 2017). This chapter aims to shed light on those norms and values that digital technologies promote or that have been directly influenced by the emergence of digital technologies.

As Elad Segev of Tel Aviv University teaches, any investigation of the relationship between society and technology can adopt one of two prisms. The first is the technological prism, whose point of departure is technology itself. When adopting the technological prism, one examines how technology influences societies and the individuals that comprise them. The technological prism, for instance, may be employed to examine the immense impact factories had on Western societies during the Industrial Revolution. Over a period of several centuries, the emergence of factories brought about mass migration to cities (Hobsbawm, 2001, p. 49). To meet the demand of burgeoning migration, cheap and bleak housing projects were rapidly developed without considering residents' basic need for sewage. The unsanitary conditions of such projects soon led to health pandemics and, in their wake, to the first planned public health interventions and the emergence of urban planning. Rapid urbanization also brought about early instances of social welfare programs aimed at providing education for factory workers' children (ibid., pp. 203–249). Yet factories also created a clear dichotomy between exploited workers and prosperous owners, slowly leading to modern notions of class distinctions and class struggles. It was on the factory floors that the rallying cry *Workers of the world unite!* first struck a chord (Hobsbawm, 2001). The rate of factory accidents and the associated costs to owners led to the invention of modern insurance schemes, through which one could calculate the statistical prevalence of work-related injuries and insure against them (Beck, 1992). Consequently, insurance became one of the most lucrative businesses in the world. The design of the factory floor, as well as the unrelenting routine of working on the assembly line, also influenced other elements of society. Early twentieth-century art depicted the hunger of the factory for the souls of its laborers, while decades later Andy Warhol adopted an assembly line approach to the production of art in his own "factory." The technology of the factory therefore impacted family life, social life, social structures, art, and the financial system.

The second prism for investigating the relationships between society and technology is the societal one. In the societal prism, one's point of departure is society itself while focusing on the users of technology and how they employ it toward specific ends. The societal prism ascribes agency to society and suggests that technology is not deterministic in nature, but that technology may be used differently than it was first intended. It even suggests that society can reject certain technological advancements. As Manuel Castells writes, "We know that technology does not determine society: it *is* society. Societies shape technology according to the needs, values and interests of people who use the technology" (Castells, 2006). One notable example is the use of text messaging in the Philippines. According to Daniel Miller and Heather Horst (2017), text messages were originally introduced in the Philippines as an add-on technology to mobile telephones. Yet since their introduction, the Philippines have become the global capital of text messaging, with more texts sent per person than any other place in the world. This is because the relatively low cost of texts, compared to mobile phone calls, offered individuals the opportunity to remain in constant contact with friends at an affordable price. Soon, text messages became central to creating and maintaining relationships in the Philippines and have even been credited with ousting a government. Thus, the needs of users, in combination with socioeconomic conditions, transformed text messages from a bonus feature to a central means of communication.

This chapter walks a tightrope between the two aforementioned prisms, at times examining the architecture of technology and the behavior it elicits, while at other times exploring how society has shaped the use of technology. Employing this dual prism, this chapter illustrates what it means to live and to practice public diplomacy in the digital society.

The Digital Society

Digital technologies have become embedded in nearly every realm of daily life. Most forms of employment now include the use of computers while at home, digital devices such as Alexa help light our living rooms or inform us of the weather forecast. Digital devices such as smartphones connect us to the Internet constantly so that we can learn about breaking news, schedule appointments with our doctors, and develop professional relationships with colleagues. Our images of daily life are digitalized on Instagram and stored on digital clouds, while Spotify creates playlists based on our digitally-identified musical preferences. We digitally stream television shows and movies, while we use digital platforms to rank books, movies and restaurants. We exercise with wearable digital devices that monitor our health and determine our diet while our schedules are digitally synced with our emails so that we never miss a meeting or a flight. Our medical records and university grades have been digitalized, as have our school classrooms, with digital smart boards replacing old chalk ones. We digitally pay our taxes and municipal utility bills and digitally launch petitions against government policies. Even those who wish to remain hidden from the digital world have been digitalized as they are tagged in images shared on social media, while their personal details are digitally embedded into their passports (Lupton, 2015). In short, we lead digital lives.

While the digitalization of daily life has been a long-term process spanning several decades, recent years have seen a process of accelerated digitalization. In 2001, Wikipedia was launched, revolutionizing how information is created and accessed by society. Wikipedia, which is now the most highly referenced source in the world (ibid.), is also one of the most successful collaborative projects in human history. Over the course of nearly two decades, a dedicated community of individuals has created the most comprehensive encyclopedia to date, accessible for free to anyone with an Internet connection. This project has finally achieved the lofty goals of the Encyclopédistes while remaining true to the spirit of Enlightenment. Yet while Wikipedia is enlightening, it also challenges our notions of knowledge and expertise as the information we read may be fact or fiction, true or false, edited by an expert in a given field or a complete novice. Moreover, Wikipedia is a political battleground, with contentious articles such as the ones on Jerusalem or Donald Trump being edited and altered by activists. If expert content is now written by novices, if encyclopedia articles are subject to political rivalry, and if the distinction between experts and non-experts has been blurred, is there such a thing as authoritative knowledge? Is there such a thing as truth? Or is the digital society one in which truth is constantly being contested and manufactured?

The period between 2003 and 2007 saw the consecutive launching of social media sites including LinkedIn (2003), Facebook (2004), and Twitter (2006). YouTube and Flicker were both introduced in 2005 (Lupton, 2015). These platforms have transformed our ability to seek employment opportunities, manage social ties, and create an online, visual, persona that exudes confidence and dexterity. On social media, all the world's a stage while all men and women are successful actors. But these platforms also have altered our understanding of the term "friends," influenced our concepts of private and public life, and created a tailored existence in which we may be exposed to a narrow algorithmic environment that filters the world around us. Had the popular sitcom *Friends* been produced today, it may have been titled *Followers*.

2007 saw the introduction of the smartphone, which ushered in an era of constant connectivity. Such connectivity has not only contributed to our ability to manage daily life, but has also redefined the work-life balance. The symbolic gesture of the factory gate closing has been replaced by the sound of the email notification, reminding us that we remain at the assembly line even after we have left the office (Horst, 2017). Dolly Parton's classic song "Working 9 to 5" is now but a piece of nostalgia, a serenade to a time when disconnectedness was permissible.

The immensely popular messaging application WhatsApp was launched in 2009. Taken together, social media sites and smartphone applications such as WhatsApp have influenced how space is conceived in the digital society. WhatsApp bullying groups, for instance, in which classmates create a dedicated group meant to ridicule a fellow student, extend the reach of the bullies from the classroom into the victim's house and private realm. The separation between the school and the home is thus erased (Broadbent, 2017; Horst, 2017) and both spaces collapse into a single, hybrid, space.

Reflecting on the advent of social media sites and digital technologies, Zygmunt Bauman and David Lyon (2016) argue that the digital society is characterized by distance and remoteness. They define the digital society as one in which things are done at a distance. A drone flying in the skies of Pakistan is operated from a military base in Nevada; university classes in Germany are attended by students in Paris; and occupational therapists complete their training from their living rooms.

Even the relationship between citizens and the state is presently negotiated at a distance. As Bernal (2014) argues, digital technologies lead to both de-territorialization and re-territorialization. In her examination of the Eritrean diaspora's use of web forums, Bernal found that such forums create an online public sphere where political issues are debated, groups are mobilized into action, and government narratives are both promoted and contested. During certain periods, Eritrean diasporas used these forums to rally political and financial support for their country of origin, then engulfed in a war with Ethiopia. As such, the boundaries of the nation state extended into foreign realms and web forums had a re-territorializing effect as diasporas became a virtual extension of Eritrea. When diasporas began to use web forums to condemn their country of origin, this had a de-territorializing effect, signaling the demarcation lines between diasporas and their former government (ibid., p. 32).

The rapid pace of digitalization has influenced how knowledge is created in society, how social ties are nurtured, how privacy is conceptualized, how the work-life balance is defined and how social institutions, such as the school, invade social spaces, such as the home (Lally, 2002). Digital technologies have therefore influenced political, social, and economic life (Castells, 2002; Gershon, 2010; Silver & Massanari, 2006). This reality has led some to conclude that we can no longer conceive of culture or society without recognizing that computer hardware and software are now used to constitute the self, social life, social relations, and social institutions (Lupton, 2015). Thus, those leading a digital life can be said to live in a digital society or a society that has been substantially reshaped by digital technologies. This assertion is strengthened by the fact that digital technologies are so ubiquitous that we no longer notice them (Miller & Horst, 2017, p. 25). We scan our produce at the supermarket and tap our credit card on a screen so reflexively that we forget to marvel at how fast we shop or pause to think about where our digital information will travel once it leaves the supermarket's computer servers.

This book asserts that one cannot understand the digitalization of public diplomacy without understanding the digital society. For instance, the influence of Wikipedia on the production of knowledge and the use of this platform to contest reality mirrors a similar process in the realm of public diplomacy. As is explored in Chapter 4, the Crimean crisis of 2014 saw MFAs use social media sites to offer conflicting accounts of events unfolding in Crimea. Russia's MFA used Twitter to suggest that neo-Nazis had staged a coup d'état in Kiev and were threatening the lives of Russian minorities in Eastern Ukraine. To protect these minorities, Russia agreed to annex Crimea into the Russian Federation. Conversely, the U.S. State Department argued that Ukraine had witnessed a demo-cratic revolution and that Russia was staging a stealth invasion of Eastern Ukraine (Bjola, 2016). Both MFAs attempted to utilize social media sites to narrate events, sway public opinion, and garner support for their for-eign policies. Yet as a result of these public diplomacy activities, digital publics were faced with two conflicting accounts of events and the very fabric of reality was shattered. This example demonstrates that the online and offline worlds of diplomacy are not separate but intertwined and that digital tools impact the non-digital world, and vice versa (Miller & Horst, 2017, p. 16).

Similarly, the emergence of a society "at-a-distance" has also impacted public diplomacy. Historically, diplomacy rested on prox-imity. Ambassadors to foreign countries would reside at court so as to assess the monarch's temperament, gather information on state affairs, and foster ties with the court's noblemen and women. Proximity was crucial to a diplomat's success as it facilitated the formation of relation-ships, the foundation on which diplomacy rests, and provided access to information, the currency of diplomacy (Roberts, 2017). Yet the digi-talization of public diplomacy has brought about the practice of diplo-macy at a distance. As is explored in Chapter 7, early experiments with digital platforms led MFAs to launch virtual embassies, at first seen as innovative tools that could facilitate direct interactions between diplo-mats and distant populations (Pamment, 2013). Similarly, web forums were first employed to facilitate online dialogue between diplomats and foreign Internet users (Khatib, Dutton, & Thelwall, 2012). However, as the process of digitalization continued, diplomats shifted their atten-tion from online interactions to online message dissemination, while their communication goals altered from relationship building to influenc-ing foreign elites. This process may have been the result of diplomacy at a distance as diplomats and MFAs could never fully see or envision the digital public they were interacting with. Lack of proximity may have led diplomats to view online publics as amorphous entities without phys-ical features and which therefore could not be truly engaged with. As

Manor (2016) has argued before, diplomacy can only be practiced once it has been imagined by diplomats.

Society at a distance has also impacted the conduct of diaspora diplomacy, as is argued in Chapter 5. Some MFAs have sought to extend the boundaries of the state by interacting digitally with diasporas. Such is the case with the "Know India" platform, which seeks to establish ties between Indian diplomats and the children of Indian diasporas. Similarly, Lithuanian embassies employ Facebook as a platform for managing diaspora events. In these instances, digital platforms have a re-territorializing effect that can lead to collaborations between diplomats and diasporas (Bernal, 2014). Yet other MFAs seem more cautious when communicating with diasporas, as in the case of African MFAs evaluated in Chapter 6 In such instances, digital platforms have a de-territorializing effect and they distance the diaspora from the state (ibid.).

In addition, digital platforms have had a re-territorializing effect on the nation state as a whole. Throughout history, the nation state has been an abstract entity. The sheer size of a nation, the lack of individual mobility and division between landlords and peasants meant that most individuals never saw the borders of their nation state or interacted with its many citizens in a meaningful way (Geary, 2003). Benedict Anderson (2006) famously argued that the printing press played a major role in the formation of the nation state, as languages shared by large and dispersed groups of people enabled individuals to conceptualize themselves as part of an "imagined community." The digitalization of public diplomacy has possibly enabled the nation state to manifest itself more clearly; it can now be posted and tweeted into existence. Chapter 8 evaluates selfie diplomacy activities in which MFAs create a social media persona for their nation. This persona individualizes the state that suddenly has a username, a profile picture, and even a timeline of activities.

The re-territorialized state also has an online tone and animate qualities, as it can now like and share content as well as engage in conversations with other users. Selfie diplomacy is thus a different form of diplomacy at a distance, one that reduces the distance between citizens and the nation, which is no longer imagined but favored into existence. Of course, living in a digital society means more than being influenced by digital technologies. It is a set of metaphors, norms, values, and behaviors that guide the individual and society. A popular metaphor of the digital society is that of the network.

The Network Society

Manuel Castells has famously argued that ours is the network society. Castells asserted that over the past three decades, the world has undergone a process of structural transformation in which the network has become the dominant structure in society. Brought about by the global diffusion of Information and Communication Technologies (ICTs) and digital technologies, networking is now the modus operandi in most realms of human activity and the means by which wealth, power, and knowledge are generated (Castells, 2006).

Networks, which are a system of interconnected nodes, are not a new societal structure (Miller, 2017). In fact, family life has always been structured as a network. In addition, networks have always been a valuable social structure, thanks to their adaptability and flexibility. Networks form to achieve a specific goal. To that end, nodes are added or removed. Once the goal is obtained, the network disperses with the same ease with which it was formed. The size of networks, however, was historically limited by barriers to information sharing. Until the late nineteenth century, networks could not coordinate activities across great distances as information traveled slowly from one location to another. Subsequently, networks dominated family and community life, while the worlds of production, power, and war were dominated by hierarchical structures (Castells, 2000a, 2006). Digital technologies have had a transformative impact on society, as they enabled networks to overcome their temporal and spatial limitations. Using digital technologies, networks of organizations, individuals, companies, and states coordinate action instantaneously and on a planetary scale as information circles the globe in seconds (ibid.). Once restrictions on network size were lifted, they replaced hierarchies as the dominant structures of production, power, and war (Lupton, 2015).

When imagining the network society, Castells adopted both the technological and societal prisms. On the one hand, he recognized that there was no single network society. The network society manifests itself differently based on the history, institutions, and culture of each nation (Castells, 2006). On the other hand, he asserted that all network societies share certain features. As networks transcend national borders, the network society is global and it is through global networks of goods, capital and communication that the logic, values, and behaviors of the network society diffuse and transform all nations (ibid.).

To demonstrate the contemporary dominance of the network structure, Castells maintained that the economy, the media, and the nation
state have been networked. The network economy is one in which
small and medium firms become members in transnational business
networks, while large corporations network with one another on specific projects. The media is networked as digital technologies have given
rise to interactive forms of communication. In turn, societies have transitioned from unidirectional broadcasting systems, such as those of the
television and radio, to interactive ones in which masses of individuals
create and disseminate information that travels through global communication networks (Castells, 2006). The information shared on these
networks includes blogs, vlogs, podcasts, selfies, social media updates,
and diplomats' accounts of global events. The nation state has been networked as part of its attempt to keep up with the process of globalization. Globalization, according to Castells, is characterized by a multitude
of financial, cultural, political, and technological networks that work as
a single unit on a global scale, leading to social processes that supersede
the nation state (Castells, 2000a). To contend with globalization, the
network state creates ultra-national networks that share sovereignty, such
as the EU, where member states collectively formulate foreign and economic policies. In addition, the network state facilitates the formation
of sub-national networks in which sovereignty is transferred to networks
of local governments, non-governmental organizations (NGOs) and civil
society organizations (Castells, 2006). State agency is thus migrating
upwards and downwards (Copeland, 2013).

As is the case with any social restructuring, the network society has
seen the redefinition of time and space. In the industrial age, society was
managed through "clock time", or the constant allocation of time to specific tasks. In 1950s America, the factory hours of nine to five were allocated to employment, while family time corresponded with primetime
television (Horst, 2017). By contrast, the network society is one that
relentlessly uses digital technologies to annihilate time. One form of such
annihilation is the compression of time until it is rendered meaningless;
this is the case with financial transactions that circle the globe instantaneously or nations' attempts to wage instant wars. Another form of annihilated time is the de-sequencing of time or the reordering of life and work
cycles. Such is the case with 20-year-old tech CEOs who manage hundreds of older employees. Similarly, the view of retirement as a second

adolescence and a time of experimentation and adventure represents a de-sequencing and reordering of life cycles.

Space is also reconfigured as digital technologies enable two events to take place simultaneously, regardless of geographic proximity. The advent of global networks of media, corporations, and governments that can collaborate in real-time and across vast distances suggests that space is no longer relevant. Indeed, the digital age has been credited with advancing the death of space. Yet many digital technologies, powered by GPS systems, Google Maps, or wearable devices, are tasked with tracking users' spatial locations. In this sense, space is awarded greater significance in the digital society (DeNicola, 2017).

Castells implies that the network has become the dominant metaphor for life in contemporary societies. Individuals seek to network with their superiors or potential employers, academics coalesce around research networks, and citizens create networks to combat climate change. Similarly, diplomats create networks with diasporas while governments launch networks of excellence to inform policy making.

As part of the process of digitalization, some MFAs have already adopted networked approaches to public diplomacy. As is elaborated in Chapter 5, the Israeli MFA uses social network analysis to identify networks that spread anti-Semitic content online. As part of these activities, the rhetoric of network members is analyzed and "moderate members" are identified. These moderate members are then contacted by Israeli diplomats with the aim of conversing and reaching mutual understanding. The end goal of such communications is to persuade moderate members to stop sharing the network's content, thereby isolating networks of hate and stemming the flow of anti-Semitic content online. Similarly, the Lithuanian MFA aims to foster networks with European opinion makers and elites through which it may counter the Russian online narrative which depicts Lithuania as a failed state.

Other MFAs have sought to create networks with tech companies, aimed at developing innovative solutions to shared challenges or preparing for the next wave of digital disruption. The Danish MFA, for instance, has appointed a tech ambassador responsible for creating goal-oriented networks with companies in the USA, Europe, and China (Danish Foreign Ministry, 2017). Considering the risk of rising water levels and its potential impact on Norway, the Norwegian MFA is looking to form global networks with climate change organizations. As Jorge Heine argued, the digitalization of public diplomacy has thus included the adoption of a new metaphor through which diplomats conceptualize their craft and the actors they must interact with: that of the network.

The annihilation of time and reconfiguration of space have also influenced MFAs' practice of public diplomacy. First, as Chapter 7 illustrates, the age of instant communication is also the age of instant revolutions. As Philip Seib wrote, the all-powerful Hosni Mubarak was deposed in three weeks while the Orange revolution in Ukraine lasted some ten weeks (Seib, 2012). The age of instant revolutions has seen diplomats adopt a form of real-time diplomacy in which events and public sentiment are monitored and analyzed in near-real time using digital technologies. This may enable diplomats to anticipate possible shockwaves to the international system (ibid.). Second, the de-sequencing of time has been embraced by MFAs, who routinely summon the past to make sense of the present. Such activities, which are evaluated in Chapter 8, rest on redefining a nation's past to manage its present-day image. Third, public diplomacy annihilates space through diplomatic activities that facilitate real-time interactions between diplomats and distant populations. Such is the case with interactive Q&A sessions with diplomats and world leaders. As this book will demonstrate, public diplomacy is also currently preoccupied by a relentless drive to condense time and space.

Even the challenge that networks pose to the nation state has influenced the digitalization of public diplomacy. The networked and globalized world is one in which numerous government ministries must face the world. Ministries of energy, health, agriculture and the environment routinely network with their foreign peers because global challenges require global solutions (e.g., climate change, terrorism). In turn, MFAs have lost their monopoly on managing the nation's foreign affairs. Digital technologies, however, have enabled MFAs to counter-balance this loss of territory within government. Chapters 3, 6, and 7 examine how digital platforms enable diplomats to directly interact with their domestic population, giving rise to domestic public diplomacy activities in which diplomats seek to develop a domestic constituency, be it through consular aid or promoting goals of national importance. Such is the case with Poland's MFA, who is engrossed in the task of distancing the nation from the atrocities of World War II.

Lastly, Chapters 4 and 7 demonstrate that MFAs, like the nation state, perform a balancing act between the global and the local. While some public diplomacy messages target a global audience, others focus on specific national audiences and are tailored to the attributes of those national audiences. For instance, the French embassies to China, Kenya, and the UK may all share the same public diplomacy messages if those are directed at a global constituency. Other messages will target specific national audiences, such as French audiences, while taking into account each nation's values and norms. Digitalization has therefore brought about "glocalized" public diplomacy in which space and national borders are disregarded and respected, simultaneously.

But as Lyon and Bauman (2016) assert, a network is not a community. Networks are goal-oriented, temporary social structures characterized by weak ties. Communities, by contrast, are more permanent structures characterized by strong ties among members, an emotional connection to other members, and continuous engagement with members over long durations of time. Communities generally have something in common, such as religion, values, or sexual orientation. Over time, people develop a "sense of community" in that the community becomes an important part of their daily lives and their identity (ibid., p. 39).

The differences between networks and communities, and diplomats favoring one structure over the other, have important ramifications for the practice of public diplomacy. A network approach to public diplomacy may lead diplomats to focus on obtaining short-term policy goals by joining and leaving online networks. A communal approach, on the other hand, may lead diplomats to focus on building long-term relationships with digital publics. As these publics begin to develop a sense of community, they may be willing to advocate in favor of a foreign nation and facilitate the acceptance of its foreign policy. As Chapters 5 and 6 find, MFAs and embassies rarely offer digital publics opportunities for meaningful dialogic engagement, as some of these institutions focus their attention on networking with elites rather than building communities with digital publics. While the dominant structure of the digital society is the network, its currency is information.

THE INFORMATION SOCIETY

One of the defining characteristics of the digital society is that information has become the principal vehicle of accumulating wealth (Lupton, 2015). All tech giants, from Facebook to Google and Amazon, have acquired an astonishing ability to gather digital data, create information, and generate knowledge. Digital data are encoded objects recorded and transmitted using digital media technologies (ibid., p. 7). Digital data are transmitted in symbols such as ones and zeros and include not only numerical information such as likes and shares, but also audio and visual data such as images, videos, blog posts, and comments on Facebook (ibid., pp. 4–7). The ability to transfer digital data from one device to another has been central to the emergence of the digital society, as data gathered by a smartphone application can be transmitted to the servers of a marketing company.

Digital data objects are pooled together to create information, while information generates knowledge (Lupton, 2015). For instance, whenever we browse Amazon for books, our search queries, the titles we look at, and the amount of time we spend looking at each title are recorded as data objects. Taken together, these objects create information about our browsing history. This information is then turned into knowledge pertaining to our interests, occupations, hobbies, and artistic taste. This knowledge is used by Amazon to send us emails recommending new titles that we may enjoy reading (Clegg, 2017). The basis of Amazon's financial model is its ability to generate knowledge concerning the interests and tastes of millions of individual users and then offering them products that are tailored to their hearts' desires.

Other tech giants use information to generate knowledge that is sold to advertisers. Google, for instance, scans users' emails, records their search queries, and tracks the websites they visit to gather information. This information is used to generate a user profile and to tailor online advertising to that profile (Lupton, 2015, p. 96). The same is true of Facebook, Twitter, YouTube, and most other free platforms. The financial model of all these companies is similar: gather as much information as possible about their users and sell this information to the highest bidder (Beer, 2013; Lash, 2007). In the industrial economy, workers produced value. In the information society, digital users create value as each emoji, image, like, and share is gathered, analyzed, monetized and sold (Lupton, 2015). Those who wish to take Wall Street's bull by the horns no longer yell "Show me the money". They yell *Show me the data*.

Algorithms are the foundations of the information society. Lupton (2015) defines algorithms as a sequence of computer code commands that tells a computer how to process through a series of instructions to arrive at a specific endpoint. Algorithms have become central to the economy of the information society as they collect data about users, sort and make sense of the data (information), and generate predictions about users' future behavior (knowledge). Such is the case with the Google Go application, which draws on a user's Gmail content and Google searches to anticipate her next request (ibid., p. 11).

The information society is also tailored; most of our digital experiences are personalized to our unique attributes. When we search Google, we are exposed to tailored advertisements based on our browsing history and emails. When we log onto Twitter we are exposed to a tailored feed that ranks tweets based on our preferences. On Facebook, we are likely to see news articles that accord with our political affiliation. Algorithms are the main functionaries of tailoring. It is their task to gather our information, sort it, and produce relevant knowledge about our likes and dislikes. As such, the feeling of unlimited access to knowledge that we experience when going online is but a mirage. The world at our fingertips is merely a diluted version of the vast cosmos of the Internet.

The 2016 US elections, however, raised concerns that the tailored society is also the ignorant society. As algorithms gather more information on our activities, they increasingly tailor our online experiences to the point where we may exist in individual filter bubbles (Tucker et al., 2018). Within these bubbles, we supposedly no longer see any content that does not match our algorithmically-determined interests, nor can we engage with any friends who have not been algorithmically deemed suitable. And so, our worldview is diminished to that of an ant while our exposure to new ideas and experiences is dramatically limited. One becomes blissfully, and algorithmically, ignorant. A poignant example of such ignorance dates to 2011 when certain Google users who searched the term "Egypt" saw no mention of the Arab Spring protests. Social revolutions were simply not part of their algorithmically-determined interests (Praiser, 2011).

Viewing algorithms as promoting ignorance, or erecting filter bubbles, employs the technological prism and focuses primarily on the technological attributes of an algorithm. The societal prism reminds us that data gathering and analysis are not neutral. Algorithms are developed by individuals and they are imbued with the biases and goals of their developers (Lupton, 2015). Some algorithms, for example, are used to exclude certain populations. For instance, certain algorithms offer special discounts to frequent flyers while overcharging regular customers. Other algorithms are used to classify populations based on the risk they pose to a state (Bauman & Lyon, 2016), while still others are meant to classify users of a digital platform based on socioeconomic status. It is thus important to remember that in every stage of the data gathering process there was an individual who determined what should constitute data, how the data should be classified, and what questions should be answered based on the data at hand (Lupton, 2015).

The advent of algorithms has ushered in the era of big data. "Big data" is a term used to refer to the vast accumulation of single data points. Using algorithms, big data can be used to generate information and knowledge on a large scale, be it a community, a city, or even a nation (ibid., p. 94). Some national health institutions now collect a variety of individual health measurements, including citizens' weight, blood pressure, and cholesterol levels. Pooled together into a national database, these single data objects become big data sets that can be used to compare the health of different nations, different social classes within a nation, or different age groups. This big data can even be used to predict future mortality rates as high cholesterol and obesity are major predictors of heart disease. Similarly, financial corporations rely on big data sets of consumer spending habits to anticipate fluctuations in markets while Google uses global search queries to predict outbreaks of flu around the world.

In this sense, the digital society is a future-oriented one. Its gaze is permanently fixed on the next wave of innovation, the next market to be disrupted by digital technologies, and the next successful start-up. Its investors hope to fund the next Facebook while its entrepreneurs seek to launch the next Google. Its stockbrokers buy commodities based on future weather patterns while its financial institutions publish future market predictions.

The rhetoric of big data often obscures its ethical dimensions. The amassing of vast quantities of data on citizens, consumers, and individuals are routinely accompanied by violations of their privacy and their right to anonymity. Data brokerage firms that gather data online are only partly constrained by regulation. The same is true for social media sites and smartphone applications. Some of these have willingly shared users' private data with intelligence services, as was made evident in the Snowden revelations (Lupton, 2015). Private companies also violate customer privacy. It is estimated that Walmart has amassed big data on some 60% of American adults and has shared that data with numerous third parties (Lupton, 2015, p. 96). Tellingly, these mass assemblages of personal information have been dubbed "big data" as opposed to "big personal data" or "big invasive data" or even "big private data." The reason for this is that "big", for lack of a better word, is good. The term "big data" suggests that the data in question has simply been supersized; like a McDonald's meal, it is data on a grand and magical scale.

The ethics of algorithms and big data are also obscured; as there is no other way to contend with the magnitude of information produced online, as the information society is also the Too Much Information (TMI) society. The sheer amount of online content created every day is staggering. In 2017, every minute of the average day saw the posting of 527,760 photographs on Snapchat, the viewing of 4,146,600 videos on YouTube, the sending of 456,000 tweets, 154,200 Skype calls, 3,607,080 search entries on Google, 600 new page edits on Wikipedia, and the creation of 360 new Facebook profiles. Bauman and Lyon (2016) claim that intelligence and security agencies are flooded by more information than they can ever hope to fully analyze. The same is true of digital publics, who can only hope to read all the articles that their peers recommend, or view all the videos that their friends upload, or read all the academic articles sent to them by publishers. It is, however, possible that we are drowning by design that the overwhelming feeling of TMI is meant to elicit adoration for algorithms that help us navigate our way across the tidal wave of information that heads our way every minute of every day. TMI may even increase our tolerance towards filter bubbles as they ensure that, amid the chaos of blogs and vlogs, we are only exposed to content that is of interest or relevance to us (Miller & Horst, 2017, p. 6).

Algorithms are thus like ideals. We cannot reach them, but oh how we profit from their presence! (le Carré, 1986).

The need to contend with TMI has already been recognized by some diplomats and MFAs. As Chapter 9 describes, some ambassadors have begun to use social media sites and blogs to offer a digital compass for all those facing the disorienting daily influx of TMI. These ambassadors curate information for their online followers, identify reliable sources of information, suggest interesting analyses of world events, and even identify sources of disinformation. Such curation offers an added value to followers and may therefore enable an ambassador to foster an online community rather than a network. Similarly, the algorithmic logic of sorting populations for different treatment has also been adopted by MFAs. In Israel's case, the MFA assumes that 25% of Twitter users will reject any Israeli message. Another 25% already support Israel. Thus, the MFA uses social media sites to target the 50% of users who may be swayed to one side or the other. It is this 50% who are analyzed and who then become the target of online public diplomacy campaigns (Y. Morad, personal communication, March 30, 2014).

Some MFAs have even developed their own algorithms and means of big data analysis, as described in Chapter 10. When using big data analysis, diplomats and MFAs ascribe importance to certain populations, countries, and regions because they must decide who to analyze and who not to analyze. In this manner, big data may come to determine the audiences, activities, and even goals of public diplomacy (Cheney-Lippold, 2011; Ruppert, 2011). Algorithms' predictive capacity suggests that they are inherently "modern," characterized by a relentless drive to impose structure on a chaotic world (Bauman, 2000). It is possible that it is the predictive element of big data and algorithms that has facilitated their adoption by MFAs as diplomats seek to impose structure onto an increasingly chaotic and accelerated world in which uncertainty is now the norm rather than the exception.

The existence of possible filter bubbles has proved a major source of concern for public diplomacy practitioners and their institutions, as discussed in Chapter 4. When first migrating online, diplomats envisioned social media sites through linear communication models such as the ones that characterized television. An embassy would tweet a message that would reach thousands of users. As part of the process of digitalization, MFAs and diplomats have come to realize that algorithms filter their messages. Embassy tweets only reach those users who follow the embassy directly or who have expressed some interest in diplomacy, foreign affairs or bi-lateral ties between two nations. Thus, diplomats and MFAs seek to shatter algorithmic confines. To this end, some MFAs, such as Canada and Russia, have developed algorithmic tactics that include the use of trending hashtags in their tweets or asking their followers to help disseminate messages through retweets.

Equally worrisome for diplomats is the assumption that filter bubbles may be driving political polarization, hyper-partisanship, and violent online discourse. These are all the result of algorithmic filtering, which engulfs social media users in filter bubbles that prevent cross-party discourse because users can interact only with like-minded individuals. Within these filter bubbles, hate and bigotry are fueled by a bonfire of profanities and the circulation of disinformation. Crucially, if diplomats cannot reach a public engulfed in filter bubbles, they cannot practice public diplomacy. As Chapter 5 illustrates, several MFAs have now developed tools and strategies to "burst" filter bubbles.

In the digital society, information is the main vehicle for accumulating wealth. Yet the ability to generate information requires two things. First, members of the digital society must agree to be surveilled by digital devices that amass vast quantities of data. Second, members of the digital society must constantly generate and share personal information online, thus "feeding" the algorithms. Generating data from users' devices is achieved by offering them a new social contract, one in which their use of digital devices and applications is conditional upon the surrender of all privacy. Users supposedly surrender privacy of their own volition by accepting a device's terms of use. But these are really "terms of misuse", as they are formulated in a legal vernacular that cannot be deciphered even by the most diligent user (Manor & Soone, 2018). The constant generation and sharing of personal information are achieved by creating an insatiable desire to be surveilled at all times. These are explored in the following section.

The Sharing Society

Will Storr (2018) has argued that social media sites have ushered in an era of social perfection. By nature, humans evaluate their self-worth by comparing themselves to others. Social media sites offer a unique medium for such comparisons, as one can evaluate one's self-worth relative to that of friends, classmates and even celebrities (ibid., p. 16). Yet social media profiles are not structured around an honest portrayal of one's life. They are used primarily to create an online persona of achievement, popularity, and pleasure. There are no selfies from the unemployment lines, nor do people tag one another when they are fired from their jobs. Social media promote a narrative of life as a never-ending parade of fine restaurants, champagne-infused parties, and professional excellence. Online, all users become hyperactive public relations agents-not surprising given that the logic of digital platforms is that of the neo-liberal market (ibid., pp. 16–33).

Neo-liberalism has had an immense impact on the digital society. Early developers of the personal computer believed that they would create a world free of hierarchies in which individuals would be free to do as they please without having to surrender to centralized authorities (Storr, 2018, p. 252). This vision made its way into the offices of IBM and AT&T, who together promoted a rhetoric of unlimited individuality in which every person would be his own "hub of ingenuity and profit making." Thus, every individual would become a commodity that could be sold on the market (ibid.). Social media sites such as Facebook, LinkedIn, and Twitter have simply provided the marketplace where these individuals are presently traded.

On the social media market, the self becomes a brand that must compete over the attention of digital publics with all other brands or all other individuals. Consequently, the age of iPhones and iPads is also the age of iBrands. Yet social media sites have also taken the market vision one step further by creating an online environment in which "the currency is the self and the gold standard is openness and authenticity" (Storr, 2018, p. 255). Competing successfully on the marketplace requires that every social media user embrace the values of openness and authenticity, while rewarding others who follow suit. Authenticity relates to creating an iBrand that has a distinct appearance and tone and that deals with specific issues, be it Japanese *manga*, Beyoncé, or post-colonial politics. Openness relates to a deeply felt commitment to lead an open and transparent life, and to share one's successes and failures, cherished memories and innermost thoughts, romantic conquests, and family drama. Social media facilitates such openness through its technological design, such as the "It's Complicated" feature to describe romantic entanglements, situated alongside the "Like" button. These buttons reward openness and enable a community of iBrands to enforce its norms and values (Locke, 2018).

Indeed, the more personal a Facebook post or a tweet, the more likely it is to generate likes and favorites and the greater the author's sense of social validation. Such was the case with a university professor who recently published a CV of his failures. This professor became more popular online than his more successful colleagues because he wholeheartedly embraced the norms of the digital society, which was to be open about his failures (*Guardian*, 2016). The question that soon emerges is, has the migration of MFAs and diplomats to social media sites subjugated them to the logic of the marketplace? Has digitalization led diplomats to adopt the norms of information sharing, openness, and authenticity?

As Chapter 9 details, diplomats have in fact embraced more open forms of diplomacy. The Geneva Conference of 2014 was live-tweeted by diplomats sitting at the negotiating table. The Iran nuclear agreement was published in full by the State Department soon after it was signed. But diplomacy did not become more transparent in one day. Rather, as part of the long-term process of digitalization, diplomats are increasingly lifting the veil of secrecy and granting digital publics a "behind the scenes" look at diplomacy.

MFAs and diplomats are also increasingly attempting to find an authentic voice. In a recent digital diplomacy conference in London, a high-ranking British diplomat stated that his colleagues often wonder why they are unable to attract many social media followers. His answer was blunt: "because you are boring." This statement demonstrates a current trend in which diplomats and their institutions aim to create an authentic digital persona to compete with other iBrands on the social media market. Ambassadors in particular have become brands, as is explored in Chapter 9, with some of them adopting brazen language that hardly seems diplomatic, but which epitomizes their craving for the attention of digital publics and their willingness to compete with others to obtain it.

The rhetoric of the marketplace is now also common among diplomats practicing public diplomacy. The goal of public diplomacy "campaigns" is to tailor messages to a "target audience" in an engaging way. Other campaigns seek to target "influencers" to increase the "reach" of an embassy. Of course, diplomats and their institutions not only compete with other iBrands, they compete with other diplomats and media outlets to gain exposure and influence online publics' perception of world events. Digital platforms are thus transformed into aggressive arenas in which multiple diplomatic actors offer their narration of world events while competing over the attention of foreign audiences. Social media users in Ukraine, for instance, were a highly sought-after commodity for the Russian MFA during the 2014 Crimean crisis, while U.S. social media users were a rare commodity for Israel's MFA during the 2015 ratification of the Iran nuclear agreement. While the digital society has been called the "sharing society", the drive for authenticity and openness can only be fully understood through the lens of the surveilled society.

THE SURVEILLED SOCIETY

Some people question why digital publics do not simply abandon social media sites or smartphone applications, especially after the Snowden revelations and the increased media attention paid to privacy violations on digital platforms (Lupton, 2015, p. 4). From the perspective of the societal prism, suggesting that one simply opt out of digital platforms fails to recognize the pervasiveness of these mediums in the digital society.

University professors open Facebook groups where students can ask questions before an exam, customers visit corporate Twitter channels to lodge complaints, and social movements such as #MeToo rely on Facebook to raise awareness and support for their causes. Human resources managers trail a candidate's digital footprints while companies expect employees to establish an online presence that promotes the corporate brand. This is also true of MFAs in which diplomats are asked to migrate to social media and establish a formidable digital presence. Lastly, digital platforms are also a mechanism for maintaining ties with dispersed social contacts in a globalized world. Those who exit these platforms do so at the peril of "social death" (ibid.).

The technological prism would offer a different explanation regarding people's reluctance to abandon digital platforms. This explanation is based on the concept of the panopticon. Designed by the English utilitarian philosopher Jeremy Bentham, the panopticon was a prison design in which a small number of prison guards could watch a large number of prisoners from a hidden location. Given that the prisoners in the panopticon did not know when they were being watched, they engaged in a form of self-discipline, internalizing the guards' "regulatory gaze" (Lupton, 2015, p. 33). Unsure if they were being watched or not and fearful of being punished for bad behavior, the prisoners came to discipline themselves. Foucault used the panopticon as a metaphor for modern life and drew on it when he analyzed the self-regulatory power of social intuitions such as schools and factories. Students and assembly line workers are also subject to an ever-present (yet never present) watchful eye of the teacher or floor manager. In such institutions, the watched soon assumed the power to watch themselves, thereby oppressing themselves into disciplined behavior (Bauman & Lyon, 2016, p. 52).

The age of social media is also the age of post-panoptic surveillance, one in which social media users are both those being watched and those doing the watching. As argued above, the logic of social media sites is that of the marketplace. The desire of all users is to be seen—to be liked and shared and retweeted into stardom. Such desires are a result of the technological design of social media sites that include the features of liking, sharing, and retweeting other users' content. The logic of the marketplace is hammered into the minds of users by the designation of some as social media celebrities. Those who obtain the greatest digital reach are adopted by corporate sponsors and catapulted into a life of leisure and exclusivity (Manor & Soone, 2018). They stroll along the beaches of the Bahamas and glide down the slopes of Davos while selling their sponsors' watches and bathing suits. Their status implies that a person's digital worth rests solely on the reach of his or her last post and that one must work all day, every day, to maintain their status through sharing personal information. This is what Lupton calls "social labor" (Lupton, 2015, p. 28).

So, the users of digital platforms conduct acrobatic feats to be seen and liked. They no longer fear the panoptic gaze of the watcher; indeed, they relentlessly try to summon it. To do so, they share their relationship status, publicize their failures, Instagram their engagements, turn their private homes into public domains, and document their lives on an hourly basis. To quote Bauman and Lyon (2016), everything private is now done in public and for public consumption as part of the promotion of the iBrand. Yet the startling realization is that most social media users are not watched by their friends or peers, but by the algorithms that lay hidden behind the façades of Facebook and Twitter.

To obtain recognition, social media users are also forced to surveille their peers. Social media is predicated on the concept of reciprocity: follow me and I will follow you, share me and I will share you, surveille me and I will surveille you. This logic of reciprocity is technologically enforced, because when we follow someone on social media or share their content, they receive a notification prompting them to return the favor. Thus, in post-panoptic surveillance, social media users are both the watchers and those being watched. Users soon become complicit in the act of digital surveillance, and their ability to defy it both online and offline diminishes. The logic of social media, coupled with the pervasiveness of digital surveillance in daily life, forces us to discipline ourselves like the inmates in the original panopticon. The behavior we are asked to adopt is complete openness. To paraphrase Margaret Thatcher, surveillance is the method: The object is the soul.

The pervasiveness of digital platforms has also had a substantial impact on diplomatic institutions. As Chapter 3 explains, throughout the process of digitalization, MFAs have established social media empires. Most MFAs now manage hundreds of social media accounts on a variety of platforms, including Facebook, Twitter, Snapchat, YouTube, Instagram, and others. The formation of social media empires may have stemmed from the fear of "social death," of being ignored by digital publics. More recently, several MFAs have considered abandoning or limiting their social media activities in favor of focusing on other digital tools. Yet such initiatives usually fail. Opting out of the online realm risks another form of "social death"—that of irrelevance.

Similarly, Chapter 4 finds that MFAs and embassies also perform acrobatic feats to be surveilled, watched, and shared online. Such feats include using sarcasm, creating humorous memes, attacking diplomatic institutions, using sensational language, and trolling foreign diplomats. The Russian embassy in London, for instance, has turned trolling and promoting conspiracy theories into an art form. Other diplomatic institutions have taken to tagging one another in images to ensure diplomatic reciprocity (Cassidy & Manor, 2016). Importantly, the norms and behaviors of the surveilled society may have diffused into MFAs and embassies through young diplomats who grew up branding themselves on the social media marketplace.

Even online virality has become a much-revered achievement among diplomats. Those ambassadors who have become Twitterati, or Twitter celebrities, are often labeled public diplomacy gurus, and their acrobatic techniques are integrated into digital training courses within their respective MFAs. Like other social media celebrities, Twitterati ambassadors are catapulted into a procession of World Economic Forums in Switzerland, global discussions on the future of diplomacy in Geneva, and university lectureships. Thus, the logic of post-panoptic surveillance is hammered into the minds of all diplomats.

Conclusion

This chapter has characterized the digital society by identifying its norms, values, and underlying logic. It has done so as a prerequisite to this book's assertion that one cannot understand the digitalization of public diplomacy without first studying the digital society. Diplomats are social beings and MFAs are social institutions. Events that take place in society impact diplomats' worldviews, values, norms, and behaviors, and it is through diplomats that societal changes diffuse into MFAs. The digitalization of nearly every aspect of daily life has given rise to the digital society and it is this society that shapes the process of digitalization of public diplomacy.

Importantly, this chapter has also demonstrated that the digital society cannot be characterized by a single norm or metaphor. Rather, the digital society is a mélange of technologies, ideas, behaviors, and metaphors. The technological prism would suggest that these are mostly the result of technological infrastructure and design. The network society is born out of ICTs that transmit information globally in seconds, while the sharing society is born out of the demand to feed social media algorithms. The societal prism would argue that the digital society is shaped by digital publics. It is they who edit Wikipedia articles and contest reality and it is they who use the "like" button to ensure that all society members share personal information. Of course, neither prism can account for the formation of the digital society. It is their combination that best illustrates what it means to live in a society that has been reshaped by digital technologies.

Lastly, this chapter has exemplified the way the norms, logic, and metaphors of the digital society come to shape the practice of public diplomacy. Table 2.1 summarizes some of these examples. The first example illustrates the demand of the digital society that everything once done in secret now be done in the open. The logic behind this demand is the need to feed algorithms, which are the foundation of the digital society. This demand has led digital society members to embrace the norms of complete openness and authenticity and to adhere to these norms by constantly sharing personal information. The demand that everyone be open and authentic has led digital society members to adopt the metaphor, or self-narrative, of an iBrand, which competes against all other iBrands by sharing the most private and sensitive information.

Similarly, the demand that everything once done in secret now be done in the open has led to a normative shift, as diplomats are more willing to relinquish partial control over the communication process and to share information on digital platforms where it might be negated, contested, or rejected. This new norm has led to structural and procedural changes in MFAs, who have established digital units tasked with live-tweeting diplomatic negotiations or publishing international accords. From the perspective of diplomats' self-narratives, or the metaphors they employ to conceptualize their craft, some have adopted the metaphor of democratized diplomacy, in which information is shared to allow digital publics to take part in the policy formulation process. Such is the case with the New Zealand MFA evaluated in Chapter 6.

The second example deals with the logic of a society at a distance, one that employs digital technologies to manipulate time and space. From a normative perspective, society at a distance is one that constantly strives to annihilate time and space, rendering these dimensions meaningless. This leads to doing things at a distance, from remote learning

Table 2.1 Mapping the influence of the digital society on the digitalization of public diplomacy

Digital society/ public diplomacy	Logic/demands	Normative (norms, values)	Procedural (working routines, structure)	Conceptual (metaphors, self-narratives)
Digital society	Everything done in secret must be done in the open	Openness and authenticity	Constant sharing of personal information	Creation of distinct iBrand
Public diplomacy	Everything done in secret must be done in the open	Relinquishing control over the communication process	Digital units that live-tweet diplomatic events, publish international accords	Democratized diplomacy
Digital society	Society at a distance	Annihilation of time and space	Remote learning, drones	Instant wars
Public diplomacy	Diplomacy at a distance	Overcoming traditional limitations of time and space	Digital outreach teams that launch virtual Embassies, manage Q&A	Relationship building
Digital society	Too much information	Drown by design	Algorithmic filtering	Tailoring
Public diplomacy	Too much information	Sense making	Ambassadors curate information for followers, recommend sources of insight	Real-time diplomacy

to remote and instant wars. Society at a distance manifests itself within MFAs through the practice of diplomacy at a distance, which utilizes digital tools to overcome the limitations of time and space, as explored in Chapter 7. This leads to structural and procedural changes, such as the creation of the U.S. State Department's Digital Outreach Team, which is based in Washington, but tasked with building relationships with Muslim Internet users all over the world or Swedish officials based in Stockholm, tasked with launching virtual, global embassies.

The third example deals with the demand that digital users sift their way through a daily barrage of TMI. From a normative perspective,

digital publics may be deluged by design to increase adoration for algorithmic filtering and adopt the metaphor of a tailored society. TMI has
led diplomats to adopt the norm of sense making or aiding digital publics make sense of the world around them. To do so, ambassadors now
curate information for their followers concerning world events as they
unfold, thus limiting the impact of TMI and adopting the metaphor of
real-time diplomacy.

Crucially, the impact of the digital society on public diplomacy is
not uniform across all MFAs, as each ministry is currently undergoing
its own unique process of digitalization influenced by a myriad of factors ranging from government-wide adoption of digital technologies to
local norms, customs and national priorities. Digitalization is also not
an instantaneous process. Rather, it is a prolonged one which over time
influences the values, norms, working routines and structures of MFAs
alongside the self-narrative and metaphors diplomats employ to imagine
their craft. Now that the digital society has been characterized and its
logic explained, this book can begin to analyze the digitalization of public diplomacy. The following chapter analyzes a decade of interactions
between diplomats and digital publics.

REFERENCES

Anderson, B. (2006). *Imagined communities: Reflections on the origin and spread
of nationalism*. New York: Verso Books.
Arsenault, A. (2013). Networks of freedom, networks of control: Internet policy
as a platform for and an impediment to relational public diplomacy. In R. S.
Zaharna, A. Arsenault, & A. Fisher (Eds.), *Relational, networked and collabo-
rative approaches to public diplomacy* (pp. 192–208). New York, NY: Taylor &
Francis.
Bauman, Z. (2000). *Modernity and the Holocaust*. Ithaca: Cornell University
Press.
Bauman, Z., & Lyon, D. (2016). Remoteness, distancing and automation. In
Z. Bauman & D. Lyon (Eds.), *Liquid surveillance* (pp. 76–99). Cambridge:
Polity Press.
Beck, U. (1992). *Risk society: Towards a new modernity*. London: Sage.
Beer, D. (2013). *Popular culture and new media: The politics of circulation*. New
York: Springer.
Bernal, V. (2014). *Nation as network: Diaspora, cyberspace, and citizenship*.
Chicago, IL: University of Chicago Press.

Bjola, C. (2016). Diplomacy as world disclosure: A fractal theory of crisis management. *The British Journal of Politics and International Relations, 18*(2), 335–350.

Bjola, C. (2017, August 8). *Diplomatic crisis management in the digital age* [Blog]. Retrieved from https://uscpublicdiplomacy.org/blog/diplomatic-crisis-management-digital-age.

Bjola, C., & Jiang, L. (2015). Social media and public diplomacy: A comparative analysis of the digital diplomatic strategies of the EU, US and Japan in China. In C. Bjola & M. Holmes (Eds.), *Digital diplomacy theory and practice* (pp. 71–88). Oxon: Routledge.

Broadbent, S. (2017). Approaches to personal communication. In H. A. Horst & D. Miller (Eds.), *Digital anthropology* (pp. 127–145). London: Bloomsbury Academic.

Cassidy, J., & Manor, I. (2016). Crafting strategic MFA communication policies during times of political crisis: A note to MFA policy makers. *Global Affairs, 2*(3), 331–343.

Castells, M. (2000a). Materials for an exploratory theory of the network society. *The British journal of sociology, 51*(1), 5–24.

Castells, M. (2000b). The contours of the network society. *Foresight, 2*(2), 151–157.

Castells, M. (2002). *The internet galaxy: Reflections on the internet, business, and society.* Oxford: Oxford University Press on Demand.

Castells, M. (2006). The network society: From knowledge to policy. In M. Castells & G. Cardoso (Eds.), *The Network Society From Knowledge to Policy* (pp. 3–22). Washington, DC: Center for Transatlantic Relations.

Causey, C., & Howard, P. N. (2013). Delivering digital public diplomacy. In R. S. Zaharna, A. Arsenault, & A. Fisher (Eds.), *Relational, networked and collaborative approaches to public diplomacy* (pp. 144–156). New York, NY: Taylor & Francis.

Cheney-Lippold, J. (2011). A new algorithmic identity: Soft biopolitics and the modulation of control. *Theory, Culture & Society, 28*(6), 164–181.

Clark, K. (1987). *Civilization: A personal view.* London: BBC Books.

Clegg, B. (2017). *Big data: How the information revolution is transforming our lives.* London: Icon Books.

Copeland, D. (2013). Taking diplomacy public: Science, technology and foreign ministries in a heteropolar world. In R. S. Zaharna, A. Arsenault, & A. Fisher (Eds.), *Relational, networked and collaborative approaches to public diplomacy* (pp. 56–69). New York, NY: Taylor & Francis.

DeNicola, L. (2017). Geomedia: The reassertion of space within digital culture. In H. A. Horst & D. Miller (Eds.), *Digital anthropology* (pp. 80–100). London: Bloomsbury Academic.

Geary, P. J. (2003). *The myth of nations: The medieval origins of Europe*. Princeton: Princeton University Press.

Gershon, I. (2010). *The breakup 2.0: Disconnecting over new media*. Ithaca: Cornell University Press.

Guardian Staff. (2016, April). CV of failures: Princeton publishes resume of his career lows. *The Guardian*. Retrieved from https://www.theguardian.com/education/2016/apr/30/cv-of-failures-princeton-professor-publishes-resume-of-his-career-lows.

Haynal, G. (2011). Corporate diplomacy in the information age: Catching up to the dispersal of power. In J. G. Stein (Ed.), *Diplomacy in the digital age: Essays in honour of Ambassador Allan Gotlieb* (pp. 209–224). Ontario: Signal.

Hobsbawm, E. (2001). *The age of capital: 1848–1875*. London: Abacus.

Horst, H. A. (2017). New media technologies in everyday life. In H. A. Horst & D. Miller (Eds.), *Digital anthropology* (pp. 61–79). London: Bloomsbury Academic.

Israel Ministry of Foreign Affairs. (2017). *Digital diplomacy conference summary* (pp. 6–19). Retrieved from https://www.state.gov/documents/organization/271028.pdf.

Kant, I. (2013). *An answer to the question: 'What is enlightenment?'* London: Penguin.

Khatib, L., Dutton, W., & Thelwall, M. (2012). Public diplomacy 2.0: A case study of the US digital outreach team. *The Middle East Journal, 66*(3), 453–472.

Lally, E. (2002). *At home with computers*. Oxford: Berg Publishers.

Lash, S. (2007). Power after hegemony: Cultural studies in mutation? *Theory, Culture & Society, 24*(3), 55–78.

Lesk, M. (2013). Big data, big brother, big money. *IEEE Security and Privacy, 11*(4), 85–89.

Locke, M. (2018, April 25). *How likes went bad* [Blog]. Retrieved from https://medium.com/s/a-brief-history-of-attention/how-likes-went-bad-b094ddd07d4.

Lupton, D. (2015). A critical sociology of big data. In D. Lupton (Ed.), *Digital sociology* (pp. 93–116). New York, NY: Routledge.

Manor, I. (2016). Are we there yet: Have MFAs realized the potential of digital diplomacy? *Brill Research Perspectives in Diplomacy and Foreign Policy, 1*(2), 1–110.

Manor, I., & Soone, L. (2018, January). The digital industries: Transparency as mass deception. *Global Policy*. Retrieved from https://www.globalpolicyjournal.com/articles/science-and-technology/digital-industries-transparency-mass-deception.

McNutt, K. (2014). Public engagement in the Web 2.0 era: Social collaborative technologies in a public sector context. *Canadian Public Administration, 57*(1), 49–70.

Melissen, J. (2005). The new public diplomacy: Between theory and practice. In J. Melissen (Ed.), *The new public diplomacy: Soft power in international relations* (pp. 3–27). New York: Palgrave Macmillan.

Metzgar, E. T. (2012). Is it the medium or the message? Social media, American public diplomacy & Iran. *Global Media Journal, 12*(21), 1.

Miller, D. (2017). Social networking sites. In H. A. Horst & D. Miller (Eds.), *Digital anthropology* (pp. 146–164). London: Bloomsbury Academic.

Miller, D., & Horst, H. A. (2017). The digital and the human: A prospectus for digital anthropology. In H. A. Horst & D. Miller (Eds.), *Digital anthropology* (pp. 3–38). London: Bloomsbury Academic.

Ministry of Foreign Affairs of Denmark. (2017). *Denmark names first ever tech ambassador.* Retrieved from http://um.dk/en/news/newsdisplaypage/?new sid=60eaf005-9f87-46f8-922a-1cf20c5b527a.

Morad, Y. (2014). *Understanding Israeli digital diplomacy* [In person].

Pamment, J. (2013). *New public diplomacy in the 21st century: A comparative study of policy and practice.* Abingdon: Routledge.

Paraphrased from: le Carré, J. (1986). *A perfect spy.* London: Hodder & Stoughton.

Powers, S., & Kounalakis, M. (2017). *Can public diplomacy survive the internet? Bots, echo chambers, and disinformation.* US Advisory Commission on Public Diplomacy. Retrieved from https://www.state.gov/documents/organization/271028.pdf.

Praiser, E. (2011, March). *Eli Praiser: Beware online "filter bubbles"* [Video file]. Retrieved from https://www.ted.com/talks/eli_pariser_beware_online_filter_bubbles?language=en.

Ratson, E. (2018). *Understanding Israeli algorithmic diplomacy* [In person].

Roberts, I. (2017). Diplomacy—A short history from pre-classical origins to the fall of the Berlin Wall. In I. Roberts (Ed.), *Satow's diplomatic practice* (pp. 3–19). Oxford: Oxford University Press.

Ruppert, E. (2011). Population objects: Interpassive subjects. *Sociology, 45*(2), 218–233. Cited in: Lupton, D. (2014). A critical sociology of big data.

Seib, P. (2012). *Real-time diplomacy: Politics and power in the social media era.* New York, NY: Palgrave Macmillan.

Seib, P. (2016). *The future of diplomacy.* Cambridge: Polity Press.

Silver, D., & Massanari, A. (2006). *Critical cyberculture studies.* New York, NY: New York University Press.

Slaughter, A. M. (2009). America's edge: Power in the networked century. *Foreign Affairs, 88*(1) 94–113.

Slaughter, A. M. (2017). *The chessboard and the web: Strategies of connection in a networked world.* New Haven, CT: Yale University Press.

Storr, W. (2018). *Selfie: How the West became self-obsessed.* London: Picador.

Tucker, J., Guess, A., Barberá, P., Vaccari, C., Siegel, A., Sanovich, S., ..., Nyhan, B. (2018). Social media, political polarization, and political disinformation: A review of the scientific literature. Hewlett Foundation

Van Dijk, J. A. (2017). Digital divide: Impact of access. *The International Encyclopedia of Media Effects*, 1–11.

Zaharna, R. S. (2013). Network purpose, network design: Dimensions of network and collaborative public diplomacy. In R. S. Zaharna, A. Arsenault, & A. Fisher (Eds.), *Relational, networked and collaborative approaches to public diplomacy* (pp. 173–191). New York, NY: Taylor & Francis.

CHAPTER 3

A Vocal and Volatile Online Public

Diplomacy is the art of telling someone to go to hell in such a way that he actually looks forward to the journey.

—Winston Churchill

After the outbreak of World War II, British Prime Minister Winston Churchill attended a military exercise of the British artillery corps. The Prime Minister noticed that seconds before the cannons roared, several soldiers knelt and raised their right hands in the air. Soon, new shells had been loaded into the canonns and, once again, seconds before their roar, the soldiers kneeled and raised their right hands in the air. Perplexed, the Prime Minister asked the soldiers what they were doing. Their reply was that they were holding the restraints of the horses so that they would not bolt in fear of the cannons. There were, of course, no horses near the cannons in 1940, but the drills and working routines of the artillery corps had not been updated since World War I.

The emergence of the digital society found diplomats restraining their own imaginary horses. The desire to interact with members of the digital society, the demand for sharing information and the need to attract attention from digital publics all required that diplomats establish new working routines, adopt new norms, and acquire new skills and capabilities. The procedures established to practice twentieth-century-public diplomacy would become mostly obsolete by the turn of the century as public diplomacy shifted its gaze from elites and opinion makers to ordinary citizens.

© The Author(s) 2019
I. Manor, *The Digitalization of Public Diplomacy*,
Palgrave Macmillan Series in Global Public Diplomacy,
https://doi.org/10.1007/978-3-030-04405-3_3

Yet what diplomats failed to account for was the temperament of digital publics who would soon prove to be vocal, opinionated, volatile, and yearning to be heard. This chapter offers a series of case studies demonstrating how the characteristics of digital publics challenged diplomats' practices, working routines, and communicative cultures. The chapter is chronological so as to demonstrate that the digitalization of public diplomacy did not occur in one day, nor was it the result of a single digital interaction. Rather, the digitalization of public diplomacy has been a long-term process in which digital technologies, digital publics and digital initiatives have all impacted the conduct of public diplomacy. The chapter begins by illustrating the digitalization of American public diplomacy before examining the digital initiatives of the governments of Hamas, Israel, Sweden, the USA and the EU. Each of these case studies demonstrates the manner in which interactions between digital publics and diplomats shaped the digitalization of public diplomacy.

The "New" American Evangelists

As was explained in the introduction, the dawn of the twenty-first century saw a conceptual shift among scholars of public diplomacy referred to as the "new" public diplomacy. The 9/11 terror attacks, the formation of a global media ecology, and the emergence of the digital society all necessitated that diplomats transition from monologue- to dialogue-based public diplomacy. This "new" form of public diplomacy would strive to foster relationships with foreign populations so as to create a receptive environment for a nation's foreign policy. Such relationships could be formed through two-way digital interactions (Melissen, 2005). Importantly, public diplomacy scholars regarded digital platforms, such as social media sites, as *the* medium of the "new" public diplomacy as they enable organizations to transition from one-way broadcast paradigms to two-way communicative paradigms that center on mutual interactions (McNutt, 2014). Moreover, relationships are the foundations of social media sites (Waters, Burnett, Lamm, & Lucas, 2009), which also provide ideal conditions for two-way interactions, as organizations and publics can discuss issues of mutual concern (Bortree & Seltzer, 2009). During the first decade of the twenty-first century, the logic of the "new" public diplomacy began to permeate MFAs around the world. One notable example is the U.S. State Department.

Like scholars of public diplomacy, its practitioners also realized that monologic public diplomacy could not thrive in the digital realm.

According to James Pamment (2013), the process by which the "new" public diplomacy diffused into the State Department began when Washington-based think tanks lobbied to reform U.S. public diplomacy. One such think tank, the Council on Foreign Relations, argued in 2002 that new technologies necessitated that public diplomacy actors focus on foreign citizens and "adopt an engagement approach that involves listening, dialogue, debate and relationship building and increases the amount and effectiveness of public-opinion research" (Pamment, 2013, p. 8).

In 2008, the diffusion of the "new" public diplomacy was made evident in the Public Diplomacy 2.0 initiative, launched by President Bush's Under Secretary of State for Public Diplomacy and Public Affairs, James Glassman. When defining the Public Diplomacy 2.0 initiative, Glassman stated:

> Don't we want to maintain control of our message? Perhaps. But in this new world of communications, any government that resists new Internet techniques faces a greater risk: being ignored. Our major target audiences - especially the young - don't want to listen to us lecture them or tell them what to think or how wonderful we are... But our broad mandate in public diplomacy is to understand, inform, engage, and influence foreign publics. All of these activities work best by conversation rather than dictation. (in Hayden, 2012)

Glassman's statement echoes Nicholas Cull's (2008) definition of the "new" public diplomacy as accomplishing foreign policy goals through engagement with foreign publics. It also mirrors James Pamment's definition, as Public Diplomacy 2.0 was framed by Glassman as a clear break from twentieth-century public diplomacy. Additionally, Glassman's statement represents an understanding of the digital society. Digital publics, especially the young members of the digital society, would not simply absorb State Department messages, but would comment on them and even contest them. As Spry (2018) wrote, digital publics are active audiences and they determine what content to respond to, and how, be it in reinterpreting public diplomacy messages, resisting them, or ignoring them altogether.

In his statement, Glassman warned the State Department that failure to relinquish control over public diplomacy messages and engage with digital society members would transform American diplomats into whales storming the beaches of irrelevance.

While the Bush administration launched Public Diplomacy 2.0, it was the Obama administration that would fully embrace the logic of the "new" public diplomacy. This was no accident. As a presidential candidate, Barack Obama realized the immense potential of digital platforms to shape online discussions, as well as offline opinions and beliefs. Once in office, the Obama administration actively encouraged federal agencies to embrace digital platforms as a means of communicating with the American public and providing it with information and services. In 2009, the Obama administration published the "Open Government Initiative," which required federal departments to "harness new technologies" and readily publish information about their operations online. The directive focused on three core activities of the open government: transparency, collaboration, and participation (Bertot, Jaeger, & Grimes, 2012; Bertot, Jaeger, & Hansen, 2012; Lee & Kwak, 2012; Mergel, 2013; Snead, 2013). These are the very building blocks of the digital society, as members constantly share information, commit themselves to the value of openness, and collaboratively create information.

Where the Obama White House led, federal agencies followed, flocking to social media sites while developing their own open government initiatives (Bjola & Manor, 2018). Within the State Department, the zeitgeist of the Obama administration was propagated by 28-year-old Alec Ross, senior adviser for innovation to the Secretary of State, and 38-year-old Jared Cohen, the youngest member of the Secretary of State's policy planning staff. It was these two digital evangelists who sought to leverage the power of digital technologies toward diplomatic ends. Both maintained that diplomacy could no longer be limited to "white guys with white shirts and red ties talking to other white guys with white shirts and red ties." The strategy they championed, known as twenty-first-century statecraft, aimed to amplify traditional diplomatic efforts with tech-based solutions. As Cohen and Ross stated, diplomacy was no longer just about political beliefs, it was about open diplomacy versus closed diplomacy, about working with networks that exist above and below the state, and about relinquishing control over online communication as "the twenty-first century is a terrible time to be a control freak" (Cull, 2013; Lichtenstein, 2010; Ross, 2011).

Ross and Cohen soon struck an alliance with Silicon Valley magnates such as the CEO of Google or the chairman of Twitter and would also frequently visit Silicon Valley looking to foster new collaborations. The logic of the digital society was becoming embedded into the very DNA of American public diplomacy. Twenty-first-century statecraft grew to include sending tech delegations abroad, crowdsourcing tech-based solutions to bilateral challenges such as the narcotics trade, and ensuring that U.S. tech companies help spread democracy around the world. In one famous instance, the CEO of Twitter was asked to delay maintenance work on the network as protesters in Iran's Green Revolution were relying on Twitter to disseminate images and videos of the regime's crackdown (Lichtenstein, 2010).

As part of their gospel, Cohen and Ross maintained that viral videos would alter the nature of politics, that mobile phones would become widespread tools for election monitoring and that virtual embassies would create new platforms for collaborations between global NGOs. Commenting on a video depicting the death of a young woman in Iran's Green protests, Cohen stated that it was "the most significant viral video of our lifetimes" (Lichtenstein, 2010).

Equally important to the adoption of the "new" public diplomacy was the 2009 appointment of Anne-Marie Slaughter as director of the policy planning staff at the State Department. In the same year as her appointment, Slaughter wrote an article entitled "America's Edge: Power in a Networked Century," in which she argued that American power would rest on its ability to form transnational networks that could stimulate innovative solutions to global challenges (Slaughter, 2009). Ross, Cohen, and Slaughter seem to have epitomized the values of the digital society, and through them, among others, its culture and logic permeated the State Department (G. Lampe, personal communication, July 26, 2018). They would lobby for a more open, engaging, and networked form of public diplomacy that met the demands of digital society members and transitioned from monologue- to dialogue-based forms of engagement. Even their own use of social media was representative of the digital society. Alec Ross would tweet policy updates alongside his anticipation for a new season of the TV show *Entourage*, thereby creating an authentic online persona (Lichtenstein, 2010).

Ross and Cohen soon became Twitter celebrities in the U.S. government. Through their celebrity status and their authentic online tone, the logic of the digital society was being hammered into the minds of U.S. diplomats: Open is good. Closed is bad. Authenticity is key. By 2010, Ross and Cohen were, after Barack Obama and Senator John McCain, among the most followed members of government on Twitter. By 2012, the U.S. State Department was managing an empire of more than 500 social media accounts (Hayden, 2012).

Another catalyst of the new public diplomacy's diffusion into the State Department was the Arab Spring, which caught American diplomats by surprise as they were not monitoring the digital platforms in which these revolutions were beginning to take shape. These were platforms on which Arab citizens openly criticized their despots. On those platforms Arab Citizens freed themselves from the binding shackles of government censorship. In 2011, President Obama's Under Secretary of State for Public Diplomacy and Public Affairs stated:

> In a world where power and influence truly belongs to the many, we must engage with more people in more places. That is the essential truth of public diplomacy in the internet age…. The pyramid of power flipped because people all around the world are clamoring to be heard, and demanding to shape their own futures. They are having important conversations right now - in chatrooms and classrooms and boardrooms - and they aren't waiting for us. (Cited in Hayden, 2012)

The Arab Spring saw the acceleration of the digitalization of public diplomacy in the U.S. State Department. Notably, the State Department did not become digital in one day, nor did it embrace digital platforms at one time. Rather, there was a process of digitalization in which new approaches, methods, and definitions of public diplomacy were embraced over the course of a decade. This process was facilitated by external events (Arab Spring), the musings of academics and think tanks (Council on Foreign Relations), government-wide approaches to digital technologies (Obama's Open Government Initiative), appointments of certain individuals to high-ranking positions (Anne-Marie Slaughter), and the zeal of two young policy-makers looking to digitalize diplomacy through alliances with Silicon Valley. While this process was unique to the State Department, it was also generic as MFAs throughout the world experienced their own processes of digitalization, influenced by local norms and values, government approaches to technology, and external events or shocks.

Yet for all the optimism that characterized the early work of Alec Ross and Jared Cohen, within a few years they changed their tune. In an interview from 2015, Alec Ross echoed Zygmunt Bauman and David Lyon (2016), stating that the problem with digital revolutions was that they were networked, and as such, were also leaderless. As there is no charismatic leader willing to take the mantle of power once the revolution ends, chaos ensues. When asked if digital revolutions could lead to better outcomes, the more cautious Ross stated:

> This is one of the cases when I'm just not a techno-utopian. I'm not terribly optimistic about it... I just don't think people will be able to tweet their way to a functional democracy... I actually think people should put their smartphones down and focus on institution building and leadership development. (BNN, 2015)

What brought about this reversal of opinion? Why was the techno-euphoria of 2010 replaced by the techno-pessimism of 2015? One answer could lie in diplomats' encounters with digital publics. For while diplomats were willing to relinquish some control over their communications and converse with connected individuals, they were unprepared for the vocal and volatile public they would encounter online—a public that disputed, rejected, or outright opposed public diplomacy campaigns (Spry, 2018). This chapter charts diplomats' experiences with this volatile public over a decade and demonstrates how these interactions further shaped the process of digitalization of public diplomacy.

2007—Sweden's Virtual Sex Party

On May 30, 2007, Swedish Foreign Minister Carl Bildt entered the virtual world of Second Life, becoming one of the first diplomats to visit this mirror world in which a vibrant community of individuals gathered daily to lead a virtual life and manage virtual relationships. Bildt entered this world to inaugurate one of the world's first virtual embassies, built by the Swedish Institute in Second Life. Sweden's virtual embassy, called Second House of Sweden, represented a novel approach to practicing the "new" public diplomacy. The embassy's stated goal was to cultivate direct engagement with Second Life users and serve as a pilot study through which Swedish officials could learn how to communicate in digital settings (Pamment, 2013).

In addition to being one of the world's first virtual embassies, Second House of Sweden was also the world's first global embassy, meant to foster relationships between the Swedish government and a global, digital, public. Second House of Sweden was thus a truly "digital" initiative, as it sought to render time and space meaningless. Government officials and digital publics could meet online and converse in real-time regardless of the physical distance between them. Moreover, officials and publics conversing on Second Life would exist in the same digital time zone irrespective of their physical time zones.

Unlike future virtual embassies, Second House of Sweden was not meant to serve as a surrogate for a brick and mortar embassy. It did not have a consular department, nor did it deal with bi-lateral issues. The embassy was used to promote Swedish art and culture and offer visitors a Swedish experience. It therefore included three virtual exhibition areas and an outdoor stage. Between 2007 and 2009, the embassy hosted talks by Swedish art curators, Swedish language lessons, film screenings and film festivals, e-learning conferences, and even national day celebrations.

Importantly, Second House of Sweden was created with offline diplomatic goals in mind. The virtual embassy was a replica of the real Second House of Sweden, the nation's flagship embassy in Washington. Moreover, Second House of Sweden was meant to promote a positive national image of Sweden, which would bolster the Swedish national brand (Pamment, 2013, pp. 119–123). Swedish virtual diplomacy was thus intrinsically linked to offline public diplomacy goals.

From its inauguration, however, the embassy encountered resistance from Second Life users. Some threatened to oppose the embassy's grand opening by having a sex party on its roof. Danish Second Life users protested the incursion of reality into their virtual world. In one instance, a Second Life user visited Raoul Wallenberg's recreated office wearing a Nazi uniform, while hackers attempted to disrupt film screenings (ibid.).

These protests were instructive for Swedish officials and diplomats. They illustrated that not all digital communities would welcome governments into their midst. Indeed, the Declaration of Independence of Cyberspace, published in 1996 by John Perry Barlow, stated quite clearly that the governments of the world would not be welcome in the digital realm.

Sweden's digital experience demonstrated the ease with which digital diplomatic activities and campaigns could be derailed by digital publics. The rejection of the Second House of Sweden by some users elucidated that digital publics could assert themselves in unpredictable ways, to paraphrase George Haynal (2011). Early rejections of digitalized public diplomacy activities shook the foundations of diplomatic institutions, as MFAs had yet to adapt to the digital age in which diplomatic blunders, mistakes, and faux pas are inevitable (Copeland, 2013). Nonetheless, the emergence of the digital society required that diplomats step out from behind their embassy walls, interact directly with digital publics, relinquish control over their messages, and lift the veil of discretion and secrecy from diplomatic processes. One leader who promised to do just that was Barack Obama.

2009—OBAMA'S CAIRO REDRESS

On June 4, 2009, President Obama delivered his "New Beginnings" address at Cairo University. In it, the President called for a new relationship between the USA and the Muslim world and an end to animosity between the two. Speaking to the Muslim world from a Muslim capital, Obama hoped to redress the damage caused to America's relationships in the Middle East and with the Muslim world following the tenure of George W. Bush (Colvin, 2009). In the aftermath of the address, the State Department's Digital Outreach Team (DOT) attempted to interact directly with Muslim Internet users. This activity was the digital manifestation of Obama's promise to begin a new dialogue with the Muslim world and a unique attempt to practice the "new" public diplomacy and create relationships with Muslim digital publics. The DOT's activity also demonstrates how digital technologies are used to obtain offline public diplomacy goals.

The State Department's DOT was established in 2006 as a means of engaging with online Muslims. It was staffed by ten civil servants who were all native Arabic speakers. In the weeks following Obama's Cairo address, DOT members visited popular websites in the Arab world so as to converse with Muslim visitors, narrate America's policies in the Middle East, highlight positive aspects of America's involvement in the region, and counter the view of America as a militaristic empire that was occupying Muslim countries such as Iraq and Afghanistan (Khatib, Dutton, & Thelwall, 2012).

However, the DOT soon encountered barriers to its digital activities. First, the DOT often responded to questions by simply posting excerpts from Obama's address. When the DOT did interact with Internet users, DOT members took 2.7 days to reply to a user's comment or question. DOT members also posted similar messages across multiple websites, thus failing to tailor their online communication to the interest and needs of website users. Similarly, the DOT often replied to emotional posts with facts and figures, thus failing to meaningfully interact with

Internet users. Equally problematic was the DOT's attempt to respond to graphic images of dead Muslim children by stating that it was Muslim terrorists who were killing children in Iraq. These responses stoked a tidal wave of profanities from Muslim Internet users. In fact, Khatib et al. (2012) found that DOT messages actually led to more negative sentiment in online conversations.

The DOT's outreach activities demonstrate how unprepared American diplomats were for dealing with contentious issues opposite critical audiences. The DOT took more than 2 days to respond to questions and comments, as each DOT response had to be researched for accuracy and approved in a meeting by all DOT members. Yet the very promise of digital connectivity is that of instantaneous conversations that take place regardless of time and distance. By failing to meet the expectations of digital publics to converse in real-time, the DOT was unable to foster dialogue with digital audiences. DOT members also seem to have failed to listen to the comments posted by Internet users. They responded to emotions with facts and figures and posted the same responses across multiple platforms. Yet the digital society is one in which information must be tailored to the views and interests of digital publics. The team also embraced a reactive form of communication rather than an active one in which they could attempt to set the agenda for online discussions. This was most evident in their decision to respond to graphic and violent images, which are often used by trolls to purposefully derail online conversations.

Following the DOT's experience, and that of other digital teams around the world, MFAs began to develop new working routines and adapt existing routines to the digital age. Conversing with digital publics required that diplomats be allowed to post online messages based on their own judgment. This would require digital training so that diplomats venturing online would be able to contend with the expectations, demands, and newfound agency of digital publics. Dealing with online criticism and possible trolls would require that MFAs draft guidelines articulating when, and how, critics should be engaged and what type of content should be disregarded. Tailoring diplomatic messaging to the interests and needs of specific publics would require that diplomats become familiar with the logic of each social media site; while Facebook is primarily used for relationship building, Twitter is used for information gathering and opinion sharing (Hughes, Rowe, Batey, & Lee, 2012; Kwak, Lee, Park, & Moon, 2010). Importantly, digital interactions would also necessitate a normative shift within MFAs in which public diplomacy would become public-centric and strive to meet the informational needs and desire of digital publics rather than those of elites. Yet MFAs would also have to be cautious of imposing too many restrictions, guidelines, and limitations on diplomats, as these would prevent diplomats from obtaining the authenticity that is required for digital interactions.

So, the process of digitalization begun to influence the procedures, culture and working routines of MFAs around the world who created digital departments tasked with overseeing the training of diplomatic corps. As each MFA underwent its own process of digitalization, each MFA developed its own unique form of digital training and supervision. The Polish MFA adopted the model of "Train and Supervise" in which the MFA closely supervises and reviews content published by Polish embassies on digital platforms. The Finnish MFA adopted the model of "Trust, Train and Provide" in which embassies enjoy autonomy with regard to content published online and are also provided with materials from the MFA. Israel's MFA adopted the model of "Train, Supervise, and Utilize" as embassies are often used by the MFA to promote certain messages on a global scale (Manor, 2016). These MFAs, however, are by no means the only ones to offer diplomats digital training. From Nairobi to Dublin and London to Moscow, diplomats are now trained in the new art of digital engagement. MFAs' ability to develop new working routines, alter their structures, and establish new departments negates Copeland's (2013) argument that as the oldest organ of government, MFAs are "ossified and sclerotic, relying heavily on established procedures and command and control style social relations."

The DOT's activities represented an open form of online interactions conducted on Internet websites. By 2013, MFAs adopted a more conservative and quarantined form of engagement—the social media Q&A.

2013–2014 Ask #Israel

Between 2013 and 2014, the Israeli MFA held two important Q&A sessions on Twitter inviting users to interact in real-time with Israeli diplomats. By the summer of 2013, Q&As had become a popular public diplomacy tool as they counterbalanced the desires of digital society members and the risk-intolerant cultures of MFAs. While these Q&As

were advertised as "live," they consisted of users posting questions and diplomats determining which questions to answer. Diplomats could take up to several minutes to review the questions posted online, determine which were least controversial, and formulate a diplomatic response. Moreover, diplomats could decide which questions and users to avoid. By providing opportunities for near-real-time interactions, and by sharing information, opinions, and even personal anecdotes from their careers, diplomats met the desire of digital publics.

One of the first Israeli Twitter Q&As took place in December 2013. Twitter users were asked to pose questions to the MFA's spokesperson, Yigal Palmor. Tellingly, the Twitter advertisements for the Q&A asked users to submit questions several days before the event actually took place. This enabled the spokesperson to review the type and tone of questions he was receiving, and to pre-author a set of possible answers. The online advertisements for the event also attempted to set the agenda for the Q&A by limiting the topics to be addressed online. One ad stated, "What does Israel really think about Hamas? Everything you've always wanted to know and were afraid to ask." Another advertisement asked, "What does Israel really think about Iran?" As such, this Q&A may be regarded as a quarantined form of engagement in which digital publics could interact with diplomats for a limited time regarding a limited number of issues (Kampf, Manor & Segev, 2015).

Half a year later, in July 2014, the Israeli ambassador to the USA, Ron Dermer, invited American Twitter users to a special Q&A dealing with Israel's War in Gaza.

As Hamas rockets turned dusk to dawn in Israeli cities, and as Gaza was being bombarded by Israeli fighter jets, the ambassador began taking questions from Twitter users. However, it quickly became apparent that many users were not interested in conversing with the ambassador, but were hoping to hijack the event and criticize Israel's government and its policies. Dermer was bombarded with a long series of personal attacks, graphic images of dead Palestinian children, and cartoons depicting Israeli soldiers as Nazi officers. Twitter users also asked Dermer what was his favorite instrument for killing Palestinian children—bombardment, starvation, or disease? Another user asked if the ambassador took drugs to convince himself that killing children on the beaches of Gaza was an act of "self-defense." Others asked if he was proud that his nation had injured more than a thousand Palestinians and whether it was he who fed the White House Zionist propaganda.

Digital publics did not merely oppose the ambassador's public diplomacy effort. They rejected it completely, telling the ambassador in a very non-diplomatic tone to go to hell. Subsequently, the Q&A attracted media attention. Al Jazeera published a news article titled "Q&A goes terribly wrong," while *Russia Today* and *Business Insider* labeled it an "Epic Fail" and "A disaster" respectively. According to Al Jazeera, the #AskDermer hashtag was used more than 20,000 times, mostly for posting negative comments (Manor, 2014; The Stream, 2014).

In spite of the negative backlash, the Israeli ambassador neither flinched nor sought refuge offline. His replies stated that Israel was doing all in its power to protect the lives of civilians, even though Hamas uses citizens as human shields. The ambassador also assured followers that all civilian deaths would be investigated by Israel. He explained that Israel had agreed to numerous cease-fire proposals but these had all been rejected by the Hamas government. He stressed that Israel withdrew from the Gaza strip in 2005, only to have it fall into the hands of an organization that openly called for the destruction of Israel. The ambassador also narrated Israel's objectives, stating that "quiet would be met with quiet", meaning that once Hamas stopped firing rockets, Israel would cease its air and ground operations. The ambassador also equated Hamas' use of human shields with Israeli attempts to shield its citizens. Yet amidst the graphic imagery of dead mothers and sons, and the clatter of curse words and anger, the ambassador's answers may have fallen on deaf ears.

One could, however, assert that the ambassador's decision to remain online and answer difficult questions demonstrated a true desire to converse with digital publics. It may have also demonstrated that Israel could justify its policies in the region, even the most contentious ones. Moreover, by attempting to interact with critical audiences of Israel, the ambassador was attempting to realize the full potential of digital tools, for why preach to the choir when you can attempt to convert the flock? Lastly, some users who received answers to their questions may have been willing to further converse with the ambassador online, thus laying the foundation for future relationships.

The ambassador's Q&A session may have been used to obtain three offline, public diplomacy goals. The first was to rally support from American Twitter users so as to prevent the Obama administration from restraining Israel's military activities. The second goal may have been to create a moral dichotomy between Hamas, which uses citizens as human shields, and Israel which shields its citizens. Such a moral dichot-omy could have helped manage Israel's image in the USA even as it was bombing Gaza (Manor & Crilley, 2018a). Third, the ambassador may have been attempting to draw a parallel between the threat of terror fac-ing the USA and that facing Israel, thus crafting public diplomacy mes-sages that would resonate with American social media users. While the ambassador may have hoped to converse with American Twitter users, his Q&A drew users from all over the world, many of them unrecep-tive to arguments that could have resonated with Americans. As Sabrina Sotiriu (2015) states, digitalization is often accompanied by a loss of control over the communication process as messages reach unintended audiences. Dermer's Q&A, therefore, demonstrates the glocalized nature of public diplomacy delivered via digital platforms and the annihilation of space in the digital society as borders are rendered meaningless.

Dermer's Q&A illustrates two difficulties that diplomats would have to contend with when practicing the "new" public diplomacy. The first was the relative ease with which digital publics could hijack a diplomatic event and its symbol. The hashtag #AskDermer was not associated with Israeli diplomacy but with Israeli brutality. The second was the media's coverage of such occurrences. The headlines following the Q&A all labe-led it a disaster because the ambassador was rebuked by digital publics. None of the news stories included the ambassador's answers to difficult questions or his willingness to remain online. Such negative media cov-erage of diplomats' efforts to interact with digital publics would cause MFAs to fear digital publics and to view engagement with suspicion. The media's lack of understating of the importance of Dermer's attempt to interact with digital publics shows that the process of digitalization of public diplomacy would include other actors orbiting the sphere of diplomacy, such as journalists and media institutions.

Just as the Israeli ambassador was preparing to log off Twitter, the unpredictable online public stormed Hamas' headquarters.

2015—Ask Hamas

In March 2015, the Hamas terror movement held a three-day Q&A session on Twitter. The tweet publicizing the event stated "Truth from the mouth of the Horse" and employed the hashtag #AskHamas. Unlike previous Q&As, Hamas' event would last for several days and allow Twitter users to interact with four different officials: a female member of

Fig. 3.1 Invitation to Hamas Twitter Q&A (*Source* https://twitter.com/HamasInfoEn/status/576136445443891200)

the Palestinian Legislative Council, a Hamas terrorist who had spent several years in an Israeli jail, the Prime Minister of the Hamas government in Gaza, and a leader in Hamas' military wing (Fig. 3.1).

From the beginning of the Q&A, Hamas spokespersons found themselves facing harsh criticism from digital publics. A large number of questions focused on the priorities of the Hamas government with followers asking, "Why do you choose to build murder tunnels rather than invest in education for your children?" and "Why did you take money given to you by wealthy Arab countries and use it to build terror tunnels instead of feeding your people?" Other users focused on the government's corruption, stating that one of Hamas' leaders, Khaled Mashal, is worth more than $2.6 billion USD while others have secret accounts in Swiss banks and live in lavish hotels in the Gulf.

Additionally, users attacked Hamas' morality and policies toward Israel or Jews by asking "Doesn't firing your missiles from kindergarten and hospitals make you culpable for civilian deaths?" "Using civilians (especially kids) as human shields is inhuman," and "After you fulfill your charter by killing all the Jews, which minority group would you like to exterminate next?" Another issue to be addressed by digital publics was the similarity between Hamas and Daesh, with users focusing on the indoctrination of children, summary executions, and the brutality through which both organizations maintain civil order in their territories. The images projected at Hamas spokespersons were either graphic images of wounded and dead Israelis, images of Hamas' summary executions in Gaza, or images of young Palestinian children holding weapons and vowing to wage holy war. One striking image even included a baby in a crib surrounded by bullets and rifles.

For their part, Hamas spokespersons were selective in the questions they chose to answer. When asked about the prospects of peace with Israel, one spokesperson replied that "Hamas supports any just solution that grants the Palestinian people all their legitimate rights." In response to questions regarding Hamas' military activities, spokespersons stated that Hamas was defending Palestinians from Jews looking to kill Arabs and that Hamas would not disarm "until the occupation ends and justice prevails. Period." Other answers focused on rebuking allegations that Hamas fired rockets from hospitals or civilian areas. Finally, when asked why people would be willing to commit suicide bombings, and why Hamas would support such activities, a spokesperson stated that these bombings were born out of years of aggression, oppression, and occupation.

In summary, Hamas spokespersons addressed questions relating to the terror movement's goals, its military activities and its moral character. However, spokespersons did not comment on the government's priorities in the Gaza strip, the allegations of corruption, the indoctrination of children, and its brutality toward the civilian population of Gaza. The barrage of cynical questions and criticism that Hamas faced online influenced the media's coverage of the Q&A, with the *Washington Post* running the headline "Hamas #AskHamas Twitter campaign is being mocked and it hasn't even started yet," while the Israeli Haaretz paper used the headline "Ask Hamas Twitter campaign backfires" (Haaretz, 2015; Taylor, 2015).

An important question is, why would a terror organization hold a Twitter Q&A in the first place? One answer might be that Hamas was hoping to legitimize its rule over the Gaza strip. By taking to Twitter and offering digital publics the opportunity to interact with and criticize its leaders, Hamas was following the example of many other governments. Moreover, Hamas may have been attempting to manage its

international image. The Q&A, and the involvement of a female spokesperson, enabled Hamas to distance itself from the likes of Daesh and to
portray itself as a progressive Muslim government rather than an oppres-
sive radical Islamic group. The very use of social media sites may have
impacted Hamas' image, as in 2015 social media sites were still viewed
as positive forces in society and were closely associated with the hopeful spirit of the Arab Spring. Finally, online images influence offline perception. Daesh's social media empire and tech savviness, for instance,
enabled it to create an offline image of a state in the making. By authoring an online narrative, or iBrand, of legitimacy and good governance,
Hamas may have been attempting to influence offline perceptions of its
rule over the Gaza strip.

The Hamas Q&A demonstrates that the digitalization of public diplomacy empowered a broad range of actors who could now engage in
public diplomacy activities, foster relationships with digital publics,
manage their image, and legitimize their activities. These ranged from
terror groups such as Daesh to quasi-governments like Hamas and ultra-
national diplomatic entities such as the EU.

2014–2017 The EU's Obsession with Israel

The EU's Delegation to Tel Aviv is one of the most digitally active diplomatic institutions in Israel. Between 2014 and 2017, the Delegation
repeatedly turned to digital platforms in order to interact with Israeli citizens, narrate the EU's policies in the Middle East, and exhibit the close
relationship between Jerusalem and Brussels. These activities, which
included two Facebook Q&As and a Facebook campaign, offer a longitudinal case study of the digitalization of public diplomacy.

The relationship between Israelis and the EU is a strained one. Many
in Israel believe that the EU focuses obsessively on the Israeli-Palestinian
conflict, in comparison with other regional and global crises. Some even
argue that the EU's interest in Israel stems from anti-Semitism and not
from a desire to bring about a peaceful solution to the conflict. Others
maintain that the EU is hypocritical for blaming Israel for human rights
violations while ignoring the atrocities committed by Arab despots or
China (Ahren, 2017; Landau, 2018; Pardo, 2016).

The tension between the EU and Israelis may have motivated the
EU's ambassador to hold a Facebook Q&A soon after he arrived in
Israel. Held in May 2014, the Q&A included 86 questions posed to the

ambassador by Israeli Facebook users. In an attempt to analyze the 2014 Q&A, all questions posted by Facebook users were categorized by two coders based on their subject matter. This categorization was based on an inductive approach in which categories arise from the text itself. The questions posted on Facebook were collected in May 2014 and analyzed during March 2018. The categories identified and their prevalence may be seen in Graph 3.1.

As Graph 3.1 reveals, the two most prevalent categories of queries were "Obsession with Israel" and "Criticize Israel." The "Obsession with Israel" category included questions such as: Why is the EU so obsessed with Israel? Why does it not focus on other global conflicts? Why does the EU condemn Israel's policies while supporting Arab

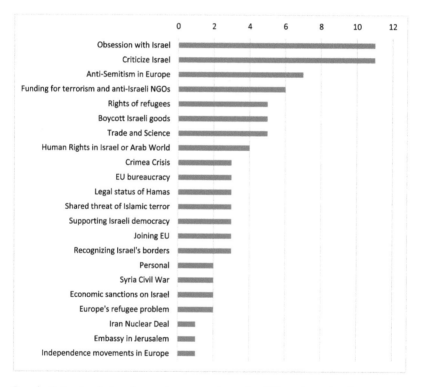

Graph 3.1 Analysis of questions posed to the EU ambassador by category prevalence (number of questions)

dictators? Why does the EU blame Israel for human rights violations while allowing the Assad regime to murder its own people? Notably, many of these questions included the term "obsession". Questions in the "Criticize Israel" category blamed the EU for being quick to judge Israeli military activities even when they are justified, for accepting racism in other countries (such as Denmark's attitude toward Muslims), for attacking Israel in multilateral forums, and for meddling in the Israeli-Palestinian conflict.

The third most prevalent category included questions pertaining to rampant anti-Semitism in Europe and the EU's lack of response to rising anti-Semitism. The fourth most prevalent category, "Funding for terrorism and anti-Israeli NGOs," alleged that EU funds were used by the Palestinian government to pay families of terrorists and that the EU financed Israeli NGOs that strive to subvert the nation state. The fifth most prevalent category lamented the EU's lack of assistance to refugees and asylum seekers who are persecuted in Israel, while the sixth most prevalent category accused the EU of supporting boycotts of Israeli products. The category of "Trade and Science" included questions pertaining to collaborations between the EU and Israel, while the "Human Rights in Israel or Arab World" category emphasized the EU's need to deal with human rights violations in the Arab world, not in Israel.

Among the least prevalent categories were those including questions about global events such as the Crimean Crisis, independence movements in Europe (such as Catalonia) or the Iran nuclear agreement. Israeli Facebook users also asked the ambassador if the EU intended to officially recognize the Hamas government in Gaza, whether the EU intended to collaborate with Israel in fighting the shared threat of Islamic terrorism, if the EU would ever recognize Israel's borders and move its embassy to Jerusalem, and whether Israel could eventually join the EU. Finally, a small number of Israelis asked how Europe would contend with its refugee problem, whether the EU would ever place economic sanctions on Israel, and how the ambassador became a diplomat.

When assessing the sentiment of the questions posed to the ambassador, one begins to understand the Israeli sentiment toward the EU in general. As part of this chapter's analysis, each question was ranked on a sentiment scale ranging from very negative to negative, neutral, positive, and very positive. Two coders ranked all questions, while the Spearman correlation coefficient was used to ensure a high inter-coder reliability. Of the 86 questions posed to the ambassador, 62% had a negative or very negative sentiment, 32% had a neutral sentiment, and only 6% had a positive or very positive sentiment. Indeed, the majority of Facebook users did not simply pose questions to the ambassador; rather they attacked him, the polity he represents, and the EU's policies vis-à-vis Israel. For instance, one user asked, "Will you please stay out of Israeli affairs?" Another wrote, "Dear Ambassador, could you please explain why you think that after more than 2000 years of Europe proving itself incapable of humanely treating its Jews, why do you think we buy your act of PC [political correctness] civility and think that all of a sudden you have all turned on your heads and can now think of Jews as regular people? PS Please advise why you are still here wasting our oxygen?" When addressing funds allocated to the Palestinian government, one Israeli asked, "Good day his Excellency, why is the EU always focused on Israel and almost only on Israel? Why doesn't the EU see to it that all the money given to the so-called 'Palestinians' is going for the right causes!"

Even when asked about issues that are not related to the Israeli-Palestinian conflict, the ambassador was blasted by Israelis. For instance, Israeli Facebook users employed harsh words when blaming the EU for abandoning asylum seekers in Israel, for not doing enough to advance peace, and for not using financial leverage to pressure Israel into making concessions to the Palestinians. One user suggested that the ambassador pack up his bags and leave as soon as possible. As such, the ambassador was damned if he did and damned if he didn't. Despite the negative sentiment of the questions, the EU ambassador answered 64 of the 86 questions posed to him.

In May 2017, exactly three years after the 2014 Q&A, the EU Delegation to Israel launched a shared Facebook campaign with Israel's delegation to the EU in Brussels. The campaign was meant to reflect the close nature of the relationship between the EU and Israel and highlight areas in which the two have a mutually beneficial partnership. This was made evident in the images comprising the campaign, which include two doves, or two hands intertwined, one bearing the flag of Israel and the other the flag of the EU (Fig. 3.2).

An examination of 30 Facebook posts comprising this campaign suggests that it was tailored to many of the views expressed by Israeli Facebook users in 2014. The issues addressed in EU campaign posts, which were also categorized by two coders, may be seen in Table 3.1. Notably, all posts were gathered during January 2018 and analyzed during March 2018.

Fig. 3.2 EU Delegation joint Facebook campaign with Israeli mission to the EU (*Source* https://www.facebook.com/Europe.in.Israel/photos/a.138558509540849.27528.134470763282957/1547361638660522/?type=3&theater)

As seen in Table 3.1, the majority of campaign posts dealt with Israel's participation in EU-funded research and development projects. These Facebook posts may have been used to negate the view of the EU as being obsessed solely with the Israeli-Palestinian conflict and always resorting to harshly criticizing Israel. As these posts demonstrate, the EU and Israel enjoy numerous forms of collaborations. Campaign posts also dealt with the everyday benefits of the close relationship between the EU and Israel and trade relations between the two. Everyday benefits included cheaper flights for Israeli citizens to Europe and the opportunity to visit more destinations in Europe. Posts focusing on trade relations emphasized the fact that the EU was, and remains, Israel's largest trade partner.

Table 3.1   Issues addressed in EU Delegation campaign by number of posts

Issue	Number of posts	Examples
Israeli participation in EU R&D projects	7	7% of EU Horizon 2020 included Israeli research projects; Israel received 1.7 billion euros in EU research program grants
Everyday benefits to Israel	6	Open skies agreement means Israeli can fly to Berlin for Paris in 100 euros; Thanks to open skies number of cities with direct flights from Tel Aviv has doubled in less than 5 years
Trade with the EU	6	EU states invested 11 billion euros in Israel; EU is Israel's biggest trade partner
Shared values	5	Israel and EU hold regular anti-terrorism dialogues; EU appoints Anti-Semitism coordinator; Israel, Germany, and Finland are all ranked as top 5 most innovative countries in the world
Joint ventures	3	Joint development of innovative technologies for early detection of cancer
Shared roots	3	Shimon Peres, Israel's 9th President, was born in Poland; Tel Aviv is home to large number of German Bauhaus buildings

The third most prevalent issue addressed in campaign posts was the values shared by the EU and Israel. One such post dealt with Israel's historic Eurovision win in 1998 when it was represented by transsexual singer Dana International. This post could have resonated with Israeli Facebook users as Israelis take pride in being a bastion of LGBT rights in the midst of an intolerant region. Two posts that warrant attention are those stating that the EU appointed a coordinator for all efforts to combat anti-Semitism in Europe and a post stating that the EU and Israel collaborate in fighting terrorism. These two issues had been raised time and again in the 2014 Q&A. The two least prevalent issues were joint ventures between the EU and Israel, and the shared roots of the EU and Israel.

However, an analysis of engagement rates with campaign posts suggests that these were mostly rejected by Israeli Facebook users. As can be seen in Graph 3.2 between January and April 2017 the average Facebook post published by the EU Delegation in Israel garnered 6.6 likes, 1.53 shares and 0.37 comments. During the month of May, Facebook posts, including those in the campaign, attracted similar engagement in terms of likes and comments but substantially lower levels of shares. As such,

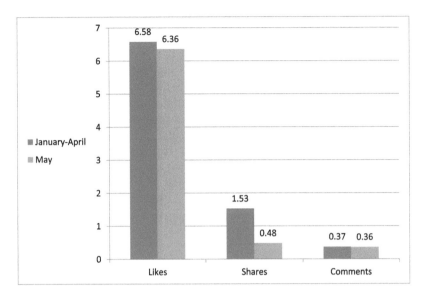

Graph 3.2 Comparison of average levels of user engagement with EU Facebook posts

Israeli Facebook users were not willing to share campaign messages with their online contacts, nor did campaign messages especially resonate with Israeli users or elicit higher levels of interactions.

The 2017 campaign ended with another Q&A with the ambassador. Now nearing the end of his tenure in Israel, the ambassador held a video Q&A in which he responded in real-time to Israeli Facebook users' questions. Despite the fact that three years had passed, and despite the Delegation's Facebook campaign, the 2017 questions echoed those of 2014 as the ambassador was asked why the EU was so anti-Semitic, why it was obsessed with Israel, why the EU focused on the Israeli occupation of Palestine and not on other occupations around the world, and why EU funds were allocated to anti-Israeli NGOs, as well as families of Palestinian terrorists. The ambassador was even asked, once more, why the EU was boycotting Israeli products. As was the case in 2014, only 1 out of the 19 questions posed to the ambassador had a positive or very positive sentiment, while 9 questions had a negative or very negative sentiment and 9 had a neutral sentiment.

The EU in Israel's case study demonstrates both the benefits and limitations brought about by the digitalization of public diplomacy. By interacting with Israeli Facebook users, the EU's ambassador in Israel may have been able to begin fostering relationships with Israeli so as to facilitate the acceptance of the EU's foreign policy in Israel. Moreover, the EU Delegation seems to have realized the potential of tailoring social media campaigns to the unique attributes of specific digital publics, be in terms of values, culture, language, history, or political views. Indeed, the EU's Facebook campaign was tailored to Israelis' views of the EU. By doing so, the Delegation sought to meet the demands of digital society members for tailored digital experiences. However, simply migrating to digital platforms does not ensure that a public diplomacy actor will achieve his goals as digital publics may choose to reject an actor and his narration of policies.

The question that follows is, what could have improved the EU's public diplomacy efforts in Israel? This question has three answers. First, the digitalization of public diplomacy demands that public diplomacy actors continuously converse with digital publics. Engagement spectacles, such as Q&As, can attract new digital followers, but they cannot serve as the basis for relationships. These require ongoing conversations on matters of shared interests and over long durations of time (Taylor & Kent, 2014). Members of the digital society exist in a world of constant connectivity, and so must public diplomacy. Second, while the EU's campaign dealt with some of the issues addressed by Israeli Facebook users, it did not directly contend with their two most prominent arguments: that the EU is quick to criticize Israel while neglecting to condemn Arab dictators, and that the EU's foreign policy is too fixated on Israel. A truly tailored campaign might have tried to counter these two arguments by articulating the EU's policies toward Arab states and demonstrating the global outlook of the EU's foreign policy which extends far beyond Israel. Lastly, the EU Delegation could have incorporated more visuals in its campaign and taken a narrative approach to its online communication. In the digital society, members are tasked with authoring an authentic personal narrative or iBrand. This narrative is brought to life through images and videos, as "seeing is believing." Diplomatic actors can adopt a similar approach in which they employ visuals to create a narrative that explains their policies and actions in the global arena. In the EU's case, videos could have been used to portray the global spread of the EU's diplomatic efforts, to exhibit its policies toward other nations in the Middle East, and to demonstrate how its diplomatic actions hold true to EU values. The EU's visual narrative could have also focused on historic milestones in its relationship with Israel, the scientific advancements made thanks to EU funds, and the EU's contribution to Israelis' quality of life. Previous studies have demonstrated that images and videos do increase follower engagement with public diplomacy materials (Manor & Crilley, 2018b).

The final case study explored in this chapter relates to America's decision to withdraw from the Iran nuclear agreement.

2018—The Art of the Iran Deal

On May 8, 2018, U.S. President Donald Trump addressed the world from the White House. In a prolonged statement, the President announced that the USA would leave the Iran nuclear agreement, also known as the Joint Comprehensive Plan of Action (JCPOA), negotiated in 2015 between the world powers (USA, EU, France, UK, Germany, China and Russia) and Iran. Much to the dismay of his European allies, Trump characterized the accord as defective at its core. He promised to re-impose all financial sanctions that were lifted off the Iranian economy (White House, 2018).

Nearly three weeks after Trump's announcement, on May 21, U.S. Secretary of State Michael Pompeo delivered a major foreign policy address outlining the terms under which the USA would rejoin the Iranian nuclear agreement. Speaking at a conservative think tank, the Heritage Foundation, Pompeo's address was live-tweeted on the State Department's Twitter channel. In a series of 16 tweets, Pompeo presented four major arguments. First, the Iran accord merely delayed the threat of an Iranian nuclear bomb as Iran could begin developing nuclear weapons several years after the agreement came into effect. Second, the Iran agreement enriched Iran, given the removal of crippling economic sanctions. Rather than use these funds to improve the lives of Iranians, the regime used it to wage proxy wars all over the region, including in Syria, and threaten Israel's security. Third, the USA was still committed to working with its allies on a new agreement that would address Iran's nuclear program as well as its efforts to destabilize the Middle East, its attempts to become a regional hegemon, and its investments in ballistic missiles programs. Lastly, the Secretary asserted that the USA hoped that its actions could bring about true change in the Iranian regime, which abuses its citizens, demeans its women, and denies freedom to all.

In total, Pompeo's tweets garnered 719 comments from Twitter users the world over. Table 3.2 includes the content of each Pompeo tweet and the sentiment of the comments it garnered. The sentiment of Twitter comments was measured by ranking each comment on a scale ranging from very negative to negative, neutral, positive and very positive. Two coders ranked all comments, while the Spearman correlation coefficient was used to ensure a high inter-coder reliability. All tweets were gathered during May 2018 and analyzed during July 2018.

As can be seen in Table 3.2, all of Pompeo's tweets, save two, were greeted poorly by Twitter users. On average, 76% of all comments posted in response to a Pompeo tweet were either negative or very negative. The most poorly received tweets were those dealing with the actions of the Islamic Revolutionary Guards Corps, including its activities in Syria and attacks on Israel, and tweets that directly threatened Iran, such as "we will track down Iranian operatives and their Hezbollah proxies operating around the world and crush them", and "the sting of the sanctions will only grow more painful if regime does not change course." The tweet stating that Iran will never be allowed to develop nuclear weapons was also poorly received, with 89% of the comments being negative or very negative.

The tweets that were best received were those dealing with the plight of the Iranian people, including a tweet asking what the Iranian regime has actually done to benefit the people of Iran (41% negative sentiment), a tweet stating that the regime uses new funds to finance military activities rather than aid its citizens (50% negative sentiment), and a tweet promising that the USA would not hand over any more money to Iranian kleptocrats (61% negative sentiment).

The results of the sentiment analysis suggest that while Twitter audiences agreed that the Iranian regime does little to benefit the Iranian people, they rejected the strong tone used by the USA and its direct threats against Iran. Audiences' comments on tweets threatening Iran centered on three main arguments. Several Twitter users stated that it was America who was the hegemon in the Middle East, not Iran, as the USA maintains several military bases in the region. Others stated that it was the USA that was defying international law by abandoning the JCPOA, not Iran, which had complied with its provisions. Another recurring argument was that the USA was simply looking to secure its oil interest in the region by seeking to destabilize Iran. There were also many Twitter users who stated that new American sanctions would

Table 3.2 Sentiment of comments posted in response to Pompeo tweets (based on sample of 719 comments)

Tweet's content	Sentiment[a]
@POTUS (*President of the United States*) withdrew from the deal for a simple reason: it failed to guarantee the safety of the American people from the risks created by the leaders of the Islamic Republic of #Iran	82% negative
#JCPOA (*Joint Comprehensive Plan of Action*) put world at risk b/c (*because*) of its fatal flaws. The weak sunset provisions of JCPOA merely delayed #Iran's nuclear weapons capability. After countdown clock ran out on the deal's sunset provisions, Iran would be free for a quick sprint to the bomb	82% negative
#JCPOA (*Joint Comprehensive Plan of Action*) permitted the Iranian regime to use money from the JCPOA to boost the economic fortunes of a struggling people. The regime's leaders refused to do so. Instead the govt. spent its newfound treasure fueling proxy wars across the Middle East	50% negative
#IRGC (*Islamic Revolutionary Guard Corps*) has cont. to pump thousands of fighters into Syria to prop up the murderous Assad regime…Iran perpetuates a conflict that has displaced more than 6 million Syrians inside the country and over 5 million to seek refuge outside its borders	92% negative
#IRGC (*Islamic Revolutionary Guard Corps*) has flown armed drone into Israeli airspace and launched salvos of rockets into Golan Heights from #Syria. Our steadfast ally #Israel has asserted its sovereign right of self-defense in response, a stance U.S. will cont. to unequivocally support	85% negative
We will cont. to work w/our allies to counter the regime's destabilizing activities in the region, block their financing of terror and address #Iran's proliferation of missiles. We will also ensure Iran has no possible path to a nuclear weapon—ever	89% negative
The sting of sanctions will only grow more painful if regime does not change course from the unacceptable and unproductive path it has chosen for itself and the people of #Iran. These will be the strongest sanctions in history by the time we are done	86% negative
We will ensure freedom of navigation on the waters in the region. We will track down Iranian operatives and their #Hezbollah proxies operating around the world and crush them. #Iran will never again have carte blanche to dominate the Middle East	89% negative
As seen from the hijab protests, the brutal men of the regime seem to be particularly terrified by Iranian women who are demanding their rights. As human beings with inherent dignity and inalienable rights, the women of #Iran deserve same freedoms the men of Iran have	78% negative
Any new deal must begin with defining what the world should demand from #Iran…America did not create this need for changed behavior, Iran did	79% negative

(continued)

Table 3.2   (continued)

Tweet's content	Sentiment[a]
In the strategy we are announcing today, we want the support of our most important allies and partners in region and around globe. We welcome any nation which is sick and tired of the nuclear threats and brutality of a regime at peace w/inflicting chaos on innocent people	70% negative
Next year marks 40th anniversary of Islamic Revolution in #Iran. At this milestone we have to ask: what has Iranian Revolution given the Iranian people? The regime reaps a harvest of suffering and death in the Middle East at expense of its own people	41% negative
It is America's hope that our labors toward peace and security will bear fruit for the long-suffering people of #Iran. We long to see them prosper and flourish as in decades past, and as never before. Today, the #USA is proud to take a new course towards that objective	70% negative
No more wealth creation for Iranian kleptocrats. No more acceptance of missiles landing in Riyadh and in the Golan Heights. No more cost-free expansions of Iranian power. No more	61% negative
We'll cont. (*continue*) to work with allies to counter the regime's destabilizing activities in the region, block their financing of terror and address #Iran's proliferation of missiles. We will ensure Iran has no path to a nuclear weapon	90% negative
What has the Iranian Revolution given to the Iranian people? The regime reaps a harvest of suffering and death in the Middle East at the expense of its own citizens	74% negative

[a]Value combines negative and very negative comments

simply lead to another war, much like the one in Iraq, which was also launched based on false pretense.

Twitter users, therefore, seem to have rejected the Secretary of State's narration of the U.S.' new policy toward Iran. They rebuked his argument that Iran was destabilizing the region, as well his statement that the USA was merely looking to ensure the safety of its citizens and its allies. They did not accept his allegations that Iran was threatening US allies in the region or his appraisal that Iran would seek nuclear weapons when the JCPOA expired. They were also unimpressed by his promise to work with America's allies toward a new agreement. For too many users, Pompeo's speech felt like a Déjà Bush.

However, regardless of the sentiment expressed in users' comments, the response from the State Department was similar—silence. Twitter users' questions remained unanswered, and their criticism was ignored while their requests for additional information were disregarded. The

State Department did not reply to a single comment on Twitter, nor did it host a Q&A following Pompeo's speech. And so, this chapter comes full circle, ending with another U.S. official delivering a major address on the future relations between America and the Muslim world. Yet this time there would be no DOT and no promise of new beginnings. The "new" public diplomacy goals of relationship building were replaced with traditional goals of influencing elites and opinion makers.

The second stage of digitalization had arrived.

CONCLUSIONS

This chapter examined how interactions between diplomats and digital publics shaped the process of public diplomacy's digitalization. At its core lies the argument that digitalization is a process and not a fixed state. MFAs and embassies are not either digital or non-digital. Rather, diplomatic institutions are in the midst of a long-term process of digitalization which is influencing their norms, values, working routines and the self-narratives or metaphors through which diplomats conceptualize their craft. As this chapter has demonstrated, each MFA is undergoing its own unique process of digitalization which is shaped by local norms and values, institutional cultures, government-wide approaches to technology, and external events. In the case of the U.S. State Department, the process of the digitalization of public diplomacy was influenced by the Obama administration's Open Government Initiative, the Arab Spring, the work of think tanks, and the appointment of certain individuals, such as Jared Cohen, to high-ranking positions. Thus, the State Department underwent a process of digitalization in which new approaches, methods, and definitions of public diplomacy were embraced over a decade.

The example of the State Department also serves to demonstrate how digital technologies impact a diplomatic institution's norms, values, working routines, and self-narratives. In 2008, Under Secretary of State for Public Diplomacy and Public Affairs James Glassman launched the Public Diplomacy 2.0 initiative, which hoped to engage, inform, and influence publics through conversations rather than message dissemination. In 2011, and following the Arab Spring, President Obama's Under Secretary of State for Public Diplomacy and Public Affairs stated that people all over the world were having important conversations online and that they were not waiting for diplomats to join them or listen to them. So, the self-narrative, or metaphor through which U.S. diplomats now conceptualized the craft of public diplomacy was that of the conversation. This was an important conceptual shift given that for most of the twentieth century, public diplomacy was conceptualized through one-way communicative models. The metaphor of the conversation soon led to new working routines and practices such as the establishment of the State Department's DOT, tasked with conversing with digital publics. This change in working routines was accompanied by new norms and values namely reaching out to digital publics assembled on websites and "listening" to such publics with the goal of fostering relationships. The experiences of the DOT led to additional changes in the structure and working routines of the State Department, as diplomats would require digital training if they were to communicate freely with digital publics.

The case studies reviewed in this chapter also demonstrate that digital initiatives influenced the digitalization of public diplomacy, thus adhering to the societal prism that examines how social beings use digital technologies to obtain their goals. The year 2007 saw the launch of Sweden's virtual embassy and an open approach to online interactions with digital publics. By 2013, MFAs had adopted a more quarantined form of online interactions, that of the Twitter Q&A. Cyber pessimists might argue that this transition demonstrates how outdated MFAs are, how constrained they are by well-entrenched working routines and how ill-equipped they are when using digital technologies. Yet a counter view that employs the societal prism would argue that this transition demonstrates a true desire by MFAs to leverage digital technologies toward interacting with digital publics while balancing the unpredictable nature of digital publics with the risk-intolerant culture of diplomatic institutions. The Twitter Q&A offers digital publics the opportunity to interact in real-time with diplomats, to learn about events shaping their world and to gain insight into regional and global issues while also allowing diplomats to determine the extent to which they wish to deal with potentially divisive issues. The fact that by 2007 MFAs were launching virtual embassies, and that by 2013 they were constantly interacting with social media users, demonstrates how flexible and agile some MFAs have been and how quickly they have adapted to new digital surroundings.

The activities of the EU's Delegation to Israel, however, demonstrate the limitations of digital outreach. While engagement spectacles such as Q&As can attract digital publics, they cannot facilitate the formation of relationships between diplomats and connected individuals. That requires continuous conversations on issues of shared concern over long durations of time. Alas, constant interactions require a commitment of resources as diplomats must author digital content, respond to publics' questions, provide requested information, and understand the needs and desires of digital publics. As Hocking and Melissen (2015) argued, it is the lack of resources, among others, that currently limits MFAs' digital outreach.

Throughout this chapter, the influence of the digital society on public diplomacy's digitalization has been evident. Such was the case with Jared Cohen and Alec Ross, who hammered the logic of the digital society into the minds of American diplomats, proclaiming that open is good, closed is bad, and authenticity is everything. Open is good relates to the demands of the digital society that everything once done in secret must be done in the open. The values of openness and transparency are celebrated in the digital society, as they ensure that a constant flow of information reaches algorithms that can transform information into knowledge, the currency of the digital society. Closed is bad relates to the view of withholding information as a cardinal sin. Digital society members must share all aspects of their lives, good and bad, as this allows a society of iBrands to enforce its norms and values. Lastly, authenticity relates to the logic of digital platforms, that of the neoliberal market in which every individual, company, and embassy is but a brand competing over the attention of digital publics with all other brands.

In addition, Sweden's virtual embassy and digital publics' response to the Israeli ambassador's Q&A are representative of the annihilation of time and space in the digital society. Second House of Sweden enabled Swedish officials to interact in real-time with digital users throughout the world regardless of their location and regardless of their physical time zone. Space and time were thus rendered meaningless. This was no mistake or accident. As Manuel Castells argued, the digital society is motivated by a constant desire to annihilate time and space, and as this book will demonstrate, public diplomacy is now concerned with attempts to condense time and space. The responses to Dermer's Q&A are representative of the glocalized nature of the digital society, one in which a tweet directed at Americans is read by international audiences and spurs a global reaction. The distinction between domestic and foreign constituencies collapses in the digital society, and both form a single hybrid audience. As this book will demonstrate, the emergence of a glocalized digital public still challenges public diplomacy practitioners today.

From the perspective of the technological prism, this chapter illustrates that all public diplomacy actors, even terror groups, must now create an authentic iBrand if they are to attract digital publics and create a digital image for themselves. Hamas' digital Q&A suggests that the terror movement sought to refashion its image as a progressive Islamic political movement by inviting digital publics to interact with a female legislator, a former prisoner in Israeli jails, and a leading political figure. Hamas' iBrand was thus meant to differ substantially from Daesh's iBrand. The importance of iBrands stems not merely from their online appeal, but from diplomats' belief that they can use digital platforms to shape people's offline perceptions of the world. If digital publics accepted Hamas' new iBrand, they may have also come to accept its policies opposite Israel and its armed struggle. That was not the case. The Hamas Q&A, much like the Israeli one, exemplifies the ease with which digital publics can derail and even hijack diplomats' digital activities. The digital public can thus assert itself in unpredictable ways.

In conclusion, this chapter echoes Abbasov (2007) and Adesina's (2017) finding that the digitalization of public diplomacy is a gradual process in which new technologies lead to new opportunities, challenges, and working routines. The digitalization of public diplomacy is thus a process of evolution, and not revolution, to use Amanda Clarke's (2015) terminology. It is a process that has seen the "gradual shift from telegrams to mobile phones, and more recently to Skype, postal letters to e-mails, short messages (SMS) to Twitter posts, hard-copy invitations to Facebook events, TV announcements to YouTube channels…and even from physical embassies to net-based virtual embassies" (Abbasov, 2007).

Just as diplomats were coming to grips with the nature of the digital demos, the Crimean crisis shocked the foundations of the digital town square. The crisis, and its impact on the process of public diplomacy's digitalization, is explored in the next chapter.

REFERENCES

Abbasov, A. (2007). *Digital diplomacy: Embedding information and communication technologies in the department of foreign affairs and trade.* Retrieved from https://www.academia.edu/1058526/Digital_Diplomacy_Embedding_Information_and_Communication_Technologies_in_the_Department_of_Foreign_Affairs_and_Trade.

Adesina, O. S. (2017). Foreign policy in an era of digital diplomacy. *Cogent Social Sciences, 3*(1), 1297175.

Ahren, R. (2017, September). More Israelis like the EU than dislike it, poll finds. *The Times of Israel.* Retrieved from https://www.timesofisrael.com/more-israelis-like-the-eu-than-dislike-it-poll-finds/.

Barlow, J. P. (1996). *A declaration of the independence of cyberspace.* Retrieved from https://www.eff.org/cyberspace-independence.

Bauman, Z., & Lyon, B. (2016). Remoteness distancing an automation. In Z. Bauman & B. Lyon (Eds.), *Liquid surveillance* (pp. 76–99). Cambridge: Polity Press.

Bertot, J. C., Jaeger, P. T., & Hansen, D. (2012a). The impact of polices on government social media usage: Issues, challenges, and recommendations. *Government Information Quarterly, 29*(1), 30–40.

Bertot, J. C., Jaeger, P. T., & Grimes, J. M. (2012b). Promoting transparency and accountability through ICTs, social media, and collaborative e-government. *Transforming Government: People, Process and Policy, 6*(1), 78–91.

Bjola, C., & Manor, I. (2018). Revisiting Putnam's two-level game theory in the digital age: Domestic digital diplomacy and the Iran nuclear deal. *Cambridge Review of International Affairs, 33*, 1–30.

Bortree, D. S., & Seltzer, T. (2009). Dialogic strategies and outcomes: An analysis of environmental advocacy groups' Facebook profiles. *Public Relations Review, 35*(3), 317–319.

Clarke, A. (2015). Business as usual? An evolution of British and Canadian digital diplomacy as policy change. In C. Bjola & M. Holmes (Eds.), *Digital diplomacy theory and practice* (pp. 111–126). Oxon: Routledge.

Colvin, R. (2009, May). Obama to reach out to Muslims in Egypt speech. *Reuters.* Retrieved from https://www.reuters.com/article/us-obama-muslims/obama-to-reach-out-to-muslims-in-egyptspeech-idUSTRE54754920090508?feedType=RSS&feedName=ObamaEconomy&virtualBrandChannel=10441.

Copeland, D. (2013). Taking diplomacy public: Science, technology and foreign ministries in a heteropolar world. In R. S. Zaharna, A. Arsenault, & A. Fisher (Eds.), *Relational, networked and collaborative approaches to public diplomacy* (pp. 56–69). New York, NY: Taylor & Francis.

Cull, N. J. (2008). Public diplomacy: Taxonomies and histories. *The Annals of the American Academy of Political and Social Science, 616*(1), 31–54.

Cull, N. J. (2013). The long road to public diplomacy 2.0: The internet in US public diplomacy. *International Studies Review, 15*(1), 123–139.

Haaretz. (2015, March). Ask Hamas Twitter campaign quickly backfires. *Haaretz.* Retrieved from https://www.haaretz.com/askhamas-twitter-campaign-backfires-1.5336781.

Hayden, C. (2012). Social media at state: Power, practice, and conceptual limits for US public diplomacy. *Global Media Journal, 11*(21), 1–12.

Haynal, G. (2011). Corporate diplomacy in the information Age: Catching up to the dispersal of power. In J. G. Stein (Ed.), *Diplomacy in the digital age: Essays in honour of Ambassador Allan Gotlieb* (pp. 209–224). Ontario: Signal.

Hocking, B., & Melissen, J. (2015). *Diplomacy in the digital age*. Clingendael: Netherlands Institute of International Relations Clingendael.

Hughes, D. J., Rowe, M., Batey, M., & Lee, A. (2012). A tale of two sites: Twitter vs. Facebook and the personality predictors of social media usage. *Computers in Human Behavior, 28*(2), 561–569.

Kampf, R., Manor, I., & Segev, E. (2015). Digital diplomacy 2.0? A cross-national comparison of public engagement in Facebook and Twitter. *The Hague Journal of Diplomacy, 10*(4), 331–362.

Khatib, L., Dutton, W., & Thelwall, M. (2012). Public diplomacy 2.0: A case study of the US digital outreach team. *The Middle East Journal, 66*(3), 453–472.

Kwak, H., Lee, C., Park, H., & Moon, S. (2010, April). *What is Twitter, a social network or a news media?* Proceedings of the 19th international conference on World Wide Web (pp. 591–600). ACM.

Lampe, G. (2018). Understanding U.S. digital diplomacy [In person].

Landau, N. (2018, May). Trade and tirades: The complicated truth behind Israel's love-hate relationship with the EU. *Haaretz*. Retrieved from https://www.haaretz.com/israel-news/.premium-israel-eu-ties-a-love-hate-relationship-that-s-better-than-it-looks-1.6116399.

Lee, G., & Kwak, Y. H. (2012). An open government maturity model for social media-based public engagement. *Government Information Quarterly, 29*(4), 492–503.

Lichtenstein, J. (2010, July). Digital diplomacy. *The New York Times*. Retrieved from https://www.nytimes.com/2010/07/18/magazine/18web2-0-t.html.

Manor, I. (2014, July). An Epic Q&A session. *The Times of Israel*. Retrieved from https://blogs.timesofisrael.com/an-epic-qa-session/.

Manor, I. (2016). Are we there yet: Have MFA s realized the potential of digital diplomacy? *Brill Research Perspectives in Diplomacy and Foreign Policy, 1*(2), 1–110.

Manor, I., & Crilley, R. (2018a). Visually framing the Gaza War of 2014: The Israel Ministry of Foreign Affairs on Twitter. *Media, War & Conflict*.

Manor, I., & Crilley, R. (2018b). The aesthetics of violent extremist and counter violent extremist communication. In C. Bjola & J. Pamment (Eds.), *Countering online propaganda and extremism: The dark side of digital diplomacy*. Oxon: Routledge.

McNutt, K. (2014). Public engagement in the Web 2.0 era: Social collaborative technologies in a public sector context. *Canadian Public Administration, 57*(1), 49–70.

Melissen, J. (2005). The new public diplomacy: Between theory and practice. In J. Melissen (Ed.), *The new public diplomacy: Soft power in international relations* (pp. 3–27). New York: Palgrave Macmillan.

Mergel, I. (2013). Social media adoption and resulting tactics in the US federal government. *Government Information Quarterly, 30*(2), 123–130.

Pamment, J. (2013). Introduction. In J. Pamment, *New public diplomacy in the 21st century: A comparative study of policy and practice* (pp. 1–19). Abingdon: Routledge.

Pardo, S. (2016, August). What does Israel think about the European Union? *European Council on Foreign Relations*. Retrieved from https://www.ecfr.eu/article/commentary_what_does_israel_think_about_the_european_union_7101.

Ross, A. (2011). Digital diplomacy and US foreign policy. *The Hague Journal of Diplomacy, 6*(3–4), 451–455.

Ross, A. (2015). *Hillary Clinton's FMR innovation advisor on digital diplomacy* [TV]. Retrieved from https://www.bnnbloomberg.ca/video/hillary-clinton-s-fmr-innovation-advisor-on-digital-diplomacy~582509.

Slaughter, A. M. (2009). America's edge: Power in the networked century. *Foreign Affairs, 88*, 94–113.

Snead, J. T. (2013). Social media use in the US Executive branch. *Government Information Quarterly, 30*(1), 56–63.

Sotiriu, S. (2015). Digital diplomacy: Between promises and reality. In C. Bjola & M. Holmes (Eds.), *Digital diplomacy theory and practice* (pp. 33–51). Oxon: Routledge.

Spry, D. (2018). Facebook diplomacy: A data-driven, user-focused approach to Facebook use by diplomatic missions. *Media International Australia, 168*(1), 62–80.

Taylor, A. (2015, March). Hamas #AskHamas Twitter campaign is being mocked and it hasn't even started yet. *The Washington Post*.

Taylor, M., & Kent, M. L. (2014). Dialogic engagement: Clarifying foundational concepts. *Journal of Public Relations Research, 26*(5), 384–398.

The Stream. (2014, July). Israeli ambassador's #AskDermer Q&A on Gaza goes terribly wrong. *Al Jazeera*. Retrieved from http://stream.aljazeera.com/story/201407171922-0023936.

The White House. (2018). *President Trump says the Iran deal is defective at its core: A new one will require real commitments*. Retrieved from https://www.whitehouse.gov/articles/president-trump-says-iran-deal-defective-core-new-one-will-require-real-commitments/.

Waters, R. D., Burnett, E., Lamm, A., & Lucas, J. (2009). Engaging stakeholders through social networking: How nonprofit organizations are using Facebook. *Public Relations Review, 35*(2), 102–106.

CHAPTER 4

From Targeting to Tailoring—The Two Stages of Public Diplomacy's Digitalization

The only man I know who behaves sensibly is my tailor; he takes my measurements anew each time he sees me. The rest go on with their old measurements and expect me to fit them.

—George Bernard Shaw

It is fabled that during the 1970s, a British labor secretary attended an official reception in Lima, the capital of Peru. Once sufficiently inebriated, the minister dared ask a woman in purple to tango with him. The woman refused on three counts. First, it was not a woman, but a man. Second, the man was wearing purple because he was the Bishop of Lima. Third, the music playing in the background was not a tango but the Peruvian national anthem. In its early stages, the process of the digitalization of public diplomacy saw diplomats facing a mystical woman in purple. Despite their desire to converse with digital publics and leverage digital platforms toward "new" public diplomacy ends, diplomats were unfamiliar with the logic of digital platforms. The need to compete over the attention of digital publics faced with a daily barrage of TMI (Too Much Information), the short attention span of digital audiences, the requirement to foster networks with digital influencers, and the need to comment on events as they unfold all demanded that diplomats adopt new practices and develop new skills. Thus began the process of public diplomacy's digitalization.

© The Author(s) 2019
I. Manor, *The Digitalization of Public Diplomacy*,
Palgrave Macmillan Series in Global Public Diplomacy,
https://doi.org/10.1007/978-3-030-04405-3_4

As diplomats migrated to digital platforms and embraced the logic of the digital society, the process of digitalization accelerated. Soon, the passionate beat of the Peruvian tango was replaced with the swinging jolt of big-band jazz music as diplomats dared to experiment with digital platforms and improvise during digital interactions. It was this spirit of free experimentation that led Sweden to launch a virtual embassy in 2007, and that prompted the UK's foreign secretary to hold one of the world's first Twitter Q&A session in 2011 (Foreign and Commonwealth Office). By 2013, diplomatic institutions had created a digital presence that enabled them to communicate with globally-dispersed audiences in perfect harmony. Like a capella groups lining the sidewalks of American cities filling warm nights with sweet dreams, diplomatic institutions could at once communicate public diplomacy messages to a digital public fragmented across multiple platforms, channels and networks (Hayden, 2012). Then, in 2014, the process of digitalization entered its second stage, and a capella harmony gave way to the operatic grandeur of the Russian "Kalinka."

The Crimean crisis, which burst onto the scene in December of 2013, saw rapid escalation in global tensions as Russia and Western nations fought over the fate of Eastern Ukraine. Strongly worded tweets were followed by economic sanctions, the expulsion of diplomats and troop convoys threatening to once again divide Europe into West versus East. This battle also manifested online as nations sought to influence digital publics and shape their perception of the reality unfolding in Crimea. Among some MFAs, the "new" public diplomacy goal of relationship building was slowly supplanted by the traditional public diplomacy goals of information dominance and influence. Russian trolls and bots flooded digital platforms with false news articles and doctored images, while words such as "echo chambers" and "filter bubbles" overshadowed discussions among public diplomacy practitioners. This transition is best exemplified by two digital diplomacy conferences held by the Israeli MFA. The first (which took place in 2016) focused on MFAs' role as service providers, while the second (held in 2018) focused on algorithmic diplomacy or the use of algorithms to obtain influence. As this chapter will demonstrate, the Crimean crisis was a watershed event that segmented the digitalization of public diplomacy into two stages. A key reason for this was Russia's use of its official digital presence to contest the reality unfolding on the ground in Crimea, to promote a narrative based on half-truths, and to allege that Western diplomats were lying to their digital followers. Reality was the first victim of the Crimean crisis.

Marcus Holmes (2015) has argued that the digitalization of public diplomacy can be influenced by two types of "change." The first is gradual, internal, and bottom-up change in which the adoption of digital technologies by diplomats and embassies ultimately impacts an MFA's utilization of digital technologies. The second is abrupt, external, top-down change that is caused by an exogenous shock. It is the contention of this chapter that the Crimean crisis was an exogenous shock that had a dramatic impact on certain MFAs' use of digital technologies. In its wake, governments and MFAs implemented top-down changes to their digital communications, including re-conceptualizing the use of digital technologies in public diplomacy and developing new digital strategies for obtaining public diplomacy goals.

But other factors also shaped the transition from the first to the second stage of public diplomacy's digitalization. The more experience diplomats gained on digital platforms, the more tactics they discovered to increase their digital reach. Similarly, consular crises forced diplomats to attempt and fracture algorithmic confines to reach citizens in need of aid. The goals of diplomats also changed as they sought to leverage digital platforms toward long-term objectives rather than short-term press statements. Thus, the digitalization of public diplomacy was also influenced by gradual bottom-up change. But most importantly, the second stage of digitalization saw a shift from targeted to tailored communication in which diplomats crafted content that met the characteristics of specific digital publics including their values, norms, history, needs, interests and usage of digital platforms. This shift is important as tailoring is representative of the internal conflict that accompanies the digitalization of public diplomacy, a conflict between diplomats' desire to create online relationships and diplomats' well-entrenched norm of obtaining influence. Indeed, some MFAs hoped that tailored communications would lead to greater influence over digital publics' worldviews. Yet while the goals of public diplomacy may have altered between the two stages of digitalization, its focus has remained public-centric.

This chapter first explores the main differences between the first and second stages of the digitalization of public diplomacy. By doing so, this chapter demonstrates yet again that digitalization is a long-term process rather than a binary state. Next, the chapter deals with the effectiveness of tailored communication models as opposed to targeted ones before concluding with a series of case studies that demonstrate how diplomats now tailor their public diplomacy activities to the unique attributes of the audiences they aim to interact with. One of the main differences between the first and second stages of public diplomacy's digitalization is tied to algorithms, the main functionaries of the digital society.

FROM LINEAR TO ALGORITHMIC COMMUNICATION

In a recent opinion article published on the Chinese website Global Times, Corneliu Bjola asserted that the first stage of digital transformation has been an astonishing success: "Within less than a decade since the launch of the first social media networks, 90 percent of all UN member states have established a Twitter presence, and 88 percent have opened a Facebook account with a combined audience of 325 million and 255 million followers respectively" (Bjola, 2017). As Bjola notes, the first stage of public diplomacy's digitalization, which lasted from 2007 to 2014, saw the mass migration of MFAs, embassies and diplomats to digital platforms such as social media sites. Throughout the world, diplomatic institutions created a formidable digital presence while launching numerous social media profiles across dozens of platforms (Manor, 2016a). By 2012, the U.S. State Department was managing a social media empire of more than 1200 profiles (Hanson, 2012). The same was true of the governments of Kenya, Qatar, Mexico, Israel, and France. The first stage of digitalization also witnessed the training of diplomats in the art of digital public engagement as they were tasked with leveraging social media empires toward relationship building. Some MFAs, such as Israel and Norway, tailored their online training to the needs of specific diplomatic functions. Ambassadors learned to use social media sites as a tool for analyzing the sentiment of foreign publics and foreign elites, while press attachés learned to decipher and influence media narratives (Manor, 2016a). As part of this process of professionalization, MFAs authored guidelines for embassies venturing onto social media sites, protocols for diplomats using digital platforms during political crises, and manuals for embassies using social media sites during consular crises (Israel MFA, 2017).

Yet during the first stage of digitalization, diplomats conceptualized digital platforms through linear communication models. An embassy would log onto Twitter, publish a tweet, and reach millions of Twitter users. An early guide to social media platforms published by the Israeli

MFA in 2014 demonstrates this conceptualization. The guide reviews popular social media platforms while arguing that they vary in content and form. While Twitter is used to publish short bursts of diplomatic communiques, YouTube is used to disseminate videos. The guide also states that each social media platform may be used to interact with different audiences as young people are more likely to be found on YouTube than on Twitter. Yet not once does the guide mention the word "algorithms" or suggest that an embassy's digital reach is limited in any way.

Conceptualizing social media sites through linear communication models posited that Twitter was no different from twentieth-century mass media, such as radio and television. It is possible that diplomats originally likened social media to the radio, as public diplomacy was practiced via mass media for most of the twentieth century. As the technological prism would argue the norms, working routines, and conceptualization of public diplomacy activities, were shaped by the medium diplomats utilized. The logic of broadcast mass media thus became ingrained into the fabric of public diplomacy.

By 2014, however, diplomats were becoming increasingly aware of the algorithmic confines of social media sites. One instance in which these became apparent was the 2015 earthquake in Nepal. Following the earthquake, MFAs and embassies attempted to utilize Twitter to communicate with citizens in need of aid. Yet diplomats soon discovered that they were unable to reach their citizens due to algorithmic filtering. The Canadian MFA, which took to Twitter immediately after the quake, realized that its messages would only be seen by Twitter users who follow the MFA directly, users who have expressed an interest in Canadian diplomacy, or Canadian users who have expressed an interest in international affairs. The vast majority of Canadians stranded in Nepal were beyond the MFA's reach (ibid.).

Similarly, Russia's utilization of digital platforms during the Crimean crisis of 2014 further elucidated the limits of social media's reach. A NATO Stratcom report from 2015 found that Russia actively used digital platforms to spread false information, rumors, and emotionally-arousing propaganda. Trolls, fictitious information agencies, and state-sponsored media channels were used to flood social media sites, news websites, and discussion boards with false news stories and doctored images in an attempt to control the information environment in Ukraine and influence digital publics' perception of reality. In one instance, Russian trolls published a story alleging that pro-Ukrainian extremists prevented a doctor from rescuing people from a burning building in Odessa. Another story featured a pregnant woman strangled to death by pro-Ukrainian extremists, while other stories dealt with the supposed poisoning of water wells (NATO Stratcom, 2015).

In response, Western diplomats turned to their social media accounts to promote their own narratives of events and dispel Russian disinformation. Yet whether they were tweeting from MFA accounts, or those of embassies in Kiev, diplomats were faced yet again with the confines of algorithms as they could reach only those Ukrainians who followed them directly or who had expressed some interest in diplomatic activity. Of course, algorithmic confines have increased over time. The organic reach of a Facebook page, or the number of users who can find a Facebook page for free, has gone down from 15% in 2012 to 2% in 2018. This imposes additional limitations on diplomats who must either author viral content or pay for Facebook advertisements if they are to reach digital publics (Joseph, 2018).

These experiences, among others, led diplomats to re-conceptualize digital platforms through algorithmic communication models. Subsequently, the second stage of digitalization saw MFAs employ digital tactics to overcome or "hack" social media algorithms. The Canadian MFA, for one, began to incorporate trending hashtags into its tweets. Hashtags are a way of organizing conversations on digital platforms, and during major events such as consular crises, certain hashtags rise in prominence and become central to online conversations (Bik & Goldstein, 2013). The tweet below, published by the Canadian MFA following the Nepal earthquake, employed the hashtag "#NepalQuake," which was already trending on Twitter. By using this hashtag, the MFA joined trending conversations and increased the potential reach of its message. Moreover, the MFA asked followers to "Please Retweet" its message, thereby further increasing its online reach (Fig. 4.1).

Other MFAs sought to fracture the confines of algorithms by conducting shared social media campaigns. Such was the case in February of 2016 when the UK Foreign and Commonwealth Office (FCO) and the U.S. State Department collaborated on a shared public diplomacy campaign meant to counter Daesh's online propaganda.

Since its establishment, Daesh had used social media to portray itself as an omnipotent Caliphate (Pamment, Nothhaft, Agardh-Twetman, & Fjallhed, 2018). In response, the UK FCO launched the "UK Against Daesh" Twitter channel, while the State Department managed the

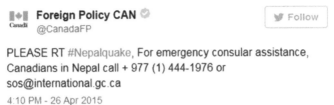

Fig. 4.1 Canadian foreign ministry asking followers to retweet messages (*Source* https://twitter.com/CanadaFP/status/592345097473302528)

"Think Again Turn Away" channel. Both of these were meant to counter Daesh's "selfie" and highlight the achievements of the Global Coalition Against Daesh. As such, both accounts aimed to influence how digital publics viewed the war against Daesh rather than disrupt Daesh recruitment efforts online. While the British and American Twitter channels published their own content, they also shared one another's messages through retweets. Thus, both MFAs could increase their reach and the diversity of audiences they engaged with as "UK Against Daesh" followers were exposed to the State Department's content and vice versa. In addition, both MFAs used the same hashtags including "Coalition Progress" and "Defeating Daesh." An analysis from 2016 found that these hashtags were strongly correlated with the hashtags "Daesh," "ISIS," "Iraq", and "Syria." These correlations imply that by using the same hashtags, the two MFAs were able to become central to online conversations about Daesh and to reach those digital audiences seeking information about Daesh and its activities (Manor, 2016b). This was not a coalition of the willing, or even a coalition of the able, but rather a coalition of tweets. The aforementioned examples highlight that each MFA adopted its own tactics for hacking algorithms as each MFA is amid its own unique process of digitalization. Yet the second stage of digitalization also saw diplomats replace digital tactics with digital strategies.

FROM DIGITAL TACTICS TO DIGITAL STRATEGIES

During the first stage of digitalization, diplomatic institutions employed digital tactics (Bjola & Manor, 2016a). The goal of digital tactics was to create content that would obtain virality and attract attention to specific issues. A classic example is the "Lame Duck Tweet" published by the Russian embassy to London following the Obama administration's decision to expel 35 Russian diplomats in response to Russia's alleged interference in the 2016 U.S. elections (Fig. 4.2).

The Russian duck soon became "the tweet heard around the world" as it attracted national and international media attention. British newspapers reporting on the tweet ran the headlines "Russian embassy in UK responds to sanctions with 'lame duck tweet'" and "Russia's London embassy sets Twitterati abuzz." The *New York Post* website read "Russia dismisses Obama as lame duck after U.S. sanctions" while the

Fig. 4.2 "Lame Duck" tweet published by Russian embassy to London (*Source* https://twitter.com/RussianEmbassy/status/814564127230271489/ photo/1?ref_src=twsrc%5Etfw&ref_url=https%3A%2F%2Fd-20614579953605498026.ampproject.net%2F1529106593171%2Fframe.html)

Indian Express stated, "Russia's London embassy calls out 'lame' U.S. sanctions." The tweet also became a topic of discussion among journalists, diplomats, and branding experts. A reporter from the *Wall Street Journal* tweeted: "The Russian embassy Twitter account seems to be run by pre-adolescents", while an employee of a global NGO chose to berate the Russian embassy by tweeting, "In related news, @RussianEmbassy tweets picture of a duck in response to sanctions. Modern diplomacy everyone." Other diplomats took a similar tone, writing, "Fine professional diplomats at work here" and "God bless the noble art of diplomacy." Even branding strategists commented on the embassy's tweet and asked, "who on earth runs the Russian Twitter?" and "Teenagers are running the Russian embassy's Twitter. Wait, actually teenagers would have edited a better image."

The comments listed above seem to express three sentiments. The first is that the Russian tweet was undignified. Gone are the days of eloquent rebuttals and double entendres as diplomacy is reduced to offensive bickering. The second is that Russia's response was childish. Instead of offering a counter argument to Obama's policy of expulsion, Russian diplomats settled for name calling. The final sentiment is that social media and images have, for better or worse, become an indispensable part of modern diplomacy. Yet when analyzing the image used in this tweet one begins to understand that it was anything but childish.

At first, the viewer is drawn to the word "lame" written in block capitals. This is an unsophisticated message that plainly states that Obama or his administration is lame. Yet this simplicity is used to suggest that Russian diplomacy is clear-spoken and understandable to the common person. Unlike other nations, Russia does not mince words or hide behind long and dreary diplomatic statements: It speaks its mind and it speaks truth to power. Taken within a wider context, the "lame" phrase echoes the anti-intellectual sentiments of Brexit, Trumpism and right-wing resurgence in Europe. The world has had enough of experts and slick politicians; it wants frank and bold nations that are not afraid of being abrasive.

Next, the viewer is drawn to the image of the duck. It is at this point that the double meaning of the image becomes clear—Obama is not just lame, he is a lame duck. This tweet, therefore, suggests that Obama's recent actions are as irrelevant as the president himself. It is this added meaning that places Obama in a specific context: that of the world of yesteryear. The lame duck tweet, therefore, offers a narrative through which digital publics can interpret both Obama's actions and Russia's role in the world; Obama belongs to the irrelevant past, while Russia belongs to the relevant future.

An additional interpretation may focus on the use of the image of a duck. Within popular Western culture, images of ducklings often evoke references to the "Ugly Duckling," a story written by Hans Christian Andersen about a dark duckling who morphs into a beautiful white swan. Analyzed through this prism, the Russian duckling references the president's race. Indeed, the duck in the tweet has a streak of black hair, again referencing the president's race. But even more importantly, unlike Andersen's duckling, President Obama has failed to develop into a beautiful white swan as is evident from his "lame" swansong: the inept expulsion of 35 Russian diplomats.

Finally, the viewer is drawn to the text that accompanies the image. Here the embassy uses a short message to ensure that digital publics understand both the image and its underlying ideology. Obama's actions are described as reminiscent of the Cold War, of the past. Yet today Russians and Americans are closer and see the world in the same way. And what is it that Russians and Americans agree about? What is it that draws them together? Obama's lack of aptitude.

By resonating with the anti-intellectual and racist sentiments of Brexit and Trumpism, and offering a narrative of the Obama administration, the embassy's tweet emerges as anything but adolescent. It is an ideological vehicle comprised of two layers, one that is understandable to all social media users, and another that is understandable to more sophisticated ones. The lame duck tweet exemplifies digital tactics as the Russian embassy obtained online virality by raising media attention to a single issue: The U.S. response to Russia's alleged interference in the 2016 election. Yet the tweet did not affect the UK's foreign policy toward Russia, nor did it lead the British population to realign themselves with Russian foreign policy or denounce American foreign policy. As such, digital tactics are limited in their ability to obtain long-term public diplomacy goals. Digital tactics may, however, be able to sow the seeds of gradual change. Tweet after tweet, argument after argument, an embassy may be able to win over certain digital publics. Of course, the more the world of diplomacy changes, the more it stays the same, and derogatory statements have always accompanied international affairs. When asked his opinion of British Prime Minister Lloyd George, the

French leader Clemenceau said "Oh! if only I could piss the way he speaks!".

The Russian embassy's digital activities are in line with Russia's digital vision. As Adesina (2017) writes, Russia's MFA uses the term "innovative diplomacy" with regard to the utilization of digital technologies in public diplomacy activities. Innovative diplomacy is defined by the MFA as "a tool for Russian foreign policy to exert influence on public opinion through the use of ICTs (Information and Communication Technologies)." At a meeting of Russian ambassadors in 2012, President Vladimir Putin encouraged diplomats to use digital technologies, stating that these were among the most effective foreign policy tools. As the "Lame Duck" tweet demonstrates, the Russian embassy does not focus its innovative activities on relationship building, but rather on influencing the agenda of the media and possibly increasing the virality of its content.

The second stage of digitalization saw a transition from digital tactics to digital strategies, in which diplomatic institutions create content to achieve a pre-defined and measurable public diplomacy goal. The goal determines the target audience, while the target audience determines the platform to be used (Bjola & Manor, 2016b). The transition from digital tactics to strategies was facilitated by diplomats' realization that each digital platform attracts different audiences in different regions of the world. The demographics of Twitter users in Israel and the UK are quite different, as are the demographics of WhatsApp users in the USA and Peru.

Digital strategies require a transition from issue-based to campaign-based public diplomacy. This chapter defines a digital campaign as a planned set of activities carried out by diplomatic institutions over a period of time to achieve measurable public diplomacy goals. A campaign consists of pre-authored and pre-approved messages as well as pre-designed infographics and multimedia which are used to attract target audiences and convey messages that will resonate with them. One example was the Obama White House's use of a dedicated Twitter channel to "sell" the Iran Deal to the American public through domestic public diplomacy. The goal of the digital strategy was to rally American public support for the Iran Deal which would translate into political support of the Iran agreement. The measurement was the ultimate ratification of the agreement in Congress. The @theIranDeal Twitter channel began tweeting as soon as the Iran Deal was announced and ceased its activity when the deal was ratified by Congress. Pre-authored content and infographics were used to make four arguments that would resonate with the American public. First, the deal demonstrated that American diplomatic engagement can bring about tangible change in the world. Second, the deal blocked all routes Iran could pursue toward developing a nuclear bomb. Third, the deal avoided another costly war in the Middle East, and fourth, the deal enabled constant international monitoring of Iranian nuclear sites (Bjola & Manor, 2018). The goal of the White House was thus to influence the American public's perception of the Iran Deal which, in turn, would influence American legislators. The use of Twitter to rally domestic support for foreign policy achievements is emblematic of the glocalized nature of the digital society as public diplomacy turns inward in addition to outward. Indeed, the White House campaign attracted attention and comments from both Americans and foreign Twitter users.

The goals of digital strategies may vary from increasing tourism to rallying support for contentious foreign policies, facilitating trade relations, and fostering scientific collaborations between states. Digital strategies do, however, rest on an MFA's ability to define a public diplomacy goal and measure whether the goal has been obtained. Several years ago, NATO's public diplomacy department grasped that European youngsters were no longer aware of NATO's mandate or its importance to members' national security. These youngsters had come of age following the demise of the Cold War and the bipolar system and did not marvel at the gadgets of KGB spies in James Bond films. NATO's public diplomacy department sought to launch a social media account dedicated to informing and interacting with European millennials. As these were primarily gathered on Instagram, NATO too turned to Instagram and announced a photo competition in which youngsters were asked to upload images of what NATO meant to them with the winner being invited to NATO headquarters in Brussels. The measurements employed were the ability to attract European youngsters to NATO's new Instagram account and the number of images shared (NATO, 2014).

To date, several MFAs have launched digital campaigns as part of their bids to assume roles in multilateral forums. Such was the case with the Ethiopian MFA that managed the campaign of Tedros Adhanom to the role of Director General of the World Health Organization, or the Belgian MFA that managed a successful campaign to be elected a non-permanent member of the UN Security Council (L. Soenen, personal communication, June 26, 2018). Conversely, in 2015, the Finnish MFA took a strategic approach to managing digital publics' perception of Finland. The MFA decided to launch a smartphone application that enabled users to incorporate emojis of Finnish culture and history into their smartphone keyboards. One such emoji featured a couple in a sauna, while another displayed a heavy metal rock fan. Through this application, the MFA was able to interact with global smartphone users and portray Finland as a vibrant, innovative, and humoristic nation countering the common perception of Finland as a dark and desolate nation (Grossman, 2015). Even more importantly, the MFA encouraged Finnish citizens to incorporate the emojis when communicating with friends and acquaintances from around the world. Soon, Finnish emojis were disseminated across a myriad of digital platforms and networks. The parameter used by the MFA to evaluate the Finnish strategy was the number of times the application was downloaded by smartphone users. According to the Google Play Store, the application has been downloaded more than 10,000 times since its 2015 launch. By contrast, the Polish MFA's consular application has been downloaded more than 100,000 times. While the Finnish MFA decided to focus its activities on both domestic and foreign populations, other MFAs turned their attention to networked gatekeepers.

From Networks of Influencers to Networked Gatekeepers

During the first stage of public diplomacy's digitalization, diplomats attempted to foster and join networks of influencers. The Lithuanian MFA, for instance, focused much of its digital activity on helping Lithuanian embassies create networks with local opinion makers, journalists, and influential digital users. These networks could aid embassies in disseminating public diplomacy messages, interacting with other elites, influencing the media's depiction of events, and demonstrating local support for Lithuanian foreign policy. Lithuanian embassies also strived to identify and collaborate with influencers in the local diaspora community (R. Paulauskas, personal communication, July 17, 2018). The Polish MFA chose to foster networks with national and international cultural institutions to demonstrate Poland's cultural contribution to the EU, an important aspect of Poland's self-portrayal within the European community (Manor, 2016a).

During the second stage of digitalization, MFAs sought to interact with networked gatekeepers so as to stem the tide of hate, radicalization, and disinformation online. The Israeli MFA, for instance, employs network analysis and sentiment analysis to identify networks that disseminate anti-Semitic content or content that promotes violence against Jews and Israelis. Once these networks have been mapped, the MFA identifies networked gatekeepers or individuals that connect two networks together, such as a network of anti-Semitic content and a network of football lovers. Networked gatekeepers sit at the intersection of two networks, and it is they who enable content to flow from one network to another. Should network gatekeepers stop sharing content, the flow of information between two networks would stop. The goal of the Israeli MFA is thus not to disseminate information, but to limit the flow of certain information (E. Ratson, personal communication, June 26, 2018). To this end, the MFA uses its digital accounts to engage with networked gatekeepers. The networked gatekeepers are contacted online by Israeli diplomats (who identify themselves as such) and are informed that they sit at the intersection between two networks, one of which is sharing misleading and racist content. Over time, Israeli diplomats seek to create relationships with networked gatekeepers so that these may stop sharing anti-Semitic content. Once a network gatekeeper has agreed to stem the flow of hate, other gatekeepers are approached until, ultimately, the anti-Semitic network is quarantined and its content no longer flows to other networks. Finally, Israeli diplomats attempt to interact with anti-Semitic network members and offer them information that may counter their false assumptions and notions about Jews. By stemming the flow of disinformation and hate speech, the Israeli MFA hopes to influence how digital publics' view Israelis and Jews. Notably, Israel's algorithmic strategies demonstrate a networked mentality in which diplomats seek to engage with a network's periphery. According to the British FCO, this strategy is effective, as engaging with the network core is likely to end in rejection (Wilton Park, 2017).

The same logic may be applied to online disinformation or misleading content created by foreign governments. The British FCO, for example, uses big data analysis to map and identify Twitter bots or automated computer software meant to mimic human behavior (Corcoran, 2018). Bots are used to flood digital platforms with false information and highly positive or negative sentiments so as to sow online discord and warp digital publics' perceptions of reality. It is estimated that prior to the Brexit referendum, Russian bots published thousands of pro-Brexit tweets and filled messaging boards and news websites with pro-Brexit sentiments (Mostrous, Bridge, & Gibbons, 2017). Once bots have been mapped by the FCO, so are their networks of influence, or the various individuals who follow and disseminate the bots' content online. Bots can then be reported to digital platforms so that they can be shut down. It is hard to imagine how a fifteenth-century ambassador would have reacted to the sight of robots walking about a king's court. Nonetheless, bots are as central to contemporary diplomacy as ambassadors were to traditional diplomacy. This is because bots serve as networked gatekeepers. It is they who facilitate the flow of disinformation from the government of one nation to the population of another (see Chapter 5 for further discussion on bots).

Importantly, the need to map and stem the flow of misleading information became apparent during the Crimean crisis as Russia used bots to spread disinformation on digital platforms. The purpose of bots is not to influence people's opinions, but rather to shape their perception of reality. For this reason, bots are often employed to flood comments sections on news websites with highly positive or negative comments and sentiments. Russian bots, for instance, have been deployed on Latvian news sites both during and after the Crimean crisis so as to condemn and negatively portray NATO (NATO Stratcom, 2016). Latvian news site visitors who are exposed to the barrage of negative comments about NATO may come to assume that their fellow countrymen and women now oppose NATO. In turn, these visitors may also come to oppose NATO as humans naturally desire to belong to the majority.

The attempt to influence or disable networked gatekeepers is representative of a conceptual shift among diplomats who, as part of the process of digitalization, have adopted a networked mentality. As Copeland (2013) wrote, twentieth-century diplomacy was characterized by hierarchical organizations that employed top-down chains of command as their modus operandi. Pamment argued that diplomats even viewed societies through a hierarchical lens as some citizens, such as journalists and politicians, could influence, while ordinary citizens could be influenced (Pamment, 2012). The process of digitalization has altered the modus operandi of diplomatic institutions as they have learned to map and join networks of influence (Slaughter, 2017). The predominance of the network metaphor in public diplomacy is also evident in the logic that now governs digital interactions and "listening." Embassies are now viewed as a global network that enables an MFA to promote different goals in different countries while gathering relevant feedback from local publics. Such feedback may then inform the policy formulation process at the MFA level (Israel MFA, 2017). This, according to Emily Metzgar (2012), is the very definition of digital engagement. As Jorge Heine (2016) wrote, digitalization has forced diplomats to abandon the mentality of the elite club for that of the decentralized network. These networked approaches to public diplomacy are emblematic of the manner in which the norms, values and self-metaphors of diplomats are shaped over time by the logic of the digital society and its underlying structure. In addition to networks, influence can also be obtained through narratives, which offer digital publics a prism for understanding world events. The emergence of narrative-based diplomacy is explored in the following section.

FROM ARGUMENT-BASED DIPLOMACY TO NARRATIVE-BASED DIPLOMACY

As is the case with the digital society, the digitalization of public diplomacy has seen diplomats transition from argument to narrative-based public diplomacy. During the first stage of digitalization, diplomats and their institutions utilized digital platforms to comment on events, actors, and policies. Each tweet or Facebook post dealt with a separate issue. For instance, on the 25th of June 2015, the German MFA published tweets dealing with the death of protestors in Egypt, German support for the Ukrainian government in the face of the Crimean crisis, a diplomat's visit to the African Union's new headquarters, and a condolence message following the death of the former Spanish Prime Minister. Each issue, or policy, warranted its own public diplomacy message.

In the second stage of digitalization, diplomatic institutions employ narratives to offer digital publics a prism through which world events can be understood. The narrative is used to demonstrate how various world events relate to one another, how different actors influence each other, and how a nation's numerous diplomatic initiatives all come to form a coherent foreign policy. Narratives are crucial to contemporary public diplomacy because they bring order and structure to a world that appears chaotic, irrational, and accelerating toward a state of perpetual crisis. Narrative-based public diplomacy was adopted given MFAs' increased desire to bypass media actors and directly influence the worldview of digital publics. As Sotiriu (2015) writes, by using digital platforms, MFAs could author their own narratives and disseminate these among digital publics thus directly and effectively bypassing media gatekeepers altogether. Thus, it is the societal prism that best accounts for the use of narratives in public diplomacy as social institutions, MFAs, employ digital technologies to obtain their goals.

The transition from argument to narrative-based public diplomacy was also motivated by Russia's increased use of narratives to shape digital publics' perceptions of events unfolding in Ukraine, as well as the stability of Eastern European countries. Throughout the Crimean crisis, Russia's digital narrative asserted that Western powers have sponsored a neo-Nazi coup in Kiev, which led to violent attacks against Russian minorities in Eastern Ukraine. The attacks included rape, murder, and rampant child abuse. Similarly, Russia used digital platforms to spread narratives about Eastern European countries. One such narrative depicted Lithuania as a failed state that cannot be independent without the financial support of the EU and the military support of NATO. For Western European countries and NATO, Russia's use of digital narratives necessitated a response in the form of digital counternarratives.

It is important to draw a distinction between narratives and strategic narratives. Strategic narratives are used by diplomats to make sense of world events. To do so, strategic narratives summon the past to make sense of the present and predict the future. Strategic narratives are usually employed by diplomats over long durations of time and to comment on a variety of global issues, events, and actors (Miskimmon, O'Loughlin, & Roselle, 2014). Narratives, on the other hand, may be employed for short-term goals such as presenting a nation's vision for the near future, unveiling new diplomatic initiatives, or commenting on how domestic events may influence international relations. Narratives are often employed by diplomats and world leaders during global summits such as the World Economic Forum in Davos, G7 meetings, and various UN assemblies. This chapter focuses on short-term narratives such as the ones employed by three world leaders during the 2016 UN General Assembly. The General Assembly represents a unique opportunity for leaders and diplomats to employ narratives, as these are likely to be disseminated by the media given the importance ascribed to this annual event. The assembly is, after all, a stage on which diplomacy is meant to be played out in front of a globally-engaged audience.

The first leader to offer a narrative of her nation's foreign policy was British Prime Minister Theresa May 2016 was the first General Assembly to be held since the Brexit referendum took place, and was an opportune moment for the British leader to lay out her nation's vision for the near future. The narrative employed by May was that of a "Global Britain," a Britain that would exit the EU but not the world at large. In the first tweet published on the Prime Minister's official channel, she was quoted as saying that the "UK will be a confident, credible and dependable partner." These specific words may be seen as an attempt to portray the UK as a stable political actor following months of internal instability amid numerous resignations and cabinet reshuffles. The second tweet stated that "The challenge for us is to ensure that our governments and global institutions…remain responsive to the people we serve." This tweet suggests that the PM is committed to honoring the Brexit referendum's results. But May then proceeded to announce a series of global diplomatic initiatives, including a new global approach to tackling migration issues, new measures to end modern slavery, counterterrorism support to African countries such as Somalia and continued efforts to ratify the Paris climate accords. The PM linked these various diplomatic initiatives into one coherent foreign policy or narrative: that of a globally-engaged Britain. It is this narrative that helped digital publics both in the UK and around the world make sense of Brexit and understand how the UK's various diplomatic initiatives all relate to one another. As this narrative helped both domestic and foreign populations make sense of Brexit, it is demonstrative of the glocalized digital nature of public diplomacy in which the national and international collide into a hybrid space.

The second leader to offer a narrative of his nation's foreign policy was Iranian President Hasan Rouhani. The 2016 General Assembly was held soon after the Iran nuclear agreement and thus also served as a stage for Iran to announce its policies in the post-nuclear era. Rouhani used the UN Assembly to present Iran as a stabilizing force in an unstable region. This began with a tweet in which the president identified terrorism as the main threat to the Middle East. Rouhani ended the tweet with the hashtag #WAVE, meaning World Against Violence and Extremism. This hashtag was used previously on Iranian social media profiles, most notably during Iran's global summit to combat extremism. Additionally, Rouhani tweeted that both the 9/11 attacks and the War in Iraq ushered in an age of instability and borderless terrorism. By referring to both of these events, the president may have been attempting to appeal to Western audiences, as Western narratives identify 9/11 as ushering the era of radical Islamic terrorism (Nayak, 2006). The next tweet stated that "Terrorists hide their nefarious intents behind religious literature, instrumentalizing a compassionate religion by spreading extremism." With this statement, the president made clear that terrorism was inconsistent with Islam and Iran's values. The president's last tweet stated, "The century that began with terror and violence in N.Y. should not continue with hostile competitors and expanding conflicts in the M.E" [Middle East]. This tweet may have been a reference to Saudi Arabia's growing involvement in regional wars, including those in Syria and Yemen. As such, while Iran was portrayed by Rouhani as a source of stability and compassion, Saudi Arabia was framed as a source of instability and zeal. The narrative presented by the Iranian president was thus one of stability. In the post-nuclear age, Tehran can serve as a partner for Western countries looking to end the various conflicts in the Middle East. Like Western countries, Iran too views 9/11 and the Iraq war as the source of tensions in the Middle East and like Western countries, Iran also views global terror as a global threat. Iran's diplomatic initiatives all formed a coherent foreign policy of stabilization. By demonstrating a desire to interact with the West and by adopting the West's narrative of 9/11, the president's narrative may be seen as part of a "charm offensive" meant to depict Iran as more open to the world (*The Economist*, 2013).

The third world leader to offer a foreign policy narrative at the General Assembly was Israel's Prime Minister Benjamin Netanyahu. Like Rouhani, PM Netanyahu identified terrorism as the main source of instability in the region. Moreover, like the Iranian president, Netanyahu argued that Israel is a source of stability given its resistance to terrorism. However, the Israeli PM also suggested that in the face of the mutual challenge of terrorism, Israel and Arab countries may find a new basis for cooperation. In fact, the PM stated that Arab nations in the region are changing their attitude toward Israel. The narrative presented by Netanyahu was that of "A New Middle East." Netanyahu's first tweet stated that "more and more nations see Israel as a potential partner in fighting terrorism." This was followed by the tweet "Governments are changing their attitudes toward Israel because they know Israel can help in protecting their people." The PM ended by tweeting that "The future belongs to those who innovate and this is why the future belongs to countries like Israel...So I call upon you: Cooperate with us, dream of the future we can build together, of security, prosperity and peace." The PM's narrative offered a prism for understanding Israel's diplomatic initiatives vis-à-vis the Arab world. Israel was willing to export its innovative technologies and its anti-terror expertise in return for diplomatic ties with Arab nations who have yet to recognize Israel.

The aforementioned examples demonstrate how digital technologies can complement offline public diplomacy goals. By creating and disseminating narratives on digital platforms, national leaders can project a coherent foreign policy and outline their nation's vision for the future. Moreover, as Sotiriu (2015) argues, digitalization also enables leaders and nations to project their values amid a global public sphere.

Like national leaders, MFAs have also adopted a narrative approach to public diplomacy. The Kenyan MFA and its embassies around the world are promoting the narrative of Kenyan leadership, thus portraying Kenya as *the* prominent leader in Africa. Kenyan diplomats interpret bilateral meetings, joint initiatives, and regional collaborations through the prism of Kenyan leadership (see Chapter 6 for more). The Saudi MFA is promoting a narrative of humanitarian intervention through which its military activities in Yemen can be understood. According to this narrative, Saudi Arabia is laboring to free Yemen from the yoke of Houthi rebels who recruit child soldiers and harm the civilian population. To this end, Saudi Arabia is liberating areas held by Houthi rebels, providing civilians with humanitarian aid, organizing humanitarian convoys into besieged areas, and reconstructing damaged infrastructure. An example of this narrative is shown in Fig. 4.3.

The transition toward narrative-based public diplomacy is emblematic of the fact that public diplomacy is influenced by the norms, values and behaviors deemed to be desirable in the digital society. The digital society is one in which individuals create an attractive personal narrative that comes to life through posts, images and Instagram stories. This narrative is used by individuals to present themselves to all other society members and to increase their digital appeal. Yet true to the nature of the digital society, this personal narrative is one of success and affluence, and of achievements and conquests. There are few personal narratives from the unemployment lines. Like individuals, states now also use digital platforms to disseminate a personal narrative of achievements and grandiose plans for the future. While the second stage of public diplomacy's digitalization saw a transition toward narrative-based public diplomacy, it also saw a transition from targeted to tailored communications.

FROM TARGETING TO TAILORING

Targeting may be defined as the formulation of messages that resonate with large and diverse audiences. The message "don't drink and drive," for example, is relevant to all drivers on the road. Tailoring may be defined as the formulation of messages that resonate with specific subsets of audiences. Tailored messages consider the audience's preferences,

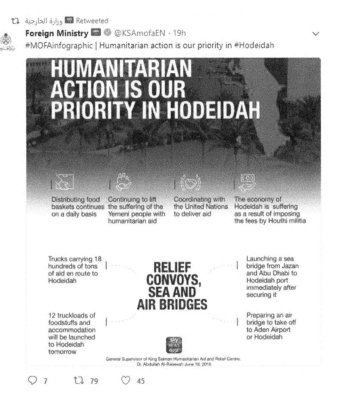

Fig. 4.3 Tweet by Saudi Arabia's foreign ministry narrating military operations in Yemen (*Source* https://twitter.com/KSAmofaEN/status/1009116564510175234)

behaviors, prior knowledge, and beliefs. Tailoring also considers an audience's culture, values, historic narratives and worldview (Enwald & Huotari, 2010; Kreuter, Strecher, & Glassman, 1999; Noar, Benac, & Harris, 2007; Yap & Davis, 2008). Tailored messages are disseminated through media channels that the audience prefers. A relevant example would be a campaign aimed at preventing 18-year-old drivers from taking to the road after consuming alcohol. During the initial stages of the campaign, questionnaires and focus groups would be used to determine whether 18-year-olds believe that alcohol can alter one's response time and sense of danger, to assess their knowledge regarding alcohol's influence on one's driving abilities and to examine whether they would prefer to take a bus or have a designated friend drive them home once they have consumed alcohol. Next, a set of campaign messages would be formulated (informed by audience research) and the audience's preferred medium, be it radio, television, or social media platforms, would be employed. Campaign messages would be tested among the audience to receive feedback, following which the campaign would officially be launched.

During the first stage of digitalization, diplomats primarily relied on targeted communication. The Swiss embassy in Paris used Facebook to communicate with the French population at large, while the Polish embassy in Amsterdam was in charge of engaging with "the Dutch" at large. Moreover, public diplomacy content was often duplicated across multiple platforms. In 2015, Kampf, Manor, and Segev found that 85% of the content published by 11 MFAs on Facebook was also published on Twitter. Thus, in addition to targeting large and diverse audiences, diplomats also failed to adapt their messages to the unique attributes of different digital platforms.

Yet as public diplomacy entered the second stage of digitalization, diplomats increasingly transitioned toward tailored communication. This process was prompted by diplomats' recognition that different digital platforms attract different digital audiences. Many MFAs now regard Twitter as a tool for elite-to-elite communication through which diplomats can interact with journalists, politicians, and the diplomatic milieu, while Facebook is viewed as an elite-to-public medium through which diplomats can converse with regular citizens, diasporas, and interest groups (Bjola, 2018). The process of tailoring was also influenced by the Crimean crisis, as MFAs needed to disseminate their policy statements among elites such as journalists and opinion makers given a global struggle between Western and Russian narratives. This necessitated that MFAs be active on elites' platform of choice. As Copeland foresaw in 2013, the "future favors clicks over bricks and tailoring rather than generic reproduction."

For some MFAs, tailoring was also necessary to obtain certain public diplomacy goals. For example, in an attempt to overcome the limitations of traditional diplomacy, the Israeli MFA decided to launch a social media account through which it could converse with the populations of Arab states neighboring Israel. As the most popular network among these publics was Facebook, the MFA launched a dedicated Arab language profile. The decision to use Arabic stemmed from the assumption that not all Arab Facebook users would be proficient enough in English to discuss political issues (G. Rudich, personal communication, May 18, 2014). The Israeli MFA thus tailored its communications to the language and digital preferences of intended audiences. Presently, MFA posts in Arabic reach approximately one million Facebook users.

The transition toward media production within diplomatic institutions also facilitated the process of tailored public diplomacy. In the twenty-first century, MFAs found themselves operating in a complex media environment that centered on visual storytelling. This is made most evident by the recent surge in popularity of Instagram stories, which are short clips through which users can update followers on their most recent romantic conquest or latest purchase of high-end brands. To compete over the attention of digital publics with non-state actors, terrorist groups, and Instagram celebrities, MFAs also had to begin producing visual content. Yet different platforms accommodate different media. Instagram is image- or- story-based, Facebook is video-based, while Twitter accommodates images or short videos. MFAs understood that as each platform accommodates different media, each platform could be used toward different ends. The UK Mission in Geneva, for instance, currently uses Twitter for publishing videos of the ambassadors' comments at the UN Human Rights Council. This is because ambassadors have but a few minutes to address the council. Facebook is used by the mission for announcing Geneva-based initiatives, elaborating on UK activities at UN forums and hosting Q&A sessions (Garrad, 2017). Diplomats, therefore, began to tailor their messages to the unique attributes of each digital platform.

The emergence of tailored communication can be analyzed through technological and societal prisms. The technological prism would suggest that the adoption of tailored communication models was a result of diplomats' embrace of digital technologies. For instance, by analyzing the number of comments and shares public diplomacy messages elicit, MFAs could fine-tune their online content so that it best resonated with their audiences. Moreover, by using sentiment analysis, MFAs could identify the topics that are of greatest interest to their followers. Thus, the affordances of digital technologies influenced the practice of public diplomacy.

The societal prism would suggest that the incorporation of digital natives into diplomatic institutions was equally important to the emergence of tailoring in public diplomacy. Mark Prensky has argued that those born after 1980 are digital natives. They were born into homes and attended schools that were populated with digital devices and, as such, they are native speakers of the digital language. These natives easily master new digital technologies and are experts at adapting to new digital surroundings. Digital immigrants are those born before 1980. Forever trapped in an analogue mentality, immigrants may come to employ digital technologies, yet they will always have a digital accent and require time and effort to master new technologies (Prensky, 2001). By 2014, digital natives were 34 years old and had begun to fill the lower ranks of MFAs. Their digital savviness and own constant use of digital technologies enabled them to introduce the logic of tailoring into their MFAs and embassies. In a recent study, Manor and Kampf (2019) found that digital natives managing embassy social media accounts instinctively tailor their messages to the feedback they receive from digital audiences, be it in the form of likes, shares, or written comments. Moreover, natives also value the comments they receive from followers and attempt to use these comments to identify issues that are of concern to their audiences. Lastly, natives tailor MFA messages to the language, values, norms, and even slangs of local audiences. The same cannot be said for digital immigrants who tended to discount their followers as unintelligent and uninformed and thus disregard their questions and comments.

The transition toward tailored communication demonstrates that public diplomacy delivered via digital technologies remained public-centric and focused on interacting with digital publics. Yet in many cases, the goal of such tailoring is influence, not relationship building. Studies conducted between 2015 and 2018 have all consistently shown that diplomats and their institutions fail to interact with digital audiences on a regular basis, do not offer opportunities for online conversations and refrain from engaging in digital collaborations with digital networks. Digital tools are mostly used for one-way message dissemination. Tailoring increases the efficacy of one-way communication as messages resonate with publics and reach publics on their preferred mediums.

The following section, however, reviews two case studies that demonstrate the potential applicability of tailored communications toward relationship building as is practiced by the Indian Ministry of External Affairs (MEA). These case studies were selected for two reasons. First, the Indian MEA has been an avid adopter of digital technologies and has long since established a digital department (Natarajan, 2014). Despite this fact, few studies to date have investigated how the MEA uses digital platforms to practice public diplomacy. Therefore, by exploring the digital activities of the MEA, this chapter diversifies the public diplomacy literature corpus. Second, the MEA has launched a smartphone application that hints at the future trajectory of public diplomacy which may be personalized to meet the needs, desires and interests of individuals rather than subsets of audiences. These case studies thus offer a glimpse into the third stage of public diplomacy's digitalization.

The "Know India" Program

As Rana writes, the Indian MEA allocates substantial resources to the practice of diaspora diplomacy. One of the MEA's most interesting programs, called "Know India," aims to foster relationships with the children of Indian immigrants. As these second-generation diasporas have not lived in India, they may not feel an emotional bond with India, which is so central to being part of a diaspora (Rana, 2013).

The "Know India" program consists of both offline and online activities. Offline, the program offers second-generation diasporas the opportunity to visit India and become acquainted with its culture, values, traditions and politics. During such visits, participants are encouraged to share their insights and experiences on social media. Moreover, the Indian MEA promotes such visits on its own social media accounts. These "Know India" visits can help participants develop an emotional bond with India while also increasing the likelihood of participants sharing their experiences with their own networks of friends and acquaintances.

Online, the "Know India" program also includes a rich and diverse web-based platform that offers visitors the opportunity to familiarize themselves with Indian history, culture, politics, society, and innovation. This platform is tailored to younger digital diasporas in two ways. First, it offers a wealth of information about India's past, present and future. One segment of the website is dedicated to India's population and demographics, as well as its geography, climate, sources of water, and land size. Another section is dedicated to Indian national identity and deals with the national flag, the state emblem, and the state song. A third section focuses on culture and heritage and provides information on India's history, its national monuments, its visual art, and its literature.

Importantly, all information is provided in a concise manner and visitors can choose which section to elaborate on and which to skim. This makes for easy navigation and skimming of information: The way young digital natives consume information online (Rosenwald, 2014). The web platform is also tailored to younger audiences, as it is visually driven. Visitors can watch webcasts of President Modi's addresses to the nation, India's Independence Day celebrations, and conferences held in India. The platform includes other multimedia such as links to radio stations, television stations and clips from Indian cinema. The website is also tailored to the needs of Indian parents as it includes a host of games, activities and quizzes that can be downloaded and used to acquaint children with Indian history, tradition, and culture. The web platform also includes educational resources on India's national institutions and the evolution of its democratic system.

The Indian MEA's decision to focus its activities on second-generation diasporas demonstrates a networked approach to diaspora diplomacy. Children of Indian immigrants are members of a myriad of intersecting networks including their family, friends, acquaintances, and interest groups. If incorporated into the diaspora network, Indian youngsters could serve as boundary spanners disseminating information and insight about India among their networks. For example, a French teenager who visited India may share his experiences and views on India's rich history and culture with other French teens, thus serving as a boundary spanner.

It should be mentioned that India is not the only nation to dedicate resources toward engaging with second-generation diasporas. The Georgian Diaspora Ministry uses Skype to offer free Georgian language lessons to children of diasporas around the world. Given that language is a fundamental component of imagined and virtual communities, the diaspora ministry may be investing in the future cohesiveness of the Gregorian diaspora.

India's Personalized Public Diplomacy

Another example of tailoring is the smartphone application launched by India's MEA, which has been downloaded more than 100,000 times from the Google Play Store. The MEA is not the first foreign ministry to launch its own application. Both the Polish and the Canadian ministries have launched applications. However, while the Canadian application focuses on consular aid and the domestic population, the MEA's application seems to target both domestic and foreign populations.

The application has six features. The first is the e-citizen feature, which offers e-services to Indian citizens ranging from telephone directories to employment opportunities at the MEA. The second feature enables users to track state visits by Indian officials abroad as well as state visits by foreign dignitaries to India. The scope of available information is substantive, ranging from images to bilateral and multilateral documents signed during state visits and public statements. The third feature enables users to locate the nearest Indian embassy to them, to read updates from embassies, and even to hear podcasts by Indian ambassadors. The fourth feature is the media center, which consists of a wide array of documents, press releases, speeches, statements and transcripts of media briefings. The fifth feature is a consular one. It is in this feature that foreign users can apply for visas, track their application, download forms, and even communicate with the MEA. The sixth and final feature focuses on public diplomacy. It is under this feature that a user can hear lectures on Indian diplomacy from former ambassadors, watch documentaries on India's history, or read issues of the MEA's magazine—*India Perspectives* (Fig. 4.4).

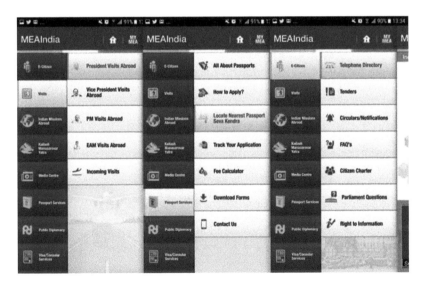

Fig. 4.4 Screenshots of Indian MEA smartphone application

The review of the MEA's application thus far suggests that it offers a breadth of information. However, the most interesting feature of the application is its personalization mechanism. Each user can create his own MEA application by selecting the specific issues he wishes to follow more closely. Users even have a notepad (see Fig. 4.5) where they can write comments on the information they have reviewed. This application, therefore, offers users a personalized digital experience that is tailored to their unique interests and needs. Journalists can follow press briefings and state visits, while prospective tourists can follow embassy updates and track their visa applications. Users can even interact with the MEA through the various modules. By offering users a personalized experience, the MEA increases the likelihood of users returning to the application, engaging with MEA content, and sharing what they have learned with online contacts. From a branding perspective, the application is also noteworthy as it contributes to the depiction of India as a rising technological power.

The Indian smartphone application demonstrates that during the second stage of digitalization, diplomats are increasingly tailoring their public diplomacy activities and messages to the audiences they wish to interact with to the extent of personalized public diplomacy. However, tailoring is but a form of communication. The fact that information is tailored does not say much about the intent of such communication. Tailoring has not led diplomats to abandon the goal of influence in favor of those of dialogue and relationship building. On the contrary, tailoring is a means for increasing influence as followers are exposed to content that is most likely to attract their interest and attention.

Conclusions

This chapter sought to chart the transition between the first and second stages of the digitalization of public diplomacy. By using a series of case studies, the chapter demonstrated that the second stage of digitalization, which began in 2014, saw dramatic changes in how diplomats and their institutions utilized digital technologies to obtain public diplomacy goals. MFAs adopted and developed new technologies, including the use of network analysis to map the flow of disinformation online, and the development of smartphone applications and web-based platforms.

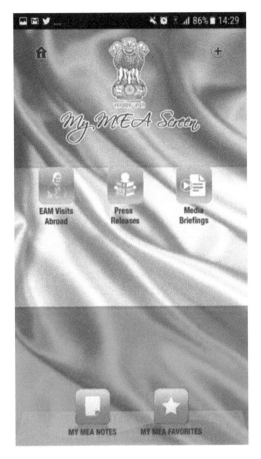

Fig. 4.5 Personalization mechanism of Indian MEA's smartphone application

Building on Marcus Holmes' (2015) argument that the digitalization of public diplomacy can be influenced by two types of "change," this chapter examined both bottom-up and top-down processes. As the chapter has demonstrated, the digitalization of public diplomacy was substantially influenced by an exogenous shock: the Crimean crisis. Russia's use of digital technologies to manipulate public opinion and influence digital publics' perceptions of reality led to changes in diplomats' norms, working routines, and self-narratives.

From the perspective of diplomats' self-narratives—the metaphors they use to conceptualize public diplomacy—the second stage of public diplomacy's digitalization saw diplomats embrace the metaphor of the narrative. From a normative perspective, diplomats regarded narratives as prisms through which they could help digital publics make sense of the world around them. From a values perspective, however, the goal of constructing narratives remained influence as narratives could shape how digital publics perceive events and actors. The new working routines that followed included designing digital campaigns, the creation of pre-authored content, and "tweaking" campaign messages based on audience feedback. Thus, MFAs embraced the logic of tailoring, which governs the digital society.

The affordance of digital technologies also led to changes in MFA norms and working routines. Be it during consular crises or the Crimean crisis, diplomats realized that algorithms limited their ability to reach digital publics. The affordance of algorithms soon led to new norms, including experimenting with different tactics to break free of algorithmic confines. These experiments, in time, led to new working routines such as using trending hashtags in tweets or asking followers to help disseminate MFA content on Twitter. The metaphor that followed was conceptualizing digital platforms through algorithmic communication models and not linear ones.

Yet this chapter has also demonstrated that the transition to the second stage of public diplomacy's digitalization was facilitated by gradual, internal and bottom-up change. Diplomats' attempts to overcome algorithmic filtering during the Neapl quake led MFAs to experiment with different tactics. Similarly, by sharing one another's content, USA and UK diplomats identified strategies for increasing their digital reach. Thus, the second stage of digitalization was brought about by both forms of change identified by Holmes.

Notably, this chapter has ascribed great importance to the adoption of tailored communications. This importance stems from the fact that tailoring demonstrates a greater commitment to fostering relationships with digital publics as content is authored to meet their interests, needs, and desires. Yet within the realm of public diplomacy, tailoring also serves to facilitate the goal of influence. Content that adheres to audiences' historical narratives, cultures, and languages may have a greater impact on their worldview than a generic press statement. Tailoring thus represents the internal conflict that accompanies the digitalization of public diplomacy, the conflict between diplomats' desire to create online relationships and diplomats' well-entrenched goal of obtaining influence. As this chapter has demonstrated, MFAs have created a host of new working routines to obtain influence, not relationships. Such is the case with the employment of Twitter campaigns to manage publics' perceptions of the war on Daesh and the use of domestic public diplomacy to obtain the ratification of the Iran Deal.

The norms of the digital society have been evident throughout this chapter. For instance, Russia's "Lame Duck" tweet was part of an authentic tone adopted by the Russian embassy since 2015, a tone that is confrontational, cynical, and abrasive. Thus, the Russian embassy has created a distinct iBrand for itself that sets it apart from all other London-based embassies. Whether this tone facilitates the achievement of Russian public diplomacy goals is another matter. Additionally, the undiplomatic language used by the Russian embassy was a homage to the norms of absolute openness and transparency and the sharing of information that in other decades would have been exchanged solely behind closed doors.

The emergence of tailored communications in public diplomacy may also be explained through the logic of the digital society. As was argued in Chapter 2, the digital society is the tailored society. Digital society members have come to expect online experiences that are algorithmically tailored to their desires and interests and that are based on their online history. They expect this from Amazon and Netflix, as well as from the *New York Times*. To attract digital society members, public diplomacy practitioners also had to offer audiences a tailored experience. Tailoring has also become crucial to public diplomacy, as the digital society is the TMI society. Digital society members are bombarded daily with vast quantities of information ranging from news articles to updates on the dietary preferences of Kim Kardashian and the undergarments favored by Justin Bieber. Coupled with a rapid influx of blogs, vlogs, and political scandals, this tidal wave of information causes digital publics to pay scarce attention to much of the content they encounter on digital platforms (Miller & Horst, 2017). By tailoring content to the needs, desires, and interests of digital publics, diplomats attempt to seize their attention long enough to disseminate public diplomacy messages. As was argued earlier, without attracting digital publics, diplomats cannot practice public diplomacy. While this chapter has demonstrated the impact of the Crimean crisis on the digitalization of public diplomacy, the next chapter examines the impact of disinformation on both public diplomacy and society at large.

REFERENCES

Adesina, O. S. (2017). Foreign policy in an era of digital diplomacy. *Cogent Social Sciences, 3*(1), 1297175.

Bik, H. M., & Goldstein, M. C. (2013). An introduction to social media for scientists. *PLoS Biology, 11*(4), e1001535.

Bjola, C. (2017, May). Digital diplomacy 2.0 pushes the boundary. *Global Times.* Retrieved from http://www.globaltimes.cn/content/1073667.shtml.

Bjola, C. (2018). *Digital diplomacy and impression management.* Presentation, Canada House, London.

Bjola, C., & Manor, I. (2016a). *How to increase ROI on digital diplomacy?* Presentation, UN Headquarters in Geneva.

Bjola, C., & Manor, I. (2016b, December 3). *10 tips to increase ROI on #DigitalDiplomacy* [Blog]. Retrieved from https://digdipblog.com/2016/12/03/10-tips-to-increase-roi-on-digitaldiplomacy/.

Bjola, C., & Manor, I. (2018). Revisiting Putnam's two-level game theory in the digital age: Domestic digital diplomacy and the Iran nuclear deal. *Cambridge Review of International Affairs, 31*, 1–30.

Copeland, D. (2013). Taking diplomacy public: Science, technology and foreign ministries in a heteropolar world. In R. S. Zaharna, A. Arsenault, & A. Fisher (Eds.), *Relational, networked and collaborative approaches to public diplomacy* (pp. 56–69). New York, NY: Taylor & Francis.

Corcoran, J. P. (2018). *UK FCO open source intelligence unit.* Presentation, the Embassy of the Slovak Republic in London.

Enwald, H. P. K., & Huotari, M. L. A. (2010). Preventing the obesity epidemic by second generation tailored health communication: An interdisciplinary review. *Journal of Medical Internet Research, 12*(2), e24.

Garrad, M. (2017). *The digital diplomacy activities of the UK Mission to the UN in Geneva* [In person].

Grossman, S. (2015, November). Finland is launching a special set of national emoji. *Time.* Retrieved from http://time.com/4100041/finland-national-emoji/.

Hanson, F. (2012). *Revolution at state: The spread of ediplomacy.* Sydney, Australia: Lowy Institute for International Policy.

Hayden, C. (2012). Social media at state: Power, practice, and conceptual limits for US public diplomacy. *Global Media Journal, 11*(21), 1–21.

Head of Communications Services, NATO. (2014). *NATO digital diplomacy efforts.* Presentation, Clingendael Institute.

Heine, J. (2016). From club to network diplomacy. In A. F. Cooper, J. Heine, & R. Thakur (Eds.), *The Oxford handbook of modern diplomacy.* Oxford: Oxford University Press.

Holmes, M. (2015). Digital diplomacy and international change management. In C. Bjola & M. Holmes (Eds.), *Digital diplomacy theory and practice* (pp. 13–32). Oxon: Routledge.

Israeli Ministry of Foreign Affairs. (2017). *Digital diplomacy conference summary* (pp. 6–19). Retrieved from https://www.state.gov/documents/organization/271028.pdf.

Joseph, S. (2018, January). Organic reach on Facebook is dead: Advertisers expect price hikes after Facebook's feed purge. *Digiday UK*. Retrieved from https://digiday.com/marketing/organic-reach-facebook-dead-advertisers-will-spend-reach-facebooks-feed-purge/.

Kreuter, M. W., Strecher, V. J., & Glassman, B. (1999). One size does not fit all: The case for tailoring print materials. *Annals of Behavioral Medicine, 21*(4), 276.

Manor, I. (2016a). Are we there yet: Have MFAs realized the potential of digital diplomacy? *Brill Research Perspectives in Diplomacy and Foreign Policy, 1*(2), 1–110.

Manor, I. (2016b, March 7). *How the UK & US are fighting ISIS online- part 2* [Blog]. Retrieved from https://digdipblog.com/2016/03/07/how-the-uk-us-are-fighting-isis-online-part-2/.

Manor, I., & Kampf, R. (2019). Digital nativity and digital engagement: Implications for the practice of dialogic digital diplomacy.

Metzgar, E. T. (2012). Is it the medium or the message? Social media, American public diplomacy & Iran. *Global Media Journal, 12*(21), 1.

Miller, D., & Horst, H. A. (2017). The digital and the human: A prospectus for digital anthropology. In H. A. Horst & D. Miller (Eds.), *Digital anthropology* (pp. 3–38). London: Bloomsbury Academic.

Miskimmon, A., O'Loughlin, B., & Roselle, L. (2014). *Strategic narratives: Communication power and the new world order.* Oxon: Routledge.

Mostrous, A., Bridge, M., & Gibbons, K. (2017, November). Russia used Twitter bots and trolls 'to disrupt' Brexit vote. *The Times.* Retrieved from https://www.thetimes.co.uk/edition/news/russia-used-web-posts-to-disrupt-brexit-vote-h9nv5zg6c.

NATO StratCom Centre of Excellence. (2015). *Analysis of Russia's information campaign against Ukraine: Examining non-military aspects of the crisis in Ukraine from a strategic communications perspectives.* Riga: NATO StratCom Centre of Excellence. Retrieved from https://www.stratcomcoe.org/analysis-russias-information-campaign-against-ukraine-1.

NATO StratCom Centre of Excellence. (2016). *Internet trolling as a hybrid warfare tool: The case of Latvia.* NATO StratCom Centre of Excellence. Retrieved from https://www.stratcomcoe.org/internet-trolling-hybrid-warfare-tool-case-latvia.

Natarajan, K. (2014). Digital public diplomacy and a strategic narrative for India. *Strategic Analysis, 38*(1), 91–106.

Nayak, M. (2006). Orientalism and 'saving' US state identity after 9/11. *International Feminist Journal of Politics, 8*(1), 42–61.

Noar, S. M., Benac, C. N., & Harris, M. S. (2007). Does tailoring matter? Meta-analytic review of tailored print health behavior change interventions. *Psychological Bulletin, 133*(4), 673.

Pamment, J. (2012). *New public diplomacy in the 21st century: A comparative study of policy and practice.* Routledge.

Pamment, J., Nothhaft, H., Agardh-Twetman, H., & Fjallhed, A. (2018). *Countering information influence activities: The state of the art.* Lund University.

Paulauskas, R. (2018). *Understanding Lithuania's digital diplomacy model* [In person].

Prensky, M. (2001). Digital natives, digital immigrants part 1. *On the Horizon, 9*(5), 1–6.

Rana, K. S. (2013). Diaspora diplomacy and public diplomacy. In R. S. Zaharna, A. Arsenault, & A. Fisher (Eds.), *Relational, networked and collaborative approaches to public diplomacy* (pp. 70–85). New York, NY: Taylor & Francis.

Ratson, E. (2018). *Understanding Israeli algorithmic diplomacy* [In person].

Rosenwald, M. S. (2014, April). Serious reading takes a hit from online scanning and skimming, researchers say. *The Washington Post.* Retrieved from https://www.washingtonpost.com/local/serious-reading-takes-a-hit-from-online-scanning-and-skimming-researchers-say/2014/04/06/088028d2-b5d2-11e3-b899-20667de76985_story.html?utm_term=.71314e79b92a.

Rudich, G. (2014). *Exclusive interview with Gal Rudich, head of new media section at the Israeli foreign ministry's digital diplomacy unit* [In person].

Slaughter, A. M. (2017). *The chessboard and the web: Strategies of connection in a networked world.* New Haven, CT: Yale University Press.

Soenen, L. (2018). *Belgium's digital diplomacy model* [In person].

Sotiriu, S. (2015). Digital diplomacy: Between promises and reality. In C. Bjola & M. Holmes (Eds.), *Digital diplomacy theory and practice* (pp. 33–51). Oxon: Routledge.

The Economist. His biggest smile. (2013, September). Retrieved from http://www.economist.com/middle-east-and-africa/2013/09/21/his-biggest-smile.

The Foriegn and Commonwealth Office. (2011). *Foreign secretary Twitter Q&A on the London Conference on Cyberspace.* Retrieved from https://www.gov.uk/government/news/foreign-secretary-twitter-q-a-on-the-london-conference-on-cyberspace.

Wilton Park. (2017). *Diplomacy in the information age: Wednesday 22–Friday 24 February WP1519.* Wilson House. Retrieved from https://www.wiltonpark.org.uk/event/wp1519/.

Yap, T. L., & Davis, L. S. (2008). Physical activity: The science of health promotion through tailored messages. *Rehabilitation Nursing, 33*(2), 55–62.

CHAPTER 5

The Specter of Echo Chambers—Public Diplomacy in the Age of Disinformation

I say, they don't have to conspire, because they all think alike. The president of General Motors and the president of Chase Manhattan Bank really are not going to disagree much on anything, nor would the editor of the *New York Times* disagree with them. They all tend to think quite alike, otherwise they would not be in those jobs.

—Gore Vidal

American poet Allen Ginsberg opened his masterpiece, "Howl", with the lines:

I saw the best minds of my generation destroyed by madness, starving hysterical naked, dragging themselves through the negro streets at dawn looking for an angry fix, angel-headed hipsters burning for the ancient heavenly connection to the starry dynamo in the machinery of night.

Presently, there seems to be a consensus that multitudes of social media users are being destroyed by madness, starving hysterically naked while looking for an angry fix of shares, likes, and re-tweets, burning for a heavenly connection to those starry yet insidious dynamos of Facebook and Twitter. At the heart of this debate lies the view of social media as a corrupting influence on the minds of its users, as the undoing of public discourse and the erosion of the very foundations of democracy.

© The Author(s) 2019   135
I. Manor, *The Digitalization of Public Diplomacy,*
Palgrave Macmillan Series in Global Public Diplomacy,
https://doi.org/10.1007/978-3-030-04405-3_5

For the institutions and practitioners of public diplomacy, social media platforms have transformed from a tool for mass engagement to a tool for mass deception. It is assumed by diplomats that social media have become weaponized platforms through which governments attempt to sway public opinion and undermine political processes in foreign countries. This is achieved by spreading disinformation, misrepresenting public sentiments, and attempting to sow discord through emotionally-arousing propaganda. Examples of digital manipulation often focus on Russia's activities during the 2016 US election, the 2016 Brexit referendum, and the 2017 German elections. Equally worrying for diplomats is the assumption that social media sites are driving political polarization, hyper-partisanship, and violent online discourse. These are all the result of algorithmic filtering, which engulfs social media users in filter bubbles that prevent cross-party discourse, as users can only interact with like-minded individuals. Here again, the debate is framed around Russia's digital activities, be it in promoting conspiracy theories that thrive on digital platforms or using bots and trolls to inflame debates on web forums. However, as this chapter will demonstrate, disinformation and public manipulation are not inherently Russian. Other nations have also deployed trolls and bots with the aim of promoting foreign policy goals. Combating disinformation thus requires that diplomats understand the goals that lead nations to deploy these tools in the first place.

The rise of political extremity, as well as the manipulation of public opinion, poses several challenges to diplomats. Inflamed and violent publics are less likely to converse with diplomats who seek to exchange opinions, foster understating, and create mutually beneficial relationships. In the age of rage, the center will not hold. Additionally, the spread of disinformation creates a media environment in which truth and reality are continuously contested. Competitions over the truth reduce the credibility of diplomatic institutions who become but one more voice among many while diplomats' statements are but one more opinion heard online. News sites and media outlets that purposefully disseminate false news stories also pose a challenge as democratic publics have been taught to put their faith in media institutions. This creates a public diplomacy "catch 22" as diplomats argue that some news agencies should be trusted, while others should be discounted (Pamment, Nothhaft, Agardh-Twetman, & Fjallhed, 2018). Lastly, the very existence of echo chambers digitally limits diplomats' ability to reach and interact with online publics who are encapsulated in a dome of ignorance and homogeneity. If diplomats cannot reach the public, they cannot practice public diplomacy.

This chapter begins by making five broad arguments that aim to question the current public diplomacy zeitgeist. These are meant to broaden the current debate and provide a wider context through which the dangers of social media may be understood. To do so, the chapter adopts the societal prism, which examines how society engages with technology, embraces technology, and regulates technology to meet its needs. The first argument states that social media sites did not aspire to be democratic when first launched. Second, that every technological medium has been viewed as corrupting, dangerous and undemocratic. Third, that when the pendulum of public discourse swings violently, as it has on the issue of social media, one must be on guard and seek to uncover underlying interest. Fourth, that social media's influence on opinion formation may be more limited than many assume. Subsequently, it is argued that social media has become a veil that focuses diplomats' attention on digital spectacles rather than offline societal processes.

Next, this chapter reviews the latest studies pertaining to algorithmic filtering on social media sites as one must understand how, and if, filter bubbles are created before he or she can burst them. The review of recent scholarly work is written from the perspective of the technological prism, which examines how the architecture and design of technology influence society. Next, the chapter explores how some nations attempt to weaponize filter bubbles to spread propaganda and disinformation. Importantly, the virality of online disinformation is not limited to social media. News sites, discussion boards, and web forums are also ripe with false information. Thus, this chapter identifies the tools through which disinformation and propaganda are spread across multiple digital platforms. The chapter concludes with two case studies that demonstrate how diplomatic institutions are attempting to fracture echo chambers, burst filter bubbles, and curate reliable information for digital publics.

For the sake of clarity, this chapter defines "filter bubbles" as gated digital communities of like-minded individuals that are created through algorithmic filtering (Tucker et al., 2018). Filter bubbles are formed by algorithms, which tailor online content to users' political beliefs, partisanship, and opinions on issues being debated in the public sphere. Within the filter bubble, one is supposedly only able to interact with those Friends and acquaintances that share his or her views and opinions. The term "echo chambers" refers here to the possible outcome of filter bubbles. The metaphor of the echo chamber suggests that within filter bubbles, one's opinions, attitudes, and even prejudices are magnified and stoked through skewed information, social validation and a bonfire of profanities (Garrett, 2017). As the sound of hate grows deafening, individuals begin their journey from the center of the political map to its extremities. The term "disinformation" is used to describe the types of information that an individual may encounter online that could lead to misconceptions about the actual state of the world (Tucker et al., 2018). Lastly, "propaganda" is defined as information created with the purpose of influencing public perception or public opinion to benefit a public figure, organization, or government (Tandoc, Lim, & Ling, 2018).

The fear of filter bubbles, echo chambers and propaganda has led many to argue that social media sites are the undoing of democracy. Yet the relationship between social media and democracy has always been a tenuous one and social media were not necessarily intended to play a democratic role as is argued next.

Social Media and Democracy

We often assume that we are the consumers of social media platforms. It is *we* who seek information online, it is *we* who follow our Friends' escapades, and it is *we* who delight in our peers' status updates and self-ies. Of course, nothing could be further from the truth. The consumers of social media platforms are advertisers. *We* are the product being sold (Lanchester, 2017). Facebook was never meant to serve solely as a tool for networking with Friends and colleagues. It was meant to make a profit. Facebook's profits stem from its ability to provide advertisers with an incredibly sophisticated advertising tool—one that tailors advertisements based on swarms of data collected on each user.

To do so, Facebook must gather as much information about its users as possible, including their interests, political views, sexual orientations, leisure activities, religious beliefs, and artistic tastes. Therefore, it must ensure that users stay on Facebook as long as possible and that they share as much information as possible, information that is analyzed and monetized. Every like, every comment, and every share is translated into dollars and cents. The best way to elicit information from users is to allow them to interact with friends, colleagues, and acquaintances. The same is true of Twitter, and YouTube which are information aggregates of personal data.

Facebook, Twitter, and others were not created with democratic aspiration in mind, nor were they originally meant to function as civil society organizations, as was made clear in early interviews with Mark Zuckerberg and Jack Dorsey (Williams, 2014; Zuckerberg, 2018). Social media companies were bestowed with democratic roles following the Arab Spring. It was the limited use of social media during these protests that shrouded social media with the aura of civil society organizations (Arsenault, 2013). It is this aura that leads people to demand that social media companies now verify the information posted on their platforms, that they prevent the spreading of rumors and lies, and that they block malicious actors from misusing their platforms.

Yet social media are not civil society organizations, they are profit-seeking companies like the Ford Motor Company or Head & Shoulders shampoo. Set against this backdrop, the demand that Facebook and Twitter serve as democratic organizations seems almost ludicrous. It is akin to demanding that the Ford Motor Company democratically provide cars to all citizens or that Head & Shoulders not discriminate against the various forms of dandruff it fights. And yet, there are resounding calls that Facebook, Twitter, and other social media sites all transition from profit-making companies to publishing corporations that adhere to ethical guidelines.

The reason for this is the fear that social media have an immense impact on how opinion is shaped. It is supposedly through posts and tweets that individuals come to know the world and construct a sense of reality. This fear is magnified when one takes into account that Western youngsters spend nearly half their time connected to digital platforms (Anderson & Jiang, 2018). When public opinion is shaped by trolls, false news stories, and disinformation, there is a feeling that social media is inherently bad. When public opinion is shaped by tweets originating from journalists, diplomats, and activists, there is a feeling that social media is inherently good. Markedly, social media are not the first mass medium to be regarded as undemocratic. In fact, nearly every mass medium in the twentieth century was labeled as a menace to society.

Every Technological Medium Has Been Viewed as Undemocratic

The fear of social media as a corrupting medium is not unique. Every mass medium has been greeted by euphoria, fear and regulation. During the 1940s, television was seen as a tool for mass education. Journalist

Edward R. Murrow imagined it as a tool for enlightenment. Yet by the 1950s, television procedures and executives were testifying in Congress following revelations that their shows were orchestrated drama rather than reality. Television was seen as having an immense influence on the morals and values of young people. Programs that celebrated promiscuity were regarded as "magic bullets" that could at once impact the behavior of youngsters. By 1954 Congress was holding hearings on comic books and their influence on juvenile delinquency. This decade also saw the House Un-American Activities Committee which wished to weed out communists from Hollywood given that films could, again, act like magic bullets and at once subvert the entire nation. Hollywood was now the undoing of democracy (Pietilä, 1994; Sproule, 1989).

Is the debate about social media any different from the TV scare? Or the comic book scare? Or even the Red Scare of the 1950s? After all, the debate today is also fixed on a Red Scare, a Russian menace that spreads through online virality. Some would argue that the social media scare is different because social media sites reduce the diversity of information individuals access. Unlike television, movies, or comic books, social media algorithms narrow users' worldviews. Gone are the days in which people consumed news from multiple sources, including newspapers, radio, and television. On social media, individuals become engulfed by filter bubbles that ensure they only see information that adheres to their political orientations, interests and habits. Such filter bubbles supposedly polarize public opinion, lead to political radicalization, and shake the pillars of the town square.

Yet, here again, there may be nothing new under the sun. For did certain classes not always read certain newspapers? Or watch certain television shows? Or listen to certain commentators? It was the fictitious British Prime Minister Jim Hacker from the television show *Yes Prime Minister* who described British newspapers as echo chambers saying that in the UK:

> The *Daily Mirror* is read by people who think they run the country; *The Guardian* is read by people who think they ought to run the country; *The Times* is read by the people who actually do run the country; the *Daily Mail* is read by the wives of the people who run the country; the *Financial Times* is read by people who own the country; *The Morning Star* is read by people who think the country ought to be run by another country; *The Daily Telegraph* is read by people who think it is.

As Gore Vidal's quote at the beginning of this chapter elucidates, we may have always existed in echo chambers reenforced by class, occupation, and chosen media channels.

The view of social media as bad, or even dangerous, has been strengthened in recent years given the emergence of a new rhetoric, one that focuses on the words "fake news," "foreign meddling", and "echo chambers." Yet this was not always the case. In 2011, social media sites were framed as the tool du jour of democratic revolutionaries. Why has the framing of social media grown so negative? Why has the pendulum of public opinion swung so violently?

When the Pendulum
of Public Opinion Swings Violently

The pendulum of public opinion is always in motion. After a decade of Conservative leadership, new labor is elected. After a decade of Republican presidents, Barack Obama is elected. This is the natural progression of thesis, antithesis and synthesis. Yet it is when the pendulum of public opinion swings violently that individuals must seek to uncover possible interests. Between 2011 and 2014, Twitter and Facebook were framed by the media as *harbingers of the Arab Spring*. From Libya to Cairo and Damascus, the spirit of democracy and revolution was propelled through tweets. But in today's media landscape Twitter and Facebook are framed as tools for mass surveillance, mass deception, and mass stupidity as "fake" or false news travels as fast as real news (Pamment et al., 2018; Vosoughi, Roy, & Aral, 2018). Rumors turn fact to fiction and fiction to fact, while tweets and posts may be weaponized as a tool for foreign interventions.

Who stands to profit from this framing? Why has the pendulum swung so violently?

First are the old media, the traditional gatekeepers who ensured that the public only accessed "accurate" information, who were guided by objective ethical guidelines, and whose professionalism was above reproach. Or was it? The old media includes the journalists who legitimized the invasion of Iraq and Afghanistan, the journalists who had scores of stories regarding Harvey Weinstein's sexual misconduct, and the journalists who knew of human rights violations in Guantanamo Bay long before they were made public. Amid the current climate of echo chambers and disinformation, there is a tendency to romanticize the role journalists played in society. Journalists traditionally excelled at scrutinizing government policies and uncovering government mishaps while at the same time eagerly supporting the government, rallying behind the flag, and knowing when not to ask difficult questions.

The old media have been stranded on the island of irrelevance for some time as social media sites became the new gatekeepers of information. Embarrassingly, old media had to migrate to social media. *The Guardian* and the *New York Times* had to publish stories on Facebook in order to reach their readers. But now the tables have turned and old media is on the rise again. The past year has seen the largest growth in old media subscriptions in more than a decade. Importantly, it is millennials who are flocking to old media sites and are paying for newspaper subscriptions (Newman, Fletcher, Kalogeropoulos, Levy, & Nielsen, 2017). The old media have much to gain from the demise of public trust in social media as they may once again retain the role of dominant information gatekeepers.

Second, governments have profited from the new framing of social media sites. Western governments have a new/old menace—a Russian menace. In light of a menace, governments must take swift action. Social media accounts must be monitored, privacy must be curtailed, and shadow courts must be allowed to issue secret indictments. Even Russia has gained something, going from a bankrupt nation tittering on the verge of financial collapse to being viewed as a global information superpower. Finally, politicians have found a new scapegoat. An assortment of government misadventures and ministerial blunders can be blamed on social media.

And so the pendulum of public opinion has swung violently against social media sites not merely because of their growing use to spread false information and malicious content, but because other societal actors may profit from the demise of social media. Indeed, the traditional media may be overstating the actual impact of filter bubbles and echo chambers on opinion formation.

Social Media's Limited Impact

The societal prim suggests that social media's impact on opinion formation may be limited as people use digital platforms to communicate with diverse contacts. In the digital society, the term "Friends" relates to co-workers and acquaintances; family members and former lovers; high school compatriots; and other echoes of one's past lives. As such, one's online Friends are likely to be much more diverse than his offline friends and people may actually be exposed to a broader range of ideas, opinions, and facts online. Equally important, people do not exist solely online. After logging onto Twitter and Facebook, individuals drive to work and listen to the radio, hold discussions over lunch or near water coolers, converse with friends over dinner, and spend holidays with families. Each of these exposes people to diverse opinions and each influences political orientations.

The technological prism would also suggest that social media's impact on opinion formation is limited as each social media user is exposed to a unique online experience. This is because social media feeds are personalized by algorithms to meet users' interests, informational desires, and shopping habits. One user may log on to Twitter and view three consecutive tweets: one by President Trump calling North Korea a menace, another by Theresa May calling for action against North Korea, and another by the *New York Times* describing North Korean military drills. This user would assume that war is imminent. Another user may first see a video of a cat playing the piano, then a dog jumping for joy and finally a tweet by Trump calling North Korea a menace (Crilley, 2016). This user would assume that all is right in the world. Thus, one cannot say that all information reaches all social media users in the same way or has the same influence on all users. As each feed is personalized, so is access to information and so is opinion formation. As such, it is possible that the concern over social media's influence on users' worldviews has been exaggerated. In fact, it is possible that social media has become a powerful veil that focuses people's attention on digital spectacles rather than offline societal processes.

THE SOCIAL MEDIA VEIL

Facebook was not the first social media site to be launched online. It was preceded by digital platforms such as Friendster and Myspace which also enabled users to create a public profile on which they could share information and through which they could interact with other users (Boyd & Ellison, 2007). However, Facebook was the first platform to demand that users verify their identity through a university email and that they import their offline identity to the online realm. Facebook thus ended the age of online anonymity. One would have expected that this merger of offline and online personas would prevent people from sharing hateful, violent, derogatory, and racist comments on Facebook. One would have expected that there would be a barrier of shame and normative compliance that would actually limit hate speech on social media sites. That is not the case. Social media sites are a breeding ground for hate groups. Within gated communities, members of hate groups enter a digital vortex of prejudice and ignorance that may translate into offline violence. But is this vortex created by social media? Or has it merely migrated online?

The answer is both. The sentiments expressed online are forged by offline events. As former U.S. President Barack Obama tweeted, people are not born to hate. They learn to hate. After they do so offline, they can use the online world to find a community of hate, one in which their prejudice is validated. Studies suggest that hate and fear travel much faster online than compassion, an alarming finding as the violent re-emergence of racism, xenophobia, homophobia, and other forms of discrimination are a direct threat to the cohesiveness of societies and democracies everywhere (Vosoughi et al., 2018).

But social media's ability to drive political extremity and hate is also limited. Financial corporations, brands and politicians have learned that altering one's opinions and behavior through social media content is vexing at best and impossible at worst. Had users really been so susceptible to social media messaging, 1 billion Facebook users would presently be singing the anthem of the Soviet Union while wearing GAP t-shirts.

What emerges is that social media may have become a powerful veil. This is true for society in general, and of diplomats practicing public diplomacy in particular. Diplomats may come to focus their attention on social media, on echo chambers, and on filter bubbles until they neglect offline societies and political structures. Rather than understand the motivation to vote for Trump, diplomats might obsess over the use of social media to support Trump. Rather than engaging with people's prejudice and their foul rhetoric, diplomats may take to simply analyzing big data sets. This "social media mystification" reduces public diplomacy to strategic communication while neglecting a decade's work of "new" public diplomacy activities.

In summary, by adopting the societal prism this section has demonstrated that the fear of social media as a corrupting medium is not a novel phenomenon. Calls to regulate social media sites and ensure accuracy of information are akin to the manner in which previous mass media have been treated with suspicion. There are also those who stand to gain from the demise of social media. What is required is substantive research that examines the existence of filter bubbles, their possible impact on opinion formation, and whether they may be weaponized by nations to sow societal discord. Such research is presented in the following section.

Echo Chambers—Fact or Fiction?

Tucker et al. (2018, p. 16) have stated that the "prevailing narrative of echo chambers is that of online disinformation being amplified within communities of like-minded individuals." Within echo chambers, disinformation goes unchallenged due to algorithms that filter out opposing voices and contradictory information (Pariser, 2011; del Vicario et al., 2016). The concern over echo chambers stems, in part, from the finding that roughly 50% of adults in the developed world access news through social media sites (Newman et al., 2017; Shearer & Gottfried, 2017). If these adults are in fact engulfed within echo chambers then nearly half of the demos may be formulating its political opinions based on lies, falsehoods and half-truths.

However, the very existence of filter bubbles and echo chambers has recently been called into question (Garrett, 2017). A study from 2016 examined 50,000 news consumers in the USA. The study found that most participants had a healthy, or diverse, online news diet and that the most frequently visited news sites were those that catered to both liberals and conservatives. News sites that catered solely to political extremes attracted little attention (Flaxman, Goel, & Rao, 2016). Another study found that people's offline interactions were more likely to be politically filtered than their online news consumption (Tucker et al., 2018). As was argued earlier, this finding is not surprising when one takes into account the nature of "Friendships" in the digital society, which refers to both strong and weak ties, friends and colleagues, fathers and lecturers. Thus, individuals' online public spheres may be more politically diverse than their offline spheres as people tend to form close offline friendships with those who share their worldviews.

In 2015, a study of 10 million Facebook users found that the social media site's removal of oppositional news stories was also limited. Algorithmic filtering removed only 5% of oppositional news stories for conservatives and 8% for liberals (Bakshy, Messing, & Adamic, 2015). Similarly, scholars have found that people often seek out information online that negates their political affiliation. As algorithms surveil one's digital activities, seeking contradictory information indirectly diversifies one's online information diet (Garrett, 2017, p. 371). Lastly, studies have found that social media users are regularly exposed to a "surprisingly" high volume of diverse political views (Barberá, 2014). This was also reported by social media users themselves in a recent study by the Pew Research Center (Duggan & Smith, 2016). The aforementioned studies indicate that algorithmic filtering does not necessarily limit people's access to diverse sources of information and news. Subsequently, filter bubbles' impact on the formation of political opinion may be limited.

But the term "filter bubble" is also used in reference to disinformation. It is assumed that disinformation is magnified online as it is shared within digital communities of like-minded individuals where it goes unchallenged (Pariser, 2011). This leads to societies that are increasingly misinformed and polarized given that false news stories are often sensational reports that deal with contentious issues that are meant to elicit negative emotions and sow feelings of discord (Sunstein, 2017). Yet studies suggest that social media and Internet use do not correlate with political polarization and that disinformation has a marginal impact of levels of political knowledge (Allcot & Gentzkow, 2017; Boxell, Gentzkow, & Shapiro, 2017). Some studies have even found correlations between social media usage and increased political knowledge (Baumgartner & Morris, 2010; Groshek & Dimitorva, 2011; Kenski & Stroud, 2006).

Conversely, studies did find that "fake" or false news stories were wildly shared during the 2016 US elections and reached large numbers of citizens. Other studies have shown that Facebook engagement was higher for "fake" content than for news originating from traditional media (Rogers & Bromwhich, 2016; Timberg, 2016). As such, skewed and biased information was as salient as accurate news coverage during the elections. Additionally, false news sites, deployed during the U.S. elections, attracted a staggering 159 million visitors during the last month of the campaign. Yet an in-depth analysis found that the average American only saw and remembered 1.14 fake stories, a relatively small number (Allcot & Gentzkow, 2017).

Lastly, conspiracy theories are known to thrive on digital platforms mainly because skeptical audiences rarely visit sites that promote conspiracies. Thus, these sites may be the most crystallized version of echo chambers (Wood, Douglas, & Sutton, 2012). Sunstein and Vermeule (2009) argue that conspiracy theories normally include a belief that a powerful group is manipulating the public while concealing its activities. These theories often make their way to the mass media, which seek to profit from them, as was the case with the media attention paid to Donald Trump's theory that President Obama was not born in the United States. Surveys suggest that half of the American public believe or endorse at least one conspiracy theory at any given time (Oliver & Wood, 2014). Yet this study was limited to America, a nation that has a historic affinity for such theories.

The majority of the studies reviewed in this section suggest that the impact of algorithmic filtering, or filter bubbles, on the formation of political opinions, the spread of disinformation, and access to diverse news sources is limited. In fact, the aforementioned studies have led Garrett (2017) to conclude that the concepts of echo chambers and filter bubble are but a myth. This chapter does not make such a sweeping statement. Yet it does argue that the impact of algorithmic filtering may be more limited than originally thought, as digital publics actively seek out news, information and viewpoints that negate their political stance and interact with "Friends" that hold diverse political affiliations. It is equally important to note that even in the age of filter bubbles, much of the information about politics shared on social media is authored by traditional news outlets (Tucker et al., 2018).

However, the aforementioned studies do suggest that digital platforms are now competitive arenas in which truth and reality are contested. The fact that filter bubbles may be less influential than first thought has not prevented nations from attempting to strategically utilize filter bubbles to increase the impact of disinformation and propaganda. Such is the case with Russia's use of propaganda in its Hybrid Warfare doctrine, which is introduced in the following section.

From Russia with Love

On February 26, 2013, the chief of the Russian General Staff, General Valery Gerasimov, published an article on the future of warfare. Within Western circles, the article would come to be known as the "Gerasimov Doctrine." The doctrine supposedly called for a blend of conventional and unconventional warfare known as "Hybrid Warfare." Specifically,

Gerasimov called for combining military force with propaganda, subversive NGOs, peacekeeping operations, private military companies, cyber warfare, and cyber warriors. The purpose of this hybrid form of warfare is to destabilize foreign countries by stirring political dissent, stoking separatist sentiment, and preventing a legitimate government from conducting the affairs of state (Bartles, 2016).

According to Western interpretations, the Gerasimov Doctrine reconceptualizes how Russia could obtain regime change in foreign countries. In the first stage, social media, the Internet, and NGOs are used to sow discord through propaganda and give rise to internal tensions. Violence may soon erupt, leading to a crisis of legitimacy for the government. As internal security destabilizes, private mercenaries and special forces are used to promote chaos until paralysis grips the capital. Next, the besieged government is sanctioned, either military or financially, leading to its collapse and the rise of mob rule. Finally, under the pretense of peacekeeping or humanitarian mediation, soldiers can be deployed, ultimately instilling a more convenient regime. This was, according to NATO, the very strategy used by Russia to invade and ultimately annex Crimea in 2014 (Giles, 2016). In light of the Gerasimov Doctrine, digital propaganda is but one tool in Russia's military arsenal meant to facilitate its foreign policy objectives, be it regime change, destabilizing other countries, or acquiring new territory. Propaganda is thus the continuation of Russian diplomacy by other means.

The Gerasimov Doctrine has major implication for diplomats because it suggests that during times of crises public diplomacy must counter Russian propaganda being disseminated on social media and on the Internet and by NGOs. This requires digital capabilities that MFAs may have yet to acquire such as methods for identifying false stories in near-realtime, mapping local networks through which counter information may be circulated, quickly forming networks with opinion makers (especially those relevant to minority groups or ethnic minorities), exposing fictitious accounts, discrediting or diminishing the credibility of certain spokespersons, promoting positive national narratives as a means of boosting social and national cohesion, and working with diaspora groups as a means of influencing online discussions in countries being targeted by Russia.

Charles Bartles (2016), however, has argued that the so-called Gerasimov Doctrine was part of the Russian military's use of foresight to anticipate changes in warfare and adopt new practices. Bartles contended that the aforementioned description of Hybrid Warfare was used by Gerasimov to characterize Western regime changes in Yugoslavia, Kosovo, Iraq, and Afghanistan and to identify the defensive measures Russia would have to develop to ward off such attacks on its own sovereignty. In other words, Gerasimov was describing Western, not Russian, Hybrid Warfare. The Russian General even argued that Russia could soon find itself under hybrid attacks given intense competition over global resources, many of which can be found on Russian soil.

Mark Galeotti (2018b), who apparently coined the phrase "Gerasimov Doctrine," recently published an article that stated that there was no such doctrine, nor had Russia implemented a new means of warfare. He asserted that people seek refuge in "doctrine" terminology given that perceptions of threat drive policy and, at the moment, Western nations feel threatened by Russia's campaigns to "divide, distract and dismay" (Galeotti, 2018a).

The controversy surrounding the Gerasimov Doctrine is reminiscent of a John le Caré book situated at the height of the Cold War. Had the master spy George Smiley read the doctrine he would have remarked "Style appalling, blatantly a fabrication from beginning to end. It just could be the real thing" (Alfredson, 2011). Whether the Gerasimov article was used to illustrate a threat to Russia or to promote a new Russian military doctrine remains debatable. What is certain is that it has had a profound impact on European MFAs and members of the NATO alliance. As one British diplomat blogged during the 2014 NATO Summit in Wales:

> Firstly, Russia's actions in Ukraine require us to focus again on our traditional core NATO task of collective defence. But the 'hybrid' conflict we have witnessed in Ukraine (including use of irregulars, propaganda and deniable soldiers/equipment without insignia) also demonstrates the need to adapt and innovate. Amongst other investments to modernize our forces, we want to develop a brigade-size high readiness response force able to react quickly to sudden or ambiguous attacks or crises. (Leach, 2014)

NATO and European MFAs have thus increasingly focused their digital resources on identifying and countering Russian digital activities. As part of this process, the goals of public diplomacy have steadily transitioned from relationship building and dialogue to strategic communication and information warfare. The German MFA has launched a new initiative to restructure its strategic communication apparatus by 2020. This will include developing greater information-gathering capabilities and investing greater resources in digital campaigns that target specific online populations. The British Foreign and Commonwealth Office (FCO) has established two new departments one tasked with collecting open source intelligence and the other with mapping digital disinformation while Baltic MFAs have increased their collaborations with national defense ministries (R. Paulauskas, personal communication, June 25, 2018). Similarly, in September of 2018, the Danish government announced a new initiative to increase Danish resilience against disinformation. As part of this initiative, the Danish MFA will strengthen its abilities to monitor disinformation in the media directed at Denmark and will also train communication officers from various ministries on how to identify and counter disinformation.

Notably, different MFAs and organizations define strategic communications in different ways. Yet a recurring feature of such definitions is the emphasis on influence and behavior change, as opposed to relationships. For instance, the EU Institute for Security Studies defined strategic communications as "a systematic series of sustained and coherent activities, conducted across strategic, operational and tactical levels, that enables understanding of target audiences and identifies effective conduits to promote and sustain particular types of behavior" (Issue, 2016). Similarly, in 2010, NATO first defined the aim of its strategic communications as ensuring that "NATO's audiences, whether in the Nations or in a region where a NATO operation is taking place, either friendly or adversarial, receive truthful, accurate and timely information that will allow them to understand and assess the Alliance's actions and intentions. This will deter aggression and promote NATO's aims and objectives" (NATO, 2010). None of these definitions invoke the language of the "new" public diplomacy or emphasize the need to interact with digital publics so as to foster dialogue and relationships. As such, MFAs' transition toward strategic communications may also be a transition away from "new" public diplomacy activities. Yet countering Russia's digital activities, be it through dialogue or influence, requires that one understand the goals Russia aims to obtain when using disinformation and propaganda. These are explored in the following section.

The Goals of Russian Disinformation

The goal of Russian disinformation is not to influence one's political opinions or ideology but, rather, to alter one's perception of reality either by contesting reality or questioning the existence of an objective truth (Pamment et al., 2018). One example of such activities can be found in the digital communications of the Russian MFA during the Crimean crisis. At the onset of the crisis, the Russian MFA alleged on Twitter that neo-Nazis had staged a coup d'état in Kiev and had unlawfully overthrown a democratically elected government. Next, Russian diplomats tweeted that pro-Ukrainian extremists, backed by the EU, were harming and threatening the lives of Russian ethnic minorities in Eastern Ukraine. The MFA also argued that the Ukrainian Parliament was trampling on the human rights of Russian minorities and that the rule of law was supplanted by extremists and neo-Nazis who had seized weapons from the Ukrainian military. The MFA later stated that Ukrainian neo-Nazis, aided by the EU and the USA, posed a threat to the national interests of Russia as they could seize its bases in Crimea and murder Russian minorities in the region. Finally, Russia stipulated time and again that it had never invaded Crimea. Rather, Crimea joined the Russian Federation of its own accord once local parliaments declared their independence from Kiev.

When Russian soldiers were captured in Eastern Ukraine, a Russian spokesperson explained that they had simply gotten lost and wandered across the border (BBC, 2014). When satellites captured images of Russian military units in Ukraine, the Russian embassy to the United Arab Emirates tweeted in Fig. 5.1 mocking NATO's supposed evidence. When U.S. diplomats accused their Russian counterparts of violating international law by invading Ukraine, Russian diplomats tweeted about human rights violations in Guantanamo Bay. In all these cases, Russian diplomacy focused on questioning the reality of events unfolding in Ukraine.

Russia's diplomatic messaging during the Crimean crisis is emblematic of its overall disinformation strategy, which focuses on promoting a specific metanarrative that depicts the "West as an aggressive and expansionist entity on the one hand, and as weak and verging on collapse on the other" (Pamment et al., 2018). Indeed, throughout the crisis, Russia argued that Western powers were aligning themselves with fascists and that the West was involved in the overthrow of the democratically elected Yanukovych government.

Moreover, the Russian narrative of a neo-Nazi coup was in direct contrast to that promoted by Western MFAs, stating that a democratic revolution had taken place in Ukraine and that the people of Ukraine had deposed a pro-Russian leader who refused to accept the people's will

Fig. 5.1 Russian embassy rebukes NATO evidence (*Source* https://twitter.com/rusembassyuae/status/507226671401824256?lang=en)

Russian Embassy, UAE
@RusEmbassyUAE

Follow

#NATO's latest evidence of #Russian armor invading #Ukraine has been leaked! Seems to be the most convincing ever!

9:00 PM - 3 Sep 2014

3,933 Retweets 1,994 Likes

485   3.9K   2.0K

to sign a trade agreement with the EU. As both sides battled over their narratives, the reality of what was happening in Crimea became subject to speculation. This is still true today, sometime after the annexation of Crimea. According to some MFAs, there is now a place called the Republic of Crimea. It has recognized borders and a parliament, and its citizens have national passports. According to other digital channels, there is no such place. It does not exist.

Of course, the Russian MFA was not the only actor to contest the reality of the Crimean crisis. Throughout the crisis, Russian trolls flooded digital platforms in Ukraine and the Baltic states with false stories of atrocities committed by Ukrainian soldiers and extremists, including the murders of women and children and the establishment of concentration camps in Eastern Ukraine (Sazonov, Kristiina Müür, & Mölder, 2016). State-run news agencies such as Sputnik disseminated images of Russian aid convoys making their way to rescue besieged Russian minorities alongside images of neo-Nazis supposedly desecrating Russian monuments to its victory in World War II. At the same time, Russia Today carried the statements of Russian diplomats and Kremlin spokesperson across the borders of neighboring nations.

The Russian MFA has also used Twitter to contest the nature of Russia's involvement in the Syrian Civil War. Russian diplomats have employed Twitter to suggest that Russia is aiding the Assad regime in its struggle against Islamic terrorists. Over the past two years, the MFA has dedicated digital resources to exhibiting Russian aid to the Syrian population in the forms of food, medicine, and humanitarian convoys out of bombarded areas. Thus, Russia's military involvement in Syria was framed as a humanitarian intervention. These arguments are routinely accompanied by images supposedly depicting the events taking place on Syrian soil. For instance, in December of 2016, Russia's embassy to South Africa published the tweet seen in Fig. 5.2 depicting Christmas celebrations in the liberated city of Aleppo. At the exact same time, Western European MFAs were circulating images of an Aleppo that had been reduced rubble, a city populated only by ghosts.

Fig. 5.2 Conflicting depictions of the reality in Aleppo (*Source* https://twitter.com/EmbassyofRussia/status/811486637242908672?ref_src=twsrc%5Etfw%7Ctwcamp%5Etweetembed%7Ctwterm%5E811486637242908672&ref_url=https%3A%2F%2Fdigdipblog.com%2F2017%2F01%2F07%2Fon-the-use-of-images-in-the-diplomatic-struggle-over-syria-2%2F; https://twitter.com/foreignoffice/status/808764943365525504)

The fate of Aleppo and the nature of the Syrian Civil War were thus also called into question, suggesting that truth was in the eye of the beholder, or the tweeter. In both Crimea and Syria, Russia created a skewed information media ecology meant to instill senses of confusion and doubt among digital publics as confusion leads to insecurity and insecurity breeds tension and paralysis. In other words, by contesting truth and reality, Russia created a climate of doubt in which it could secure its foreign policy goals of annexing Crimea and rescuing the Assad regime.

While Russian disinformation focuses on contesting reality, Russian propaganda focuses on polarizing societies. These activities were all manifested in Russian paid ads circulated on Facebook during the 2016 US elections campaign.

The Goals of Russian Propaganda

While Russia initially focused its digital activities on its neighbors, such as Ukraine and Georgia, in 2016 it spread its reach to the USA (NATO). Unlike Russian disinformation, Russian digital propaganda seems to adhere to the traditional goals of propaganda: identifying discontent segments of society, highlighting contentious issues, using past events to stoke social tensions, sowing the seeds of discord and driving wedges between social groups (Pamment et al., 2018). In a recent project, the Oxford Digital Diplomacy Research Group evaluated 800 Facebook ads circulated during the 2016 elections that were paid for by Russian organizations. Intriguingly, Russian ads usually targeted two, opposing social groups simultaneously, such as African Americans and white conservatives.

The ad shown in Fig. 5.3, which was targeted at African Americans, is comprised of two images. The top one depicts members of the Ku Klux Klan, while the lower one depicts Trayvon Martin, a young black man who was shot to death in 2012 by a white neighborhood watch volunteer in Florida. The ad states that Americans should fear the hoods of the Klan rather than the hoods of young African Americans. This ad resonates with growing racial tensions in America following the deaths of several young black men by police officers and the emergence of the Black Lives Matter movement. This Russian ad also summons African Americans' past to make sense of African Americans' present—that of enduring white hate, discrimination, and violence.

Fig. 5.3 Russian
Facebook ad targeting
African Americans dur-
ing 2016 elections

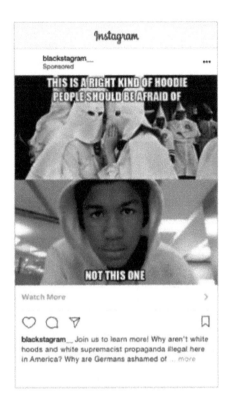

At the same time, another Russian ad targeted white conservatives while using the rhetoric of law and order, one which has been embraced by the Republican Party since the election of Richard Nixon (Zeitz, 2016). The ad featured three men—a black man who was choking a white police officer and another black man poised to impale the white officer with the American flag. The ad included the tagline "Blue Lives Matter," a direct rebuke of the Black Lives Matter movement. This ad resonated with historical white fear of African American violence, suggesting that law and order were coming under attack, not young black men.

Both of these ads focused on contentious issues and evoked a strong emotional response. Their goal, however, was not to alter opinions, but to drive social frustration and increase societal polarization. As a recent report by the University of Lund argues, polarization is a key Russian digital strategy (Pamment et al., 2018). What is unique about Russian digital propaganda is thus not its goal, as propaganda has traditionally sought to undermine social cohesion, but its method of delivery. By disseminating these ads on Facebook, Russia made use of social media algorithms to deliver its messages to a specific subset of audiences with whom it might most resonate. This was a form of tailored propaganda, as opposed to targeted propaganda, which was used during the ages of print, radio, and television and reached entire societies. As Chapter 4 argues, tailored communication is much more likely to resonate with intended audiences than targeted communication.

Russian Facebook ads also demonstrate an attempt to weaponize the filter bubble effect, as these ads would likely go uncontested among targeted audiences, be they African Americans or white conservatives. Moreover, these ads were likely to be shared widely as they resonated with the worldviews of target audiences (McClenghan, 2017). The cost of publishing and disseminating these ads was remarkably low. According to Facebook, Russian ads during the 2016 election may have reached 216 million users at the cost of $46,000 (Senate hearing, 2016).

Markedly, many of the accounts that disseminated Russian ads all had the appearance of American grassroots organizations thus masking their true origin. This masking is demonstrative of the fact that contemporary disinformation and propaganda campaigns are increasingly hard to detect and are "purposively at odds with familiar categories of right and wrong" (Pamment et al., 2018, p. 10). Equally disturbing is the fact that these ads were only visible to those users who were targeted by Russia. As a report from Lund University concludes, digital platforms create a reality in which millions of people may be exposed to divisive and false ads without anyone being the wiser. Will Moy, director of the fact-checking website FullFact.org, is quoted in the Lund report and said that "Inaccurate information could be spreading with no-one to scrutinize it. Democracy needs to be done in public" (ibid.).

It should, however, be mentioned that other countries have also used disinformation to obtain policy goals. China, Iran, and Venezuela have all been credited with using disinformation to counter the promotion of democracy and to promote authoritarianism (King, Pan, & Roberts, 2017; Nocetti, 2015; Vanderhill, 2013; Way, 2015). The Computational Propaganda Project at the Oxford Internet Institute suggests that the number of countries deploying some form of social media influence operations has grown from 28 in 2016 to 48 in 2017. These include the governments of Australia, Germany, Hungary, Israel, Saudi Arabia, Serbia, Turkey, Ukraine, the UK, and the USA (Bradshaw & Howard, 2018). Russia was also not the only nation to use digital platforms to contest reality through disinformation and skewed information. Elsewhere on social media, one might learn that Turkey has both strengthened its democracy and fallen under totalitarian rule, that Daesh has both established a Caliphate in Syria and Iraq and has collapsed while Iran has both met its nuclear commitments and violated them—depending on if one follows President Trump or Macron online and if one follows the Turkish foreign ministry or the Israeli one.

To summarize, the goal of Russian disinformation is to contest reality and to suggest that there is no such thing as an objective truth. The goal of Russian propaganda is to sow the seeds of discord by targeting disillusioned segments of society and drawing greater attention to contentious issues. One method of disseminating Russian propaganda was through paid Facebook ads, as was explored in this section. Yet Russia has also deployed additional drivers of disinformation including trolls, bots, and news sites that spin fiction rather than fact. These are explored in the following section.

Additional Drivers of Russian Disinformation

The Russian MFA and state-owned media are not the only drivers of Russian disinformation. These also include trolls, bots, and "fake" or false news sites. Trolls are individuals who post inflammatory comments on digital platforms to sow discord and evoke emotional responses (Phillips, 2015). The term "trolls", however, may refer to private individuals who enjoy stoking emotional fever online. Hired trolls, on the other hand, are operatives who are contracted by politicians, political parties, and governments to flood digital platforms with fake commentary with the goal of preventing users from accurately assessing reality (Mihaylov, Georgiev, & Nakov, 2015).

Reports have suggested that Russia operates "troll farms" where operatives are tasked with influencing digital discussions on national and international issues. These trolls are strategically deployed by Russia to spread conspiracy theories, sway public opinion in favor of Russia and against NATO, promote authoritarianism in Europe, and counter the promotion of democracy (Gerber & Zavisca, 2016; Lankina & Watanabe, 2017). Russian trolls are active on numerous digital platforms, news sites and discussion boards. A recent report by the NATO Stratcom Centre (2017) stated that Russian trolls have been active on news sites in Ukraine, Poland, Finland, and the USA. Trolls have also been used by the Russian government to edit Wikipedia articles, a strategy that demonstrates the goal of contesting reality (Tucker et al., 2018).

As opposed to trolls, bots are computer software programs that generate content on social media by performing highly repetitive tasks (Forelle, Howard, Monroy-Hernández, & Savage, 2015; Michael, 2017). As the Lund report stipulates, bots can be used to perform positive tasks, such as chat bots that offer customer support, or aggregate bots that collect news stories on certain issues for their users (Boichak, Jackson, Hemsley, & Tanupabrungsun, 2018). Yet bots may also be used to spread disinformation, spam online forums, flood discussion boards with highly emotional content, increase the reach of false content at a low cost, and redirect web traffic toward websites that specialize in curating inaccurate information (Ratkiewicz et al., 2011). The scale of use of bots has become astounding. According to Bessi and Ferrara (2016), 400,000 bots were used to disseminate 3.8 million tweets during the last month of the 2016 US election. Saho et al. have argued that humans are especially vulnerable to bots and often retweet their messages unknowingly. Beyond the USA, studies have uncovered the use of Russian bots during the German elections (Applebaum, Pomerantsev, Smith, & Colliver, 2017), the Catalonia referendum and the French elections. NATO has found the 70% of Russian language Twitter accounts commenting on NATO's presence in the Baltics are automated bots (Fredheim, 2017).

Alarmingly, not only is the use of bots increasing, but bots have also been found to be the most influential form of propaganda. Recent studies suggest that human users fail to identify online bots and mistake them for actual users. Even when users are aware of the existence of bots, they do not have less trust in bots than they do in humans (Edwards, Edwards, Spence, & Shelton, 2014). Trust in bots is concerning, given that these were strategically employed to flood social media with pro-Brexit hashtags (Howard & Kollanyi, 2016), anti-Macron content, and pro-Trump tweets (Tucker et al., 2018). Bots have also been identified in the social media ecosystems of Azerbaijan, Brazil, Canada, China, France, Germany, Italy, Mexico, Poland, and Ukraine. These bots have been used to increase leaders' numbers of followers, influence political discourse, attack political oppositions, and influence public discourse (Kollanyi, Howard, & Woolley, 2016; Treré, 2016; Woolley & Howards, 2017).

In summary, the conclusions of this chapter are somewhat contradictory. On the one hand, the impact of filter bubbles appears to be less substantial than first assumed and even in the age of rage digital publics have healthy news diets and actively seek out diverse sources of information. Moreover, although digital publics are exposed to vast quantities of digital propaganda, its long-term effect seems to be limited as well. On the other hand, some nations are attempting to weaponize the filter bubble effect; hate spreads online faster than hope contributing to greater political extremity; bots warp people's senses of reality while conspiracy theories are thriving in gated digital communities. These contradictory conclusions demonstrate the continued need to combat nefarious digital activities. The question that arises in the context of this chapter is, how has the digitalization of propaganda and disinformation influenced the conduct of public diplomacy? In other words, how do diplomats use digital technologies to combat the spread of propaganda, false information, and conspiracy theories? The following section presents two case studies that offer an answer to this question.

The first case study reviews the British FCO's use of its own blogosphere to narrate the Syrian Civil War and Russia's involvement in that war. Rather than be pulled onto social media sites and drawn into competitions over the truth, the FCO attempts to pull digital publics onto its own platforms where its content is less susceptible to digital manipulation. Moreover, the FCO builds on the reputation and prestige of high-ranking British diplomats to increase the credibility of its arguments, as well as individuals who have experienced the horrors of the Syrian Civil War firsthand. The FCO thus contends with digital propaganda through credible spokespersons and eyewitness accounts. Conversely, the Israeli MFA focuses on developing algorithmic capabilities through which it can decrease the spread and virality of malicious content and even "hack" social media algorithms so that these increasingly remove malicious content themselves. Thus, unlike the FCO, which builds on traditional diplomatic resources, the Israeli MFA relies on innovative technological infrastructure.

The FCO's Blogosphere

Brevity has also played an important part in the digitalization of public diplomacy. Often, this was a result of the architecture of digital platforms such as Twitter, which limited the number of characters to 280. Yet diplomats were also forced to disseminate concise messages given digital publics' short attention spans and their exposure to a daily barrage of TMI. Despite this, the FCO decided to launch its own blogosphere in 2009 with the explicit goal of providing a place for "officials and ministers to engage in a direct and informal dialogue with public audiences about international affairs and the work of the Foreign and Commonwealth Office". To date, UK ambassadors, ministers, and diplomats have published hundreds of posts dealing with diverse issues ranging from the protection of human rights to globalization, the future of NATO, and the changing nature of diplomacy in the digital age.

The FCO's blogosphere represents a unique approach to public diplomacy as it substitutes brevity with insight and reflection. Posts written by ambassadors or high-ranking diplomats are not meant to be skimmed or immediately shared. On the contrary, officials aim to tackle complex issues, to present foreign policy dilemmas, to share their own professional and personal experiences with readers and offer a context through which global events may be understood as well as the UK's response to these events.

Since 2012, the FCO has also used the blogosphere to narrate or interpret the Syrian Civil War. By using its blogosphere to frame the Syrian Civil War, denounce the Assad regime's abhorrent violations of human rights, and narrate Russia's involvement in Syria, the FCO is able to more effectively contend with Russian propaganda and disinformation. The reason for this is that competitions over the truth may often benefit the digital aggressor. By responding to Russian claims that it is defeating terrorists in Syria, or that Aleppo has been liberated, one inadvertently admits that reality can be contested and that truth is a matter of opinion. Everything becomes true, and everything becomes false, and all is a matter of perspective. The FCOs' choice to use its blogosphere to comment on events in Syria avoids this competition altogether. Moreover, it enables the FCO to pull audiences away from social media platforms or web discussion boards, thus limiting the extent to which

Russian trolls and bots can hijack FCO content, flood its accounts with false information, or drown out messages through a windfall of emotion and rage. Lastly, the use of the blogosphere may increase the credibility of the information presented to readers as posts are often written by ambassadors who enjoy a certain degree of prestige.

Since 2012, UK diplomats have posted 197 blogs relating to the civil war in Syria. The issues debated in FCO posts about Syria altered substantially between 2012 and 2018. This is not surprising given that what began as a popular uprising in 2012 morphed into a horrid civil war, which soon translated into a refugee crisis in the Middle East and Europe. It was also only in September of 2015 that Russia became involved in the war. This chapter analyzed 69 Syria-related posts published between 2012 and 2018. FCO blog posts were accessed during April of 2018 and analyzed throughout May of 2018. All posts published during a certain year were analyzed using word clouds to identify prevalent topics. Figure 5.4, for example, represents the word cloud of 2014 Syria-related posts.

As can be seen in Fig. 5.4 during 2014 FCO posts dealt mostly with the refugee crisis, which was depicted as endangering the stability of Jordan and Lebanon and posing a foreign policy challenge to European nations. Posts also dealt with the Geneva talks, which were

Fig. 5.4 Word cloud—2014 Syria related FCO blog posts

meant to facilitate a political solution to the civil war by bringing the Assad Regime and the Syrian Rebels to the negotiating table. The UN Human Rights Council, headquartered in Geneva, was also frequently mentioned in posts describing the UK's attempts to create an international coalition against the Assad regime and focus attention on its appalling human rights violations. Finally, diplomats emphasized the need to offer increased financial support for children and women displaced by the war.

The 2015 word cloud, shown in Fig. 5.5, demonstrates how the issues addressed in Syria-related posts altered from one year to the next. Indeed, in 2015 UK diplomats focused on Daesh's activities in Syria and the efforts of the Coalition Against Daesh, the plight of Christian minorities in Syria being massacred by Daesh terrorists, the suspected use of chemical weapons by the Assad regime against its own civilian population, the increased financial support offered by the UK to Syrian refugees in Lebanon, and the UK's work with the international community to ensure that Assad would not be able to use chemical weapons with impunity (Fig. 5.5).

Finally, the 2018 word cloud, shown in Fig. 5.6, demonstrates Russia's rise in prominence in FCO blogs. 2018 blog posts often dealt with Russia's emboldening of the Assad regime to use chemical weapons by preventing UN resolution on the matter, Russia's own use of a nerve agent on UK soil during the Salisbury Attack, and Russia's

Fig. 5.5 Word cloud—2015 Syria related FCO blog posts

Fig. 5.6 Word cloud—2018 Syria related FCO blog posts

lack of willingness to accept the findings of the OPCW's (Organization for Prohibition of Chemical Weapons) investigations into the use of chemical weapons in Syria (Fig. 5.6).

In terms of content, Syria-related blog posts can be classified into three categories. The first category of posts was emotionally driven and aimed to shed light on the humanitarian catastrophe that is the Syrian Civil War. Such posts tended to describe the scenes British diplomats were confronted with when visiting refugee camps in Jordan or when hearing the testimony of those who had fled Syria. Emotionally-driven posts may have been an effective method of explaining the UK's policies regarding Syria as they humanized a foreign policy issue, made it relatable to readers and emphasized the urgency for diplomatic action. They also offer a dichotomy between a moral UK and an immoral Syria and Russia. Values and norms play an important role in public diplomacy messages, as they enable actors to legitimize their own actions while delegitimizing the actions of other actors (Van Ham, 2013). Emotionally-driven posts also offered readers an in-depth, eyewitness account of the reality in Syria and may have thus been more effective in countering false Russian narratives than a single tweet or a two-minute video. One example of an emotionally driven post was authored by Peter Millet, the UK ambassador to Libya who visited refugee camps in Jordan in 2013. When describing the camps, he wrote:

The flow of Syrian refugees entering Jordan has now reached crisis point. What started as a trickle over 18 months ago has now become a flood. Even a few weeks ago the UN was reporting 300 – 400 new arrivals each night. Now it is 3,000 – 4,000 most nights. These are bald figures. Like all statistics they mask the reality of multiple human tragedies and personal suffering. On our visit to Za'atari this week we met a woman from Homs who had spent two months making her way south with her young family until she reached Jordan; she has no news of the rest of her family. We met new arrivals who had left their villages near Dera'a just over the border, walking through the night and dodging patrols by the Syrian army. In all these cases, they told of their towns and villages being attacked by helicopters, shelled by tanks and flattened by artillery…What is the solution? The best answer is the removal of Bashar Al-Assad and a transition to a new democratic, pluralistic government. That is our political objective.

The second category of FCO posts consisted of calls to action. These posts tended to highlight the urgency of ending the destructive war in Syria and the need to hold the Assad regime accountable for its human rights violations and use of chemical weapons. Such posts may have been used by the FCO to rally online support for UK actions in various UN forums against the Syrian and Russian governments. One post, published in 2018 by the UK ambassador to the Philippines, asked "Does Russia support the rule-based international system at all?" This post portrays Russia as a consistent violator of international law and a morally questionable diplomatic actor.

With cavalier disregard not only for the victims but its own international reputation, last week Russia deployed its veto for the twelfth time to protect the Assad regime from accountability. As the horror was unfolding in Douma, Syria, the OPCW (*Organization for the Prohibition of Chemical Weapons*) was carefully compiling its report on the toxin used in the attack in Salisbury, England. We now have its findings: the international watchdog has confirmed that the toxin unleashed in Salisbury was military-grade nerve agent of the type known as Novichok, which was developed in the Soviet era and produced by Russia. There can be no doubt as to the integrity of the OPCW process yet Russia declared in advance that it would not accept the findings of this independent, international body…

Indeed for a decade now, the Russian State has scandalously forfeited its responsibility as a permanent member of the Security Council in its narrow attempts to avoid answering for its own appalling behaviour. There is a clear pattern of pushing back the boundaries of law and decency including in Georgia and Ukraine...Taken together, it is clear that Russia now represents a direct threat to the Chemical Weapons Convention.

The last category of FCO posts were testimonies of Syrians who had experienced firsthand the brutality of the Assad regime and its Russian comrades. Testimonies are especially hard to counter by propaganda or trolls as one runs the risk of being seen as insensitive, callous, and complicit to the misery of others. FCO posts that included testimonies tended to focus on the use of chemical weapons or the lives of displaced refugees in camps. By incorporating testimonies into its posts the FCO was able to demonstrate to its readers that British diplomats dealt with facts rather than fiction. One testimony, published in 2015 recounted the aftermath of a chemical attack:

> There were around 10,000 injuries. People having spasms are everywhere, all convulsing and then falling like leaves. Many of those who were sleeping did not wake up; they died quietly. Some woke up but could not get out; they died trying. A mother had to choose two from her five children. She carried them and got out, but they were already dead. At the entrances to the houses, on sidewalks, asphyxiated bodies were littered all over the town. Responders who tried to rescue the victims were themselves injured. Some of them survived.

By using its own digital platform to narrate events in Syria and the actions of international actors, the FCO was able to achieve three important goals. First, pulled digital publics onto its own platform, which is less susceptible to digital disinformation, propaganda, and trolling. Bots could not flood the comments section of the UK blogosphere with emotionally-charged content or drive audiences away from the blogosphere with links to dubious websites that spin conspiracy theories. Second, the FCO capitalized on the prestige of senior diplomats such as ambassadors to increase the credibility of its arguments and narration of the Syrian Civil War. Similarly, the FCO relied on firsthand accounts to describe the horrors of the war, again increasing the reliability of its arguments. Lastly, by refusing to engage in social media competitions over the truth and reality, the FCO prevented Russia from arguing that events in Syria were a matter of perspective. Moreover, the FCO offered its visitors a comprehensive narrative through which they could understand events unfolding in Syria and their impact on neighboring states, Europe and the world. As such, the FCO may have offered digital publics a rare commodity—the ability to make sense of a world that appears to be in constant flux.

Unlike the FCO, the Israeli MFA has chosen to fight disinformation by developing algorithmic diplomacy, or the ability to create and manipulate algorithms toward diplomatic ends.

Israel's Algorithmic Diplomacy

In 2017, the Israeli MFA held its first hackathon on algorithmic diplomacy. 11 teams of 50 web developers were tasked with exploring algorithmic solutions to combating anti-Israeli and anti-Semitic propaganda on social media sites. The hackathon is representative of the MFA's emphasis on developing new digital skillsets. For some time, the Israeli MFA has sought to develop algorithmic capabilities, which could enable it to anticipate the virality of online content, map networks that share specific kinds of content, and identify filter bubbles in which such content might flourish. To this end, the MFA has appointed a Director of Algorithmic Diplomacy who is stationed at the Israeli embassy in London. The Director, a former high-tech executive, is charged with developing the MFA's algorithmic capabilities, recruiting diplomats with relevant skills, such as software developers, identifying possible partners and collaborators from the tech sector, developing algorithmic tactics that can be employed by Israeli embassies around the world, fostering ties with digital diplomacy departments in other MFAs, and collaborating with academics researching the fields of computational propaganda, digital disinformation, and social media.

The hackathon was also representative of the Israeli MFA's approach to contending with anti-Israeli and anti-Semitic content on social media. The MFA's first priority is to prevent malicious content from spreading online in the first place. It has recently been estimated that some form of anti-Israeli or anti-Semitic content is shared online every 83 seconds (Chan, 2017). By anti-Israeli content, the MFA means propaganda shared by terrorist groups such as the Hamas movement, which openly calls for acts of violence against Israelis. The MFA does not aim to limit the flow of content published by the Palestinian government in the West Bank, nor does it attempt to limit online criticism of Israel's policies in the region and vis-à-vis the Palestinians. By anti-Semitic propaganda, the MFA refers to content that calls for violence against Jews, content that includes disinformation and conspiracy theories about Jews, or content that promotes stereotypes of Jews, such as their stranglehold on the global economy or their attempts to flood European nations with immigrants. Such propaganda is nowadays shared on both social media sites and other digital platforms, namely alt-right news sites. The MFA's second priority is to alter the perceptions of digital publics who share, or are exposed to, anti-Semitic and anti-Israeli propaganda.

In an interview, the Director of Algorithmic Diplomacy stated that since 2017, the MFA has been able to dramatically increase its algorithmic capabilities on Facebook. Presently, the MFA can predict fairly accurately what types of anti-Semitic content will go viral on Facebook. To do so, the MFA has written its own code and developed its own algorithms that interface with Facebook's platform. Once anti-Israeli or anti-Semitic content has been identified as viral in nature, the MFA is able to deploy digital assets and cause the Facebook algorithm to remove this content. In other words, the MFA does not have the ability to remove content by itself. Yet it can cause the Facebook algorithm to take note of digital propaganda and remove it because the content in question breaches Facebook's terms of use. The Director estimated that the MFA currently prevents the spread of 50% of anti-Israeli and anti-Semitic propaganda on Facebook. When asked to describe this mechanism, the Director stated: "we have learned that if we tickle the Facebook algorithm in one location, it will remove content in another."

The Israeli MFA also uses algorithmic diplomacy to counter disinformation spread online. In such instances, the MFA uses its own algorithms to map filter bubbles that either promote positive narratives about Jews or promote disinformation about Jews. The MFA then identifies digital assets or, as the Director explains, "social media users that can serve as bridges between positive and negative filter bubbles." Essentially, bridges are digital users that have contacts in negative filter bubbles. These contacts can help introduce new information into the negative filter bubble. Bridges are used by the MFA to counter disinformation with positive narratives about Jews and information that can dispel stereotypes. Subsequently, negative filter bubbles are burst. In these instances, it is not diplomats who counter disinformation, but other social media users. This may thus be conceptualized as a form of peer-to-peer public diplomacy in which individuals help stem the tide of online hate (Attias,

2012). Peer-to-peer diplomacy may be a more effective way of fighting disinformation and hate as social media users may view messages from diplomats as state-sponsored propaganda. Moreover, audiences who have a negative view of Jews are unlikely to be receptive to messages originating from Israeli diplomats. But from the ethical perspective, one has to wonder if the Israeli MFA's reliance on Facebook users to combat disinformation does not mask Israel's digital activities.

Conclusions

Algorithms are the main functionaries of the digital society. It is algorithms who tailor digital publics' online experiences, who help them reach relevant and desired information and who facilitate their online relationships. Social media algorithms were originally meant to gather as much information as possible about users to create knowledge that could be used to generate profit. Algorithms were not meant to increase the potency of propaganda and disinformation. Yet as this chapter has demonstrated, some nations have sought to weaponize social media algorithms to question the existence of an objective truth and drive societal discord. This utilization of algorithms is demonstrative of the fact that technology is not wholly deterministic. As the societal prism suggests, social actors can use digital technologies in ways that were not originally intended.

Yet the functionality of algorithms has also impacted society in a manner best explained through the technological prism. Technological affordance, including algorithmic filtering, has given rise to a host of new metaphors through which society conceptualizes digitalization. The most common metaphors are those of filter bubbles and echo chambers. While the filter bubble metaphor is somewhat benign, the echo chamber metaphor is daunting because it suggests that the digital sphere is one that inevitably unravels the fabric of society at the seams.

The societal and technological prisms are also evident in the case studies reviewed in this chapter. The UK FCO's use of its blogosphere to narrate Russia's involvement in the Syrian Civil War is demonstrative of the societal prism, as social actors leverage technologies to obtain their goals. Rather than be forced onto social media sites, the FCO pulls digital publics onto its own platforms, where content is less susceptible to digital manipulation. The FCO also utilizes traditional public diplomacy assets online, namely the credibility of ambassadors. In the age of rage and "fake" news, the credibility of spokespersons is paramount. The more credible a spokesperson, the less his image can be tarnished by trolls and the less his statements can be labeled as "alternative facts" or mere opinions. Ambassadors enjoy a certain degree of credibility given their prestige, which stems from their roles as official emissaries of states, their historic image as peacemakers, and their access to the highest echelons of power. The FCO builds on the prestige of ambassadors to argue that while others spin fiction, it deals with facts.

The Israeli case study is demonstrative of the technological prism in which digital infrastructure determines digital solutions. The Israeli MFA has determined that the best way to counter the echo chamber effect is to manipulate social media algorithms and burst filter bubbles through digital assets, or individuals who can transmit positive information about Jews into gated communities that hold negative opinions of Jews or Israelis. The activities of the Israeli MFA are less dependent on traditional public diplomacy assets and are more focused on developing new digital skillsets.

Both case studies, however, demonstrate that the process of digitalization has influenced the self-narratives and metaphors that diplomats employ to understand their craft, and by extension, their working routines and their norms. The interview with the Director of Israeli Algorithmic Diplomacy suggests that the Israeli MFA has adopted the metaphor of filter bubbles which encapsulate digital users and expose them to hateful information. This metaphor has given way to new working procedures such as using network analysis to identify digital assets, or bridges, and creating algorithms that limit the virality of hateful content. From a normative perspective, the MFA is willing to act as a "invisible hand." Its public diplomacy activities are conducted through peer-to-peer diplomacy, as it is individual social media users who interact with digital publics, not Israeli diplomats. Public diplomacy may thus be moving into the shadows, a process which raises ethical questions.

The British FCO may have adopted the metaphor of echo chambers given its desire to pull publics away from social media platforms, which are considered more susceptible to digital propaganda and disinformation. This has led to new working routines such as relying on the testimonies of ambassadors, high-ranking diplomats, and eyewitnesses to narrate the war in Syria and Britain's response to the war. From a normative perspective, the FCO's approach could indicate that the tools of mass democracy, such as Facebook and Twitter, are now viewed by British diplomats as the tools of mass deception.

Both case studies also reflect the influence of the digital society on the digitalization of public diplomacy. The topics addressed in FCO blog posts altered as the reality on the ground in Syria changed. Thus, the FCO engaged in a form of real-time public diplomacy in which the narration of world events occurs as events unfold. This is required of diplomatic institutions as the digital society is one that constantly strives to annihilate time. The Israeli case study demonstrates a form of networked diplomacy in which the MFA forms transnational networks of digital assets who can help disseminate accurate information about Jews and Israelis. Like the digital society, public diplomacy has also become networked as power migrates downwards from the nation state, Israel, to individual digital users.

Importantly, both case studies also demonstrate that MFAs do not have to engage in competitions over the truth. Rather than reply to Russian tweets about the fate of Aleppo, and the humanitarian conditions in Syria, the FCO published testimonials about the brutality of the Assad regime. Rather than respond to conspiracy theories about Jewish financial power, the Israeli MFA seeks to reduce the virality of disinformation. This is crucial given the fact that competitions over the truth often benefit the aggressor as they suggest that facts are a matter of perspective.

That contestation of reality on digital platforms by diplomats has far-reaching consequences that exceed the realm of public diplomacy. First, diplomacy cannot function in a world without reality. Countries cannot recognize a semi-existing republic nor can they diffuse tensions if the Syrian crisis both exists and does not exist. Recent debates about North Korean aggression demonstrate that bilateral and multilateral diplomacy necessitates a minimal shared definition of reality. If diplomats cannot agree that a war is taking place, they cannot even attempt to resolve it. Similarly, if a political entity both exists and does not exist, the rights of its population cannot be secured through diplomatic deliberations. Shared threats and shared challenges are those most likely to be addressed by diplomats. Yet a world where there are no shared threats, challenges, or realities, is one of diplomatic paralysis, as is presently evident in the UN Security Council. Additionally, contested realities contribute to the senses of instability and confusion now felt by people around the world. It is a world that seems more and more out of balance given the proliferation of alternative facts and news. Finally, contestations of reality contribute to global tensions by alleging that one side is hiding information or manipulating public opinion or conspiring by hiding its true actions. Thus, diplomacy comes to undermine relationships rather than facilitate them.

As this chapter has argued, the fear of echo chambers and filter bubbles has altered the trajectory of the digitalization of public diplomacy. Among some Western MFAs, digital technologies are no longer leveraged toward relationship building and conversations; rather they are leveraged for strategic communication that prioritizes information dominance and influence over people's behaviors. Yet the studies reviewed in this chapter suggest that the fear of echo chambers and filter bubbles may be somewhat exaggerated. Digital publics seek diverse sources of information, interact with "Friends" who hold diverse opinions, and are exposed to oppositional content on social media sites. Similarly, the influence of digital propaganda and disinformation seems to be limited, especially over long durations of time. Americans who were exposed to "fake" news stories could not recall them at a later time.

Notably, a recent report published by the FCO (Wilton Park, 2017) offers a glimpse into the future digitalization of British public diplomacy. The report, compiled in 2017, states that the FCO should seek to exploit big data analysis, sentiment analysis tools and forecasting models. To do so, the FCO is encouraged to develop data skills among its diplomats through training, focus on recruiting data scientists and create projects that foster collaborations between subject matter experts and data scientists. The future trajectory of British public diplomacy thus seems to be ingrained in the logic of influence rather than relationship building. New recruits will be asked to analyze big data sets rather than converse with digital publics while the FCO's gaze will be fixed on the future and not the present, much like the digital society. Yet the abandoning of "new" public diplomacy goals in favor of influence may be unwarranted given the analysis presented in this chapter. It may even be counterproductive, as is explored in the following chapter.

References

Allcott, H., & Gentzkow, M. (2017). Social media and fake news in the 2016 election. *Journal of Economic Perspectives, 31*(2), 211–236.
Anderson, M., & Jiang, J. (2018). *Teens, social media & technology.* Pew Research Center. Retrieved from http://www.pewinternet.org/2018/05/31/teens-social-media-technology-2018/.

Applebaum, A., Pomerantsev, P., Smith, M., & Colliver, C. (2017). 'Make Germany great again': Kremlin, alt-right and international influences in the 2017 German elections. *Institute for Strategic Dialogue and the Arena Project at the LSE's Institute of Global Affairs*. Retrieved from http://www.isdglobal.org/wp-content/uploads/2017/12/Make-Germany-Great-Again-ENG-081217.pdf.

Arsenault, A. (2013). Networks of freedom, networks of control: Internet policy as a platform for and an impediment to relational public diplomacy. In R. S. Zaharna, A. Arsenault, & A. Fisher (Eds.), *Relational, networked and collaborative approaches to public diplomacy* (pp. 192–208). New York, NY: Taylor & Francis.

Attias, S. (2012). Israel's new peer-to-peer diplomacy. *The Hague Journal of Diplomacy, 7*(4), 473–482.

Bakshy, E., Messing, S., & Adamic, L. A. (2015). Exposure to ideologically diverse news and opinion on Facebook. *Science, 348*(6239), 1130–1132.

Barberá, P. (2014). How social media reduces mass political polarization. Evidence from Germany, Spain, and the US. *Job Market Paper, New York University, 46*.

Bartles, C. K. (2016). Getting Gerasimov Right. *Military Review, 96*(1), 30–38.

Baumgartner, J. C., & Morris, J. S. (2010). MyFaceTube politics: Social networking web sites and political engagement of young adults. *Social Science Computer Review, 28*(1), 24–44.

BBC News. (2014, August). Captured Russian troops 'in Ukraine by accident'. *BBC News*. Retrieved from https://www.bbc.co.uk/news/world-europe-28934213.

Bessi, A., & Ferrara, E. (2016). Social bots distort the 2016 US Presidential election online discussion. *First Monday, 21*(11), 14.

Bevan, T., Fellner, E., & Slovo, R. (Producers), & Alfredson, T. (Director). (2011). *Tinker Taylor soldier spy*. [Motion picture]. UK: Focus Features.

Boichak, O., Jackson, S., Hemsley, J., & Tanupabrungsun, S. (2018, March). Automated diffusion? Bots and their influence during the 2016 US Presidential election. In *International conference on information* (pp. 17–26). Cham: Springer.

Boxell, L., Gentzkow, M., & Shapiro, J. M. (2017). Greater internet use is not associated with faster growth in political polarization among US demographic groups. *Proceedings of the National Academy of Sciences, 114*(40), 10612–10617.

Boyd, D. M., & Ellison, N. B. (2007). Social network sites: Definition, history, and scholarship. *Journal of Computer-Mediated Communication, 13*(1), 210–230.

Bradshaw, S., & Howard, P. N. (2018). Challenging truth and trust: A global inventory of organized social media manipulation. *Computational*

Propaganda Research Project. Retrieved from http://comprop.oii.ox.ac.uk/wp-content/uploads/sites/93/2018/07/ct2018.pdf.

Chan, M. (2017, March). There's a new anti-Semitic message on social media every 83 seconds: Study. *Time.* Retrieved from http://time.com/4712439/anti-semitic-posts-world-jewish-congress/.

Crilley, R. (2016). Like and share forces: Making sense of military social media sites. In *Understanding popular culture and world politics in the digital age* (pp. 67–83). Oxon: Routledge.

del Vicario, M., Bessi, A., Zollo, F., Petroni, F., Scala, A., Caldarelli, A., ..., Quattrociocchi, W. (2016). The spreading of misinformation online. *Proceedings of the National Academy of Sciences, 113*(3), 554–559.

Duggan, M., & Smith, A. (2016). *The political environment on social media.* Pews Research Center. Retrieved from http://www.pewinternet.org/2016/10/25/the-political-environment-on-social-media/.

Edwards, C., Edwards, A., Spence, P. R., & Shelton, A. K. (2014). Is that a bot running the social media feed? Testing the differences in perceptions of communication quality for a human agent and a bot agent on Twitter. *Computers in Human Behavior, 33,* 372–376.

Flaxman, S., Goel, S., & Rao, J. M. (2016). Filter bubbles, echo chambers, and online news consumption. *Public Opinion Quarterly, 80*(S1), 298–320.

Forelle, M., Howard, P., Monroy-Hernández, A., & Savage, S. (2015). *Political bots and the manipulation of public opinion in Venezuela.* Retrieved from https://arxiv.org/ftp/arxiv/papers/1507/1507.07109.pdf.

Fredheim, R. (2017). *Robotrolling.* NATO StratCom Centre of Excellence. Retrieved from https://www.stratcomcoe.org/robotrolling-20171.

Galeotti, M. (2018a). The mythical 'Gerasimov Doctrine' and the language of threat. *Critical Studies on Security,* 1–5.

Galeotti, M. (2018b). I'm sorry for creating the 'Gerasimov Doctrine'. *Foreign Policy.*

Garrett, R. K. (2017). The "echo chamber" distraction: Disinformation campaigns are the problem, not audience fragmentation. *Journal of Applied Research in Memory and Cognition, 6*(4), 370–376.

Gerber, T. P., & Zavisca, J. (2016). Does Russian propaganda work? *The Washington Quarterly, 39*(2), 79–98.

Giles, K. (2016). *Russia's 'new' tools for confronting the West: Continuity and innovation in Moscow's exercise of power.* Royal Institute of International Affairs Chatham House.

Ginsberg, A. (2015). *Howl and other poems.* San Francisco, CA: Martino.

Groshek, J., & Dimitrova, D. (2011). A cross-section of voter learning, campaign interest and intention to vote in the 2008 American election: Did Web 2.0 matter. *Communication Studies Journal, 9*(1), 355–375.

Howard, P. N., & Kollanyi, B. (2016). Bots, #StrongerIn, and #Brexit: Computational propaganda during the UK-EU referendum.

Issue. (2016). *Strategic communications: East and south*. Paris: EU Institute for Security Studies. Retrieved from https://www.iss.europa.eu/sites/default/files/EUISSFiles/Report_30.pdf.

Kenski, K., & Stroud, N. J. (2006). Connections between internet use and political efficacy, knowledge, and participation. *Journal of Broadcasting & Electronic Media, 50*(2), 173–192.

King, G., Pan, J., & Roberts, M. E. (2017). How the Chinese government fabricates social media posts for strategic distraction, not engaged argument. *American Political Science Review, 111*(3), 484–501.

Kollanyi, B., Howard, P. N., & Woolley, S. C. (2016). Bots and automation over Twitter during the first US Presidential debate. *Computational Propaganda Research Project*. Retrieved from http://comprop.oii.ox.ac.uk/wp-content/uploads/sites/89/2016/10/Data-Memo-First-Presidential-Debate.pdf.

Lanchester, J. (2017). You are the product. *London Review of Books, 39*(16), 3–10.

Lankina, T., & Watanabe, K. (2017). 'Russian spring' or 'Spring betrayal'? The media as a mirror of Putin's evolving strategy in Ukraine. *Europe-Asia Studies, 69*(10), 1526–1556.

Leach, K. (2014, September). *Building stability in an unpredictable world—The NATO SUMMIT IN Wales 4–5 September* [Blog]. Retrieved from https://blogs.fco.gov.uk/katherineleach/2014/09/04/building-stability-in-an-unpredictable-world-the-nato-summit-in-wales-4-5-september/.

McClenaghan, M. (2017). The 'Dark Ads' election: How are pollical parties targeting you on Facebook? *The Bureau of Investigative Journalism*. Retrieved from https://www.thebureauinvestigates.com/stories/2017-05-15/the-dark-ads-election-how-are-political-parties-targeting-you-on-facebook.

Michael, K. (2017). Bots trending now: Disinformation and calculated manipulation of the masses. *IEEE Technology and Society Magazine, 36*(2), 6–11.

Mihaylov, T., Georgiev, G., & Nakov, P. (2015). Finding opinion manipulation trolls in news community forums. In *Proceedings of the nineteenth conference on computational natural language learning* (pp. 310–314).

NATO. (2010). *Military concept for NATO strategic communications*. Deputy Secretary General of NATO. Retrieved from https://info.publicintelligence.net/NATO-STRATCOM-Concept.pdf.

Newman, N., Fletcher, R., Kalogeropoulos, A., Levy, D. A., & Nielsen, R. K. (2017). Reuters Institute digital news report 2017.

Nocetti, J. (2015). Contest and conquest: Russia and global internet governance. *International Affairs, 91*(1), 111–130.

Oliver, J. E., & Wood, T. J. (2014). Conspiracy theories and the paranoid style (s) of mass opinion. *American Journal of Political Science, 58*(4), 952–966.

Open hearing social media influence 2016 US election before Senate Intelligence Committee. Senate, 115th Congress (2017).

Pamment, J., Nothhaft, H., Agardh-Twetman, H., & Fjallhed, A. (2018). *Countering information influence activities: The state of the art.* Lund University.

Pariser, E. (2011). *The filter bubble: What the Internet is hiding from you.* London: Penguin.

Paulauskas, R. (2018). *Understanding Lithuania's digital diplomacy model.* [In person].

Phillips, W. (2015). *This is why we can't have nice things: Mapping the relationship between online trolling and mainstream culture.* Cambridge, MA: MIT Press.

Pietilä, V. (1994). Perspectives on our past: Charting the histories of mass communication studies. *Critical Studies in Media Communication, 11*(4), 346–361.

Ratkiewicz, J., Conover, M., Meiss, M. R., Gonçalves, B., Flammini, A., & Menczer, F. (2011). Detecting and tracking political abuse in social media. *ICWSM, 11,* 297–304.

Rogers, K., & Bromwhich, J. E. (2016, November). The hoaxes, fake news, and misinformation we saw on election day. *The New York Times.* Retrieved from https://www.nytimes.com/2016/11/09/us/politics/debunk-fake-news-election-day.html.

Sazonov, V., Kristiina Müür, M. A., & Mölder, H. (2016). *Russian information campaigns against the Ukrainian state and defence forces.* Tartu: NATO StratCom Centre of Excellence. Retrieved from https://www.stratcomcoe.org/analysis-russias-information-campaign-against-ukraine-1.

Shearer, E., & Gottfried, J. (2017). *News use across social media platforms 2017.* Pew Research Center. Retrieved from http://www.journalism.org/2017/09/07/news-use-across-social-media-platforms-2017/.

Sproule, J. M. (1989). Progressive propaganda critics and the magic bullet myth. *Critical Studies in Media Communication, 6*(3), 225–246.

Sunstein, C. R. (2017). *#Republic: Divided democracy in the age of social media.* Princeton: Princeton University Press.

Sunstein, C. R., & Vermeule, A. (2009). Conspiracy theories: Causes and cures. *Journal of Political Philosophy, 17*(2), 202–227.

Tandoc, E. C., Jr., Lim, Z. W., & Ling, R. (2018). Defining "fake news" a typology of scholarly definitions. *Digital Journalism, 6*(2), 137–153.

Timberg, C. (2016, November). Russian propaganda effort helped spread "fake news" during election, experts say. *The Washington Post.* Retrieved from https://www.washingtonpost.com/business/economy/russian-propaganda-effort-helped-spread-fake-news-during-election-experts-say/2016/11/24/793903b6–8a40-4ca9-b712-716af66098fe_story.html?utm_term=.6a0b32245a72.

Treré, E. (2016). The dark side of digital politics: Understanding the algorithmic manufacturing of consent and the hindering of online dissidence. *IDS Bulletin, 47*(1), 127–138.

Tucker, J., Guess, A., Barberá, P., Vaccari, C., Siegel, A., Sanovich, S., ..., Nyhan, B. (2018). *Social media, political polarization, and political disinformation: A review of the scientific literature.* Hewlett Foundation.

Vanderhill, R. (2013). *Promoting authoritarianism abroad.* Boulder, CO: Lynne Rienner.

Van Ham, P. (2013). Social power in public diplomacy. In R. S. Zaharna, A. Arsenault, & A. Fisher (Eds.), *Relational, networked and collaborative approaches to public diplomacy* (pp. 17–28). New York, NY: Taylor & Francis.

Vosoughi, S., Roy, D., & Aral, S. (2018). The spread of true and false news online. *Science, 359*(6380), 1146–1151.

Way, L. A. (2015). The limits of autocracy promotion: The case of Russia in the "near abroad". *European Journal of Political Research, 54*(4), 691–706.

Williams, E. (2014). *Ev Williams on Twitter's early years* [Print]. Retrieved from https://www.inc.com/issie-lapowsky/ev-williams-twitter-early-years.html?cid=em01011week40day04b.

Wilton Park. (2017). *Diplomacy in the information age: Wednesday 22–Friday 24 February WP1519.* Wilson House. Retrieved from https://www.wiltonpark.org.uk/event/wp1519/.

Wood, M. J., Douglas, K. M., & Sutton, R. M. (2012). Dead and alive: Beliefs in contradictory conspiracy theories. *Social Psychological and Personality Science, 3*(6), 767–773.

Woolley, S. C., & Howard, P. N. (2017). Computational propaganda worldwide: Executive summary. *Computational Propaganda Research Project.* Retrieved from http://comprop.oii.ox.ac.uk/wp-content/uploads/sites/89/2017/06/Casestudies-ExecutiveSummary.pdf.

Zeitz, J. (2016, July). How Trump is recycling Nixon's 'Law and Order' playbook. *Politico.* Retrieved from https://www.politico.com/magazine/story/2016/07/donald-trump-law-and-order-richard-nixon-crime-race-214066.

Zuckerberg, M. (2018). *Mark Zuckerberg's 2004 CNBC interview shows how far he and Facebook have come* [TV]. Retrieved from https://www.cnbc.com/video/2018/04/16/facebook-founder-mark-zuckerbergs-first-tv-interview-in-2004-on-cnbc.html.

CHAPTER 6

The New Public Diplomacy—Fact or Fiction

> For all those whose cares have been our concern, the work goes on, the
> cause endures, the hope still lives, and the dream shall never die.
> —Edward Kennedy, 1980 Democratic National Convention

The rumor took time to cross the Atlantic. The artists of the day were
quite poor and most could not afford to send telegrams. Those who
could afford them found that the telegraph stations were occupied with
transmitting news of the War in Europe. The rumor, therefore, had to
travel by boat. After three harrowing weeks at sea, the rumor docked
in Marseilles and then made its way to Paris by train. There, it climbed
slowly up the cracked and weary sidewalks of the village of Montparnasse
where the modern artists resided. It was there that the rumor finally
revealed itself and informed listeners that Marcel Duchamp had placed
a urinal inside an exhibition hall in New York. The purpose of the urinal
was to ask a simple, albeit profound question: what is art?

Throughout the process of the digitalization of public diplomacy,
diplomats have time and again questioned what constitutes a diplomatic
act. Is the changing of one's profile picture tantamount to announcing
a new policy initiative? This question was raised in July of 2018, when
the Russian Ministry of Foreign Affairs (MFA) and its embassies replaced
their Twitter profile pictures with that of Maria Butina, a Russian citizen
detained in the USA for her possible role in interfering with the 2016
presidential elections. At other times, diplomats questioned whether text

© The Author(s) 2019 177
I. Manor, *The Digitalization of Public Diplomacy*,
Palgrave Macmillan Series in Global Public Diplomacy,
https://doi.org/10.1007/978-3-030-04405-3_6

messages sent between two ambassadors should be regarded as an official diplomatic communique which bound two governments to a certain course of action, or whether e-mail could be used to submit an official protest to a foreign government.

Similarly, throughout the process of digitalization, diplomats have often found themselves questioning what constitutes engagement with digital publics. In some MFAs, the term "engagement" is a catchall phrase that relates to how digital publics interact with MFA content online (R. Paulauskas, personal communication, July 25, 2018). Among these institutions, engagement can be measured by calculating the number of likes and shares a Facebook post attracts. Other MFAs use the term "engagement" to reference the type of content they share online. Engaging content is that which sparks an interest among digital society members and might go viral (Manor, 2016a). Still in other MFAs, engagement relates to the extent to which embassies or diplomats respond to queries they receive online, such as requests for consular aid. Lastly, in several MFAs, engagement is synonymous with the word "dialogue" and the amount of conversations that diplomats have with digital publics (A. Lutyens, personal communication, July 10, 2018).

The term "engagement" has accompanied the process of public diplomacy's digitalization since its humble beginnings. This is because the digitalization of public diplomacy was intrinsically linked to the emergence of the "new" public diplomacy and the desire to foster online relationships with foreign publics so as to create a receptive environment for a nation's foreign policy. Engagement was a means of creating such relationships. In 2002, a USA think tank named the Council on Foreign Relations argued that digital technologies necessitated that public diplomacy actors focus on foreign citizens and *"Adopt an engagement approach that involves listening, dialogue, debate and relationship building and increases the amount and effectiveness of public-opinion research"* (Pamment, 2013).

The Council on Foreign Relations thus tied the term "engagement" to the process of relationship building. In 2008, the State Department defined four goals of public diplomacy activities delivered via digital technologies: understanding, informing, engaging, and influencing foreign publics. The State Department thus tied the term "engagement" to the traditional public diplomacy goal of influence. By 2013, the UK FCO was regularly using the term "engagement" to reference a host of digital activities. For instance, when describing the FCO's operations in Iran, one diplomat wrote:

We launched our new website "UK for Iranians" this time last year to reach out to Iranians, explaining, discussing and engaging with them on UK policy. Since then, we've grown from strength to strength including our coverage in pictures of the Olympics which attracted our largest ever audience, our 'prezis' against the death penalty in Iran, Facebook Q&A on the nuclear sanctions issue and our Farsi videos addressing a variety of topics from the cultural to the political. (Russo, 2013)

The year 2013 also saw the publication of an internal report in the New Zealand MFA outlining a new framework for the ministry's digital activities. The document, titled "Digital Communication Strategy," invoked the term engagement 39 times. At first, engagement is used to reference a private corporation that had attempted to manage a public relations crisis on social media. The report states that the corporation's social media presence "had focused on broadcast rather than engagement." The New Zealand MFA thus defined the term "engagement" as an antonym to broadcast or one-way models of communication.

According to Alexandra Lutyens, head of the digital unit at the New Zealand MFA and author of the digital framework report, the promise of conversing with digital publics was central to the MFA's decision to adopt digital technologies. Like other MFAs, New Zealand's was first made aware of the importance of digital platforms during the Arab Spring of 2011. The uprisings in Egypt and Tunisia suggested that digital platforms had become central to an MFA's ability to anticipate events in foreign countries and shape policies accordingly. The MFA was also motivated to migrate online given a digital trend that had gathered momentum across New Zealand's government. It was the digital migration of other ministries that eased the MFA's angst toward digital platforms and their possible adverse impact on diplomacy. Lutyens also stated that New Zealand felt the need to follow in the footsteps of its closest allies—the USA, UK and Canada which had already established a formidable digital presence.

Yet above all, New Zealand's MFA hoped that digital platforms could democratize public diplomacy. The MFA's vision was one of continued online conversations through which digital publics could partake in the foreign policy formulation process. This was the manifestation of the ministry's definition of engagement as a two-way communicative act that is the very opposite of broadcasting. To meet its vision, New Zealand's ministry sought to understand the issues that are of greatest concern to domestic and foreign populations, to crowd-source solutions to shared challenges, to offer opportunities for collaborative creation of policies and to make the process of policy formulation more open and transparent (A. Lutyens, personal communication, July 10, 2018).

New Zealand's MFA has yet to successfully implement its vision. While its embassies and diplomats have migrated to digital platforms, they do not practice collaborative public diplomacy. Rather, they too have taken to publishing vast amounts of information online while attempting to shape people's perception of New Zealand and its policies. One impediment to obtaining the vision of democratized public diplomacy is the ambiguity surrounding the term engagement. As Lutyens stated in an interview:

> The question of our time is what do we mean by engagement? The digital world said to MFAs we have an engagement tool for you. And that's why we took to it. But simply being on social media is not engagement. We often feel that when we tweet we have engaged with publics. That's not true. What people are looking for is conversations, actions and responses.

To date, the New Zealand ministry has refused to abandon its goal of democratized public diplomacy. On the contrary, Lutyens argued that the first stage of the MFA's digitalization was to familiarize diplomats with the benefits and shortcomings of digital platforms. Now the second stage of digitalization may begin, in which the MFA and its embassies will ask: "*What is the impact of our digital activities and how can we best leverage each platform to meet our unique vision. This is not an easy question as we may find many faults in our current activities.*" Lutyens stated that the MFA still prioritizes public-centric digital activities as opposed to strategic communications, as it is removed from the digital struggles between Western Europe, the USA, and Russia. Thus, the digitalization of New Zealand's public diplomacy has been influenced by its vision and values, the adoption of digital technologies by other government ministries, and its geographic location. For New Zealand, the work of democratizing public diplomacy goes on, the cause endures, the hope still lives, and the dream has yet to die.

Like diplomatic institutions, public diplomacy scholars have also routinely employed the term "engagement" without clearly defining its meaning. This is most evident in scholarly definitions of the "new" public diplomacy. For instance, Cull defines it as international actors' attempts to accomplish foreign policy goals "by engaging with foreign publics." Jan Melissen's definition centers on "engaging with connected publics." Manor and Segev use the term "engagement" to reference online conversations between diplomats and digital publics that may enable a nation to refashion its image. Yet these definitions fail to define what amounts to an online conversation or an act of engagement.

Emily Metzgar argued that the term engagement refers to two interrelated activities: Communicating with publics assembled in various digital networks and "listening" to digital publics to understand foreign populations and shape foreign policy accordingly. Metzgar's definition of engagement is similar to scholars' use of the term "dialogue" when referring to the "new" public diplomacy. Such is the case with James Pamment's (2013) assertion that twenty-first century public diplomacy is "dialogical, collaborative and inclusive" and Cowan and Arsenault's (2008) view that the "new" public diplomacy transitions from monologue to dialogue and collaborations. Yet these studies also fail to clearly define what constitutes dialogue or an act of engagement on digital platforms.

Surprisingly, the term "engagement" has never been defined in many MFAs, despite its centrality to digital activities and its common usage by diplomats. In a recent study, Manor and Kampf asked diplomats from six MFAs (Australia, Canada, India, Israel, New Zealand, and Switzerland) to define the term "engagement". Results demonstrate that diplomats belonging to the same ministry offered very different definitions of this term based on their own experiences, their scope of daily use of digital platforms and even their level of digital proficiency. Digital natives were more likely to define engagement as a two-way process of communication, while digital immigrants defined it as a means of one-way information dissemination. Embassy resources, local culture, and the identity of the person in charge of digital communication also influenced diplomats' definitions of the term "engagement" (Manor & Kampf, 2019).

The ambiguity surrounding the terms "engagement" and "dialogue" has serious ramifications, both for the study and practice of public diplomacy. From the practitioner's perspective, ambiguity may prevent an MFA from improving its digital activities. If each embassy adopts its own local definition of engagement, then MFAs may be unable to compare the activities of their embassies as a means of identifying best practices that can be emulated by others. Moreover, the definition of engagement determines public diplomacy activities. If engagement relates to two-way conversations, then MFAs will invest digital resources in providing opportunities for real-time interactions with diplomats. But if engagement relates to appealing content, then MFAs will dedicate resources to counting followers and likes. The definition of the term "engagement" is thus central to how an MFA utilizes digital technologies to achieve public diplomacy goals.

The same is true of scholars who cannot research the "new" public diplomacy without first defining its core elements: engagement and dialogue. Defining these terms is also necessary if one is to compare the digital activities of several embassies or ministries. Lastly, defining "engagement" is a necessary stepping-stone toward investigating the digitalization of public diplomacy. If engagement refers to online interactions between diplomats and publics, then measuring engagement can offer insight into diplomats' willingness to relinquish control over the communication process and adopt new norms and working routines. In other words, engagement may suggest that an MFA is undergoing a process of digitalization, as diplomats have transitioned from broadcast to communicative paradigms (McNutt, 2014).

Damian Spry (2018) suggested that when researching the practice of public diplomacy, scholars should ask four questions: Who are the agents of public diplomacy? Who are its targets? What is the relationship between these? And how is public diplomacy done? This chapter examines agents that have thus far been neglected by scholars: African and Eastern European MFAs. The analysis presented in this chapter explores how these agents interact with foreign populations and diasporas. The relationship between these, and the manner in which public diplomacy is practiced, is analyzed through a new model that seeks to measure the scope of dialogic engagement between diplomats and digital publics. This chapter addresses the lack of clarity regarding the terms "dialogue" and engagement by building on the works of public relations scholars and introducing the term "dialogic engagement." Next, the chapter introduces a new model for measuring the scope of dialogic engagement between diplomats and digital publics, which is based on the works of Bjola and Jiang and that of Manor. Finally, the chapter analyzes the dialogic activities of five African MFAs and four Lithuanian embassies. The following section examines the intersection between public diplomacy and public relations, for it is at this intersection that a definition for the term "engagement" may be found.

BETWEEN PUBLIC RELATIONS AND PUBLIC DIPLOMACY

Diplomats have always been experts in public relations. Ambassadors to foreign courts, for instance, would be tasked with representing the cultural and intellectual wealth of their countries. They would dress in their nation's latest fashions, display artwork in their residences, and host poets and musicians. The French ambassador to the British Court was the very embodiment of France in Britain (Sharma, 2015). Even today, public diplomacy activities focus on the promotion of a nation's cultural and intellectual achievements, as is evident in World Expos, the architectural design of new embassies, and networks of cultural institutions, such as the Institute Français.

The advent of the "new" public diplomacy has also seen a convergence between public diplomacy and public relations scholarship. This is because like public relations, the "new" public diplomacy is relational in nature and focuses on creating (and possibly leveraging) relationships with stakeholders. As Saunders (2013) argued, contemporary public diplomacy focuses on building relationships with connected individuals as these are an untapped resource that can help governments face global challenges. Public relations scholars such as Taylor and Kent (2014) have argued that studies examining organizations' digital interactions with stakeholders often include the terms "dialogue", "engagement" and "relationships" without offering clear definitions. At times, studies even employ the term "engagement" to reference one-way flows of information in which organizations communicate *at*, not *with*, stakeholders. Thus, in both public diplomacy and public relations scholarship, ambiguity shrouds the aforementioned terms.

To define the meaning of "engagement" and "dialogue," Taylor and Kent (2014) employ the term "dialogic engagement" which is a two-way relational process between organizations and their publics that aims to improve understanding between participants and make decisions that benefit both organizations and their stakeholders (ibid., p. 391). Dialogic engagement includes five components: previous research to identify issues, key publics, and cultural variables; positive regard for publics' input, experiences, and needs; interactions with the aim of relationship building rather than problem solving; seeking council with publics on issues of shared concern; and a recognition by organizations and publics of their interdependence and collaborative action for the good of the community. Dialogue is not, however, a fixed state. Rather, it is a process that requires constant two-way flows of information, alongside an ethical communicative environment. One such environment may be social media sites, as these mitigate power relations between organizations and individuals (ibid, p. 388). On Facebook, an individual may be as influential as a nation state or a large corporation. Moreover, an individual may publicly challenge assertions made on social media by corporations and nations.

The components of "dialogic engagement" are quite similar to the definitions of "new" public diplomacy. For instance, a positive regard for public input resonates with Metzgar's concept of "listening" to online publics and shaping foreign policy accordingly. Seeking counsel on issues of shared concern is like James Pamment's definition of the "new" public diplomacy as collaborative and inclusive. Previous research to identify issues, key publics, and cultural variables is in line with Bruce Gregory's (2011) assertion that public diplomacy is an instrument for understanding foreign cultures, attitudes, and behaviors.

Importantly, Damian Spry and Brian Hocking stipulate that the "new" public diplomacy offers an opportunity to redefine the role of publics who become active participants in a communicative act, rather than passive objects of foreign policy strategies (Hocking, 2005; Spry, 2018). A review of MFAs' digital activities suggests that some already incorporate elements of dialogic engagement and listening into their public diplomacy efforts. For instance, the British FCO (Foreign and Commonwealth Office) uses Twitter survey questions (such as the one shown in Fig. 6.1) to research the interests of its followers, especially regarding the war against Daesh (Manor, 2016b). The FCO's digital campaign to end sexual violence in conflict zones also saw multiple online collaborations with NGOs and civil society organizations, thus seeking council on issues of shared concern (Pamment, 2016). Conversely, the Indian MEA offers second-generation diasporas opportunities to visit India. Such visits aim to create relationships with children of diasporas rather than solve specific problems. The concept of dialogic engagement also echoes New Zealand's vision of democratized public diplomacy, which is mutually beneficial as diplomats understand the needs of digital publics while digital publics provide the insight necessary for formulating effective foreign policies.

The conceptualization of dialogic engagement can thus serve as part of a model for measuring "new" public diplomacy activities on digital platforms. This model is introduced in the following section.

Fig. 6.1 FCO use of Twitter survey questions (*Source* https://twitter.com/ UKagainstDaesh/status/699249615074430976?ref_src=twsrc%5Etf-w&ref_url=https%3A%2F%2Fdigdipblog.com%2F2016%2F02%2F28% 2Fhow-the-uk-U.S.-are-fighting-isis-online%2F)

From Digital Agenda Setting to Digital Engagement

Studies that have explored MFAs' and embassies' use of social media sites to practice the "new" public diplomacy have rarely offered a model through which engagement and dialogue can be measured. Such was the case with Emily Metzgar's 2012 analysis of the State Department's virtual embassy to Iran. Metzgar found that the virtual embassy was primarily used for one-way message dissemination, and thus failed to realize the potential of digital platforms for engagement. Yet Metzgar (2012) did not offer the means through which one could measure engagement—is it the number of queries that an embassy answers? The number of questions an embassy poses to followers? Or any form of two-way interactions, including a Facebook user liking an embassy post?

Vanc (2012) found that senior diplomats still believe that relationships can only be built through face-to-face engagement and not through digital means. Her study suggested that diplomats may resist new technologies due to well-entrenched working routines and that such working routines may serve as barriers to the process of digitalization. Yet Vanc does not offer a model for measuring the scope of engagement, be it face-to-face or digital. Archetti (2012) found that London-based embassies devoted greater resources to digital engagement given that much of their representational capacity has been diminished. In the past, embassies served as middlemen between two capitals passing information from one government, or leader, to another. Yet in the digital age, world leaders and MFAs can communicate directly with one another. Moreover, as Causey and Howard (2013, p. 144) argued, capitals can monitor events in foreign countries at a reduced cost, be it through news sites or Twitter. The embassy's role as a middleman between two capitals has thus been reduced. To counterbalance this loss, embassies increasingly engage with digital publics. However, Archetti also does not offer a model for measuring engagement between diplomats and their publics.

In 2015, Kampf, Manor, and Segev defined engagement as "all instances in which MFAs interact directly with their followers (for example, answering questions, responding to criticism and supplying requested information)." When comparing the Facebook and Twitter activities of 11 MFAs (Ethiopia, India, Israel, Japan, Kenya, Poland, Rwanda, Somalia, South Korea, the UK, and the USA) the authors found that engagement was a rarity and that most MFAs used social media sites for one-way information dissemination. Similarly, Bjola and Jiang (2015) evaluated the social media engagement of embassies to China by measuring the number of questions embassies answered, and instances in which they responded to images that they were tagged in. While both studies offer insight into the possible measurement of dialogic engagement, they do not consider the very foundations of the "new" public diplomacy including its collaborative nature, its goal of meeting the needs of digital publics, its shaping of foreign policy by "listening" to publics, and its emphasis on relationship building.

This chapter stipulates that by creating a model based on the concept of dialogic engagement, one may be able to measure the scope of two-way, dialogic engagement between diplomatic institutions and digital publics as, well as the extent to which diplomats practice the "new" public diplomacy. This model may focus on social media sites given that these center on creating relationships, facilitating two-way interactions, and mitigating power relations between organizations and their stakeholders (Bortree & Seltzer, 2009; Waters, Burnett, Lamm, & Lucas, 2009).

The model developed in this chapter combines the works of Bjola and Jiang (2015) with that of Manor (2017). When examining the digital activities of embassies in China, Bjola and Jiang first measured embassies' abilities to set the agendas of their online discussions with digital publics. Agenda-setting is broadly defined as the ability to influence the salience of topics on the public's agenda (Reynolds & McCombs, 2002). Traditionally, the media has had the power to set the public agenda by dedicating press coverage to a certain issue or place. Similarly, an MFA can attempt to set the agenda for its discussions with digital publics by repeatedly addressing certain issues, such as trade or culture, and downplaying other issues, such as political strife or contentious foreign policies. An MFA's agenda-setting activities are important given that dialogic engagement calls for conversations on issues of shared concern. By highlighting or repeatedly addressing certain topics, diplomats can identify the issues they are concerned with and, subsequently, seek the publics' council on how to best address these issues. Bjola and Jiang evaluated embassies' agenda-setting abilities by analyzing the issues that they most commonly addressed online and measuring whether those issues elicited high-levels comments and shares from digital publics.

Yet Bjola and Jiang did not measure the second component of dialogic engagement: actual two-way conversations between digital publics and diplomats. In 2017, Manor measured the State Department's dialogic engagement by reconceptualizing four of the five components that comprised Kent and Taylor's definition of "dialogic engagement." This conceptualization may be seen in Table 6.1.

The following section integrates Bjola, Jiang, and Manor's work into a single model that measures the dialogic engagement of five African MFAs. While the past decade has seen increased academic interest in the utilization of digital platforms in public diplomacy, few studies have focused on the digitalization of African public diplomacy. Indeed, the current scholarship tends to separate the West from the rest. This is surprising for two reasons. First, the utilization of digital technologies in public diplomacy has been linked to the search for cost-effective public diplomacy. As Adesina wrote (2017), digital technologies might prove especially beneficial for countries with limited resources and limited numbers of embassies abroad, including African countries. It might therefore be assumed that African MFAs would eagerly adopt digital technologies to augment their public diplomacy activities, reach a globally connected public, and create receptive environments for their

Table 6.1 Manor's (2017) model of dialogic engagement

Taylor and Kent (2014) components	Conceptualization	Measurement
Engagement requires demonstration of positive regard for stakeholders/publics input, experiences, and needs	Diplomatic institutions will meet the needs of online followers by answering questions and supplying requested information, and will positively regard follower input by responding to comments	Recording all instances in which diplomatic institutions respond to followers' queries, supply information on demand, publish user-generated content, or respond in any other way to followers' comments on posts
Engagement requires interaction with stakeholders/publics for relational purposes outside an immediate problem	Diplomatic institutions will invite followers to converse on issues of shared concern. Moreover, diplomatic institutions will hold continuous conversations with online publics by addressing issues or concerns raised by followers	Recording all instances in which diplomatic institutions invite followers to converse with it, as well as all instances in which they responded to concerns raised by followers
Engagement requires interaction with stakeholders/publics for their advice and council on issues of organization/community concern	Diplomatic institutions will query followers by posting questions relating to their activities. Diplomatic institutions will also query followers by posting questions relating to their informational needs or services they require. Finally, diplomatic institutions will query followers on how they perceive a country's role in the world and the policies it promotes	Recording all instances in which diplomatic institutions query social media followers, be it in an individual post/tweet/message or in response to a comment posted by followers
Engagement requires interaction that contributes to a fully functioning society, whereby organizations and publics realize their interdependence and act together for the good of the community	Diplomatic institutions will offer collaborative opportunities for the formation of online advocacy groups and advocacy campaigns aimed at raising awareness to issues of mutual concern to their followers	Recording all instances in which diplomatic institutions offered opportunities for collaborative action, be it in forming communities of influence with followers, conducting shared online advocacy campaigns, or co-creating content to raise awareness to issues of shared concern

foreign policies. Second, digital platforms create a more levelled diplomatic playing field, as all users are transformed into iBrands that compete against each other over the attention of digital audiences. All a brand needs to successfully compete on the digital market is a smartphone and an Internet connection. By adopting digital technologies, African countries may be able to better compete opposite their more affluent colleagues over the attention of digital publics and digital influencers such as journalists, opinion makers, bloggers, tech companies, and other diplomatic institutions. This chapter, therefore, addresses an important empirical gap by evaluating the dialogic engagement of five African MFAs.

THE DIGITALIZATION OF AFRICAN PUBLIC DIPLOMACY

While the utilization of digital technologies may allow African MFAs to overcome limited representation abroad, it may also enable them to meet a unique public diplomacy challenge to Africa—maintaining close ties with diasporas and ensuring that they continue to contribute to their former countries' financial prosperity. As Oxford University's Geraldine Adiku argued, in recent years, the image of African diasporas has altered from traitors who abandoned their nations to saviors who financially support their countries of origin. Presently, diaspora remittances account for 0.6% of Ethiopia's national GDP, 1.6% of Kenya's GDP, and 1.9% of Rwanda's GDP (OECD, 2012). Considering their growing reliance on diasporas, several African governments have launched new diplomatic initiatives aimed at strengthening ties with diaspora communities (Kenya MFA, 2014).

Rana (2013) stated that a migrant community becomes a diaspora if it retains a memory of, and some emotional connection with, its country of origin. Using digital platforms and practicing the "new" public diplomacy, African diplomats can maintain continuous ties with diasporas, thus strengthening the emotional bond that characterizes a diaspora community. Moreover, MFAs can use digital platforms to update diasporas on events shaping their country of origin, thus increasing diasporas' emotional investment in their former countries. Lastly, MFAs can use digital platforms to offer collaborative opportunities that may lead to the formation of communities of diplomats and diasporas.

Studies suggest that African MFAs are just as proficient in utilizing digital platforms as their Western or Asian peers. By 2015, most African MFAs had created some form of digital presence. Thirteen

MFAs in the continent chose to establish Facebook profiles, including the ministries of Botswana, Egypt, Ethiopia, Kenya, Libya, Namibia, Nigeria, Rwanda, Somalia, South Africa, Sudan, Tunisia and Uganda. Other MFAs turned to Twitter, including Ghana, Mali and Niger, while others still settled for websites, including Benin, Chad, Guinea, Mozambique, Sudan, Tanzania, Zambia, and Zimbabwe. African MFAs were also among the first to utilize digital platforms to deliver consular aid (Manor, 2015a, 2015b). Such was the case in 2013 when the Kenyan MFA used Twitter to coordinate the evacuation of its citizens from South Sudan once internal fighting broke out (Manor, 2018). Over the course of several days, Kenyan diplomats manned the MFA's Twitter account, providing citizens with real-time information on evacuation flights and answering consular questions.

In an analysis from 2015, Manor found that some African MFAs, such as Kenya, Somalia, and Ethiopia, published more Facebook posts and tweets per day than the MFAs of India, Japan, South Korea, and the USA. Manor also found that the MFAs of Somalia and Ethiopia were less likely to duplicate content across social media sites than the MFAs of Japan, South Korea, the UK, and the USA. As such, African MFAs were as proficient at tailoring content to medium as their Western and Asian peers. For the neoliberal evangelicals of Silicon Valley, this is wonderful news, as it suggests that in the digital marketplace, all iBrands compete with one another equally. Digital proficiency, the evangelicals would argue, has trickled down from the West to the rest.

Given the fact that few studies to date have examined the digitalization of African public diplomacy, and considering the assumption that African MFAs would use digital platforms to enhance their public diplomacy activities, this chapter examined the dialogic engagement of five African MFAs on Facebook. The decision to focus on Facebook stemmed from the fact that it is a medium for creating and maintaining relationships, while Twitter is used for information gathering and opinion sharing (Hughes, Rowe, Batey, & Lee, 2012; Kwak, Lee, Park, & Moon, 2010). Some scholars have also suggested that MFAs view Twitter as an elite-to-elite medium through which diplomats can interact with opinion makers, journalists, diplomats, and policymakers, while Facebook is an elite-to-public medium through which diplomats can interact with digital society members and diasporas (Bjola, 2018).

The MFAs evaluated in this chapter were those of Botswana, Ethiopia, Kenya, Rwanda, and Uganda. These were selected for two reasons. First, all five migrated early to digital platforms and were already operating a digital presence in 2015. It was thus assumed that these MFAs would be active on digital platforms and would attempt to leverage these platforms toward public diplomacy goals. Second, the MFAs of Ethiopia, Kenya, and Rwanda had been previously analyzed by Kampf, Manor, and Segev in 2015. Thus, by returning to these MFAs three years later, this chapter could explore whether the digital divide between African MFAs and their Western or Asian peers has continued to narrow.

The analysis of African MFAs' dialogic engagement consisted of three stages. In the first stage, a sample of 100 Facebook posts published by each MFA was collected. These posts, published between 2017 and 2018, were categorized by subject matter to identify the issues highlighted by each MFA as part of its agenda-setting activities. Next, the chapter measured the extent to which digital publics do in fact comment on and share posts that deal with the issues highlighted by each MFA. Lastly, the dialogic engagement of all five MFAs was measured. In addition, the type of visual content (i.e., images, videos) published by African MFAs, as well as their average daily scope of activity, was analyzed. These were then compared with the activities of Western and Asian ministries to measure a possible narrowing of the digital divide.

CONTENT ANALYSIS

To categorize African MFA posts, this chapter employed the methodology of thematic analysis, which may be defined as a method for identifying, analyzing, and reporting on patterns of themes within a given research corpus (Clarke & Braun, 2014). In the first phase of analysis, 100 random posts published by all five MFAs were examined. Next, a set of categories were created based on the content of these posts. For example, many posts dealt with the stability of the African continent or activities aimed at increasing the stability of African countries. Thus, a category named "stability and prosperity" was created. Likewise, posts dealing with the need to invest in public health initiatives were sorted under the "Public Health" category. This stage of analysis led to the formulation of seven categories. Next, another 100 posts were analyzed to ensure the validity of the identified categories. This led to the formulation of four more categories. Such was the case with posts dealing with the impact tourism has on the prosperity of African countries and posts depicting state visits by African leaders. The methodology of thematic analysis has previously been employed to analyze the digital activities of the Israeli MFA, the Obama White House, and the U.S. State Department (Bjola & Manor, 2018; Manor & Crilley, 2018). In total, all 500 posts published by the five African MFAs were classified into 14 categories. These are listed in Table 6.2. Notably, all Facebook posts were gathered during May of 2018 and analyzed during June of 2018.

Table 6.2 Subject matter categories of posts by published by African MFAs on Facebook

Category name	Issues addressed in posts	Example
Academia/ education	Posts dealing with academic achievements of African scholars, exchange programs with foreign universities, establishment of new research centers	Ethiopia's MFA announces new poultry facility will open to explore genetic diversity
Bilateral ties	Submitting and receiving letters of accreditation from new ambassadors, dialogue between parliaments and parliamentarians, foreign aid to other African countries, signing bilateral agreements on security, trade, and infrastructure development, inaugurating new embassies	Kenya's MFA announces meeting between members of the European Parliament and members of the Kenyan Parliament
Condolences	Offering condolences to other countries following the deaths of present and past leaders, signing condolence books at embassies, commemorating historical events such as the genocide in Rwanda	Botswana Foreign Minister signs condolence book at South African High Commission following passing of Winnie Mandela
Cultural	Celebrating national culture, promoting national culture abroad, promoting new cultural achievements, investing in cultural activities exemplifying national norms and values	Kenyan President tells CNN that homosexuality does not conform with the norms and values of the Kenyan people
Diaspora	MFA publications dealing with diaspora issues, policymakers and leaders meeting with diaspora groups, recognizing diasporas' contribution to the nation	Rwandan Foreign Minister celebrates national day with Rwanda diaspora in Brussels

(continued)

Table 6.2   (continued)

Category name	Issues addressed in posts	Example
Economic growth	GDP growth rates, national conferences to stimulate growth in partnership with private companies, seeking news sources and resources for economic growth like oceans, harnessing new technology for economic growth	Kenya's GDP growth rebounds to 5.5%
Multilateral	Meetings and new initiatives of the African Union, appointments to UN agencies, resolutions to be passed at the UN Security Council, African leaders attending G7 and Commonwealth meetings, visits by directors of multilateral organizations such as the UN Human Rights Council or World Bank	Ugandan President holds meetings with heads of Commonwealth nations in London
National achievements	Sports achievements such as winning medals at Commonwealth Games, election of African policymakers to posts at UN organizations, events commemorating military victories	Ethiopia Airlines to operate direct lines to a host of new destinations
Public health	Inaugurating new medical facilities, foreign aid from other countries in the form of public health interventions, attending global summits on public health issues	Rwanda Foreign Minister delivers speech at Malaria summit in London
Stability and prosperity	Speeches by national leaders on policy initiatives aimed at increasing security and stability across Africa, peacekeeping missions to Somalia, collaborative negotiations to end tensions in South Sudan and Sudan, joint infrastructure projects between neighboring states, celebrating African Union Day	Botswana MFA to celebrate Africa Day with the theme "Wining the Fight Against Corruption"
State visits	State visits by African leaders to foreign countries, welcoming foreign leaders to African countries	South African President begins State Visit to Botswana

(continued)

Table 6.2   (continued)

Category name	Issues addressed in posts	Example
Tourism	Bilateral agreements to stimulate tourism between two countries, showcasing tourist attraction, contribution of tourism to national growth, seeking partners to enhance tourism	A video montage by Ethiopian MFA of most attractive tourist sites in Ethiopia
Trade/investment	Meetings between national leaders and trade delegations, foreign direct investments by global corporations, signing of new trade agreements between African countries	Uganda's Minister of State for investment and privatization holds trade forum in Cairo

Once all 500 posts had been categorized, the prevalence of each category was calculated to identify the main topics addressed by each of the five MFAs. The results of this analysis may be seen in Table 6.3.

Table 6.3 offers several insights into the public diplomacy activities of the five African MFAs. First, bilateral issues were highly prevalent among all five ministries, ranging from 17% in Kenya's case to nearly 50% in Rwanda's case. This result is not surprising given that the primary task of diplomacy is to manage relations with other countries. Posts dealing with bilateral issues were very diverse, and included the inauguration of new embassies alongside meetings between two foreign ministers. However, in all MFAs, a large proportion of bilateral posts dealt with the presentation of letters of accreditation of new ambassadors. Posts also often dealt with bi-lateral agreements between African countries to embark on joint infrastructure projects, such as new border terminals that would ease the transfer of goods and individuals.

Another prevalent category addressed by all MFAs was the stability and prosperity of Africa. This was especially true of the Ethiopian and Rwandan MFAs. Posts comprising this category tended to focus on three core issues: demonstrating the stability of the African continent, diplomatic measures aimed at increasing African stability and arguing that stability was key to Africa's financial prosperity. As such, many posts in this category dealt with the growing resilience of African economies. It is possible that the Ethiopian MFA focused on this issue given recent domestic instability that challenges political structures. The Rwandan MFA referred mostly to the nation's new role as the leader of the African

Table 6.3 Prevalence of topical categories by African MFA[a] (based on sample of 500 Facebook posts)

Topical category	African MFAs				
	Botswana (%)	Ethiopia (%)	Kenya (%)	Rwanda (%)	Uganda (%)
Academia/ education	5	2	2	–	1
Bilateral	36	19	17	50	31
Condolences	1	–	2	–	2
Cultural	3	6	3	9	1
Diaspora	–	4	5	7	–
Economic growth	1	8	8	1	7
Multilateral	14	6	10	7	10
National achievements	–	10	11	1	4
Public health	–	1	3	1	1
Stability and prosperity	10	18	12	18	14
State visits	26	4	9	3	7
Tourism	–	10	1	–	6
Trade/investment	5	12	17	3	14
Other	–	–	–	1	3

[a]Sum of percentages may be greater than 100 due to rounding

Union stating that "*The forces reshaping the global economic and security environment mean Africa's future depends on the quality of cooperation within our continent.*" The Kenyan MFA often depicted Kenya's policies, including its contribution to peacekeeping operations in Somalia and mediating tensions in South Sudan, through the prism of a regional leader. As the Kenyan foreign minister stated in a Facebook video, "*The world looks to Kenya as a thought leader and a regional leader.*"

The category of Trade and Investments was also prevalent among the MFAs of Ethiopia (12%), Kenya (17%), and Uganda (14%). These posts dealt with meetings between national leaders and trade delegations, foreign direct investments by global corporations, and the signing of new trade agreements. Taken together, economic issues accounted for more than a third of all Facebook posts published by the Ethiopian, Kenyan, and Ugandan MFAs.

Multilateral issues were also prevalent across all five ministries, ranging from 6% in Ethiopia's case to 14% in Botswana's. These figures are also not surprising given the number of multilateral organizations that are active in Africa. During the sampling period, there were several visits by high-ranking policy makers to African countries, including the President of the UN Human Rights Council, members of the World Bank and executives from the Intentional Organization for Migration. Another reason for the high prevalence of this category was that the sampling period included a summit of the Commonwealth of Nations, which was attended by the presidents of Botswana, Kenya, Rwanda, and Uganda.

Notably, two categories had a surprisingly low prevalence. The first was posts dealing with cultural issues, which ranged from 1% in Uganda's case to 8% in Rwanda's case. This finding is surprising as cultural achievements, or celebrations of a nation's culture, history, traditions, and art, may hold special significance for diasporas who long to reconnect with their countries of origin. Thus, posts dealing with culture or depicting cultural celebrations may enable a diaspora community to retain an emotional bond to its country of origin. Moreover, cultural issues tend to be very prevalent on the digital profiles of European MFAs. Showcasing a nation's culture is viewed by some European MFAs as a tool for national image management (Manor, 2016a).

Second, the prevalence of posts dealing with diaspora issues was extremely low among all MFAs. Posts that focused on diasporas tended to deal with national day celebrations, as well as ambassadors and foreign ministers meeting with diaspora communities abroad. The low prevalence of this category is important given that African economies are dependent on remittances from diasporas and have formulated national policies to strengthen ties with them.

While there were certain similarities in the content published by the five African MFAs, each ministry also had its own unique style of communication. For instance, many posts published by the MFA of Botswana were labeled as a "press release" and were thus primarily targeted at journalists and media institutions, rather than digital society members. Botswana's MFA was also the only one to comment on non-African issues. While the other four MFAs focused solely on events shaping the African continent, Botswana's ministry commented on a host of international issues, including condemning North Korean aggression, praising the ousting of Zimbabwe's Robert Mugabe, lamenting the UN Security Council's lack of resolve in ending the Syrian Civil War, and denouncing President Trump's decision to move the U.S. embassy to Jerusalem. Botswana's ministry also focused on a domestic issue: the peaceful transition of power from the president to the vice president. This was portrayed as a process that should be emulated by other nations in Africa.

Ethiopia's Ministry, on the other hand, focused on issues relating to the prosperity and stability of Ethiopia and the Horn of Africa. The MFA commented on the economic sanctions on Eritrea, state visits to South Sudan, and meetings of the African Union. The MFA also frequently dealt with the economic growth of Ethiopia achieved by innovative technologies and a bustling tourism industry carried on the wings of Ethiopian Airlines. Most diaspora posts included the promotion of the MFA's magazine, *A Week in the Horn*, which is disseminated online by all Ethiopian embassies and offers a review of Ethiopian current affairs, cultural achievements, and diplomatic activities.

Kenya's MFA focused on the topics of foreign investments and economic growth. Kenyan posts dealt with the nation's growing GDP, collaborations with the World Bank to ensure continued financial growth, and Kenya's plan to convene a global Blue Economy Summit to study ways in which oceans may be used for financial growth. The MFA also highlighted economic growth and financial stability when dealing with diaspora issues. Such was the case when Kenyan diplomats were interviewed by the media and asked how the diaspora could support Kenya's economy.

The past was very present in Rwandan posts, as the MFA repeatedly referenced the Rwandan genocide. Such was the case with cultural posts depicting ceremonies at monuments for the Rwandan genocide, prizes for organizations that combat the dangers of genocide, or cultural events meant to ensure that the lessons of the genocide not be forgotten. The prism of genocide was also evident in posts dealing with the stability and prosperity of the continent. When agreeing to accept Libyan refugees, the MFA stated, "*Given Rwanda's political philosophy and our history, we cannot remain silent when human beings are being mistreated or auctioned off like cattle.*"

As was the case with Botswana, the majority of posts published by Uganda's MFA were prolonged press statements. These, however, tended to adopt financial prisms. For instance, when congratulating Korea on its Independence Day, the Ugandan Foreign Ministers were quoted as saying, "*Fifty years ago, the economies of many newly independent African Countries including Uganda were at the same level of development with that of Korea. However, since the 1960s, the Republic of Korea has strategically used industrialization and exports as the engine of growth, propelling it to the 11th largest economy in the world, joining the ranks of countries in OECD and G-20."*

In summary, the content analysis suggests that the five African MFAs offered digital publics a breadth of information pertaining to events and issues shaping the continent. While economic posts were quite prevalent across all five MFAs, and while diaspora posts were surprisingly rare, each MFA adopted its own narrative. The following section evaluates whether these MFAs were successful in setting the agenda for discussions with digital publics.

AGENDA-SETTING ANALYSIS

Analyzing MFAs' abilities to set the agenda for their discussion with digital publics first necessitated the identification of the issues that each MFA chose to highlight. Following in Bjola and Jiang's footsteps, it was decided that topics that amounted to 10% of all posts published by an MFA would be regarded as highlighted issues. For instance, 36% of all posts published by Botswana's MFA dealt with bilateral issues, 25.8% with state visits, 13% with multilateral issues, and 10% with the stability and prosperity of Africa (see Table 6.3). Thus, these four topics were regarded as the issues highlighted by Botswana's MFA.

Next, it was necessary to identify posts that elicited higher than average reactions from MFA followers on Facebook. Posts that attract higher than average shares and comments are those that are most successful at eliciting a reaction from followers, and thus can lay the foundations for dialogic engagement. This is because shares and comments are more demanding forms of interaction with MFA content. Lastly, it was necessary to calculate what percentage of posts that elicit higher than average shares and comments also deal with the issues highlighted by each MFA. If an MFA can elicit shares and comments on the issues that it is most concerned with, then it may be able to instigate a process of shared deliberation on issues of mutual concern. Table 6.4 includes the average number of shares and comments MFA posts garnered, the number of posts to elicit higher than average shares and comments, and the percentage of such posts that dealt with issues highlighted by each MFA.

As is evident in Table 6.4, in the case of all five African MFAs, most posts that elicited higher than average shares and comments dealt with issues highlighted by MFAs. Thus, this chapter finds that African MFAs

Table 6.4 Analysis of African MFAs' agenda-setting on Facebook (based on sample of 500 Facebook posts)

MFA	Average number of shares	Average number of comments	Number of posts to attract higher than average comments or shares	Percentage of posts to attract higher than average comments or shares that dealt with MFA priorities
Botswana	14	2	24	91
Ethiopia	17	2	50	64
Kenya	17	3	8	63
Rwanda	3	0	32	78
Uganda	2	1	47	64

can set the agenda for discussions with their Facebook followers. These findings echo those of Bjola and Jiang. Yet the question that remains is whether these MFAs also offer opportunities for dialogic engagement. This question is answered in the following section.

DIALOGIC ENGAGEMENT ANALYSIS

Table 6.5 includes an analysis of the dialogic engagement of the five African MFAs based on the sample of 500 posts. As can be seen, MFA posts attracted an average of 0.1–3 comments. While this may be perceived as a relatively low figure, it does suggest that digital publics routinely comment on MFA posts. Yet results also demonstrate that all five MFAs failed to practice dialogic engagement. The MFAs did not respond to followers' comments or questions, did not supply requested information, failed to query followers to identify their needs and interests, and refrained from offering opportunities for collaborations and shared creation of value.

The most dialogic MFA was Uganda's, yet here, too, instances of two-way interactions were rare. In one case, the Ugandan MFA asked followers if they were interested in the activities of Ugandan embassies abroad. Yet the MFA did not respond to followers' answers or comments. In another instance, the MFA asked followers how a new train between Kampala and Mombasa would impact their business without bothering to further converse with followers who answered the question. There was also only one instance in which the MFA answered a follower's question by inviting him to the MFA after the theft of his

Table 6.5   Analysis of African MFAs' dialogic engagement with Facebook users (based on sample of 500 Facebook posts)

Components of dialogic engagement (Manor, 2017)	MFA				
	Botswana	Ethiopia	Kenya	Rwanda	Uganda
Average number of comments per post	2.0	2.0	3.1	0.2	1.5
MFA replies to follower comments/reactions	–	–	–	–	–
Number of responses to follower queries	–	–	–	–	–
Instances of supplying requested information	–	–	–	–	1.0
Number of publications of user-generated content	–	–	–	–	–
Number of overall response to followers' comments	–	–	–	–	1.0
Number of invitations to engage in conversations	–	–	1.0	–	1.0
Number of responses to followers' stated concerns	–	–	–	–	–
Instances of querying Facebook	–	–	–	–	2.0
Number of collaborative opportunities for creation of shared values	–	–	–	–	–

travel documents. In Kenya's case, the MFA published a single post inviting digital publics to follow the foreign minister on Twitter. These results demonstrate that the five African MFAs evaluated in this chapter use Facebook as a one-way medium for information dissemination. They thus fail to leverage digital platforms to practice the "new" public diplomacy and foster relationships with foreign populations or create digital communities with their diasporas. It should be mentioned that African MFAs are by no means the only ones who fail to practice dialogic engagement. Studies have shown that Western MFAs, including those of Finland, Israel, Norway, Poland, and the USA, also use digital platforms for one-way message dissemination (Clarke, 2015; Comor & Bean, 2012; Hocking & Melissen, 2015).

Public diplomacy scholars have argued that digital activity breeds followers (Hocking & Melissen, 2015). This is also the logic of the digital society in which constant sharing of personal information is a means of attracting interest. MFAs who are not digitally active may thus fail to attract digital publics and consequently may have no one to engage with. This chapter therefore compared African MFAs' rates of daily activity on Facebook with those of Western and Asian MFAs. The sample included the MFAs evaluated by Kampf, Manor, and Segev in their 2015 study. Moreover, the use of media (e.g., images, videos) was also compared as visuals increase the appeal of digital content as they succinctly convey large volumes of information, an important function in the age of Too Much Infromation (TMI) (Miller & Horst, 2017). Lastly, the analysis compared the average change in MFA Facebook fans per day and the average number of likes MFAs receive per day, as can be seen in Table 6.6. This analysis was conducted during July of 2018 using the Social Bakers application.

As seen in Table 6.6, the Ethiopian MFA published more posts per day than the British FCO and the MFAs of Israel, Poland, Japan, and South Korea, while the Kenyan MFA was more active than the Japanese ministry and as active as South Korea's MFA. Conversely, the Rwandan and Ugandan MFAs were the least active of all 12 MFAs. The Ethiopian MFA also garnered more likes per day than the FCO, the Japanese, the Polish, and the South Korean MFAs, while Kenya's MFA outperformed the ministries of Japan and South Korea. However, the MFAs with the lowest average number of likes were Botswana, Rwanda, and Uganda.

Regarding the use of visual media, there was no discernible difference between African and Western or Asian MFAs. In fact, Kenya's use of videos was greater than that of the Polish, South Korean, Israeli, and Indian MFAs. This is an important finding as creating videos is the most resource-intensive form of visual production. Similarly, Uganda's use of videos was greater than that of the Polish, South Korean, and Japanese MFAs. Lastly, the Ethiopian MFA had one of the highest average changes in fans per day while Kenya had a higher average than that of Japan and India. Finally, in terms of average likes per day, the Ethiopian MFA attracts more likes per day than the ministries of the UK, Japan, and South Korea. However, all other African MFAs are outperformed by their Western peers.

In summary, these results suggest that African MFAs are as active on digital platforms as many of their Western and Asian peers, that they are as proficient at creating visual content, and can attract similar numbers of new fans per day. The digital divide in public diplomacy seems to be narrowing even further as the digitalization of African MFAs continues.

Table 6.6   Facebook activities of African and selected Western and Asian countries

MFA	Facebook activities and user engagement rates			
	Average posts published per day	Average Likes per day	Types of media employed[a]	Average change in fans per day
Botswana	0.6	13	76% photos 24% links	–[b]
Ethiopia	3.0	397	85% photos 9% links 7% videos	+144
FCO	1.6	228	83% videos 11% photos 4% links 2% notes	+25
India	4.3	1200	75% photos 18% videos 5% notes 2% links	−120
Israel	1.3	1600	75% videos 20% photos 3% status 3% links	+75
Japan	0.7	29	81% photos 13% videos 6% links	+4
Kenya	0.9	29.3	71% photos 15% videos 7% links 7% status	+13
South Korea	0.9	16	68% photos 18% links 14% videos	–[b]
Poland	1.7	142	63% links 38% photos	+22
Rwanda	0.4	7	90% photos 10% links	–[b]
Uganda	0.2	4	71% photos 15% videos 15% links	+4
U.S.	4.2	2000	45% videos 32% photos 23% links	+108

[a]The sum of percentages may be greater than 100 due to rounding
[b]Missing value due to insufficient data

While the analysis of African MFAs suggests that they do not practice dialogic engagement, it is possible that embassies are more dialogic than ministries. Past studies suggest that embassies interact more with digital publics as they attempt to counterbalance their loss of agency as middlemen between two capitals (Archetti, 2012). The practice of dialogic engagement by embassies is analyzed through the case study of Lithuanian public diplomacy.

THE DIGITALIZATION OF LITHUANIA'S MFA

The digitalization of Lithuania's public diplomacy started in 2013. According to Rytis Paulauskas, Director of the Communications and Cultural Diplomacy Department, the MFA first adopted digital technologies to promote the nation's presidency of the EU. Since then, the MFA has sought to utilize digital tools to work toward achieving four goals. First, publicizing Lithuanian policies among local and global elites including journalists, think tanks, neighboring countries to the East and the West, and other members of the diplomatic community. Paulauskas stated that other MFAs are an especially sought-after constituency for Lithuania. Through digital tools, the Lithuanian MFA can announce policy initiatives to the global diplomatic community, comment on the policies of other countries, and even contest certain policies, thus bringing attention to issues that are of importance to Lithuania. Second, the MFA utilizes digital technologies to express Lithuanian support for the policies of its allies, such as the EU and NATO. Third, digital platforms are used to increase the reach of the MFA's public diplomacy activities given its limited physical representation abroad. According to Paulauskas, digital technologies enable the MFA to communicate with a global public, thus offsetting the disadvantage of a small number of embassies. The fourth goal is to foster and maintain ties with Lithuania's diaspora (R. Paulauskas, personal communication, July 25, 2018).

Much like African countries, Lithuania's diaspora is an important digital constituency given its size and global dispersal. It is estimated that there are 1.3 million Lithuanians living abroad, while the population of Lithuania is estimated at 2.8 million citizens (Ferguson, Salominaite & Boersma, 2016). This diaspora is a source of both political and financial support for Lithuania, and as such, the MFA and Lithuanian embassies dedicate digital resources to communicating with the diaspora. This includes attempts to reverse the "brain drain," in which talented

Lithuanians left the nation seeking employment and academic opportunities in Western Europe and North America.

Another important digital goal, which is linked to diaspora diplomacy, is promoting a positive narrative of Lithuania as a prosperous Northern Baltic state that offers many opportunities for young people. While this narrative can help stem the tide of the "brain drain," it also counters Russia's digital activity. Paulauskas stated that in recent years, Russia has been promoting the narrative of Lithuania as a failed state on the verge of financial collapse that cannot be independent without the aid of the EU and NATO. Other major themes disseminated on digital platforms include the importance of the truth pertaining to the events that unfolded in Crimea, the economic achievement of Lithuania (including joining the OECD) and promoting Lithuanian culture (R. Paulauskas, personal communication, July 25, 2018).

As of 2018, the MFA's digital activities are limited to social media sites, and the MFA is active on multiple platforms including Facebook, Twitter, YouTube, and Flickr. To date, the MFA has yet to implement organization-wide training in using social media sites, and has not yet published guidelines for embassies and diplomats migrating online. The MFA does publish examples of best practices in its quarterly report, which is disseminated among all embassies. Moreover, ambassadors slated to serve at important embassies meet with the communications department before their departure to discuss ways in which digital technologies could be used to leverage embassy activities.

Thus far, the MFA has evaluated its digital activities through four parameters: the overall number of followers it attracts, the reach of its digital content, the amount of reactions this content elicits, and the sentiments of comments. Engagement is currently defined by the MFA as the numbers of likes, shares, and comments that digital content garners. The Lithuanian ministry has, however, recently begun an internal process that will see the establishment of new "digital teams" and the creation of internal training courses. This process rests on a collaborative effort between the Lithuanian MFA, the strategic communications department at the UK Prime Minister's Office, and the Oxford Digital Diplomacy Research Group. The process of digitalization of Lithuanian public diplomacy is thus about to change both the structure of the ministry and its values and working routines. In terms of structural change, the MFA will soon create horizontal digital teams whose members will originate from three departments: strategic communications, public information, and the monitoring division. These horizontal teams will create digital campaigns aimed at promoting Lithuanian policy goals and countering the narratives of other countries. Moreover, the teams will "listen" to online networks in other countries and supply MFA desks with relevant information. Teams will also create digital content based on big data analysis, thus tailoring content to the needs and interests of digital publics. As such, the MFA's working routines will include both digital broadcasting and digital listening, while diplomats will be asked to regard content shared by digital publics as a source of information that should inform the policy formulation process (R. Paulauskas, personal communication, July 25, 2018).

Paulauskas mentioned in an interview that two-way interactions and dialogic engagement rarely take place on MFA social media channels. This is due in part to a lack of resources, yet is also tied to the conservative communications culture in the MFA. Some in the ministry still believe that the foundations of diplomacy rest on face-to-face interactions in which close working relations can be established and leveraged. As is the case with other MFAs, well-entrenched working routines are a barrier to enhanced digital activity. Paulauskas noted, however, that Lithuanian embassies are more dialogic with their followers as they continuously use Facebook to communicate with diasporas.

Given the importance of diaspora outreach to the Lithuanian MFA, and as no studies to date have examined the digitalization of Lithuanian public diplomacy, this chapter evaluated the Facebook activities of four Lithuanian embassies (Canada, Ireland, the UK, and the USA). These embassies were selected because they are in countries with large diaspora communities. Moreover, all four embassies include relatively large staffs and may thus be better positioned to invest digital resources in diaspora outreach. Once again, thematic analysis was used to analyze the content shared by the embassies on Facebook. However, only content that directly targeted diasporas was analyzed. Facebook posts that were designated as targeting diasporas were those written in Lithuanian, as opposed to English, or posts that dealt with events and activities organized by the diaspora community. Finally, the embassies' dialogic engagement activities were also analyzed. Notably, the analysis of Lithuanian embassies did not include an evaluation of their agenda-setting activities as the focus was solely on diaspora-related posts. Table 6.7 includes the topical categories identified in the thematic analysis of 280 posts published on Facebook by the four Lithuanian embassies between 2017 and 2018. All

Table 6.7 Subject matter categories of diaspora related posts published by Lithuanian embassies

Category name	Issues addressed in posts	Example
Celebrating centenary	Celebrating 2018, which marked 100 years since the independence of Lithuania	Publishing advertisements in London subway stations celebrating the centenary
Bi-lateral	Information for Lithuanian citizens living in other countries, scope of ties between two countries, ceremonies celebrating relations between two countries, military ties between countries	Information pertaining to the rights of Lithuanian's in the UK following Brexit
Diaspora engagement	Instances in which the embassy staff interacts with diaspora	Ambassador to Ireland meets local diaspora community when traveling to local councils
Brain drain	Supplying information on business opportunities in Lithuania, publicizing academic opportunities in Lithuania, information on Lithuanian economic property, ambassadors meeting with students to discuss re-immigration	New program offers internship in Lithuanian export firms
Culture/education	Events celebrating Lithuanian culture, publicizing Lithuanian cultural achievements, diaspora members who obtain cultural achievements, exchange programs, schools that offer Lithuanian language lessons	Screening of Lithuanian film at the embassy
Community events	Diaspora events including folk singing, dance contests, sports day for parents and children	Diaspora gathering to song national anthem and folk songs
Commemorating Lithuanian history	Honoring fighters who fought for Lithuanian independence, honoring those who died during Soviet occupation, commemorating those who perished during German occupation	Lithuanian partisans visit Ireland to meet with diaspora community
Consular services	Consular missions to other cities, promoting new consular services, opening and closing times of embassies	Lithuanian embassy in Canada to go on consular mission and offer services to diaspora in Toronto

posts were gathered during May of 2018 and analyzed during June of 2018.

Table 6.8 includes the analysis of each embassy's diaspora-targeted posts. For each embassy, the analysis included 70 Facebook posts published between 2017 and August of 2018. All posts in Lithuanian were translated using two separate tools: Facebook translations and Google Translate.

As can be seen in Table 6.8, the clear majority of posts published by all four embassies were in Lithuanian, suggesting that the embassies do target diasporas. Moreover, the centenary celebrations of independence were highly prevalent among all four embassies. This was because the centenary celebrations saw a host of diaspora events including piano concerts, folklore festivals, art exhibitions, celebrations in local churches, and advertising campaigns in foreign capitals. Cultural or educational events for diasporas were also prevalent across all embassies. These included youth talent competitions, a book fair in London, Irish schools offering courses in the Lithuanian language, and meetings with Lithuanian authors.

Notably, during the sampling period, all embassies published several posts inviting diasporas to join Lithuanians all over the world in singing the national anthem. This is a Lithuanian custom where all Lithuanians come together globally, regardless of their location, to honor their nation's independence and history. These events were meant to commemorate the struggle for Lithuanian independence. The "Celebrating

Table 6.8 Prevalence of topical categories by Lithuanian embassies[a] (based on sample of 280 Facebook posts)

Subject matter categories	Embassies			
	Canada (%)	Ireland (%)	UK (%)	U.S. (%)
Celebrating centenary	19	8	34	26
Bilateral	4	13	11	6
Diaspora engagement	7	2	11	8
Brain drain	4	2	9	4
Culture/education	20	49	30	32
Community events	15	17	–	9
Commemorating Lithuanian history	15	4	4	15
Consular services	17	2	2	–
% of posts in Lithuanian	78	73	81	80

[a]Sum of percentages may be greater than 100 due to rounding

Centenary" and "Commemorating Lithuanian History" categories demonstrate that Lithuanian public diplomacy is truly digital. It anni-hilates time and space by globally singing a national anthem and sum-moning the past to make sense of Lithuania's present, a present in which Lithuania is a successful and prosperous Northern Baltic nation. This prosperity was made evident in posts focused on reversing the "brain drain" and highlighting opportunities that await young Lithuanians who are willing to re-immigrate to their country of origin.

Unlike African MFAs, Lithuanian embassies seldom dealt with bilat-eral issues. The exception was the embassy in London, which pub-lished videos dealing with the rights of expats following Brexit, and the embassy in Dublin, which published images from the Irish President's visit to Lithuania. The "Diaspora Engagement" category mostly included images and videos from meetings between embassy staff and diaspora communities. Consular issues were addressed almost exclusively by the embassy to Canada, which had organized consular missions to Toronto and other cities.

In summary, the diaspora posts published by the four embassies seem to focus on creating a sense of community with diasporas and allowing them to maintain an emotional bond with their country of origin, which is central to the diaspora experience. Celebrating Lithuanian's inde-pendence, commemorating its past struggles, honoring its scholarship and literature, and celebrating its culture all facilitate the formation of communal ties. Yet for a *digital* community to take shape, such activities must be accompanied by dialogic engagement. Table 6.9 offers an over-view of the dialogic activities of all four embassies.

As Table 6.9 demonstrates, dialogic engagement is also rare among Lithuanian embassies. Over a two to three month period, most embassies failed to engage with followers, be it by querying them to understand their needs or desires, providing opportunities for cocreation of con-tent, or supplying requested information. Follower concerns were also routinely ignored.

The embassy with the highest dialogic engagement rates was Lithuania's embassy to the UK, yet even in this case, the overall reply to follower comments was six, a low figure. When the UK embassy did reply to comments, it was usually to provide information on the time and place of diaspora events or to supply the e-mail address of the embassy. Instances of dialogic engagement with the embassy to the USA included a photograph competition among embassy followers and a post querying

Table 6.9 Analysis of Lithuanian embassies' dialogic engagement with Facebook users (based on sample of 280 Facebook posts)

Components of dialogic engagement (Manor, 2017)	Embassies			
	Canada	Ireland	UK	U.S.
Average number of comments per post	0	2	3	2
Embassy replies to follower comments/reactions	2	1	5	–
Number of responses to follower queries	1	–	4	–
Instances of supplying requested information	1	–	3	–
Number of publications of user-generated content	–	–	1	–
Number of overall response to followers' comments	1	–	6	–
Number of invitations to engage in conversations	–	–	–	–
Number of responses to followers' stated concerns	–	–	2	–
Instances of querying Facebook followers	1		1	1
Number of collaborative opportunities for creation of shared values	–	2	–	2

followers about the final resting place of a famous Lithuanian activist. Similarly, the sole opportunity for dialogic engagement with the Irish embassy was a drawing competition among children of diasporas, while the sole answer supplied by the Canadian embassy dealt with consular issues. It should be noted that the average Lithuanian post attracted few comments from followers. Yet it is possible that embassies receive few comments, as they usually fail to respond to followers.

Conclusions

Standing on the floor of the 1980 Democratic National Convention, Edward Kennedy was forced to acknowledge the demise of the Kennedy dynasty. Having failed to win the Democratic nomination, "the handsomest of the handsome Kennedys" took to the stage to address his campaign followers for the last time. True to the norms of American political oratory, Kennedy exited the Presidential stage with a burst of optimism. As is quoted at the beginning of this chapter, his swan song proclaimed that "*The work goes on, the cause endures, the hope still lives, and the dream shall never die.*"

In its early stages, the process of the digitalization of public diplomacy was accompanied by similar optimism. MFAs, embassies, and diplomats regarded digital technologies as boundary spanners, which would enable them to overcome many of the limitations of traditional diplomacy. Using digital platforms, diplomats could converse with foreign populations, embassies could establish ties with diasporas, and MFAs could reach citizens of enemy nations, thus laying the foundations for peace. Yet by 2014, much of this optimism had disappeared. As the words "trolls," "bots" and "disinformation" came to dominate diplomats' world, digital platforms were increasingly regarded as the undoing of diplomacy, as tools used to systematically erode trust, faith, and relationships. Moreover, it soon became evident that diplomats were unwilling (or unable) to use digital platforms for conversations and relationship building. Monologue still ruled supreme over public diplomacy activities.

The results of this chapter should supposedly add to the current pessimistic public diplomacy outlook. The in-depth review of the digital activities of African MFA and Lithuanian embassies demonstrate yet again that diplomatic institutions fail to leverage digital platforms toward relationship building and dialogic engagement with digital publics, be they foreign populations or diaspora communities. While public diplomacy is public-centric, it is also egocentric in that MFAs speak at—not with—digital publics. Moreover, the case studies analyzed in this chapter demonstrate that relatively small MFAs fail to utilize digital technologies to offset physical limitations, such as a small number of embassies abroad. These results are in line with a host of studies published between 2011 and 2018.

And yet, this chapter ends on an optimistic note. While dialogic engagement may not take place, diplomatic institutions do use digital platforms to offer online publics a prism, or narrative, through which events shaping the nation and the world may be understood. Ethiopia's narrative focuses on the stability and prosperity of the Horn of Africa, while Rwanda's narrative uses the past to illuminate the present. In both cases, MFAs help digital publics make sense of a chaotic world. Additionally, followers of the Kenyan MFA may learn about national endeavors to increase financial growth while those who follow Botswana may learn about global events ranging from the Syrian Civil War to North Korea's nuclear weapons program.

Narratives serve an important function for both foreign and domestic publics. As Daryl Copeland (2013) argued, diplomats are experts at creating a national prism, or narrative through which citizens can make sense of global events. Citizens and foreign populations following African MFAs online now have unprecedented insight into these nations' diplomatic goals, visions, and policy priorities. The process of democratizing diplomacy is thus progressing, albeit at a slow pace.

Equally important, this chapter finds that the digital divide between African MFAs and Western or Asian ministries continues to narrow. While the MFAs of Israel, Norway, Poland, and the USA may not excel at dialogic engagement, they do offer digital publics opportunities to engage with diplomats in the forms of Q&A sessions, interactions on MFA blogospheres, smartphone applications, and even Twitter survey questions. As the digital divide continues to narrow, African MFAs may adopt similar practices. This chapter, therefore, argues yet again that digitalization is a long-term process that gradually impacts the norms, values, and self-narratives of diplomats and their institutions.

Lastly, the analysis of the Facebook activities of the four Lithuanian embassies does demonstrate an attempt to nurture an emotional bond between diasporas and their country of origin. While Lithuanian embassies do not practice dialogic engagement with diasporas, they do offer a breadth of information pertaining to community events and issues that are of concern to community members such as cultural fairs, scholarship opportunities, language lessons, and national day celebrations. Embassy Facebook profiles thus become an indispensable bulletin board for the diaspora community, thereby further strengthening the bond between the embassy, the nation, and the diaspora.

Bean and Comor (2017) have argued that the digitalization of public diplomacy was accompanied by the promise of measuring the impact of public diplomacy activities. Quantitative parameters such as an MFA's digital reach, its number of followers, and its average rates of likes and shares could "prove" the efficacy of public diplomacy activities. Yet measurement criteria invariably determine one's digital activities. MFAs that focus on measuring their digital reach will soon become consumed by "vanity metrics" such as numbers of likes and shares and will fail to pay attention to their dialogic activities. Subsequently, they may fail to foster relationships with digital publics and facilitate the acceptance of their nation's foreign policy. This chapter's quantitative model measured the scope of dialogue and engagement between MFAs, embassies, and digital publics given this book's focus on the practice of the "new" public diplomacy. MFAs who adopt this model for self-assessment may soon also adopt dialogic working routines, norms, and metaphors.

Of all the MFAs examined in this book, it is the Lithuanian one that best demonstrates how the process of digitalization impacts diplomatic institutions. The migration of the MFA to digital platforms and its utilization of digital technologies have begun to impact its norms, values and working routines. Recently, the MFA adopted the metaphor or self-narrative of "listening." By monitoring digital conversations, the MFA may gain insight into other countries' policy priorities, the way in which Lithuania is viewed by foreign populations, and new policy initiatives of Lithuanian allies. The metaphor of listening will soon lead to the formation of new working routines in the shape of "digital teams" tasked with monitoring and analyzing digital conversations and supplying relevant desks with insight. From a normative perspective, Lithuanian diplomats will be asked to regard social media content as another form of diplomatic reporting that should inform the policy formulation process.

The footprints of the digital society have also been visible throughout this chapter. The analysis of African MFAs suggests that they too create a self-narrative through which they present themselves to digital publics. This is yet another form of digital branding. The Kenyan iBrand is one of regional leadership, while the Botswana iBrand is one of good governance. Additionally, New Zealand's vision of collaborative policymaking suggests that the MFA has adopted the norms and values celebrated by the digital society. First, the MFA practices a more open form of diplomacy in which information once kept behind closed doors is shared with digital publics, thus adhering to the norms of transparency and openness. Second, the MFA has embraced a networked logic in which it hopes to establish links with connected individuals to collaboratively provide solutions to shared challenges. Finally, the MFA seeks to challenge, or blur, the rigid distinction between the domestic and the foreign as both publics will be invited to partake in the policy formulation process. Space and borders will thus be annihilated and diplomacy will become glocalized.

Finally, both the technological and societal prisms may be employed to further elucidate the results of this chapter. From the perspective of the technological prism, African MFAs' use of digital platforms to interact with diasporas could have a re-territorializing effect as the borders of African nations extend and come to include Africans living abroad. As Victoria Bernal (2014) argued, through digitalization the concepts of nationhood and citizenship undergo fundamental change. For instance, digital interactions between diplomats and diasporas may lead expats to become more involved in the politics of their countries of origin. The concept of citizenship would thus no longer be tied to one's physical location. As diasporas are dispersed globally, the concept of the nation would also become detached from physical borders, while the local and the global would collide into one hybrid space as diasporas and citizens collaborate in real time to promote national interests. In the process, the emotional bond that ties a diaspora to its country of origin may grow ever stronger.

Yet this chapter finds that African MFAs do not place an emphasis on diaspora outreach. One reason for this may be that digital platforms empower diasporas who can openly criticize their former government and share such criticism online. Moreover, diasporas can digitally organize to condemn the policies of their former governments, counter government narratives, and even thwart a government's diplomatic initiatives. Such was the case with the Eritrean diaspora which used digital platforms to openly condemn and rally opposition against its former government. For this reason, some MFAs may be more conservative when using digital technologies for diaspora outreach. And so, technology does not determine diplomatic practice. As the societal prism would suggest, social beings and social institutions determine how technology will be used. By not interacting with diasporas, some MFAs may cause a de-territorializing effect that clearly illuminates the demarcation line between the nation and its diasporas.

The optimistic note on which this chapter ends is carried to the next, which examines how digitalization may be used to overcome the limitation of traditional diplomacy.

REFERENCES

Adesina, O. S. (2017). Foreign policy in an era of digital diplomacy. *Cogent Social Sciences, 3*(1), 1297175.

Archetti, C. (2012). The impact of new media on diplomatic practice: An evolutionary model of change. *The Hague Journal of Diplomacy, 7*(2), 181–206.

Bean, H., & Comor, E. (2017). Data-driven public diplomacy: A critical and reflexive assessment. *All Azimuth, 1*.

Bernal, V. (2014). *Nation as network: Diaspora, cyberspace, and citizenship.* Chicago: University of Chicago Press.

Bjola, C. (2018). *Digital diplomacy and impression management.* Presentation, London: Canada House.

Bjola, C., & Jiang, L. (2015). Social media and public diplomacy: A comparative analysis of the digital diplomatic strategies of the EU, US and Japan in China. In C. Bjola & M. Holmes (Eds.), *Digital diplomacy theory and practice* (pp. 71–88). Oxon: Routledge.

Bjola, C., & Manor, I. (2018). Revisiting Putnam's two-level game theory in the digital age: Domestic digital diplomacy and the Iran nuclear deal. *Cambridge Review of International Affairs*, 1–30.

Bortree, D. S., & Seltzer, T. (2009). Dialogic strategies and outcomes: An analysis of environmental advocacy groups' Facebook profiles. *Public Relations Review, 35*(3), 317–319.

Causey, C., & Howard, P. N. (2013). Delivering digital public diplomacy. In R. S. Zaharna, A. Arsenault, & A. Fisher (Eds.), *Relational, networked and collaborative approaches to public diplomacy* (pp. 144–156). New York, NY: Taylor & Francis.

Clarke, A. (2015). Business as usual? An evolution of British and Canadian digital diplomacy as policy change. In C. Bjola & M. Holmes (Eds.), *Digital diplomacy theory and practice* (pp. 111–126). Oxon: Routledge.

Clarke, V., & Braun, V. (2014). Thematic analysis. In *Encyclopedia of quality of life and well-being research* (pp. 6626–6628). Springer: Dordrecht.

Comor, E., & Bean, H. (2012). America's 'engagement' delusion: Critiquing a public diplomacy consensus. *International Communication Gazette, 74*(3), 203–220.

Copeland, D. (2013). Taking diplomacy public: Science, technology and foreign ministries in a heteropolar world. In R. S. Zaharna, A. Arsenault, & A. Fisher (Eds.), *Relational, networked and collaborative approaches to public diplomacy* (pp. 56–69). New York, NY: Taylor & Francis.

Cowan, G., & Arsenault, A. (2008). Moving from monologue to dialogue to collaboration: The three layers of public diplomacy. *The Annals of the American Academy of Political and Social Science, 616*(1), 10–30.

Cull, N. J. (2008). Public diplomacy: Taxonomies and histories. *The Annals of the American Academy of Political and Social Science, 616*(1), 31–54.

Ferguson, J. E., Salominaite, E., & Boersma, K. (2016). Past, present and future: How the Lithuanian diaspora in the Netherlands accumulates human capital from social capital. *Journal of Ethnic and Migration Studies, 42*(13), 2205–2225.

Gregory, B. (2011). American public diplomacy: Enduring characteristics, elusive transformation. *The Hague Journal of Diplomacy, 6*(3–4), 351–372.

Hocking, B. (2005). Rethinking the "new" public diplomacy. In J. Melissen (Ed.), *The new public diplomacy: Soft power in international relations* (pp. 28–44). New York: Palgrave Macmillan.

Hocking, B., & Melissen, J. (2015). *Diplomacy in the digital age*. Clingendael: Netherlands Institute of International Relations.

Hughes, D. J., Rowe, M., Batey, M., & Lee, A. (2012). A tale of two sites: Twitter vs. Facebook and the personality predictors of social media usage. *Computers in Human Behavior, 28*(2), 561–569.

Kampf, R., Manor, I., & Segev, E. (2015). Digital diplomacy 2.0? A cross-national comparison of public engagement in Facebook and Twitter. *The Hague Journal of Diplomacy, 10*(4), 331–362.

Kwak, H., Lee, C., Park, H., & Moon, S. (2010, April). *What is Twitter, a social network or a news media?* Proceedings of the 19th international conference on world wide web (pp. 591–600). AcM.

Lutyens, A. (2018). *Investigating New Zealand's model of democratized public diplomacy* [In person].

Manor, I. (2015a, January 19). *In digital diplomacy a narrowing digital divide-part 1* [Blog]. Retrieved from https://digdipblog.com/2015/01/19/divide/.

Manor, I. (2015b, January 26). *In digital diplomacy a narrowing digital divide-part 2* [Blog]. Retrieved from https://digdipblog.com/2015/01/26/divide-2/.

Manor, I. (2016a). Are we there yet: Have MFA s realized the potential of digital diplomacy? *Brill Research Perspectives in Diplomacy and Foreign Policy, 1*(2), 1–110.

Manor, I. (2016b, February 28). *How the UK & US are fighting ISIS online* [Blog]. Retrieved from https://digdipblog.com/2016/02/28/how-the-uk-us-are-fighting-isis-online/.

Manor, I. (2017). America's selfie—Three years later. *Place Branding and Public Diplomacy, 13*(4), 308–324.

Manor, I. (2018, April 27). *Delivering digital consular aid* [Blog]. Retrieved from https://digdipblog.com/2018/04/27/delivering-digital-consular-aid/.

Manor, I., & Crilley, R. (2018). Visually framing the Gaza War of 2014: The Israel Ministry of Foreign Affairs on Twitter. *Media, War & Conflict*.

Manor, I., & Kampf, R. (2019). Digital nativity and digital engagement: Implications for the practice of dialogic digital diplomacy (Forthcoming).

Manor, I., & Segev, E. (2015). America's selfie: How the US portrays itself on its social media accounts. In C. Bjola & M. Holmes (Eds.), *Digital diplomacy theory and practice* (pp. 89–108). Oxon: Routledge.

McNutt, K. (2014). Public engagement in the Web 2.0 era: Social collaborative technologies in a public sector context. *Canadian Public Administration, 57*(1), 49–70.

Melissen, J. (2005). The new public diplomacy: Between theory and practice. In J. Melissen (Ed.), *The new public diplomacy: Soft power in international relations* (pp. 3–27). New York: Palgrave Macmillan.

Metzgar, E. T. (2012). Is it the medium or the message? Social media, American public diplomacy & Iran. *Global Media Journal, 12*(21), 1.

Miller, D., & Horst, H. A. (2017). The digital and the human: A prospectus for digital anthropology. In H. A. Horst and D. Miller (Eds.), *Digital anthropology* (pp. 3–38). London: Bloomsbury Academic.

Ministry of Foreign Affairs of Kenya. (2014). *Kenyan diaspora policy*. Retrieved from http://www.mfa.go.ke/wp-content/uploads/2016/09/Kenya-Diaspora-Policy.pdf, July 22, 2017.

OECD. (2012). *Connecting with emigrants: A global profile of diasporas 2015*. Retrieved from http://www.oecd.org/publications/connecting-with-emigrants-9789264239845-en.htm.

Pamment, J. (2013). Introduction. In J. Pamment, *New public diplomacy in the 21st century: A comparative study of policy and practice* (pp. 1–19). Abingdon: Routledge.

Pamment, J. (2016). Digital diplomacy as transmedia engagement: Aligning theories of participatory culture with international advocacy campaigns. *New Media & Society, 18*(9), 2046–2062.

Paulauskas, R. (2018). *Understanding Lithuania's digital diplomacy model* [In person].

Rana, K. S. (2013). Diaspora diplomacy and public diplomacy. In R. S. Zaharna, A. Arsenault, & A. Fisher (Eds.), *Relational, networked and collaborative approaches to public diplomacy* (pp. 70–85). New York, NY: Taylor & Francis.

Reynolds, A., & McCombs, M. (2002). News influence on our pictures of the world. In *Media effects* (pp. 11–28). Abingdon: Routledge.

Russo, P. (2013, February 28). *Digital diplomacy in the Middle East and North Africa* [Blog]. Retrieved from https://blogs.fco.gov.uk/pipparusso/2013/02/28/digital-diplomacy-in-the-middle-east-and-north-africa/.

Saunders, H. H. (2013). The relational paradigm and sustained dialogue. In R. S. Zaharna, A. Arsenault, & A. Fisher (Eds.), *Relational, networked and collaborative approaches to public diplomacy* (pp. 132–143). New York, NY: Taylor & Francis.

Sharma, D. (2015, June). Digital diplomacy: Making friends in the age of Facebook. *Tablet Magazine.* Retrieved from https://www.tabletmag.com/jewish-news-and-politics/192177/digital-diplomacy.

Spry, D. (2018). Facebook diplomacy: A data-driven, user-focused approach to Facebook use by diplomatic missions. *Media International Australia, 168*(1), 62–80.

Taylor, M., & Kent, M. L. (2014). Dialogic engagement: Clarifying foundational concepts. *Journal of Public Relations Research, 26*(5), 384–398.

Vanc, A. M. (2012). Post-9/11 US public diplomacy in eastern Europe: Dialogue via new technologies or face-to-face communication? *Global Media Journal, 11*(21), 1–19.

Waters, R. D., Burnett, E., Lamm, A., & Lucas, J. (2009). Engaging stakeholders through social networking: How nonprofit organizations are using Facebook. *Public Relations Review, 35*(2), 102–106.

CHAPTER 7

Overcoming the Limitations of Traditional Diplomacy

> We few, we happy few, we band of brothers; For he to-day that sheds his blood with me Shall be my brother; be he ne'er so vile, This day shall gentle his condition; And gentlemen in England now a-bed Shall think themselves accurs'd they were not here, And hold their manhoods cheap whiles any speaks That fought with us upon Saint Crispin's day.
>
> —Henry V, William Shakespeare

On May 21, 1420, a treaty was signed in the cathedral of the French city of Troyes. At first glance, this treaty was no different from most diplomatic treaties as it too sought to form an alliance between two nations through the marriage of their monarchs, Henry V of England and the French Princess Catherine of Valois. Marriages between royal houses were a common means of creating military alliances, pursuing peace, ending costly wars, and increasing a nation's treasure. Yet the Treaty of Troyes was also historic as it joined together the crowns of England and France to create a new united kingdom. For the first time, a British king would also be "heir and regent of the Kingdom of France" (Jones, 2014, p. 10).

Alas, Henry V would not reign over France for long. Within two years of the Treaty of Troyes, he was dead. His successor to the thrones of England and France was the infant Henry VI. England now found itself in a precarious position. The French people had known, respected, and felt the wrath of Henry V, who had waged a war on their nation. Yet

© The Author(s) 2019
I. Manor, *The Digitalization of Public Diplomacy*,
Palgrave Macmillan Series in Global Public Diplomacy,
https://doi.org/10.1007/978-3-030-04405-3_7

they knew nothing of his infant son, who was locked away in a remote British castle, nor did they feel any allegiance to him. The English feared that under such conditions the French nobility might attempt to restore a Frenchman to the throne.

To contend with this crisis of legitimacy, England launched a public diplomacy campaign. The goal of the campaign was to persuade the French population that the infant Henry VI was the legitimate king of France not because of his father's military victories, but because it had been ordained by God. To this end, the English hung fine tapestries in churches throughout France illustrating the lines of succession of the English and French thrones, both of which ended with Henry VI, the son of an English king and a French queen. Henry's claim to the French throne was thus sealed by the very blood that coursed through his veins. The tapestry also depicted the infant standing next to St. Louis, suggesting that Henry VI was a source of unity, a king who could bring peace to a France ravaged by a brutal civil war (Jones, 2014, p. 40). In addition to tapestries, the English hired poets to write songs narrating Henry's majestic ascent to the throne.

Between the tapestries hung in churches and poems recited in local markets, the French population could scarcely avoid English public diplomacy. Nonetheless, the English decided to stage a splendid visual spectacle that would cement Henry's authority: a grand coronation in the French city of Paris. On the morning of December 2, 1431, Henry VI rode into Paris on a white horse, accompanied by a procession of British and French nobles, administrators, and bureaucrats all adorned in the finest cloth and bearing emblems of opulence. The coronation ceremony itself was meant to symbolize the joining of the crowns of France and England. Actors thus depicted the young king symbolically wearing two crowns while conferring with both English and French advisors under a golden canopy bearing the arms of France and England (Styles & Allmand, 1982).

Yet the British campaign was more propaganda than public diplomacy. In creating their tapestries depicting Henry's lineage, the English had rewritten history, ignored French law, disregarded facts, and lied (and the French knew it). In their spectacle coronation in Paris, the English ignored the customs and ceremonies of the French nobility and orchestrated a British ceremony (and the French felt it). Henry VI's claim over the French throne remained weak and would ultimately come to an end in 1453.

While the English public diplomacy campaign in France might seem somewhat outdated by employing tapestries rather than tweets, it is representative of a recurring feature in the practice of public diplomacy—using technology to overcome the limitations of traditional diplomacy. During the time of Henry VI, diplomacy was mostly conducted by ambassadors posted to royal courts. Yet if the English were to win over the hearts and minds of the French population, they needed to step outside the palace walls and engage with their new citizens. France, however, was a vast nation and its English rulers could not visit every city, attend prayers at every church, and address nobles in every town hall. The distances were too large, the cost would be too great, and the manpower was too limited. They thus turned to the technology of the day—tapestries—which would visualize and narrate historical events in a way that could be understood by all French citizens, nobles, and peasants alike. Moreover, they strategically hung the tapestries in churches where they would be seen by most of the population. In the fifteenth century, religion was not so much a California lifestyle choice but a guarantee against purgatory. Technology was thus employed to enable English public diplomacy to overcome spatial and financial limitations.

Nearly six centuries later, technology plays a similar role. As this chapter will demonstrate, present-day diplomats have sought to employ digital technologies to annihilate time and space, transcend national borders, address global constituencies, overcome hostile media landscapes, and interact with the populations of enemy nations. As such, the need to overcome the limitations of traditional diplomacy has contributed to the process of the digitalization of public diplomacy. Importantly, digital technologies have also consistently increased the distances that diplomats can traverse. While tapestries enabled the English to reach out to across France, digital technologies enable diplomats to circle the globe. Thus, the use of digital technologies to overcome the limitation of traditional diplomacy may be understood through the prism of diplomacy at a distance, which is elaborated on in the following section.

DIPLOMACY AT A DISTANCE

Zygmunt Bauman and David Lyon (2016) have asserted that the digital society is one that operates at a distance. This is because digital technologies enable digital society members to act in ever greater remoteness. An American drone flying in the skies of Pakistan can be operated from a trailer outside Las Vegas, while a nurse sitting in her living room in Paris can attend a course taught in Berlin. Importantly, Bauman and Lyon argued that remoteness, coupled with automation, creates a moral distance between an action and the person responsible for that action (Bauman & Lyon, 2016, pp. 85–87). When a drone flying at high altitudes selects a target and fires on that target automatically, the drone's operator becomes a mere spectator. He or she has no immediate sense of responsibility for the action of the automated drone, as the reach of an individual's ethical principles is limited to that which is in their sight. Things that happen at a distance are beyond human sight and therefore beyond the reach of individual ethics. Given that digital technologies enable people to act at greater and greater distances, they systematically reduce the reach of human ethics. Bauman and Lyon's analysis of remoteness and automation is emblematic of the technological prism as they stipulate that technologies shape societal norms as well as the moral compass of society members.

Of course, remoteness and automation are not limited to military technologies. Bauman and Lyon suggested that the function of many digital technologies is to sort digital society members into categories of differential treatment (ibid., pp. 92–93). Such is the case with algorithms that determine who may be awarded a frequent flyer credit card, a loyalty card to certain shops, or a discount on Amazon's website. Even more importantly, algorithms now determine who is eligible for a mortgage or a college loan. These decisions are no longer made by the local banker or branch manager (or even onsite) but by an automated algorithm that sifts through databases located in faraway locations. And so, the decision of who will receive a mortgage or a loan is once again done at a distance and is decoupled from ethical qualms.

Automation and remoteness are now also used to determine who may enter a nation and who may not. Algorithms sifting through mass databases separate wanted visitors from unwanted immigrants. Bauman and Lyon (2016) suggested that such sorting is no longer done locally at a given border, but globally. Unwanted immigrants are stopped at their points of departure rather than when they arrive at their destination. In this way, space is manipulated by digital technologies. The distance between an immigrant's point of departure and his destination is exponentially increased, as he or she may not even board a plane. Conversely, the decision as to who may or may not board planes is made by a remote algorithm and communicated in real-time across vast distances to border police officers. Space is thus extended for the immigrant and diminished for the immigration officer.

The technological functionality of automation and remoteness, therefore, transforms the digital society into a society that operates at a distance. As algorithms are increasingly used to determine the fates of digital society members, and as new technologies increase remoteness, more and more aspects of daily life can be done at a distance, ranging from remote wars and remote banking to remote health. If analyzed through the technological prism, the ability to act at a distance imposes the logic of doing things at a distance on numerous social realms. If banking and war can be done at a distance, why not diplomacy?

Manuel Castells (2013) also believed that the manipulation of time and space is a fundamental characteristic of the digital society. Employing the societal prism Castells suggested that in the industrial age, time was allocated to specific tasks. Workers would labor in the factory from 9 to 5, eat dinner at 6, and listen to the radio with their families at 8. By contrast, the digital and networked society is one that systematically employs digital technologies to annihilate time. This is achieved by compressing time and rendering it meaningless, as is the case with global financial transactions that are completed within seconds. Space is annihilated as two events can take place at the same time across great distances, as is the case with international Skype calls. In other words, Castells believed that the *desire* to overcome spatial and temporal limitations is inherently digital and thus often pursued by members of the digital society.

This chapter examines how the digitalization of public diplomacy has been impacted by the logic of doing things at a distance and the quest to annihilate time and space. Its main argument is that the desire to overcome the limitations of traditional diplomacy was central to the process of public diplomacy's digitalization. Indeed, as diplomats began to experiment with digital technologies, they soon sought to implement these to overcome lack of bilateral ties, bypass critical media landscapes, and interact with foreign populations that were otherwise inaccessible. These attempts are representative of the logic of the digital society, as they all constitute a form of diplomacy at a distance, or diplomacy that is done remotely using digital technologies. Moreover, this chapter demonstrates that public diplomacy is now preoccupied with attempts to condense time and space.

Yet this chapter also proposes that diplomacy at a distance, like war at a distance, is accompanied by the limitation of sight. As is explored throughout the chapter, the use of digital technologies to overcome the limitations of traditional diplomacy was often hampered by diplomats' inabilities to interact meaningfully or converse with digital publics. This may have been a result of diplomats' inabilities to see who they were interacting with. When a diplomat addresses a university class, his audience is within sight. The same cannot be said of digital audiences who have an amorphous quality and who cannot be seen. Thus, just as sight limits the ethical reach of a drone operator, so it may limit the relational reach of a diplomat.

Of all the technologies employed by diplomats to overcome the limitations of traditional diplomacy, none centered on annihilating time and space as did virtual embassies. Through virtual embassies, diplomats sought to transcend borders and condense time. Therefore, this chapter begins by reviewing and analyzing the activities of four virtual embassies launched between 2007 and 2015. This review is chronological to demonstrate that digitalization is a long-term process that is influencing the norms and working routines of diplomatic institutions. Next, the chapter reviews a new case study: the activities of Palestine's virtual embassy launched in late 2015. Lastly, the chapter explores two case studies of public diplomacy campaigns aimed at reaching global audiences, thus, again, attempting to render time and space meaningless. The following section analyzes one of the world's first virtual embassies, launched by the Swedish Institute in 2007.

ON VIRTUAL EMBASSIES

Virtual embassies have accompanied the digitalization of public diplomacy since the early 2000s. One of the first virtual embassies was launched by the Swedish Institute in 2007 in the virtual world of Second Life. Named the Second House of Sweden, the embassy was the virtual extension of Sweden's new flagship embassy built in Washington, DC. The purpose of Second House of Sweden, however, was not to strengthen bilateral ties with other countries or offer visitors consular services. Second House of Sweden was meant to serve as a cultural institute that would strengthen Sweden's national brand by showcasing its culture and art (Pamment, 2013).

The Swedish government was no stranger to digital experiments, and its foreign minister, Carl Bildt, was an avid digital evangelist who had championed the integration of digital technologies into the conduct of diplomacy. In 1994, Bildt sent one of the first diplomatic emails to U.S. President Bill Clinton (Sotiriu, 2015). By 2005, Bildt was one of the first foreign ministers to manage his own blog site, posting articles on Swedish foreign policy and Sweden's perspective on global affairs. Ambassadors serving in Sweden at the time became enthusiastic readers of the blog, as it offered unique insight into the policy priorities of the Swedish government (E. Manor, personal communication, January 18, 2018). In 2007, Bildt also became one of the first foreign ministers to enter the virtual world of Second Life and inaugurate an embassy.

While Second House of Sweden was supposed to obtain a traditional public diplomacy goal using culture to promote a national brand, it was also meant to overcome the spatial and temporal limitations of traditional diplomacy. By launching the embassy on the virtual world of Second Life, the Swedish Institute created the world's first global embassy, which could be visited by any individual around the world with an Internet connection. Moreover, visitors could interact with one another and with Swedish officials and artists, regardless of the physical distance between them. Time was also rendered meaningless as there are no time zones in Second Life. This entire virtual world is tuned to the time in California.

Second House of Sweden was thus a global cultural institute dedicated to interacting with a global constituency. Between 2007 and 2012, the embassy held numerous events including film festivals, art exhibits, Swedish language lessons, virtual meetings with Swedish artists, and book launches. Yet as Chapter 3 details, not all Second Life users were pleased with the Swedish government's intrusion into their virtual world. Some protested the embassy either by threatening to have a sex party on its roof, hacking and disrupting embassy events, or visiting the embassy while wearing Nazi uniforms. Moreover, while the virtual embassy offered visitors a unique digital experience, most events were poorly attended and the embassy failed to create a virtual community with which it could interact on a regular basis (Pamment, 2013).

In 2012, the Swedish Institute decided to close Second House of Sweden. Within two years, Bildt would leave the post of foreign minister. His departure seems to have marked a transition in the process of

Swedish digitalization. The Swedish MFA, in particular, adopted a more conservative approach to digital communications that focused less on digital extermination. Practitioners of public diplomacy would come to refer to a transition in communicative cultures following a foreign minister's departure as the "Carl Bildt Effect." Parting from ministers thus proved such sweet sorrow.

The relationship between virtual embassies, time, and space begins to become apparent when one evaluates Second House of Sweden. Traditionally, the reach of diplomatic institutions was quite limited. Embassies and their staffs operated mainly in nations' capitals and could only interact with a finite amount of people. While embassy staffers could give talks at universities, diaspora events, schools and chambers of commerce, or give interviews to the press, they could not interact with an entire nation (let alone an entire globe). Yet that was exactly what Sweden sought to do. The Swedish Institute's desire was to use digital technologies to render time and space meaningless by operating a global embassy in a realm without time zones. Manuel Castells would argue that Sweden's vision was the diplomatic manifestation of the logic of the digital society.

The relationship between Second of House of Sweden and doing things at a distance is more complex. On the one hand, Swedish officials operating the virtual embassy from Stockholm could interact in real-time with Second Life users from Spain, Israel, or Argentina. Much like drone operators in Las Vegas, Swedish diplomats could thus conduct their tasks at a distance. On the other hand, Swedish officials' sight was not limited by this distance. While on Second Life, Swedish officials engaged with the avatars of other users. Thus, there was some semblance of physical interaction with embassy visitors, which may have mitigated the impact of distance on sight and digital interactions. This was not the case with America's virtual embassy to Iran, which is evaluated next.

VIRTUAL EMBASSY IRAN

In December 2011, the U.S. State Department launched Virtual Embassy Iran, a web-based platform that aimed to facilitate interactions between American diplomats and Iranian citizens. Unsurprisingly, the embassy was conceived during the tenure of Secretary of State Hillary Clinton and her two digital advisors, Alec Ross and Jared Cohen. Together these three had created a digital zeitgeist within the State Department that advocated for the use of digital technologies to openly interact with foreign citizens (for elaboration on the activities of this dynamic trio, see Chapter 3).

Unlike Second House of Sweden, the State Department's virtual embassy was meant to replace a brick and mortar embassy, as the USA has had no diplomatic presence in Iran since both countries severed ties in 1979. Virtual Embassy Iran would thus offer Iranians information about travelling to the USA, applying for U.S. visas and opportunities for studying at U.S. universities. Equally important, the embassy would seek to foster two-way conversations between American diplomats and Iranians, narrate American policies in the region, demonstrate how American values inform its diplomatic initiatives, outline America's vision for its future relationship with Iran, and demonstrate a commitment to engagement with Iran (engagement being the cornerstone of Barack Obama's foreign policy—see Chapter 3). As one senior policy maker stated during the launch of the virtual embassy, "Despite our differences with the Iranian regime, we still have a deep desire for engagement and dialogue with the Iranian people. So for us this is a mission to the Iranian people" (Metzgar, 2012).

The goals of Virtual Embassy Iran were made apparent in a video of Secretary Clinton welcoming visitors and stating:

> This is a platform for us to communicate with each other, openly and without fear, about the United States, about our policies, our culture and the American people. You can also find information here about opportunities to study in the United States, or to obtain a visa to come visit us (Clinton, 2011).

Clinton also said that the embassy was designed to meet the needs and desires of Iranians and that it was "shaped by what you wanted" and provided an opportunity for "you to tell us more about what you think and why." While the Iranian regime blocked the website soon after its launch, it still attracted some 300,000 visitors who used proxy servers to bypass Iranian censorship (Metzgar, 2012). In addition to the web-based platform, Virtual Embassy Iran would come to include a Farsi language Facebook profile, YouTube channel, Instagram account, and Twitter feed. As of August 2018, the combined audience of these platforms is 1.1 million digital users, and Farsi language YouTube videos have been watched by more than 3 million individuals.

Virtual Embassy Iran was thus a public diplomacy tool, which relied on digital technologies to overcome the limitations of traditional diplomacy, in this case, the absence of bilateral ties between the USA and Iran. The launch of the virtual embassy was made possible thanks to the digital endorsement of Secretary of State Clinton, the Obama administration's emphasis on engagement as a foreign policy tool, and a digital mindset within the State Department, which hoped to augment diplomacy with technology where possible by complementing "traditional foreign policy tools with newly innovated and adapted instruments of statecraft that fully leverage the networks, technologies and demographics of our interconnected world" (cited in Metzgar, 2012).

However, when evaluating the activities of Virtual Embassy Iran, Metzgar found little evidence of two-way interactions between U.S. diplomats and Iranians. She concluded that the embassy was primarily used for one-way message dissemination and debunking myths about America. Metzgar (2012) did, however, emphasize that the virtual embassy allowed the USA to manage its image among Iranians, counter America's depiction in Iran as a great devil, and build soft power resources among tech-savvy Iranians.

Like Metzgar, scholars have consistently found that online interactions and two-way conversations between diplomats and digital publics rarely occur (Bjola & Jiang, 2015; Clarke, 2015; Comor & Bean, 2012; Hocking & Melissen, 2015; Manor & Crilley, 2018b). Some have argued that resources may prove an important barrier for digital interactions (Cha, Yeo, & Kim, 2014) as these require that questions be posed to followers, answers be analyzed, concerns be addressed, opportunities for collaborations be created, and social media accounts be constantly monitored. All these demand committed digital staffers. Yet most digital departments tasked with utilizing digital technologies in MFAs are overburdened, overextended, and understaffed. This is even true of large MFAs such as the U.S. State Department and the British FCO (Foreign and Commonwealth Office). Moreover, analyzing the needs, desires, and interests of digital publics may require the utilization of big data and sentiment analysis tools. These tools can, for instance, help diplomats identify popular topics or detect policy issues that are viewed as contentious. The use of big data and sentiment tools also requires resources, be it in acquiring certain software or training diplomats in the use of free analytics software. As such, lack of resources often leads to one-way message dissemination, which is far less demanding than digital interactions. The fault, dear Brutus, is not in diplomats' stars, but in their depleted funds.

Others have suggested that MFAs' communicative cultures may serve as barriers to online conversations. McNutt (2014) suggested that digital interactions require an organizational willingness to shift public engagement activities from a broadcast paradigm to a communicative one. She employed the term "Government 2.0" to reference the embrace of a communicative ethos that includes transparency, participatory opportunities (such as crowd-sourcing), co-production, collaboration, and openness. Scholars have, however, characterized MFAs as change-resistant organizations that fear losing control over the communication process, and as such prefer one-way message dissemination to two-way digital conversation (Copeland, 2013). The US' inability to converse with Iranians may have thus stemmed from a conservative communicative culture.

Comor and Bean (2012) suggested that online conversations are rare as MFAs prioritize persuasion and the management of dissent over interactions with foreign populations. Lastly, Spry (2018) and Lengel and Newsom argued that diplomats often fail to take into account the local cultures of the audiences they seek to interact with. This then serves as a barrier to digital interactions. Seo (2013) reached a similar conclusion when evaluating the digital activities of the U.S. embassy in South Korea.

Another possible explanation lies within the nature of doing things at a distance. As was the case with Sweden's virtual embassy, the U.S. embassy also employed digital technologies to transcend borders and manipulate space. Diplomats in Washington could interact with an individual in Tehran in real-time as if they were sitting beside one another. Yet unlike Sweden's virtual embassy, Iranians visiting the virtual embassy had no physical semblance. They did not bear any physical traits, assume a physical shape, nor did they even adopt a digital avatar that would act as a surrogate body. As such, the Iranian public with which U.S. diplomats were meant to interact was an amorphic one: It existed solely in the minds of American diplomats like a metaphor or an image. This may have reduced diplomats' abilities to interact with Iranian digital publics, as these were beyond the sight of American diplomats, much like ethical considerations that are beyond the sights of drone operators or modern-day bank managers.

Importantly, the difficulty of interacting with a digital, amorphic public may also be tied to diplomacy's traditional reliance on proximity. Historically, ambassadors were stationed at foreign courts as it was there that diplomats could foster ties with influential nobles, create alliances with powerful families, and gauge the temperament of monarchs (Roberts, 2017). Today, diplomacy still rests on proximity. Press attachés cultivate close working relationships with influential journalists, ambassadors to multilateral forums create coalitions with their peers, and public diplomacy officers work alongside diaspora leaders. Diplomacy at a distance is thus the antithesis of diplomacy's traditional relationship with space. As remoteness replaces proximity, the audiences of diplomacy slowly slip out of sight. Unlike Sweden's embassy to Second Life, Virtual Embassy Iran is still active. Following in the US footsteps, Israel launched its Twitter embassy in 2013.

ISRAEL IN THE GCC

On July 21, 2013, the Israeli MFA established its first virtual embassy in the form of a Twitter account. Named "Israel in the GCC," the embassy was meant to foster relations between Israeli diplomats and the populations of six Gulf countries who do not officially recognize Israel: Bahrain, Kuwait, Oman, Saudi Arabia, the United Arab Emirates, and Qatar (Ravid, 2013). According to Ravid, all six Sunni countries had a common strategic interest with Israel—preventing Iran from obtaining a nuclear weapon. The embassy's stated mission was to facilitate dialogue with Arab and Muslim Twitter users on a host of issues including business, science, politics, and civil society (ibid.). To this end, the embassy invited followers to online Q&A sessions with Israeli leaders, including the president and the prime minister. In addition, the embassy shared goodwill messages from Israel's leaders, such as a video from the Israeli Prime Minister wishing Ramadan Karim to Muslims around the world.

As was the case with the Swedish and American embassies, Israel's virtual embassy was also designed to overcome the limitations of traditional diplomacy, namely the lack of diplomatic ties between Israel and six Gulf states. Yet unlike Virtual Embassy Iran, Israel's Twitter embassy did not offer consular information or discuss opportunities for studying in Israel. Rather it allowed Israeli diplomats to begin cultivating digital relationships with Twitter users in the Gulf, relationships that could possibly be leveraged to influence the policies of GCC governments. Moreover, the

Fig. 7.1 Israel in the GCC's first tweet (*Source* https://twitter.com/ IsraelintheGCC/status/357739965435744257)

embassy sought to base these relationships on shared concerns such as the menace of an Iranian nuclear bomb. As is the case with all virtual embassies, Israel in the GCC transcended time and space as Israeli diplomats conversed with Twitter users residing behind borders that were closed to Israeli citizens.

Israel's Twitter embassy also served as a means of overcoming another diplomatic challenge—a highly critical media landscape. Publications, media outlets and journalists active in the Gulf rarely interview Israeli officials, publish materials by Israeli diplomats or allow Israeli policymakers to comment on events, issues and actors shaping the region. Moreover, the framing of Israel in Gulf publications is highly negative. Media gatekeepers thus prevent Israeli diplomats from framing or narrating Israel's foreign and security policies. By launching a Twitter embassy, the Israeli MFA may have hoped to circumvent this critical media landscape and disseminate Israeli narratives directly among connected publics. As Sotiriu (2015) stated, the digitalization of public diplomacy included the promise of bypassing state-controlled media. Causey and Howard (2013) have written that social media does enable diplomats to bypass the media and disseminate information vertically, to digital publics, and horizontally, to other elites (Fig. 7.1).

As of August 2018, Israel in the GCC had attracted some 2000 followers, a relatively low figure when compared to other Israeli embassies. Israel's embassy to the EU has more than 7000 Twitter followers, its embassy to Kenya has 5000 followers and its Consulate in New York has 40,000 followers. One reason for this small number of followers might be a reluctance by Gulf citizens to interact openly with Israeli diplomats. Yet it may also be the results of limited digital activity on the part of the embassy. As can be seen in Graph 7.1, while Israel in the GCC was quite active in the first week of July 2013, the following months saw a rapid decrease in the number of tweets published by the embassy. As digital activity breeds followers and interest from digital society members, the embassy's lack of activity might account for its small following.

Moreover, Manor (2018) found that the embassy rarely offered opportunities for conversations with diplomats. Except for digital spectacles such as Q&A sessions, followers' comments and concerns remain unanswered. Manor concluded that as was the case with Virtual Embassy Iran, Israel's embassy also focused primarily on one-way message dissemination. Yet this may have been the result of the great distance between Israeli diplomats and citizens of the Gulf as most Israelis have never seen

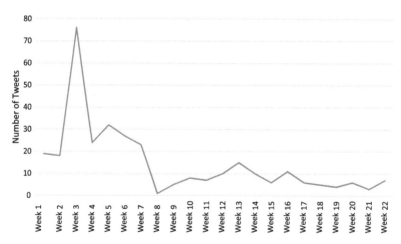

Graph 7.1   Number of tweets published per week by Israel in the GCC, July 2013–January 2014

the Gulf countries, let alone interacted with their citizens. Here, the consequences of practicing diplomacy at a distance become more apparent. If distance does limit interactions between diplomats and digital publics, then it also prevents MFAs from fully leveraging digital technologies toward public diplomacy goals. This is because digital publics now expect interactions as digital platforms center on two-way exchanges.

The analysis of virtual embassies thus far poses an important question: Why are public diplomacy initiatives based on digital technologies so short-lived? Sweden's virtual embassy was closed within five years, Israel's Twitter embassy became dormant within less than three months and America's embassy to Iran abandoned the goal of engagement soon after its launch. This chapter offers three possible answers to this question through three examples. Each example is of a relatively large and affluent MFA to demonstrate that the trials and tribulations of digital activities are by no means limited to small MFAs with limited resources.

The first example relates to MFAs' attempts to continuously interact with digital society members. Throughout the process of digitalization, MFAs and embassies have often found themselves migrating from one platform to another in pursuit of digital publics. For instance, in January 2017, the Japanese MFA migrated to Instagram, most likely because Instagram is the fastest growing social network in Japan (Neely, 2018). Yet once it launched a new Instagram channel, the MFA was faced with the arduous task of constantly producing videos, uploading images, and responding to followers' comments while at the same time managing all other MFA digital channels. The more digital endeavors MFAs undertake, the further they extend their limited resources. As a result, digital initiatives are often abandoned soon after they are announced. Indeed, a review of Japan's Instagram account reveals low levels of daily activity.

Digital initiatives are also abandoned due to changes in government as new administrations implement new working routines. One notable example is Canada. Under Stephen Harper's conservative government, Canadian diplomacy was hampered as digital messages often had to be pre-approved by the prime minister's office. Diplomats were therefore unable to converse in real-time with their followers (Manor, 2018). The Harper government also launched its own digital initiatives. One of these was meant to facilitate democracy in Iran. The Canadian government decided to help create the Digital Public Square Project, or digital forum, where Iranian citizens could speak their minds free from the surveillance of the Iranian regime. The election of Justin Trudeau led to an immediate change in the government's policies and working routines. Diplomats were set free, and no longer needed to approve digital content with Ottawa. Since then, the Digital Public Square Project has become less visible on Canadian social media channels. This is not surprising. Why focus on a new digital square when Canadian diplomats can use existing digital platforms to interact with Iranians and promote democratic values?

In other cases, digital initiatives are abandoned due to an overestimation of the power of digital platforms. One such instance was the State Department's Twitter channel, "Think Again Turn Away", which was part of the ministry's attempt to dissuade people from joining or communicating online with Daesh. The assumption among some American diplomats was that a Twitter channel could be powerful enough to impact people's beliefs and alter their behaviors (Katz, 2014). The "Think Again Turn Away" Twitter channel documented cases of sexual violence by Daesh terrorists as well as the group's violence toward fellow Muslims, its destruction of heritage sites, and its loss of territory in Iraq and Syria, all with the goal of preventing Americans from communicating with Daesh and falling under its spell. Yet the State Department soon had to contend with the fact that altering someone's behavior based solely on social media content is difficult at best, and simply not plausible at worst. Changing people's behaviors requires interactions and long-term relationship building—not infographics (Taylor & Kent, 2014). Ironically, dialogic engagement and relationship building were the very building blocks of Daesh's online recruitment efforts (Callimachi, 2015). "Think Again Turn Away" was finally abandoned and replaced by a joint Twitter account managed by several members of the Global Coalition against Daesh.

Lastly, another reason for the short lifespan of digital initiatives is rapid changes in audience preferences. For instance, the growing rhetoric of fake news and disinformation has led to changes in the behaviors of some online audiences. Last year saw the largest growth in traditional media subscriptions in more than a decade (Newman, Fletcher, Kalogeropoulos, Levy, & Nielsen, 2017). This change may soon bring about new digital initiatives, such as creating diplomatic blog platforms where audiences can access accurate information curated by diplomats. The UK FCO has been managing its own blogosphere since 2009 (for greater discussion see Chapter 5). There are, however, exceptions to the norm. Such is the case with Palestine's virtual embassy, which is setting a new standard in digital interactions and longevity, as is explored in the following section.

PALESTINE IN HEBREW

From a diplomatic perspective, Palestine represents a puzzling case study. On the one hand, it is a member state of the United Nations (UN) and other multilateral organizations. On the other hand, it has no internationally recognized borders. Similarly, while in some countries Palestine has an official embassy, in others it has offices of interests or offices managed solely by the Palestinian Liberation Organization (PLO) as is the case in the USA. Presently, there are also two Palestinian governments: one in the Gaza Strip, headed by the Hamas terror movement, and another in the West Bank, headed by the Palestinian National Authority. The Palestinian government in the West Bank has no official foreign ministry, and different bureaus manage different aspects of its foreign policy. Such is the case with the PLO Negotiations Affairs Department, which manages bilateral ties and negotiations with Israel.

An analysis conducted as part of this chapter in August 2018 suggests that the digitalization of Palestinian public diplomacy is quite inconsistent. For instance, Palestine does not have a digital presence in all countries that host PLO or Palestinian embassies. Moreover, the appearance of Palestinian digital profiles varies greatly from one nation to the next, as does the type of content that is published on these channels. Even the tone of Palestinian digital communications varies, as some embassies focus on the protracted conflict with Israel and accusing Israel of committing war crimes, while others focus more on bilateral ties between Palestine and other countries.

Palestine's relationship with Israel is also complex, as Israel partially recognizes the Palestinian government in the West Bank but does not recognize the Hamas government in Gaza. Although Israel and Palestine have signed several accords, they have not established official bilateral ties. Subsequently, there is no Palestinian diplomatic presence in Israel and there are very limited opportunities for Palestinian diplomats to engage with Israeli citizens.

It is against this backdrop of limited diplomatic recognition that the Palestinian government in the West Bank launched the "Palestine in Hebrew" Facebook page in November 2015. The page, which posts content exclusively in Hebrew, is managed by the PLO's Committee for Interaction with Israeli Society which has the stated goal of "Reaching a just and sustainable solution to the Middle East conflict through the establishment of an independent Palestinian State alongside Israel on the basis of the 4 June 1967 lines and a just and agreed-upon solution to the refugee problem on the basis of UN resolution 194" (TOI Staff, 2015).

As of July 2018, the Facebook page has amassed some 1200 followers and another 11,600 likes. Given that there is limited interaction between Israelis and Palestinian diplomats, and that Palestinian officials are rarely interviewed in the Israeli media, the Palestine in Hebrew Facebook page represents another attempt by a government to overcome the limitations of traditional diplomacy through digital technologies. Manor and Holmes (2018) have argued that as the Facebook page is one of the only channels for direct contact between Palestinian officials and Israelis, it essentially serves as a virtual embassy enabling Palestine to narrate its policies, offer a Palestinian perspective on the conflict with Israel, manage Israelis' perceptions of the Palestinian government, and converse with Israelis on issues of shared concern (of which there are many). As opposed to Israel's virtual embassy, which is on Twitter, Palestine launched its embassy on Facebook. This choice might suggest that the Palestinian embassy places an emphasis on conversing with Israelis given that Twitter is a platform for opinion formation and sharing, while Facebook is a platform for relationship management (Hughes, Rowe, Batey, & Lee, 2012; Kwak, Lee, Park, & Moon, 2010).

To characterize the Palestinian embassy's online activities, this chapter analyzed 54 posts published between January and May 2017. This period was selected as it saw intense attempts by the Trump administration to facilitate direct negotiations between Israel and Palestine. It was thus assumed that the Palestinian embassy would be especially active on Facebook given the need to comment on various U.S. diplomatic initiatives and create a receptive environment for negotiations among Israeli followers. This analysis builds on and extends the work of Manor and Holmes (2018). All Facebook posts published by Palestine in Hebrew were categorized based on subject matter using thematic analysis. Posts were gathered during August 2017 and analyzed during February 2018. In total, the thematic analysis found that embassy posts dealt with nine issues, including: manifesting the values of the future State of Palestine, building a better future for both Israelis and Palestinians, Israeli leaders who express support for Palestinian statehood, dialogue between Palestinian officials and Israelis, denouncing the Israeli military occupation of Palestine, partaking in intra-Israeli political discussions, portraying Palestine as a "State in the Making," Israeli intolerance toward Palestinians, and Israeli Defense Forces (IDF) violence toward Palestinians.

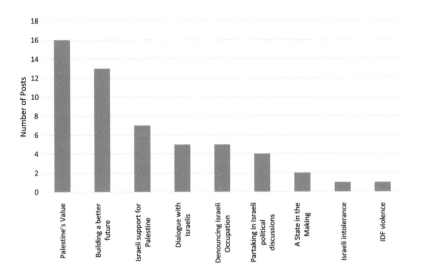

Graph 7.2 Prevalence of topics addressed in Palestinian Facebook posts, January–May 2017

As Graph 7.2 indicates, the most prevalent category of Facebook posts focused on exhibiting Palestinian values. These included posts celebrating the role of women in Palestinian society, posts featuring elements of Palestinian culture such as a theater festival and the Palestinian national orchestra, posts depicting the Palestinian government as open to criticism and posts celebrating the virtue of nonviolent resistance. These posts depict the future State of Palestine as one that will celebrate culture, not war, and one that will be committed to the principles of democracy such as free speech and public criticism of governments. Posts in this category were quite like those in a less prevalent category that depicted Palestine as "A State in the Making" with a national soccer team, a national contender in the *Arab Idol* reality show, a national philharmonic orchestra, and a booming economy, which may serve as the foundation of Palestinian independence.

The second most prevalent category consisted of posts emphasizing the need to create a better future for both Israelis and Palestinians. Such posts tended to stipulate that only a mutually beneficial future would be a prosperous one. A notable example was a post wishing Israelis a happy Passover and hoping that by the next year, Israelis and Palestinians would live peacefully as neighbors. Additional posts included a letter from Palestinian President Abbas to Israelis protesting for peace in Tel Aviv, posts depicting Jerusalem as the birthplace and future capital of two independent yet closely related states, posts celebrating peace rallies held jointly by Israelis and Palestinians, and posts depicting Palestinian children yearning for a better future.

Israeli support for Palestinian statehood was the third most prevalent topic addressed by the embassy. These posts depicted Israeli or Jewish historical leaders who openly supported peace with Palestinians, including Berl Katznelson (an influential politician during Israel's formative years) and Albert Einstein. This category also included posts in which high-ranking Israeli politicians and security officials expressed support for a Palestinian state and argued that such a state was vital to Israel's national security. The reference of historic Jewish leaders demonstrates that the past was very much present in embassy posts. It may have also been used to negate a common Israeli narrative that there was no Palestinian state prior to Israel's existence, nor was there a Palestinian national movement.

Posts illustrating Palestine's desire to engage in dialogue with Israelis comprised the fourth most prevalent category. These included images from meetings between Palestinian officials and Israeli university students or members of Israeli NGOs, as well as images of Israelis hosting Palestinian leaders for informal talks in their living rooms. Additional posts depicted meetings between Palestinian President Abbas and left-wing Israeli activists.

Surprisingly, posts denouncing the Israeli occupation of Palestine were among the least prevalent. These posts tended to focus on the historical origins of the conflict rather than its present-day violent manifestations. Posts included in this category dealt with the Palestinian Nakba (or catastrophe), the Palestinian right of return, and the illegality of Israel's occupation of Palestine. The sixth most prevalent category included posts that commented on domestic Israeli politics. One example was the denunciation of Israeli politicians who expressed support for hosting barbeques opposite jails in which Palestinians were staging a hunger strike. Likewise, Palestine in Hebrew published cartoons referencing Israel's taxation policies.

The least prevalent categories included posts depicting Israeli intolerance toward Palestinians and posts exhibiting IDF violence toward Palestinians through images and videos. Coupled with the emphasis on the historical origin of the Israeli occupation, it seems that Palestine in Hebrew focused on depicting a desire for dialogue and peaceful relations, rather than accusing Israel of maintaining a violent military occupation.

To assess the scope of interactions between Palestine in Hebrew and Israeli Facebook users, this chapter first analyzed the extent to which Israelis interact with Palestinian Facebook posts. The average Palestinian post received 47 likes and 4 shares. More importantly, the average post received 15 comments. Commenting on posts is a more intensive form of interaction as it requires more effort, and is more public than liking Facebook content. These results suggest that Israeli Facebook users are willing to share Palestinian content with their friends, thus increasing the reach of Palestinian messages. However, a qualitative analysis of Israeli comments suggests that these tended to be extremely negative and included profanities, calls to violence, hate speech, and racial stereotypes.

Next, this chapter analyzed Palestine in Hebrew's monthly rate of replies to Israeli comments. As seen in Graph 7.3, this analysis yielded a more complex picture. In January 2017, Palestine in Hebrew replied to Israeli comments and questions 66 times. Similarly, in March, it replied a total of 13 times, as was the case in May. But there were no replies to Israeli comments during February and April. Moreover, there

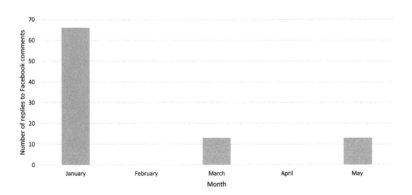

Graph 7.3 Palestine in Hebrew's monthly rate of replies to Israeli Facebook comments

was a substantial decrease in replies between January and May. While these results preclude a definitive conclusion, it seems that Palestine in Hebrew does engage in conversations with its target audience. Furthermore, it is possible that the decline in response rate may be related to the fact that many Israeli comments were negative and bordered on violent. Facebook users' violent delights may have had violent ends.

It should be noted that while Palestine in Hebrew dealt with a broad range of issues, it did not address those that are viewed as especially contentious by Israelis and as roadblocks on the way to peace. These include, among others, incitement of violence in Palestinian schools, financial aid to families of convicted terrorists, Hamas' calls to annihilate Israel, and how the West Bank government will remain free from the influence of Hamas (Palestinian Center for Policy and Survey Research, 2017; Palestinian-Israeli Pulse, 2018). However, there were also no posts that depicted a Palestinian desire to control the holy sites in Jerusalem, another important issue for Israelis. Moreover, there were frequent references to Jerusalem's importance to both Palestinians and Israelis and a hope that one day it may serve as the capital of two states, one in Eastern Jerusalem and one in Western Jerusalem.

In summary, Palestine in Hebrew focuses mostly on depicting the attributes of the future state of Palestine and its values. Like Israel, Palestine will have a democratic government that shall be open to criticism. Also like Israel, Palestine shall celebrate minorities and gender equality and will cherish culture. These messages may have resonated with Israelis who often view their country as the "only democracy in the Middle East." The virtual embassy also advocated the value of nonviolent resistance, thereby rejecting calls for Palestinian violence against Israel. Additionally, Palestine in Hebrew depicted Palestine as a "State in the Making," one that has national institutions and will be financially viable and not wholly dependent on the Israeli economy. Such messages may have also resonated with Israelis, who fear the financial ramifications of an independent Palestine, and who fail to imagine what a unified Palestine will look like given the rift between the West Bank and Gaza governments.

The least prevalent issues addressed by the virtual embassy were overtly negative issues, such as those condemning the Israeli occupation or posts highlighting Israeli violence against Palestinians. Thus, it seems that Palestine in Hebrew uses Facebook to present Israelis with a positive and credible vision of the future. Positive as it will yield prosperity, and credible as it is backed by Israeli leaders and security officials.

As such, Palestine in Hebrew demonstrates the potential applicability of digital technologies to overcome the limitations of traditional diplomacy. Through public diplomacy activities on Facebook, Palestine may be able to cultivate a receptive environment among Israelis for its main foreign policy objective: statehood.

The analysis of the embassy's monthly response rate demonstrates that while the scale of embassy interactions with followers may vary, the embassy does continuously converse with its digital public. As such, Palestine's virtual embassy seems to succeed where others have failed. The question that emerges is: why?

One answer may lie in the platform utilized. Israel's virtual embassy was created on Twitter, which is a platform for opinion sharing and news gathering. By contrast, Facebook is a platform that centers on cultivating relationships. Palestine may have chosen to launch its embassy on Facebook specifically because it sought to focus its efforts on building relationships rather than disseminating information. This assumption is strengthened by the fact that the Palestinian embassy is managed by the PLO Committee for Interaction with Israeli Society, whose goal is to engage with Israelis. Moreover, Facebook may reduce the sense of distance between diplomats and digital publics, as a Facebook profile is far more personalized than a Twitter profile. Indeed, while a Twitter profile includes a picture and a short bio, a Facebook profile lists users' friends and displays their photo albums and their most recent interactions with other users. Thus, it is possible that Facebook audiences are less amorphic and more visible to diplomats. Lastly, the physical distance between Palestinian diplomats and Israelis is far smaller than the distance between American diplomats and Iranians, or Israeli diplomats and the Gulf. Palestinian diplomats and officials in the West Bank are but a short car ride away from Israel and they engage with the Israeli presence in Palestine daily. Physical distance may thus impact the perception of digital distance.

The virtual embassies of Israel, Palestine, Sweden, and the USA all demonstrate that the desire to overcome the limitations of traditional diplomacy has been central to the digitalization of public diplomacy in numerous MFAs. It also demonstrates that attempts to overcome diplomatic limitations were emblematic of the logic of the digital society. Virtual embassies annihilated time and space, transcended and ignored national borders, and integrated acting at a distance into diplomatic practices. Like virtual embassies, global public diplomacy campaigns also enable MFAs to overcome limitations of traditional diplomacy. These are explored in the following section.

WHEN PUBLIC DIPLOMACY GOES GLOBAL

The migration of MFAs to digital platforms was motivated, in part, by a desire to compete with old and new media actors over the attention of digital publics. The digital society is one in which new media actors such as citizen journalists, bloggers, and social media personalities may narrate world events and disseminate narratives to a global public sphere. By doing so, new media actors can influence how digital society members make sense of events and actors shaping their world (Clarke, 2015). Moreover, new media actors may contest the narration of events by nations. As Causey and Howard (2013) have argued, bloggers' digital narratives of corruption and violence during the Arab Spring trumped those of Arab governments. The emergence of new media actors, alongside the migration of traditional media actors online, created a competitive digital arena that diplomats had to join if they were to impact digital publics' understanding of world events and national policies (Manor, 2016).

Within contemporary societies, old and new media actors draw strength from their abilities to frame the news. Framing, according to Robert Entman, is "to select some aspects of a perceived reality and make them more salient in a commutating text, in such a way as to promote a particular problem definition, casual interpretation, moral evaluation and treatment recommendation" (Entman, 1993). In other words, to frame is to create a prism through which one will learn about events and issues shaping his or her world. When journalists and bloggers frame an event, they do not merely describe it, but also interpret and contextualize it by illustrating its potential impact on audiences. Framing can thus shape people's perceptions of reality and behaviors and thus bears the imprint of power (ibid.).

For instance, in July 2018, CNN reported that the Israeli government had helped a group of Syrian volunteers known as the White Helmets escape from Syria to Jordan via Israel. Throughout the Syrian Civil War, White Helmet volunteers would remain in areas bombarded by Russian and Syrian forces while searching for possible survivors. The problem, according to the CNN article, was that the lives of the Syrian volunteers could soon be in jeopardy. The cause of the problem was that the Assad regime was about to conquer the territory where the volunteers lived. The solution was the quick evacuation of

the volunteers and their families from Syria, while the moral evaluation suggested that Israel had demonstrated its humanity and compassion when aiding the White Helmets' families escape certain death
(Liebermann & McKenzie, 2018).

In addition, old and new media draw their strengths from determining which issues will be debated by society. When an issue attracts media
attention, it is likely to become more central to societal conversations.
The more salient an issue becomes in media reporting, the more dominant it becomes in dining room and parliamentary debates. By the same
token, issues that are ignored by the media are unlikely to gain the attention of citizens or policymakers. Studies have found that issue salience in
the media also influences foreign policies and diplomatic initiatives. Once
a civil war, famine, or natural disaster gains media attention, it begins to
influence public opinion, which ultimately leads diplomats to formulate
corresponding foreign policies. This process has been dubbed the "CNN
Effect", as CNN coverage of events has been shown to shape American
foreign policy (Gilboa, 2005a, 2005b; Robinson, 1999).

Throughout most of the twentieth century, MFAs, embassies, and
diplomats could only reach mass numbers of foreign citizens through
the traditional media. Moreover, they could only influence the framing
of their countries and their policies by hobnobbing with journalists, editors, and media outlets. Access to the press was therefore a prerequisite
for practicing public diplomacy. Consequently, diplomats dedicated substantial resources to cultivating close relationships with the media. At the
embassy level, this was the privy of the press attaché, who would wine
and dine important columnists, while ambassadors invited senior editors
to dine at their residences. At the MFA level, spokespersons managed
relations of friendship and enmity with global media institutions or local
correspondents of foreign media outlets.

But the digitalization of public diplomacy promised to disrupt the
relationship between diplomats and the press as digital platforms enabled diplomats to interact directly with foreign populations, be it at the
embassy or MFA level. These platforms included social media accounts,
blogospheres, websites, messaging applications, and smartphone applications. Crucially, by utilizing digital platforms, diplomats could craft their
own frames and disseminate these directly among digital publics, thus
circumventing the media altogether.

James Pamment (2014) has argued that as part of the process of digitalization, MFAs have become "mediatized" in that they have adopted the logic and practices of media institutions. Manor and Crilley (2019) argue that this presently manifests itself in four ways. First, MFAs routinely frame issues and events, thus creating a prism through which digital audiences can make sense of their world. Second, these frames are created and disseminated in near-real time. As was argued in Chapter 2, the digital society is the real-time society, and publics expect to learn about events as they unfold on the ground, giving rise to a form of real-time diplomacy (Seib, 2012). Third, MFAs have also become visual producers as they create a range of visuals that are embedded into their frames, ranging from infographics to photographs and videos. These help capture the attention of digital publics and succinctly convey large volumes of information. Lastly, as is the case with the media, morality plays a central role in MFA framing. This is because values and morals can limit or facilitate state action.

As Peter Van Ham (2013) argued, public diplomacy may be used to promote new norms and values to which nations must adhere. For instance, nations may avoid contravening norms that have been accepted by the international community out of fear of being ostracized and sanctioned. Conversely, when nations are viewed as promoting accepted values, they may encounter little resistance to their foreign policies, including the use of military power (Mor, 2012). Such is the case when nations proclaim that they use troops to promote peace, restore order, or end humanitarian suffering (Quelch & Jocz, 2009).

The digitalization of public diplomacy has enabled MFAs to frame events or issues on a global scale. Chapter 4 focused on the use of digital platforms to tailor content to the values and norms of specific national publics. Yet at times, MFAs may also choose to launch a single global campaign meant to deliver a single frame to audiences the world over. Such was the case with the State Department's social media blitz following the legalization of same-sex marriages by the Supreme Court in June 2015.

Within minutes of the U.S. Supreme Court's ruling, the profile pictures of the State Department, White House, and the First Lady were all replaced with pictures bearing the rainbow pride flag. Soon, the U.S. embassies in Brussels, Dublin, Jerusalem, London, Riga, and the UN all tweeted congratulatory tweets celebrating the fact that "love is love." The same was true of ambassadors who used their professional accounts to celebrate the victory of love over bigotry (Manor, 2015). Next, the

White House itself was alight with the colors of the rainbow flag, attracting mass media attention from CNN, the BBC, *The New York Times,* and other outlets. By the following day, the vast social media empire managed by the State Department had all celebrated the Supreme Court's ruling.

The State Department's framing of the LGBT ruling was made evident in a tweet published by the U.S. ambassador to the UN, shown in Fig. 7.2. The tweet states that on the same day as the Supreme Court's ruling, the UN republished its charter in the rainbow colors. This tweet creates a link between LGBT rights in America and human rights around the world. The problem, according to this frame, is that decades after its publication, the vision of the UN's charter has yet to be achieved. The cause of the problem is that human rights are not yet universally respected. The solution is to advocate more passionately than ever in favor of equality and human rights, as the USA had done with LGBTs' right to marry. The moral evaluation suggests that equality is key to obtaining human rights, or that "love is love." This tweet, published hours after the Court's ruling, is emblematic of the mediatization and digitalization of public diplomacy, as an image was used to promote a moral frame in near-real time and on a global scale.

One might wonder why the State Department dedicated so much attention to the LGBT ruling? A possible answer lies in the image of America in the post-Bush era. During the first decade of the twenty-first century, the global image of America was tarnished by the invasions of Iraq and Afghanistan, the Global War on Terror, and America's refusal to join the Kyoto climate protocol. Public opinion polls found that the USA was seen by many as a greedy, polluting, and militaristic empire whose foreign policy rested solely on the number of fighter jets it could deploy to a given region (Anholt & Hildreth, 2005; Rawson, 2007; Silver & Hill, 2002). From his election in 2008, Barack Obama sought to refashion America's image by demonstrating a commitment to diplomatic engagement, coalition building, and human rights promotion (Manor, 2017). The State Department's social media blitz may have been part of an attempt to demonstrate that America was a changed nation that would lead through values and norms rather than military might. It thus capitalized on the Supreme Court's ruling to redraw America's global image.

Global public diplomacy campaigns, such as the U.S. LGBT blitz, represent diplomats' desires to further challenge the constraints of time and space. A single message, or frame, can be disseminated on a

 **Samantha Power**
@AmbPower44

Some coincidence: on same day US Supreme Ct legalizes gay marriage, @UN reissues 70th anniversary Charter in rainbow!

12:05 AM - Jun 27, 2015

♡ 133   ♡ 99 people are talking about this

Fig. 7.2 Tweet by U.S. ambassador to the UN (*Source* https://twitter.com/AmbPower44/status/614570083667562496)

planetary scale in near-real time. In this instance, the sense of distance between diplomats and digital publics is less influential, as the goal is not to interact with digital users but to reach as many users as possible. The audience of global campaigns is thus inherently amorphous.

The blessings of digital framing, however, soon also posed a challenge as diplomats realized that they were but one actor among many who could disseminate frames online. Citizen journalists, bloggers, social media personalities, foreign governments, NGOs, civil society organizations and activists could all harness digital platforms for framing purposes (Manor, 2016). Bloggers and activists could also influence the media's depiction of events and the salience of issues in media reporting. During the Arab Spring, for instance, global media outlets often relied on the reporting of bloggers and citizen journalists located in Arab nations and adopted their framing of events (Causey & Howard, 2013). Likewise, during the Crimean crisis, stories trending online were soon picked up and reported on by traditional news outlets. The digitalization of diplomacy therefore saw digital platforms transform into aggressive framing arenas. Winning competitions within these arenas demanded that MFAs be among the first to comment on local, regional, and global events. This would bring about both normative and structural changes in MFAs. For instance, the Lithuanian MFA would establish a "monitoring division" tasked with monitoring social networks in foreign countries and identifying trending topics or events that the MFA must comment on (R. Paulauskas, personal communication, July 25, 2018). The Israeli MFA would work alongside graphic designers to create appealing visual content ranging from infographics to cartoons and videos (Manor & Crilley, 2018a), while the U.S. State Department would integrate digital staffers into emergency task forces meant to manage crisis situations (Israeli MFA, 2017). Within competitive framing arenas, timing is everything. MFAs who are last to comment on events or who fall silent forfeit the right to influence digital publics' perceptions of an event. Such was the case with the Turkish MFA following the 2016 coup attempt.

On the evening of July 15, 2016, bloggers and independent news outlets began tweeting about irregular Turkish troop movements in key locations throughout Istanbul and Ankara (Calamur et al., 2016). Soon, images circulated online depicting Turkish air force jets flying above government facilities, while Turkish tanks assumed positions near bridges and state television studios. Later in the evening, a news anchor was forced to read a statement by the Peace at Home Council to formally announce that a coup was underway to depose the government of Recep Tayyip Erdogan. The coup would prove unsuccessful, and forces loyal to the government overran the Peace Council within a matter of hours. Yet the following days saw an unprecedented number of arrests in Turkey, including those of 10,000 soldiers and more than 2000 judges. In addition, some 15,000 education staff were suspended, as well as thousands of teachers in private schools (Said-Moorhouse, 2016). As images of mass arrests emerged from Turkey, foreign governments took to digital platforms to call for restraint and respect for the rule of law. Simultaneously, traditional media outlets began denouncing the Erdogan government's response to the coup as an attempt to silence all domestic opposition. The framing of the coup's aftermath was best captured on the cover of the *Economist* magazine as "Erdogan's Revenge." Erdogan, the media claimed, was determined to play the villain.

For the first five days following the coup attempt, the Turkish MFA, Turkish embassies, and most Turkish diplomats remained digitally silent. They did not comment on the coup attempt or its aftermath, nor did they contend with the allegations raised by foreign governments and media institutions. The frame of "Erdogan's Revenge" went unchallenged. In the time of Henry VI, five days would have little impact on a public diplomacy campaign. Yet in the digital society, five days is an eternity. By the time the Turkish MFA was ready to respond to the media's framing of events, lists of detainees were already circulating on Twitter (Fig. 7.3).

Nonetheless, on July 20, the Turkish MFA launched its own global social media blitz aimed at offering a counter-frame to that of "Erdogan's Revenge." The problem, according to the Turkish framing, was that a group within the military had attempted to oust a democratically elected government. A tweet by the Turkish embassy in London included an interview with a Turkish diplomat who reminded viewers that the Erdogan government was not the instigator of the coup, but rather was its victim. The cause of the problem lay in the violent nature of the coup plotters who used force against Turkish citizens and the Turkish government. Turkish embassies in Berlin, Brasilia, London, Tel Aviv, and the UN all published videos depicting the brutality of the coup plotters, who used tanks to run over civilians or fired on unarmed civilians from helicopters. The moral evaluation suggested that the coup was an attack on democracy itself. Thus, several MFA and embassy tweets included images of a bombed national parliament, and other national institutions

```
01. Pvt School Teacher                     >21,000^   licence rev⊕
02. Education Ministry   15,200 + 6538^ = 21,738      suspended

03. Interior Ministry                        8,777    suspended
       * Police Officers        (7,899)
       * Gendarme Soldiers        (614)
       * Public Admin.           (246)
       * Coast Guard Personnel    (18)

04. Soldiers                                >6,319*   arrested
       * Generals & Admirals     (103)

05. a) Civilian Judges                       2,745    suspended
    b) Military Judges & Prosecutors          262^    suspended

06. University Deans                          1,577   resignation
07. Finance Ministry                          1,500   sacked
08. Religious Affairs Ministry                 492    sacked
09. Family & Social Ministry                   393^   sacked
10. TRT Broadcaster                            370    investigation
11. PM Office staff                            257    sacked
12. Youth & Sports Ministry                    245^   sacked
```

                    (^Last 24 hrs)(*Outdated)
20/07/2016 15:30 GMT (updated by: @ashishjena94)

Conflict News
@Conflicts

TURKEY: Updated list on the mass purge that is ongoing in
#Turkey - @ashishjena94

6:04 PM - Jul 20, 2016

♡ 120 ○ 432 people are talking about this

Fig. 7.3 List of individuals arrested by Turkish government following 2016 coup attempt (*Source* https://twitter.com/Conflicts/status/755810585598685186)

damaged during the night of the coup. Finally, the solution to the problem was for all Turkish political parties to come together and restore faith in Turkish democracy and its national unity. To this end, the MFA and Turkish embassies posted images of a joint parliamentary session as well as a joint statement by the Grand National Assembly. When disseminating such global campaigns, MFAs effectively become a global network in which messages and content are created at the MFA level and disseminated through embassies to a myriad of intersecting planetary networks.

The Turkish campaign is demonstrative of how MFAs attempt to compete with other actors over the framing and narration of events. The Turkish MFA created a global frame that directly refuted the arguments made by other digital actors, including new and old media institutions, foreign governments, and citizen journalists. Yet it is unclear whether the Turkish digital blitz was able to counter the framing of "Erdogan's Revenge." In the five days, it took the Turkish MFA to formulate its own frame, 3,282,200,000 tweets were published; 25,970,976,000 Google searches were conducted; and 4,320,000 Wikipedia pages were edited. The digital society waits for no one. By the time Turkish diplomats were disseminating their frames, digital audiences had shifted their attention to a new issue or a new scandal. This campaign shows the limits of public diplomacy's ability to annihilate time and space. While MFAs attempt to render time meaningless, its omnipotence remains intact. The clock of the digital society cannot be stopped or turned backward.

CONCLUSIONS

Scholars have argued that the digital society is one that seeks to transcend or annihilate time and manipulate space. According to Bauman and Lyon, the digital society is one in which things are done at a distance, ranging from the granting of mortgages to the operation of drones. Employing the technological prism, Bauman and Lyon argued that digitalization impacts human morality, which is still tied to proximity. A member of the digital society feels responsible only for that which takes place in his or her eyesight. The digital manipulation of space thus has serious societal implications. Manuel Castells has argued that the digital society continuously strives to annihilate time and space by employing technologies that enable the planetary circulation of money and information in seconds.

The logic of the digital society and its relationship to time and place has been evident throughout the process of public diplomacy's digitalization. As this chapter has shown, diplomats hoped to leverage digital technologies to overcome the limitations of traditional diplomacy, including lack of bilateral ties, hostile media landscapes, and the inability to foster a global constituency. The means with which diplomats chose to overcome these limitations sought to render space and time meaningless. Such is the case with the virtual embassies of Sweden, the USA, and Israel, which all sought to transcend national boundaries, traverse great distances, and interact with distant populations in real-time. While these are but a few examples, they demonstrate that, like the digital society, contemporary public diplomacy is preoccupied with the attempt to condense time and space.

Yet as is the case with the digital society, time and space are still omnipotent in public diplomacy. Doing things at a distance is in stark contradiction to diplomacy's traditional reliance on proximity. Digitalization demands that diplomats interact and converse with amorphic and distant publics that bear no physical semblance. Diplomats' inability to see the audiences they are meant to interact with may be one reason why they fail to converse with digital publics. Just as a drone operator's ethics are limited to all that is in his or her sight, so a diplomat may only be able to foster relationships with those publics that are in their sight. The greater the physical distance between a diplomat and a digital public, the more distance may limit diplomats' relational practices. Thus, American diplomats could hardly interact with Iranian citizens, while Palestinian diplomats could more easily converse with their Israeli neighbors. Space is therefore still as powerful a force in diplomacy as it is in the digital society. As Lupton (2014) argued, many digital applications and technologies center on geo-locating users suggesting that space actually becomes more important in the digital society.

Time also plays a central role in the digitalization of public diplomacy. The digital society is one that operates in real-time. News, money, and knowledge all circle the globe within seconds. This, as Philip Seib has argued, means that diplomacy too must be practiced in real-time. Failure to do so prevents diplomats from shaping digital publics' understanding of world events. Time delays may render public diplomacy activities meaningless, as was the case with Turkey's belated framing of the 2016 coup attempt. Thus, like space, time still plays a dominant role in the digital society and in public diplomacy.

The need to practice real-time diplomacy is also the result of the metaphor or self-narrative that diplomats have adopted, which conceptualizes digital platforms as competitive framing arenas. As Manor (2016) has written, America's need to counter the framing and narration activities of Al-Qaeda motivated the State Department to migrate online in the first place. Since then, and in the wake of the Arab Spring, MFAs and diplomats have increasingly viewed digital platforms as arenas in which they compete with a host of actors over the ability to shape digital publics' perceptions of world events. These competitors include new media actors, old media institutions who migrated online, civil society organizations, and other nations.

The metaphor of framing competitions has led to new working routines and new norms and values. From the perspective of working routines, digital departments at MFAs now routinely monitor other actors to refute or counter their framing of events, as was the case with the @theIranDeal Twitter channel reviewed in the introduction. Moreover, as James Pamment (2014) argued, MFAs have become mediatized, as they are producers of visual media. During the 2014 Gaza War, the Israeli MFA published more than 700 tweets, many of them accompanied by videos, infographics, and cartoons developed by the MFA (Manor & Crilley, 2018a). These visuals were meant to counter those spread by other actors online and to further increase the efficacy of the Israeli MFA's framing. As "seeing is believing," visuals can help MFAs validate their arguments and framing of events. In terms of norms and values, diplomats can now attempt to challenge their traditional relationships with the media as they can author and disseminate their own frames online. Diplomats may thus be less reliant on the media to reach mass audiences. This may even mitigate the power that the media had to shape foreign policy. By framing events and actors online, MFAs can attempt to influence the media's reporting of events rather than having the media dictate foreign policy priorities. This, subsequently, leads to a "reverse CNN effect." President Donald Trump is a prime example of this reverse effect, as he is able to use Twitter rants to set the agenda for the American media.

Yet public diplomacy goals also influence the working routines of MFAs. The desire to overcome the limitations of traditional diplomacy led MFAs to experiment with virtual embassies. New working routines were soon adopted, including attempts to converse with virtual publics. The norm that was subsequently adopted was that of conversing with the populations of enemy nations that were otherwise inaccessible. The self-narrative that diplomats adopted was that of virtual diplomacy, or the establishment of virtual diplomatic ties in place of official physical ties.

Finally, this chapter has demonstrated, yet again, that the digitalization of public diplomacy is a long-term process that is still taking shape. This is evident when examining the evolution of virtual embassies. The Second House of Sweden was meant to serve as a global cultural institute, Virtual Embassy Iran was meant to replace a brick and mortar embassy, while Israel in the GCC was meant to overcome a critical media landscape and leverage joint threats toward the establishment of relationships with foreign populations. Yet all these embassies failed to interact with their target audiences. All but the latest embassy to be launched by Palestine. The analysis presented in this chapter demonstrates that Palestine succeeds where others have failed. This may be due to three reasons: first, the limited sense of distance between Palestinian officials and their Israeli neighbors; second, the use of Facebook, which is a digital platform centered on relationship building; and third, because the embassy is managed by a Palestinian bureau whose raison d'être is to interact with Israeli society.

So, as the process of digitalization continues, so do diplomats' abilities to leverage digital technologies toward the goals of the new "public" diplomacy. In this sense, the process that began with the technologies and tapestries of the fifteenth century is still taking shape in the twenty-first century. As the next chapter argues, the presence of the nation state in everyday life is also still evolving.

REFERENCES

Anholt, S., & Hildreth, J. (2005). Let freedom and cash registers ring: America as a brand. *Place Branding, 1*(2), 164–172.

Bauman, Z., & Lyon, B. (2016). Remoteness distancing an automation. In Z. Bauman & B. Lyon (Eds.), *Liquid surveillance* (pp. 76–99). Cambridge: Polity Press.

Bjola, C., & Jiang, L. (2015). Social media and public diplomacy: A comparative analysis of the digital diplomatic strategies of the EU, US and Japan in China. In C. Bjola & M. Holmes (Eds.), *Digital diplomacy theory and practice* (pp. 71–88). Oxon: Routledge.

Calamur, K., Vasilogambros, M., Weston Phippen, J., Graham, D. A., Yasmin, S., & Ford, M. (2016, July). What's going on in Turkey? *The Atlantic.* Retrieved from https://www.theatlantic.com/news/archive/2016/07/turkey-government/491579/.

Callimachi, R. (2015, June). ISIS and the lonely young American. *The New York Times.* Retrieved from https://www.nytimes.com/2015/06/28/world/americas/isis-online-recruiting-american.html.

Castells, M. (2013). *Communication power.* Oxford: Oxford University Press.

Causey, C., & Howard, P. N. (2013). Delivering digital public diplomacy. In R. S. Zaharna, A. Arsenault, & A. Fisher (Eds.), *Relational, networked and collaborative approaches to public diplomacy* (pp. 144–156). New York, NY: Taylor & Francis.

Cha, H., Yeo, S., & Kim, B. (2014). Social media's dialogic communication of foreign embassies in Korea and public diplomacy: Based on dialogic communication theory. *Advanced Science and Technology Letters, 63,* 175–178.

Clarke, A. (2015). Business as usual? An evolution of British and Canadian digital diplomacy as policy change. In C. Bjola & M. Holmes (Eds.), *Digital diplomacy theory and practice* (pp. 111–126). Oxon: Routledge.

Clinton, H. [US State Department]. (2011, December 12). *Secretary Clinton announces virtual embassy Tehran* [Video File]. Retrieved from https://www.youtube.com/watch?v=c70SKkcvUIw.

Comor, E., & Bean, H. (2012). America's 'engagement' delusion: Critiquing a public diplomacy consensus. *International Communication Gazette, 74*(3), 203–220.

Copeland, D. (2013). Taking diplomacy public: Science, technology and foreign ministries in a heteropolar world. In R. S. Zaharna, A. Arsenault, & A. Fisher (Eds.), *Relational, networked and collaborative approaches to public diplomacy* (pp. 56–69). New York, NY: Taylor & Francis.

Entman, R. M. (1993). Framing: Toward clarification of a fractured paradigm. *Journal of Communication, 43*(4), 51–58.

Gilboa, E. (2005a). The CNN effect: The search for a communication theory of international relations. *Political Communication, 22*(1), 27–44.

Gilboa, E. (2005b). Global television news and foreign policy: Debating the CNN effect. *International Studies Perspectives, 6*(3), 325–341.

Hocking, B., & Melissen, J. (2015). *Diplomacy in the digital age.* Clingendael: Netherlands Institute of International Relations.

Hughes, D. J., Rowe, M., Batey, M., & Lee, A. (2012). A tale of two sites: Twitter vs. Facebook and the personality predictors of social media usage. *Computers in Human Behavior, 28*(2), 561–569.

Israeli Ministry of Foreign Affairs. (2017). *Digital diplomacy conference summary* (pp. 6–19). Retrieved from https://www.state.gov/documents/organization/271028.pdf.

Jones, D. (2014). *The Hollow Crown: The wars of the roses and the rise of the Tudors.* London: Faber & Faber.

Katz, R. (2014, September). The State Department's Twitter war with ISIS is embarrassing. *Time*. Retrieved from http://time.com/3387065/isis-twitter-war-state-department/.

Kwak, H., Lee, C., Park, H., & Moon, S. (2010, April). *What is Twitter, a social network or a news media?* Proceedings of the 19th international conference on world wide web (pp. 591–600). ACM.

Lengel, L., & Newsome, V. A. (2012). Framing messages of democracy through social media: Public diplomacy 2.0, gender, and the Middle East and North Africa. *Global Media Journal, 11*(21), 1.

Liebermann, O., & McKenzie, S. (2018, July). Israel helps evacuate Syria's White Helmets to Jordan. *CNN*. Retrieved from https://edition.cnn.com/2018/07/22/middleeast/israel-evacuation-syria-white-helmets-jordan-intl/index.html.

Lupton, D. (2014). A critical sociology of big data. In D. Lupton (Ed.), *Digital sociology* (pp. 93–116). New York, NY: Routledge.

Manor, E. (2018). *Serving in Sweden in the days of Carl Bildt* [In person].

Manor, I. (2015, July 1). *The US's LGBT digital diplomacy blitz* [Blog]. Retrieved from https://digdipblog.com/2015/07/01/the-uss-lgbt-digital-diplomacy-blitz/.

Manor, I. (2016). Are we there yet: Have MFA s realized the potential of digital diplomacy? *Brill Research Perspectives in Diplomacy and Foreign Policy, 1*(2), 1–110.

Manor, I. (2017). America's selfie–Three years later. *Place Branding and Public Diplomacy, 13*(4), 308–324.

Manor, I. (2018, June 1). *The ebb and flow of digital diplomacy* [Blog]. Retrieved from https://uscpublicdiplomacy.org/blog/ebb-and-flow-digital-diplomacy.

Manor, I., & Crilley, R. (2018a). Visually framing the Gaza War of 2014: The Israel Ministry of Foreign Affairs on Twitter. *Media, War & Conflict*.

Manor, I., & Crilley, R. (2018b). The aesthetics of violent extremist and counter violent extremist communication. In C. Bjola & J. Pamment (Eds.), *Countering online propaganda and extremism: The dark side of digital diplomacy*. Oxon: Routledge.

Manor, I. & Crilley, R. (2019). The mediatization of MFAs: diplomacy in the new media ecology. *The Hague Journal of Diplomacy*.

Manor, I., & Holmes, M. (2018, May–August). Palestine in Hebrew: Overcoming the limitations of traditional diplomacy. *Revista Mexican de Politicia Exterior, 113*, 1–17.

McNutt, K. (2014). Public engagement in the Web 2.0 era: Social collaborative technologies in a public sector context. *Canadian Public Administration, 57*(1), 49–70.

Metzgar, E. T. (2012). Is it the medium or the message? Social media, American public diplomacy & Iran. *Global Media Journal, 12*(21), 1.

Mor, B. D. (2012). Credibility talk in public diplomacy. *Review of International Studies, 38*(2), 393–422.

Neely, C. (2018, January). Japan's top social media networks for 2018. *Humble Bunny.* Retrieved from http://www.humblebunny.com/japans-top-social-media-networks-2018/.

Newman, N., Fletcher, R., Kalogeropoulos, A., Levy, D. A., & Nielsen, R. K. (2017). *Reuters institute digital news report 2017.*

Palestinian Center for Policy and Survey Research. (2017). *Palestinian-Israeli pulse.* Retrieved from http://www.pcpsr.org/en/node/678.

Pamment, J. (2013). *New public diplomacy in the 21st century: A comparative study of policy and practice.* Abingdon: Routledge.

Pamment, J. (2014). The mediatization of diplomacy. *The Hague Journal of Diplomacy, 9*(3), 253–280.

Quelch, J. A., & Jocz, K. E. (2009). Can brand Obama rescue brand America? *The Brown Journal of World Affairs, 16*(1), 163–178.

Ravid, B. (2013, July). Israel open a 'Virtual Embassy' to Gulf States. *Haaretz.* Retrieved from https://www.haaretz.com/.premium-israel-opens-gulf-virtual-embassy-1.5297843.

Rawson, E. A. G. (2007). Perceptions of the United States of America: Exploring the political brand of a nation. *Place Branding and Public Diplomacy, 3*(3), 213–221.

Roberts, I. (2017). Diplomacy—A short history from pre-classical origins to the fall of the Berlin Wall. In I. Roberts (Ed.), *Satow's diplomatic practice* (pp. 3–19). Oxford: Oxford University Press.

Robinson, P. (1999). The CNN effect: Can the news media drive foreign policy? *Review of International Studies, 25*(2), 301–309.

Said-Moorhouse, L. (2016, August). This is how many people Turkey has arrested since the failed coup. *CNN.* Retrieved from https://edition.cnn.com/2016/07/29/europe/turkey-post-coup-arrest-numbers/index.html.

Seib, P. (2012). *Real-time diplomacy: Politics and power in the social media era.* New York, NY: Palgrave Macmillan.

Seo, H. (2013). The "Virtual Last Three Feet": Understanding relationship perspectives in network-based public diplomacy. In R. S. Zaharna, A. Arsenault, & A. Fisher (Eds.), *Relational, networked and collaborative approaches to public diplomacy* (pp. 157–169). New York, NY: Taylor & Francis.

Silver, S., & Hill, S. (2002). Marketing: Selling brand America. *Journal of Business Strategy, 23*(4), 10–15.

Sotiriu, S. (2015). Digital diplomacy: Between promises and reality. In C. Bjola & M. Holmes (Eds.), *Digital diplomacy theory and practice* (pp. 33–51). Oxon: Routledge.

Spry, D. (2018). Facebook diplomacy: a data-driven, user-focused approach to Facebook use by diplomatic missions. *Media International Australia, 168*(1), 62–80.

Styles, D., & Allmand, C. T. (1982, May). The coronations of Henry-VI. *History Today, 32,* 28–33.

Taylor, M., & Kent, M. L. (2014). Dialogic engagement: Clarifying foundational concepts. *Journal of Public Relations Research, 26*(5), 384–398.

The Tami Steinmetz Center for Peace Research. (2018). *Palestinian-Israeli pulse: A joint poll.* Retrieved from http://www.ps.undp.org/content/dam/papp/docs/Publications/UNDP-papp-research-PSR-%20summaryreport.pdf.

TOI Staff. (2015, November). PLO launches Facebook page—In Hebrew. *The Times of Israel.* Retrieved from https://www.timesofisrael.com/plo-launches-facebook-page-in-hebrew/.

Van Ham, P. (2013). Social power in public diplomacy. In R. S. Zaharna, A. Arsenault, & A. Fisher (Eds.), *Relational, networked and collaborative approaches to public diplomacy* (pp. 17–28). New York, NY: Taylor & Francis.

CHAPTER 8

On Selfie Diplomacy

I write scripts to serve as skeletons awaiting the flesh and sinew of images.
—Ingmar Bergman

Great leaders have traditionally realized the impact that images and symbols have on one's reputation. Julius Caesar erected great statues of himself in Rome to celebrate his magnificence and afford him a God-like status. England's King Charles I commissioned a painting of himself sitting in front of the English Parliament thus signifying his regal supremacy. In 1800, the King of Spain commissioned a painting of Napoleon crossing the Alps as a means of symbolizing the rapprochement between both nations, or their renewed friendship. The painting, which depicts Napoleon pointing to the summit of a mountain while seated upon a fiery steed, is one that exudes radiance, confidence, and daring.

Nation states have also used images to manage their reputation. In June of 1940, Nazi Germany disseminated images of its military parade through the recently conquered city of Paris. These images, signifying that the fortunes of World War I had been reversed, struck a chord of anguish and despair throughout Europe. Nearly five years later, the Soviet Union published an image of its flag being hoisted upon the German parliament denoting the ultimate triumph of communism over fascism, while in 1969 images of American astronauts planting their flag on the moon circulated the globe, signifying that even the skies could not limit American ingenuity.

© The Author(s) 2019   257
I. Manor, *The Digitalization of Public Diplomacy*,
Palgrave Macmillan Series in Global Public Diplomacy,
https://doi.org/10.1007/978-3-030-04405-3_8

Yet, the digitalization of public diplomacy has equipped diplomats with new tools for managing their nation's image and reputation. Social media sites enable diplomats to author a self-portrait of their nation that celebrates national achievements, promotes national culture, and manifests national norms. These self-portraits may also be used to demonstrate how a nation's foreign policy stems from its values and beliefs. Even more importantly, diplomats can use these self-portraits to comment on daily events ranging from holidays and viral Internet memes to geopolitical crisis. The national image is thus not confined to momentous occasions such as landing on the moon or winning World War II. Rather, social media facilitates the presentation of the state in everyday life, to paraphrase Erving Goffman (1990).

From the perspective of the digital society, such self-portraits can be regarded as "selfies", and the authoring of these portraits may be labeled as a form of "selfie diplomacy." Much like the selfies of individuals, national selfies are also meant to create an online persona of dexterity. There is no room for failure or immorality in national selfies. In addition, like individual selfies the national selfie is also an instrument of conformity rather than individuality (Manor & Soone, 2018). Through selfies, nations demonstrate their adherence to the norms and values that have been deemed as desirable by the international community. Lastly, through selfie diplomacy the nation state becomes individualized. It bears the characteristics of a digital individual as it has a social media profile, a profile picture and even likes and dislikes. It is this individualization that enables the nation to compete with other individuals on the social media marketplace.

This chapter examines how the logic of the digital society has impacted the practice of nation branding through the concept of selfie diplomacy. Conceptually, selfie diplomacy is situated at the intersection between nation branding and public diplomacy. Thus, this chapter begins by defining the term "nation branding" and analyzes the conceptual relationship between nation branding and public diplomacy. Next, the chapter introduces the term selfie diplomacy and demonstrates how nation branding activities on digital platforms differ from those conducted via mass media. Finally, the chapter reviews two case studies of selfie diplomacy activities: the selfie of America in the age of Trump and Poland's historic selfie. The following section explores the debate among nation branding scholars regarding one's ability to craft and manage a national brand.

From Coca-Cola to Global Britain

At the turn of the twenty-first century, scholars, diplomats and branding experts found themselves engaging with the notion that the nation state could be branded like a can of Coca-Cola (Gudjonsson, 2005). Soon, a debate erupted among scholars leading to the creation of three camps. Absolutists, according to Gudjonsson, maintain that nations have similar qualities to brands and obey similar rules. Like commercial brands, nations also strive to differentiate themselves from one another. According to absolutists, the motto "liberté, égalité, fraternité" was like Nike's slogan "Just Do It" as France attempted to differentiate itself from previous systems of governments. Moderates believe that unlike a commercial brand, the nation state is made of a plethora of individuals who have unique characteristics. Thus, the nation state cannot be marketed as a monolithic unit or a pair of Nike running shoes. Yet, moderates do believe that some branding techniques may be used to manage the national image and strengthen a nation's industrial brands. Royalists, according to Gudjonsson, reject the concept of nation branding, arguing that processes that influence a nation are far more profound than those that affect a can of Coca-Cola. In the royalist view, the nation is almost a divine structure as it wields influence over the souls of its citizens.

While the debate surrounding nation branding persists to this day, MFAs and governments throughout the world have invested substantial resources in nation branding campaigns. From Mexico to Taiwan and Malaysia to Kenya, the belief that nations can be branded continues to attract disciples both within governments and MFAs. While not all governments believe that their nation is like a product, many believe that its image can be proactively managed and improved. They would thus subscribe to Fan's definition of nation branding as "a process by which a nation's image can be created, monitored, evaluated and proactively managed in order to improve or enhance the nation's reputation among a target international audiences" (Fan, 2010). The *image* in Fan's definition relates to what citizens regard as most distinctive, enduring and central about their nation. *Reputation* relates to feedback received from the outside world concerning the credibility of a nation's claims about itself. In other words, the nation projects a certain image of itself which can either be accepted or rejected by the outside world.

Fan's definition includes three important components. The first is that nation branding is a process. As diplomats throughout the world have learned, altering people's perceptions of a certain nation is a demanding task. The reason for this is that national images are cognitive mechanisms that, like stereotypes, help people make sense of their world (Kotler & Gertner, 2002; Papadopoulos & Heslop, 2002). When people think of different nations, certain images or associations immediately come to mind. While Germany may be associated with automotive engineering, soccer championships and a dark past, Switzerland is likely to be associated with Alpine landscapes, private banking and wooden clocks. Yet if national images are indeed cognitive devices, then altering them requires long-term commitment and effort.

Second, Fan's definition suggests that the goal of nation branding is to improve or enhance the nation's reputation. By *improving*, scholars often refer to enhancing the nation's ability to attract investments. Nation branding thus remains rooted in the economic logic of globalization, which views nations as competing with one another over a limited pool of resources. Attracting these resources demands that nations differentiate themselves from one another through the development of a distinctive national image (Anholt & Hildreth, 2005; Aronczyk, 2008; Kaneva, 2011; Van Ham, 2008). Israel, for instance, brands itself as a hub of ingenuity and the "Start Up Nation" as opposed to "Incredible India" or "Global Britain."

Third, Fan's definition states that nation branding campaigns are targeted at foreign populations. The question that follows is: Are their conditions under which foreign populations would reject a national image? Scholars suggest that national brands must hold true to reality. Nations that delight in waging wars cannot brand themselves as peace-loving, while countries plagued by civil unrest cannot brand themselves as attractive investment destinations. As Nicholas Cull (2008) argued, national images are likely to be rejected when their divergence from a perceived reality is too great. Causey and Howard (2013) also stated that digital activities are likely to backfire if a nation's statements negate its policies.

Aronczyk (2013) added an important dimension to Fan's definition by arguing that national images can facilitate diplomatic achievements. According to Aronczyk, nation branding is used to create an image of legitimacy and authority which helps the nation find a seat at the table of global diplomacy. For this reason, national images often articulate the values and norms nations adhere to and demonstrate how such norms guide nations' foreign policies (Natarajan, 2014). By demonstrating its commitment to the global promotion of human rights, a nation may find a seat at the United Nations (UN) Human Rights Council. Similarly, by emphasizing its effort to mediate tensions between opposing factions a nation may earn a non-permanent seat at the UN Security Council.

Yet, scholars have also argued that unlike a can of Coca-Cola, national brands are dramatically impacted by events that cannot be controlled by marketers and diplomats. Wars, crises, financial upheavals, and even domestic political drama can all impact the national image rendering nation branding activities irrelevant. National leaders can also influence the national brand. At times, the image of the national leader even eclipses that of the nation in what is called a "Halo Effect" (Papadopoulos & Heslop, 2002). Such was the case when the brand of George W. Bush had a negative impact on brand America as a whole following the invasions of Iraq and Afghanistan and the War on Terror. Conversely, the election of Barack Obama had a temporary positive halo effect on brand America (Quelch & Jocz, 2009). Other leaders who may have had a "Halo Effect" on their nation's image include Canada's Justin Trudeau and Turkey's Recep Tayyip Erdogan.

Of course, "Halo Effects" are not necessarily uniform across the world. Trudeau is popular in the West, but unpopular in India. Bush is unpopular in the West, but loved in East Timor. The brand of a nation can thus win allies and enemies in the same breath. This complicates the process of nation branding as diplomats must ask: who are we trying to win over and who are we willing to lose?

The fact that nation branding activities target foreign populations and aim to benefit the welfare of a nation suggests that there may be areas in which public diplomacy and nation branding overlap. This may especially be true in the digital age, as diplomats use social media sites for both activities. The Israeli MFA, for instance, operates the @Israel Twitter channel dedicated solely to promoting Israeli culture, values, and technological achievements. Yet, the MFA also manages a plethora of social media accounts that focus on public diplomacy activities such as narrating Israel's policies in the Middle East. Similarly, the Polish MFA manages the Polska.pl Facebook account that celebrates Polish cultural achievements and promotes the Polska brand alongside Twitter channels that focus on the nation's foreign policy initiatives (Manor, 2016). The overlap between public diplomacy and nation branding is explored in the following section.

L'Etat C'est Selfie (The State Is the Selfie)

Geyorgy Szondi (2008) stipulated that there are four models for conceptualizing the relationship between nation branding and public diplomacy. The first model assumes that nation branding and public diplomacy are distinct concepts, as nation branding focuses on achieving financial goals (such as attracting foreign investments) and public diplomacy promotes an array of policy goals. The second model conceptualizes public diplomacy as part of nation branding given that foreign policies can also be branded among foreign populations. Such was the case when the Obama administration marketed the Iran Deal to domestic and foreign publics via Twitter. The third model conceptualizes nation branding as a part of public diplomacy, as foreign publics are the intended audience of both activities. Lastly, the fourth model states that public diplomacy and nation branding are distinct yet overlapping concepts. The overlapping areas are the creation of positive images, the promotion of a national identity, culture, and values as well as two-way interactions and relationship building.

Szondi (2008) argued that the concepts of nation branding and public diplomacy have grown closer together following the emergence of relational approaches to public diplomacy. Like the "new" public diplomacy, nation branding activities also rest on two-way interactions and relationship building as personal experiences shape people's perceptions of other countries (Lodge, 2002; Skuba, 2002). When people have positive interactions with citizens or diplomats of a foreign nation, they are more likely to have a positive regard for that foreign nation. Nation branding experts therefore emphasize the need to interact with foreign publics and build relationships with them to ensure brand loyalty, or a consistently positive view of a foreign nation.

Aronczyk (2013) elaborated on Szondi's fourth and overlapping model by suggesting that nation branding is a proactive tool that enables a nation to repair its reputation, which may be damaged by foreign or domestic policies. Similarly, Manor and Segev (2015) suggested that nations can use social media to draw a new self-portrait, or selfie, thus distancing themselves from their past and re-inventing their brand. They refer to the use of social media to author such self-portraits as selfie diplomacy. One example of selfie diplomacy was the UK's Twitter campaign to end sexual violence in conflicts, which may have been an attempt to associate brand Britain with humanistic values and distance the UK from the legacy of the War on Terror.

Selfie diplomacy can also be used by nations to challenge their perception among foreign populations. Countries perceived as dull can use humor to alter their reputation, while countries that are associated with war can emphasize their culture and democratic traditions (Manor & Segev, 2015). Such was the case with Finland's national emoji campaign which was promoted by the Finnish MFA on social media sites and was used to negate the view of Finland as a cold and dissolute nation (Grossman, 2015). To paraphrase Ingmar Bergman—the nation is the skeleton awaiting the flesh and sinew of images.

As is the case with an individual's selfie, the national selfie consists of a narrative through which a nation demonstrates how its actions and policies stem from the values to which it subscribes. However, like the individual selfie, the national one is also a means of demonstrating conformity rather than individuality. As Manor and Segev wrote, selfie diplomacy is used by states to demonstrate their adherence to the values and norms that have been deemed as desirable by the international community. For example, Natarajan stated that India has adopted the self-narrative of a "soft power" and a culturally diverse democracy given its need to adhere to "established norms in a Western-influenced world order" (Natarajan, 2014). Moreover, as is the case with individual selfies, national selfies focus on specific issues while employing a unique tone, thus creating an authentic self-narrative. Lastly, as is the case with the individual selfie, the national selfie also focuses primarily on achievements and accomplishments rather than failures and disappointments. Subsequently, by analyzing the issues and tone of an MFA's selfie, one can analyze the image that a nation is promoting on social media sites.

Manor and Segev define selfie diplomacy as an MFA's use of social media channels to author a national self-portrait or brand. Selfie diplomacy is thus a form of nation branding conducted via digital platforms. Yet, in this chapter, the term selfie diplomacy also has another meaning, one that deals with the individualization of the nation state on social media. As was explored in Chapter 2, within the digital society social media sites constitute a marketplace where individuals compete with one another over the attention and adoration of digital publics. To do so, individuals author a unique and distinct iBrand that has its own tone, interests and appearance. Thus, on social media, the self becomes a brand. For the nation state, an opposite process occurs. When using social media for public diplomacy activities, diplomats author a national iBrand through which they can compete for the attention of digital publics with other iBrands, such as individuals or other nations.

Competing with other iBrands is achieved by creating a unique social media presence that has a distinct appearance, tone, and interests be it trade realtions, culture or diaspora outreach. Yet in the process, the nation state is individualized. On Facebook, the nation state has a profile page and profile picture and it can even like and share content. In addition, individuals can interact with the nation online as if it were another user. For instance, social media users can tag the State Department Facebook page in a comment, or ask it a question, or respond to its posts. The nation state thus acquires the traits of a digital self. The use of social media to author and manage a national iBrand is therefore a form of selfie diplomacy or diplomats' creation of a national digital self.

Through selfie diplomacy, MFAs and diplomats can adhere to the values and norms of the digital society. This is achieved by constantly sharing information about the activities, goals and achievements of the nation. Sharing information is required from all digital society members as it demonstrates a commitment to openness and feeds algorithms which are the foundations of the digital economy. Moreover, diplomats can use national selfies to comment on global events as they unfold, thereby lifting the veil of secrecy from diplomatic processes and demonstrating a commitment to transparency. Such a commitment is also required of all digital society members since transparency ensures that all adopt the norms and the logic of the social media marketplace. Lastly, when authoring a national selfie, diplomats help the nation state acquire the traits of a digital self, thus holding true to Storr's (2018) assertion that in the digital society, "The currency is the self and the gold standard is openness and transparency."

In summary, the use of social media to author and manage a national iBrand is a form of selfie diplomacy. This is because on social media, the nation is individualized as it acquires the traits of a digital self: It has a profile picture, an authentic voice and can be engaged with by other digital individuals. Through selfie diplomacy, the individualized nation comments on global and regional events and demonstrates its commitment to certain values and beliefs. And so, the nation becomes a brand, the brand becomes a selfie and the selfie *is* the individualized nation state. Yet, as is the case with any form of nation branding, selfie diplomacy also has its limits, as explored next.

The Limitation of Selfie Diplomacy

Although selfie diplomacy affords diplomats the ability to manage the national iBrand and compete on the social media marketplace, the practice of selfie diplomacy still faces several limitations. First, the national selfie must hold true with a perceived reality. The greater the divergence between the national image and national policies, the less credible the selfie becomes. Selfies that lack credibility may be rejected by digital publics, leading to a crisis of legitimacy for the nation state. Similarly, diplomats must contend with a possible divergence between their depiction of the nation and that of the global media. A nation branded by media institutions as a brutal dictatorship will be unable to promote a national selfie of benevolence. Such a gap between a nation's self-depiction and the media's depiction of that nation is regarded by this chapter as a *credibility gap*. One notable example is the Erdogan government's social media campaign following the 2016 failed coup attempt which argued that mass arrests of teachers and civil servants were necessary due to a plot against the nation. This campaign failed to counter the media narrative of "Erdogan's Revenge" as it was too far removed from the media's depiction of a government crackdown (see Chapter 7).

Additionally, competing on the social media marketplace requires that the national selfie comment on global and regional events as they unfold on the ground. This is because digital publics want to learn about events as they occur. Yet events, and policies that follow, must be incorporated into the selfie to ensure consistent narration. In other words, events must be interpreted and presented through the values and norms to which a nation adheres. Consistent narration is necessary as national images are cognitive schemas that take time to change or take shape.

Selfie diplomacy also requires a commitment to digital interactions and long-term relationship building. This is because people's attitudes toward nations are shaped by personal experiences. When the questions and comments of digital publics go unanswered, they have a negative experience, which may lead them to hold a more negative view of a certain nation. Conversely, diplomats' willingness to answer comments, provide information, and contend with criticism can lead to a positive online experience and a positive view of a foreign nation. Yet, as has been argued elsewhere in this book, online interactions between diplomats and digital publics are a rarity.

The past must also be present in the national selfie. The reason for this is that the digital society is one that longs for the past, for an era of clear dichotomies between good and bad and friend and foe. The digital society is a fluid one (Bauman & Lyon, 2016). New modalities of power emerge daily as new actors seek to exert their influence, whether these are terrorist groups that challenge the nation state or countries looking to reassert their global dominance. In a digital and liquid world, revolutionary ideas easily transcend borders and contest long-standing traditions or values while the demarcation lines between the domestic and the foreign are blurred, as no single nation can contend with climate change or safeguard itself from financial fluctuations. Amid this climate of instability, digital society members long for the familiar time before tradition was contested. By building on a nation's past, the selfie can make sense of the nation's present.

To analyze the current practice of selfie diplomacy, this chapter explores two case studies. The first is that of America's selfie in the age of Trump. The decision to focus the State Department's iBranding activities stemmed from a desire to evaluate how the election of Donald Trump has impacted America's online image. Previous studies have explored America's selfie during the Obama Presidency (Manor, 2017; Manor & Segev, 2015). Yet, changes in administration are likely to elicit changes in the national image as new policies are perused, new priorities are formulated, and a new diplomatic tone is adopted. Thus, changes in administration may signal the emergence of a new national selfie. The analysis of America's selfie under Trump thus offers a longitudinal analysis of selfie diplomacy.

The second case study explores the Polish MFA's attempts to refashion Poland's historic image. Specifically, the Polish MFA has used Twitter to distance Poland from Nazi atrocities committed on Polish soil during World War II. By redrawing its historic image, Poland may be attempting to refashion its contemporary selfie. For instance, Poland's historic selfie may be used to demonstrate Poland's current adherence to desired values and norms. The past may be an important component of a nation's selfie as historic blemishes have future ramifications. Even after 70 years, Germany's national image cannot be separated from its atrocities during the Holocaust. The following section includes the analysis of America's selfie in the age of the Trump Presidency.

AMERICA'S SELFIE IN THE AGE OF TRUMP

In 2015, Manor and Segev analyzed America's selfie. The authors chose to focus on the USA given the "crisis in the Brand America." As it emerged victorious from the Cold War, America's brand was associated with the values of democracy and freedom while its image was tied to the promotion of human rights. Yet the Bush administration's War on Terror, the invasions of Iraq and Afghanistan, the alleged torture of prisoners in the Guantanamo Bay detention center, and America's refusal to join the Kyoto climate protocol all had an immensely negative impact on America's image. Throughout the world, the USA was viewed as a greedy, self-serving and anti-Muslim militaristic empire (Quelch & Jocz, 2009).

The crisis in Brand America was made evident in a series of public opinion polls. One of these, conducted in 2007 by the BBC World Service, found that across all countries polled, one in two respondents believed that the USA played a negative role in the world. Similarly, the Pew Research Center found that between 2002 and 2004, the image of America grew unfavorable among some of its closest allies, such as the UK and Spain, and friendly Muslim countries such as Pakistan and Indonesia (BBC, 2007; Fullerton, Kendrick, Chan, Hamilton, & Kerr, 2007). Yet, the election of Barack Obama was hailed by many as an opportunity to alter America's image and re-associate Brand America with positive values (Quelch and Jocz, 2009).

Manor and Segev (2015), therefore, assumed that the State Department would be engrossed in the task of authoring a new American selfie and managing the nation's image. Using thematic analysis, Manor and Segev analyzed 63 Facebook posts and 112 tweets published by the State Department during December of 2013. Their analysis revealed four themes that comprised America's selfie. The first theme focused on mending America's relations with the Arab and Muslim worlds. Content comprising this theme highlighted America's efforts to negotiate a peace treaty between Israel and Palestine, America's commitment to using diplomacy rather than force to contend with Iran's nuclear ambitions and America's open criticism of Arab dictatorships.

The second theme dealt with America's moral leadership and included tweets and posts in which the USA called on foreign leaders and foreign countries to uphold democratic processes during times of conflict and to promote democratic reforms. The State Department also demonstrated

U.S. financial support for fledgling democracies and for victims of natural disasters. The third theme dealt with America's "military might." Notably, Manor and Segev found an overall lack of reference to U.S. military power. America's presence in Iraq was mentioned in only one post, which demonstrated how dogs help soldiers to clear mines. While the North Atlantic Treaty Organization (NATO) was mentioned in several posts and tweets, it was branded as an international peacekeeping organization rather than a military alliance.

The final theme was America's economic leadership. Manor and Segev argued that social media content focused on U.S. support of clean energy and its contribution to green energy initiatives around the globe, as well as a new trade agreement between the USA and EU that would boost both economies. This trade agreement was especially important given the damage caused to European economies following the 2008 financial crisis. America was thus portrayed as leading a climate-oriented economy.

Manor and Segev concluded that the State Department branded America as an economically responsible and climate-oriented superpower, guided by values and committed to diplomacy and building meaningful relations with the Muslim world (Manor & Segev, 2015). This selfie was in direct contrast to the image of America during the Bush years. In 2016, Manor returned to the State Department's Facebook page to reexamine America's selfie and explore the extent to which the State Department authored a consistent and coherent national selfie. Given that nation branding is a long-term process, and considering that national brands are cognitive mechanisms, consistent narration is required if a nation is to successfully manage its image and influence its reputation.

After analyzing 146 Facebook posts Manor, found that the 2016 selfie consisted of four themes, the first of which was "America's Moral Leadership- Leading by Example." This theme demonstrated how American national values influence its policies. For instance, one post stated that America's story is that of diverse groups, religions, cultures and identities coming together to have "*Honest, respectful dialogues*" (Manor, 2017). This post articulated the values that America holds dear to its heart: religious tolerance, multiculturalism, and open dialogue, which are the basis of democracy. America's promotion of democratic values was evident in posts describing U.S. support for fledgling democracies. America's support of religious tolerance was manifest in a statement by Secretary of State John Kerry: "Fighting for religious

tolerance will define the 21st century." Finally, support for multiculturalism was manifest in America's support and acceptance of refugees from
Syria.

These posts demonstrate how everyday events, such as accepting
Syrian refugees, can be integrated into the national selfie and used to
identify national values. Manor also found that America's moral leadership rested on collaborative approaches to diplomacy. Throughout the
month of January 2016, the USA announced plans to act in unison with
its allies to tackle global issues ranging from human trafficking to aiding
Syrian refugees and promoting religious tolerance.

The second theme focused on "Engagement with the World." Posts
that aligned with this theme demonstrated American commitment to
solving crises through diplomacy and coalitions rather than force. In
his State of the Union address, President Obama focused on the Global
Coalition against Daesh, the coalition of countries that resolved the
Iranian nuclear crisis, and the collation of countries that helped stop the
spread of Ebola. Manor (2017) concluded that "Obama's comments
contribute to the portrayal of America as a nation that has abandoned
unilateral actions and is attempting to engage with other nations on a
range of global issues." Other posts in this theme demonstrated how
America's commitment to engagement led to diplomatic breakthroughs
in the Iran negotiations, the re-establishment of ties with Cuba, and
the Trans-Pacific Partnership trade agreement signed between America
and 11 countries in the Pacific region. Manor even found that the word
"engagement" was repeatedly invoked by American diplomats, leaders,
and spokespeople in reference to a plethora of diplomatic initiatives.

The third theme comprising America's selfie dealt with a "Common
War on Terror." Posts in this theme depicted the War on Terror as a
collaborative one rather than a unilateral war headed by the U.S. Posts
focused on the Global Coalition against Daesh and multilateral meetings
during which American diplomats and their peers coordinated counterterrorism activities. Posts also highlighted John Kerry's statement that
Daesh and terrorism can only be defeated by a broad coalition of faith-
based organizations, states, and non-state actors.

The fourth and last theme included posts that highlighted America's
commitment to a "Climate Oriented Economy." In one blog post published on the State Department's Facebook page, Secretary Kerry said
that the main achievements of U.S. diplomacy in 2015 included the
Trans-Pacific Partnership trade agreement, which "Protects workers

and the environment," and China's willingness to sign the Paris climate accord following intense diplomatic engagement. Other posts depicted U.S. financial aid to foreign countries as aiming to support climate-oriented economic development.

Manor concluded that "The State Department portrays the U.S. as a diplomatic superpower that is guided by values and dedicated to tackling global challenges, such as climate change, through dialogue and engagement." The 2016 selfie was thus quite like the selfie identified by Manor and Segev in 2013, which portrayed the USA as a climate-oriented superpower guided by values and committed to diplomacy and building relations with the Muslim world.

It may thus be argued that during the Obama administration, U.S. diplomats had authored a consisted national selfie of America, which negated America's image under President Bush. While Bush refused to sign the Kyoto protocol, Obama's America led a climate-oriented economy. While Bush framed the War on Terror as "You are either with us or with the terrorists" (Bush, 2001), Obama's America fought terror through a broad coalition. While Bush alienated the Muslim world, Obama's America engaged with it. And while Bush led by military force, Obama's led by diplomacy. The past was thus an integral element in America's selfie under President Obama. America's selfie also had a unique tone, which employed the terminology of "engagement" and focused on a set of issues. Thus, the selfie also constituted an iBrand that could successfully compete on the social media marketplace.

This chapter returned to the State Department's Facebook page in July of 2017 to analyze America's selfie in the age of President Trump. Once again, thematic analysis was employed to characterize America's current selfie and explore the extent to which it has altered following the election of Donald Trump. In total, 70 posts published during the month of July were analyzed and categorized into themes. In the first stage of analysis, 25 posts were reviewed and classified into themes based on their subject matter. For instance, several posts focused on American attempts to mediate an agreement between Qatar and its neighbors. Thus, the theme "Negotiations" was created. Another group of posts dealt with attempts to combat terrorism, which falls under the theme "War on Terror." In total, six themes were identified during this stage of analysis. In the next stage, 20 additional posts were reviewed to ensure the validity of the categorization process. This stage led to the consolidation of several themes. For instance, posts dealing with economic negotiations and trade agreements were grouped together in the theme "America's Business is Business." The thematic analysis resulted in the identification of four themes into which all 70 posts were categorized. All posts were gathered during July of 2017 and analyzed during January of 2018.

The first and most prevalent theme comprising America's selfie was that of "The Great Negotiator", which depicted Trump's America as a global diplomatic mediator. Posts comprising this theme dealt with American attempts to resolve the Gulf dispute between Qatar and its neighbors; American attempts to reduce tensions between Russia and Ukraine; intense diplomatic mediation between the Israeli and the Palestinian governments; attempts to broker a cease-fire in Syria; and measures taken to end the fighting in South Sudan. Posts in this theme tended to focus on the intensity of U.S. diplomatic activity, especially those undertaken by Secretary of State Rex Tillerson. During the month of July 2017, Tillerson held six meetings with Gulf leaders to resolve their dispute with Qatar while also attending several meetings with Ukrainian officials. During these meetings, Tillerson pledged U.S. support for Ukrainian territorial integrity and encouraged "the Government of Ukraine to continue implementing reforms that will strengthen Ukraine's economic, political, and military resilience."

Other posts dealt with repeated U.S. attempts to engage positively with Russia. These included a meeting between Presidents Trump and Putin and subsequent negotiations between U.S. and Russian policymakers that aimed to "seek a long-term solution that would address areas of bilateral concern that have strained the relationship" between both countries. Later in July, Secretary Tillerson appointed a Special Representative for Ukraine Negotiations tasked with working opposite the governments of France, Germany, and Russia. In total, 35% of all State Department posts during July of 2017 dealt with U.S. diplomatic mediations around the world.

The second most prevalent theme, comprising 25% of all State Department posts, demonstrated "America's Moral Leadership." Posts comprising this theme dealt with a wide range of issues including U.S. foreign aid projects to fight Ebola outbreaks, U.S. aid programs to help increase food security in the developing world, U.S. commitment to safeguarding the lives of journalists and promoting freedom of speech, U.S. plans to help establish humane prisons following the vision of Nelson Mandela, and U.S. calls for democratic reforms in countries throughout the world.

Notably, many posts in this theme were used to comment on everyday events and integrate these events into the national selfie. For instance, the State Department officially mourned the loss of Liu Xiaobo, a Chinese activist who died in prison after calling for democratic reforms in China. The State Department called on Chinese authorities to release Xiaobo's wife and end political persecutions. By doing so, the State Department demonstrated U.S. commitment to democratic values. In another post, the State Department condemned mass arrests in Turkey that undermine human rights and the rule of law. This direct rebuke of Turkey manifested America's commitment to protecting human rights around the world. Finally, the State Department condemned Russia for arresting Jehovah's Witnesses and restricting religious freedom.

However, unlike America's selfie during Obama's tenure, the State Department chose not to clearly identify the values that Trump's America would champion. In fact, the entire depiction of America as a nation that leads by moral example was missing from the 2017 selfie. The State Department did not use America's self-narrative or its history to demonstrate how American values guide the administration's foreign policies. Moreover, the State Department did not refer to values or norms when commenting on global events. While lamenting the passing of democratic reformers, the State Department failed to mention that America would support democracy when it is challenged. Similarly, when commenting on Turkish abuses of human rights, the State Department did not argue that human rights are a part of America's moral compass.

The third most prevalent theme, which included 23% of all posts published during July, dealt with the "Global War on Terror." Importantly, only three posts in this theme mentioned the Global Coalition against Daesh. One of these posts commented on the liberation of Mosul from Daesh and emphasized the Coalition's attempts to disrupt Daesh financing and recruitment. Two other posts were dedicated to labeling the Coalition against Daesh as the "largest coalition in history" and to identifying its member states including, Ethiopia, Turkey, and the UAE. Like the Obama selfie, the State Department did not share any images of American soldiers or American military activities. Notably, most posts comprising the "Global War on Terror" theme focused on Iran rather than Daesh. In these posts, Iran was portrayed as the number one exporter of terrorism and a global menace. As one State Department post proclaimed, "While ISIS receives headlines, Iran remains number one sponsor of terrorism."

Although the State Department noted that Iran was complying with the Iran nuclear agreement, it argued that the nation was undermining the spirit of the agreement through its terrorism-related activities. During the month of July, the State Department also called on Iran to comply with an investigation into the 1994 bombing of the Jewish community building in Argentina and announced sanctions on individuals involved in the Iranian ballistic missiles program. The State Department thus tied Iran's terrorist activities with its military activities and argued that the two cannot be separated. This argument negates the claim made by the Obama White House that the Iran Deal should focus solely on Iran's nuclear program and not its regional ambitions (Bjola & Manor, 2018). The negative depiction of Iran was markedly different from the Obama selfie, which emphasized America's commitment to engaging with Iran in constructive dialogue as part of a wider "diplomacy first" policy.

The posts comprising the "Global War on Terror" theme were markedly different than those published by the Obama State Department. In its 2016 selfie, the State Department went to great lengths to portray the Global Coalition as a new relationship between America and the Arab and Muslim world, as it includes Jordan, Qatar, and the UAE. These countries were repeatedly referenced in Obama State Department Facebook posts. By contrast, the Trump State Department refrained from emphasizing the role of Arab or Muslim countries in the Coalition and only mentioned them in one post. Moreover, in 2016, the State Department emphasized the role of additional partners in fighting Daesh including faith-based organizations, NGOs, and other non-state actors. The Trump State Department portrayed the War on Terror as an American endeavor that did not include non-state actors or additional partners. Lastly, the Obama selfie often highlighted U.S. initiatives in multilateral forums to combat terrorism, including the UN Security Council and NATO. The Trump selfie made no reference to any multilateral organizations during July of 2017.

The fourth and least prevalent theme identified in the Trump selfie was that of "America's Business is Business." This theme was comprised of posts that depicted U.S. foreign policies as being intrinsically linked to financial prosperity. For instance, during the month of July 2017, Secretary of State Rex Tillerson traveled to Saudi Arabia and Turkey.

Both trips were depicted through financial prisms as Tillerson met with Saudi Arabia's foreign minister to discuss mutual "stability, security and financial prosperity" while in Turkey, Tillerson sought to discuss projects that will "increase global energy security" and financial security. Similarly, economic issues and trade agreements were also prevalent in Facebook posts depicting meetings between President Trump and other world leaders. When meeting with British Prime Minister Theresa May, Trump was quoted as saying "We are working on a trade deal – a very, very big deal, a very powerful deal. Great for both countries. And I think we'll have that done very, very quickly." Another post describing a meeting between President Trump and the Prime Minister of Singapore stated that the leaders focused on new trade deals in Southeast Asia.

Other posts in this theme dealt with the need to reform financial markets and to remove obstacles to economic growth. One such post celebrated 25 years of open skies agreements between the USA and EU, which "reduced government intervention" and allowed economic expansion. During a joint press conference with French President Emanuel Macron, Trump stressed the need to tackle bureaucracies that stifle economic growth and to peruse trade agreements that are reciprocal and "fair to our workers." During the same press conference, Trump stated that strong borders would help the French and American civilizations overcome numerous challenges in the fields of finance and terrorism. Notably, the financial theme was the least prevalent one and consisted of 17% of all posts published by the State Department in July 2017.

Importantly, America's selfie in the age of Trump employs a new vernacular. While in 2016 the State Department extensively used the word "engagement," the Trump State Department routinely used the word "sanctions." Financial sanctions were the proposed remedy for many foreign policy challenges including Iran's nuclear ambitions, Venezuelan dictatorship, Syria's use of chemical weapons, and internal fighting in South Sudan. In addition, while the Obama administration spoke about leading a climate-oriented economy, the Trump administration made only one reference to global sustainability and no references to the dangers of climate change or globalization's impact on the environment.

The dominance of President Trump in State Department posts was far less noticeable than that of President Obama. When Trump's comments were posted on Facebook, they complemented America's current selfie as they focused on the need to reduce government bureaucracy and to secure Western countries' borders. The President also commented on Western civilization's ability to overcome any foe, whether domestic or foreign.

In summary, America's selfie in the age of Trump is that of a financial superpower dedicated to expanding its economic interests by eradicating the threat of terrorism and mediating global crises. American diplomacy no longer rests on engagement and dialogue but on financial stimulants and financial sanctions, as was evident in the depiction of Iran. But above all, America now leads alone. It has little need for multilateral organizations, military alliances and coalitions with non-state actors. This selfie is considerably different than that of Obama's America as it no longer focuses on mending relations with the Muslim world, engaging with former foes, caring for the environment, or adopting more collaborative forms of diplomacy. In fact, America's war on terror under Trump is similar to the Bush era, as America once again focuses its policy on a Muslim nation: Iran. While it still offers aid to the world, America is no longer portrayed as being guided by values or morals. Thus, America is not a moral compass, but a fortress of solitude looking to secure its own borders and interests by its own means. This selfie seems to resonate with the pillar of Trump's stated foreign policy: that of "America first."

The fact that America's selfie under Trump is different than that of the Obama administration is not surprising, for when administrations change, so do foreign policy priorities and the diplomatic tools that a nation wields to obtain its objectives. Yet, Brand America has long since been associated with certain values regardless of the identity of the American president. Indeed, since its establishment, America has served as a political exemplar that claims to promote the values of democracy, freedom and free enterprise. Of these three, only free enterprise is manifest in America's current selfie.

Values play a pivotal role in diplomacy, as morality breeds legitimacy on the international stage. Nations that are seen as promoting positive values, be it human rights or religious tolerance, are less likely to encounter objections to their foreign policy goals (Van Ham, 2013). Moreover, by depicting its adherence to desirable values and norms, a nation can more easily exercise power (Mor, 2012). The current American selfie suggests that America is no longer a moral compass, nor is it guided by a clear moral code. Such a selfie may, over time, prevent the USA from obtaining its foreign policy goals as digital publics come to regard America as a business leader rather than a moral leader.

The current American selfie is also representative of a "Halo Effect" in which brand Trump influences Brand America. Like Brand Trump, America now uses financial leverages to manage its relations with other countries. Like Brand Trump, it employs violent rhetoric as "engagement" is replaced with "sanctions" and like Brand Trump, America uses the art of the deal to secure its interests abroad. Given that brand Trump is not a popular one in many countries, the current American selfie risks further alienating digital publics.

Throughout recent history, America's brand has consistently been tainted by its military activities. In the 1960s, it was the Vietnam War, in the 1980s, it was the support of guerrilla fighters in Latin America, and in the twenty-first century, it was the use of drones in the War on Terror. As was the case with the Obama selfie, America's selfie in the age of Trump refrains from drawing attention to U.S. military activities. In this sense, Brand America diverges from Brand Trump, who has a very big red button on his desk from which he can launch nuclear missiles at North Korea. While America's selfie no longer focuses on norms and values, Poland's selfie attempts to re-associate Poland's brand with desirable norms by altering perceptions of its past. This selfie is evaluated in the following section.

POLAND'S HISTORIC SELFIE

The Polish MFA is no stranger to digital platforms, having established a formidable digital presence over the past decade. The ministry first migrated to Twitter in 2009, while its main Facebook profile was operational in 2010. In his interviews with Polish diplomats in 2016, Manor learned that the MFA uses Facebook strictly for the promotion of the Polska brand and, subsequently, posts deal with Polish scientific, cultural, and economic achievements. Other social media platforms such as Twitter and YouTube, are used for public diplomacy activities that target foreign populations, Polish diasporas and media organizations. Manor also learned that most individuals charged with overseeing digital activities at the Polish MFA were former journalists, media experts and public relations professionals. By 2015, these were managing a social media empire of 150 Twitter accounts, 74 Facebook pages, 38 YouTube channels, and an account on the Chinese social media platform Weibo.

One of the drivers of the digitalization of Polish public diplomacy is a desire to manage Poland's historic image. Already in 2015, Polish embassies and the Polish MFA had dedicated substantial digital resources to altering the perception of Poland's role in Nazi atrocities during World War II. Managing Poland's historic image is achieved by monitoring articles in the press pertaining to World War II and correcting journalists who mislabel "Nazi death camps" as "Polish death camps." For instance, on July 16, 2015, the Polish embassy in Ireland took to Twitter and demanded that the *Irish Examiner* correct an article that referred to Auschwitz as a "Polish death camp" rather than a "Nazi death camp". Other times, Polish embassies demand that these camps be referred to as "Nazi camps in occupied Poland." For instance, on February 27, 2017, the Polish embassy in Washington openly attacked *The New York Times* for using the term "concentration camps of Poland." In its tweet, the embassy employed the hashtag#WordsMatter. During July 2017, Poland's embassy in Canberra demanded that a popular Australian news website correct its reference to Auschwitz as a "Polish camp." During 2017 alone, more than ten Polish embassies and consulates demanded retractions or corrections from newspapers and publications around the world. In 2012, the Polish MFA invested additional resources in managing Poland's historical image by launching a dedicated Twitter account named "Truth About Camps", which is part of an ongoing campaign "aimed against false statements regarding Poland's alleged responsibility for the Holocaust."

Poland's selfie diplomacy activities thus seem to focus on two separate activities. On Facebook, the Polish MFA manages Poland's contemporary selfie, which deals mostly with cultural and scientific accomplishment. On Twitter, the MFA is managing Poland's historic selfie. One may wonder why the Polish MFA is dedicating so many resources to managing Poland's historic selfie. This chapter offers two possible answers. First, the historic association between Poland and Nazi concentration camps invariably impacts Poland's contemporary brand. Rather than associate Poland with liberal values, people may associate it with hate, inhumanity, brutality, and sadism. These values are all contrary to those celebrated by the international community and may thus prevent Poland from obtaining its foreign policy goals. By distancing itself from the horrors of World War II, Poland may be able to associate itself with the values of multiculturalism and democracy.

Second, in the age of images and selfies, a nation's past is as important as its present. This is because the past is used to understand the present. The digital society is one that longs for the simplicity and dichotomy of the past and therefore builds on the past to understand and make sense of the present. By removing the Holocaust's moral blemish from its past, Poland can increase its legitimacy in the present and go from being "bad" or evil to "good" or just. This may be an important goal for Poland's right-wing government, which is increasingly being scrutinized on the world stage and in the EU.

To manage its historical image, the Polish MFA has sought to disseminate a new selfie that illustrates the relationship between the Nazis and Poland. According to this selfie, Poland was the first victim of Nazi brutality, being the first nation to be conquered in 1939. The selfie states that the Nazi regime unleashed it ferocity against the Polish population and envisioned Poland as a land of slaves that would serve the German Reich. This selfie also argues that the death of Polish Jews was another facet of the Nazis' attack on Poland as these Jews were all Polish citizens.

Poland's historical selfie was perhaps best made evident in a YouTube video published by the Polish embassy to Washington in January of 2017. This video begins with the caption "Truth about German Nazi Camps." This caption may be regarded as an intentional reference to the 2016 Oxford Dictionary word of the year: post-truth. As such, the caption infers that this video will offer viewers that which is now a rare commodity: the truth. The caption "Truth about German Nazi Camps" therefore serves as a rhetorical device that lends legitimacy to the Polish embassy and, by extension, to its claims about history.

Next, the video includes the caption "words matter." This may be a reference to the phenomenon of "fake news" and "alternative facts" and is yet again a rhetorical device meant to establish credibility. However, the caption "words matter" is soon followed by a visual element: a drawing of the entrance to the most infamous Nazi concentration camp, Auschwitz. It is this drawing that suggests to the viewer that he has yet to be exposed to the truth about Nazi death camps, given that drawings and paintings are but an interpretation of the truth. This argument is furthered by the narration "*Words Matter, we hear this all the time. So why does the same not apply when discussing German World War II concentration camps?*"

The video then suggests that to learn the truth about Nazi camps, the viewer must return to the beginning of World War II and the Nazi invasion of Poland. While discussing the German invasion, the video transitions from drawings to photography, as shown in Fig. 8.1. This transition suggests that the viewer is now being told the truth given that photographs serve as historical records. They are regarded as historical evidence that certain events took place at a given time and place.

Fig. 8.1 From drawing to photography

The narration of this part of the video states that "*Poland alone lost 6 million citizens, including 3 million Jews.*" This narration brings to the forefront the Polish argument that Poland was a victim of Nazi Germany and that it too suffered from the brutal violence of the Nazi regime. This narration makes clear that the Jews who died in Nazi concentration camps were not just any Jews, but Polish citizens. The arguments presented in this part of the video counter a popular historical narrative that depicts Poland as "Hitler's silent accomplice." Thus, this video not only promotes a Polish selfie, but also negates other narratives spread about Poland.

The transition from drawings to photography occurs yet again when the systematic annihilation of the Jews is mentioned. The transition from a drawing of children in concentration camps to a photograph of these children is meant to negate another historical narrative of Poland as a nation that has yet to come to terms with its past. It is the image of Jews in concentration camps that claims that Poland does not shun away from its past; rather, it deals with it through facts and historical accuracy. It should be mentioned that the use of images of children may be an attempt to evoke an emotional response that will make the viewer more receptive to the embassy's message.

Next, the viewer is exposed to a map of Poland, which includes the location of Nazi concentration camps while the caption reads "Occupied Polish Territories." The use of maps lends additional credence to the

Polish embassy's arguments, as maps are also historical artifacts that are perceived as trustworthy. According to the narration, the Nazis undertook the systematic murder of the Jews by establishing extermination camps on "occupied Polish territories" (Fig. 8.2).

Finally, after making a claim to truth through pictures and proving its trustworthiness through maps, the Polish embassy presents its main argument: that journalists routinely misuse the term "Polish camps" instead of "German camps on Polish soil." "This is wrong", according to the video, as "there were no Polish camps." Next, the embassy claims that misleading language obscures the tragedy of millions who died in the Holocaust and that "It's not just semantics. It is a matter of historical integrity and accuracy." In this manner, the embassy depicts itself as fighting for the memory of Jews rather than attempting to reshape Poland's historic selfie.

Notably, this video includes an attack on journalists, who are depicted as both untrustworthy and immoral because they add insult to the

Fig. 8.2   A map of Nazi concentration camps in occupied Poland

injury of those who perished in the Holocaust. The video therefore echoes attacks on media institutions heard around the world and furthers
a potentially dangerous narrative—that of the "fake news" media that
deliberately biases publics against certain nations or leaders.

In addition to the video, content shared on the @TruthAboutCamps
Twitter channel is diverse and ranges from statements by the Polish
Prime Minister to Polish events honoring the memory of Holocaust
victims. The Twitter account also retweets relevant content published by Polish embassies around the world. For instance, on January
27, 2018, the Polish embassy in Switzerland honored the memory
of a Swiss diplomat who issued fake passports to Jews, thus enabling
them to flee the Nazis. The embassy tweet ended with the hashtag
#HolocaustRemembrance. Thus, the Polish MFA and its embassies do
not only distance Poland from the atrocities of World War II, but they
associate Poland with the endeavor to remember those who perished in
the Holocaust and not repeat the mistakes of the past.

In the days leading up to the International Holocaust Remembrance
Day of 2017, Polish embassies and consulates in Austria, Germany,
Norway, Portugal, and Spain all turned to Twitter to demand retractions from newspapers who used the phrase "Polish death camps." All
these activities were retweeted in Polish by the MFA. In fact, much of
the content published on the @TruthAboutCamps Twitter account is in
Polish. This suggests that the Twitter account targets both domestic and
foreign audiences. While English language tweets may focus on re-crafting Poland's historic selfie, Polish language tweets may demonstrate to
Polish citizens that their MFA is championing an important national
cause.

Indeed, the association between Poland and Nazi atrocities is an
important domestic issue in Poland, made evident by recent legislation to
prosecute those who misrepresent Poland's role in World War II (John,
2018). By championing the cause of re-crafting Poland's historical selfie,
and actively monitoring newspapers and publicly demanding retractions
from publications, the Polish MFA may be able to establish a domestic
constituency for itself. This is of great importance given that globalization has seen a reduction in the agency of MFAs. In the globalized
world, more and more government ministries face the world given the
need to coordinate global solutions to planetary challenges. Ministries
of health, energy, the environment, and agriculture all collaborate with
foreign peers. MFAs have thus lost their monopoly on managing all the

nation's foreign affairs. To counterweight this loss and protect their territory within governments, many MFAs attempt to leverage digital technologies to create domestic constituencies. Some MFAs, such as Canada, prioritize providing quick and efficient consular aid. Other ministries, such as the UK FCO, offer a prism through which world events are narrated and their impact on the UK is explained. Poland's MFA seems to focus on championing domestic causes. Like Spry (2018), this chapter also concludes that the digitalization of public diplomacy has brought about the emergence of domestic public diplomacy.

The Polish MFA may be close to obtaining its goal of managing Poland's historic selfie. Using the FollowerWonk application, and a sample of 5000 Twitter followers, this chapter found that the @TruthAboutCamps account attracts followers from all over the world including Twitter users in Austria, Belarus, Belgium, Finland, Germany, Greece, Ireland, Israel, Norway, Portugal, Romania, Spain, UK, Ukraine, the Baltic States, the Middle East, and North America. Importantly, the biggest hub of Twitter followers for @TruthAboutCamps is in Poland itself.

CONCLUSIONS

This chapter sought to examine the nation branding activities of MFAs. Its main argument has been that the use of digital platforms to create, refashion, and manage a national brand results in the emergence of an individualized nation which bears the characteristics of a digital self. Like any Facebook user, the nation state has a profile page, a profile picture, likes, and dislikes, and can interact with other users. And so, the nation becomes a brand, the brand becomes a selfie, and the selfie is the individualized state. Thus, selfie diplomacy is a term that relates both to the use of digital platforms to manage the national image, or brand, and the subsequent emergence of the individualized digital state.

The conceptualization of selfie diplomacy introduced in this chapter can best be explained by a mélange of the technological and societal prisms. From the perspective of the societal prism, diplomats now utilize digital platforms to create a national brand that can be disseminated among global digital publics. Yet when employing digital platforms, diplomats adopt the logic and norms of the digital society. As the technological prism would argue, the use of Facebook to manage a brand can only occur if diplomats adopt the logic of Facebook, which includes the constant sharing of information, the adoption of a unique tone, and the creation of an authentic digital self. Selfie diplomacy is thus the result of diplomats' desires to employ digital platforms, and their adherence to the logic of digital technologies once these have been employed. Yet as Manor and Soone (2018) have argued, selfies do not center on individuality or originality but are, rather, tools of conformity. Through selfies, nations demonstrate their adherence to the value and norms celebrated by the international community. This was most evident in Poland's historic selfie, which may help to distance Poland from the atrocities of World War II and associate the Polish brand with the values of multiculturalism and diversity.

Poland's focus on the past is also emblematic of the fact that selfies are the clearest manifestation of the nostalgic nature of the digital society. While the digital society is a fluid one, digital society members long for dichotomies that have traditionally separated the good from the bad and the benevolent from the evil. Such was the case with the dichotomies of World War II or of the Cold War. By refashioning its past, Poland may attempt to acquire the connotation of "good" rather than the connotation of "bad."

The analysis of America's selfie in the age of Trump demonstrates how changes in administration lead to changes in national selfies. This in itself is not surprising as new administrations adopt new foreign policy goals, instruments, and priorities. Moreover, America's current selfie seems to resonate with the selfie of President Trump. The State Department portrays America as committed to the art of the deal, unilateral action and to turning a profit. As such, the credibility gap between America's self-portrayal and its portrayal by the global media is relatively small. Digital publics may thus not contest or reject America's selfie, as they did in the Bush era when America spoke of democracy but acted with force. Yet the American selfie in the age of Trump does seem to negate 60 years of American public diplomacy. America is no longer the world's moral compass, but its CEO. Situated within its fortress of solitude (or boardroom), it has no need for allies, coalitions, or and multilateral forums.

America's selfie did, however, demonstrate how everyday events are incorporated into the national selfie. State visits by Secretary of State Rex Tillerson were often portrayed as furthering America's financial interests, while bilateral meetings between President Trump and world leaders ended with statements about trade agreements and deregulation of financial markets. In this way, the selfie is manifest on a day-to-day basis.

This is important as it may allow the nation state to reassert itself in the age of networks. As was argued in Chapter 2, the networked society is one in which state agency is migrating upwards, to ultra-national entities such as the EU, downwards, to networks of digital users, and outwards, to NGOs and civil society organizations (Copeland, 2013). Yet selfie diplomacy enables the nation to project itself in everyday life. Through digital platforms, the nation comments on daily events, partakes in daily rituals (e.g., Throwback Thursdays), and engages with its citizens. The nation is thus brought to life on an everyday basis rather than during global summits or international sporting events. This may help the nation reassert its presence in the age of networks and decreasing state agency.

This chapter also demonstrates that a government's domestic agenda can impact an MFA's process of digitalization. The Polish government's emphasis on distancing the nation from Nazi atrocities led to new working routines such as monitoring newspapers and publications around the world and demanding retractions when the terms "Polish death camps" were used. Similarly, multimedia was used to redraw the nation's past while pictures and maps were employed to validate the MFA's historical claims. The norm that followed was that of domestic public diplomacy or direct communication between the MFA and its national citizenry. Poland is not the only MFA to set its sights on developing a domestic constituency. In the age of globalization, MFAs need to interact with their citizens to safeguard their territory within governments. They can no longer face the world with their backs to the nation (Copeland, 2013). The digitalization of public diplomacy has thus led to the emergence of domestic public diplomacy.

Importantly, the Polish case study also demonstrates how the identity of those managing MFA digital activities influences the digitalization of public diplomacy. In 2015, Manor found that the Polish MFA's digital activities were managed by social media experts and public relations specialists rather than diplomats. These may have introduced the logic of branding into the MFA and identified brand management as an important public diplomacy goal. This, in turn, led to new working routines and values.

Constance Duncombe (2017) suggested that a nation may engage in a "struggle for recognition" when it believes "it is recognized in a way that is different from how it represents itself." As part of this struggle, a nation may try to convince others that is should be represented and recognized in a different way. Utilizing social media, a nation may create an "us" versus "them" dichotomy through which it can represent itself. This chapter illustrated how Poland uses Twitter to engage in such a "struggle for recognition" by creating a historic dichotomy between itself and Nazi Germany.

Causey and Howard (2013) have asked if diplomats' efforts to increase their social media reach are genuine attempts to facilitate interactions with digital publics or merely new packaging for traditional public diplomacy goals. This chapter suggests that there are a myriad of factors that influence diplomats' attempts to attract more followers, ranging from a desire to manage the national image to a government's domestic agenda, the need to adhere with the norms of the digital society, and the adoption of the logic that underpins digital technologies. Yet it is equally important to remember that without attracting followers, diplomats cannot practice public diplomacy.

Notably, this chapter limited its analysis to the selfie activities of MFAs and did not evaluate how digital publics engage with these selfies. In Fan's terminology, this chapter examined nations' images rather than their reputations. Future studies should examine the manner in which digital publics accept or contest national selfies. This can be achieved by assessing the feedback of digital publics. As Olubukola Adesina (2017) wrote, digital technologies are instrumental as they enable direct, unmediated, interactions with digital publics. Such interactions include public feedback. At the most basic level, feedback from digital publics can help diplomats fine-tune their messages so as to increase their digital reach. At the next level, feedback can help a nation manage its image and identity claims. At the highest level, feedback from digital publics can, and should, inform policy formulation.

As the next chapter demonstrates, MFAs are not the only ones to create and manage brands. In the digital age, ambassadors are also transformed into iBrands.

REFERENCES

Adesina, O. S. (2017). Foreign policy in an era of digital diplomacy. *Cogent Social Sciences, 3*(1), 1297175.

Anholt, S., & Hildreth, J. (2005). Let freedom and cash registers ring: America as a brand. *Place Branding, 1*(2), 164–172.

Aronczyk, M. (2008). 'Living the brand': Nationality, globality, and the identity strategies of nation branding consultants. *International Journal of Communication, 2*, 25.

Aronczyk, M. (2013). *Branding the nation: The global business of national identity*. New York: Oxford University Press.

Bauman, Z., & Lyon, D. (2016). Remoteness, distancing and automation. In Z. Bauman & D. Lyon (Eds.), *Liquid surveillance* (pp. 76–99). Cambridge: Polity Press.

BBC. (2007). Poll: World view of United States role goes from bad to worse. *BBC World Service*. Retrieved from http://www.bbc.co.uk/pressoffice/pressreleases/stories/2007/01_january/23/us.shtml.

Bjola, C., & Manor, I. (2018). Revisiting Putnam's two-level game theory in the digital age: Domestic digital diplomacy and the Iran nuclear deal. *Cambridge Review of International Affairs, 31*, 1–30.

Causey, C., & Howard, P. N. (2013). Delivering digital public diplomacy. In R. S. Zaharna, A. Arsenault, & A. Fisher (Eds.), *Relational, networked and collaborative approaches to public diplomacy* (pp. 144–156). New York, NY: Taylor & Francis.

Copeland, D. (2013). Taking diplomacy public: Science, technology and foreign ministries in a heteropolar world. In R. S. Zaharna, A. Arsenault, & A. Fisher (Eds.), *Relational, networked and collaborative approaches to public diplomacy* (pp. 56–69). New York, NY: Taylor & Francis.

Cull, N. J. (2008). Public diplomacy: Taxonomies and histories. *The Annals of the American Academy of Political and Social Science, 616*(1), 31–54.

Duncombe, C. (2017). Twitter and transformative diplomacy: Social media and Iran–US relations. *International Affairs, 93*(3), 545–562.

Fan, Y. (2010). Branding the nation: Towards a better understanding. *Place Branding and Public Diplomacy, 6*(2), 97–103.

Fullerton, J. A., Kendrick, A., Chan, K., Hamilton, M., & Kerr, G. (2007). Attitudes towards American brands and brand America. *Place Branding and Public Diplomacy, 3*(3), 205–212.

Goffman, E. (1990). *The presentation of self in everyday life*. London, UK: Penguin Books.

Grossman, S. (2015, November). Finland is launching a special set of national emoji. *Time*. Retrieved from http://time.com/4100041/finland-national-emoji/.

Gudjonsson, H. (2005). Nation branding. *Place Branding, 1*(3), 283–298.

John, T. (2018, February). Poland just passed a Holocaust bill that is causing outrage. Here's what you need to know. *Time*. Retrieved from http://time.com/5128341/poland-holocaust-law/.

Kaneva, N. (2011). Nation branding: Toward an agenda for critical research. *International Journal of Communication, 5*, 25.

Kotler, P., & Gertner, D. (2002). Country as brand, product, and beyond: A place marketing and brand management perspective. *Journal of Brand Management, 9*(4), 249–261.

Lodge, C. (2002). Success and failure: The brand stories of two countries. *Journal of Brand Management, 9*(4), 372–384.

Manor, I. (2016). Are we there yet: Have MFA s realized the potential of digital diplomacy? *Brill Research Perspectives in Diplomacy and Foreign Policy, 1*(2), 1–110.

Manor, I. (2017). America's selfie—Three years later. *Place Branding and Public Diplomacy, 13*(4), 308–324.

Manor, I., & Segev, E. (2015). America's selfie: How the US portrays itself on its social media accounts. In C. Bjola & M. Holmes (Eds.), *Digital diplomacy theory and practice* (pp. 89–108). Oxon: Routledge.

Manor, I., & Soone, L. (2018, January). The digital industries: Transparency as mass deception. *Global Policy*. Retrieved from https://www.globalpolicyjournal.com/articles/science-and-technology/digital-industries-transparency-mass-deception.

Mor, B. D. (2012). Credibility talk in public diplomacy. *Review of International Studies, 38*(2), 393–422.

Natarajan, K. (2014). Digital public diplomacy and a strategic narrative for India. *Strategic Analysis, 38*(1), 91–106.

Papadopoulos, N., & Heslop, L. (2002). Country equity and country branding: Problems and prospects. *Journal of Brand Management, 9*(4), 294–314.

Quelch, J. A., & Jocz, K. E. (2009). Can brand Obama rescue brand America? *The Brown Journal of World Affairs, 16*(1), 163–178.

Skuba, C. (2002). Branding America. *Georgetown Journal of International Affairs, 3,* 105–114.

Spry, D. (2018). Facebook diplomacy: A data-driven, user-focused approach to Facebook use by diplomatic missions. *Media International Australia, 168*(1), 62–80.

Storr, W. (2018). *Selfie: How the West became self-obsessed*. London: Picador.

Szondi, G. (2008). *Public diplomacy and nation branding: Conceptual similarities and differences*. Clingendael: Netherlands Institute of International Relations.

Transcript of President Bush's Address. (2001, September 21). *CNN*. Retrieved from http://edition.cnn.com/2001/US/09/20/gen.bush.transcript/.

Van Ham, P. (2008). Place branding: The state of the art. *The Annals of the American Academy of Political and Social Science, 616*(1), 126–149.

Van Ham, P. (2013). Social power in public diplomacy. In R. S. Zaharna, A. Arsenault, & A. Fisher (Eds.), *Relational, networked and collaborative approaches to public diplomacy* (pp. 17–28). New York, NY: Taylor & Francis.

CHAPTER 9

The Digitalization of Ambassadors

Oh we're not loved. We're not even hated. We're only just sweetly ignored.
—Henry James, *The Ambassadors*

Technological advancements have, throughout history, influenced the roles of ambassadors. Up to the nineteenth century, ambassadors to foreign courts and nations were both "extraordinary and plenipotentiary", meaning that they were authorized to negotiate on behalf of their monarchs and even sign treaties in their names. Ambassadors were invested with the full powers of making decisions and taking actions on behalf of their nations (Roberts, 2017). This authority was granted to ambassadors given the communication technologies of the day: Letters sent by horseback and sea that would take days or weeks to reach their destination. Given the slow pace at which information traversed great distances, diplomatic decision-making was the privy of the ambassador. Yet the invention of the telegraph in the mid-nineteenth century had a profound impact on the functions of ambassadors. The telegraph enabled a government to manage its global affairs from the capital. As information circled the globe at great speeds, details of treaties and negotiations could be transmitted via the telegraph to the capital, where a response would be formulated and sent back to the ambassador. As such, diplomatic-decision making migrated from the ambassador to the MFA.

Ambassadors suddenly found themselves quite ordinary, as the power they once held was stripped by technological advancements.

I. Manor, *The Digitalization of Public Diplomacy*,
Palgrave Macmillan Series in Global Public Diplomacy,
https://doi.org/10.1007/978-3-030-04405-3_9

The telegraph did not, however, render ambassadors superfluous. On the contrary, ambassadors were still tasked with managing relations of friendship and enmity with foreign nations, to use Corneliu Bjola's (2013) terminology. While the MFA would formulate foreign policies, it was ambassadors who were charged with creating a receptive environment for the obtainment of these policies. Moreover, ambassadors were responsible for cultivating and maintaining ties between nations. This could be achieved by creating close personal relationships with national leaders, politicians, opinion makers, and the aristocracy. Equally important, ambassadors were still responsible for gathering and analyzing information that would inform policy making, including political scandals, rumors of war, the emergence of new political leaders, and the issues dominating the public agenda.

During the twentieth-century, advancements in Information and Communication Technologies (ICTs) once again influenced the role of ambassadors. By the 1940s, world leaders could regularly confer with one another over the phone, while policy-makers at MFAs could continuously interact with their peers in foreign countries. The role of ambassadors as mediators between two governments was thus further diminished. Moreover, the emergence of summit diplomacy, made possible thanks to advancements in transportation technologies, meant that world leaders could meet regularly to negotiate treaties, form coalitions, discuss trade agreements, and formulate joint responses to shared threats. World leaders thus took over the stage of diplomacy. Yet ambassadors remained the masters of backstage diplomacy. It was ambassadors who dealt with the minutia of the agreements that world leaders signed in front of blinking cameras, and it was ambassadors who solved problems and conflicts arising during international summits. As Piki Ish Shalom wrote, "diplomats are the back-stage managers of inter-state relations: those who toil behind the scenes to ensure that the seas of international relations remain calm" (Ish Shalom, 2015, p. 10).

The digitalization of public diplomacy has seen the migration of power back from the MFA to the embassy and, subsequently, to the ambassador. While world leaders may have asserted their presence on the stage of diplomacy, and while MFAs may be responsible for diplomatic decision-making, embassies have reasserted themselves in the field of public diplomacy. Digital technologies have increased an embassy's ability to communicate with foreign populations, create relationships with key audiences and elites, and manage their nation's image (Archetti,

2012; Metzgar, 2012; Seo, 2013). Importantly, it is embassies that are responsible for tailoring diplomatic communications to the unique characteristics of local audiences. As argued in Chapter 4, the second stage of public diplomacy's digitalization saw an increased emphasis on tailored communication in which messages resonate with the attributes of specific audiences. Through social media sites, embassies can tailor foreign policy messages to the norms, values, interests, and cultures of local audiences. For instance, France's embassy in Washington can promote French foreign policies while taking into account the norms and values of American digital publics, as well as the historic relations between both nations and the way France is perceived by Americans. The increased emphasis on tailored communication has further contributed to the migration of power from the MFA to embassies.

As Sabrina Sotiriu (2015) argues, embassies are now also tasked with gathering valuable information from digital platforms which may contribute to the policy formulation process at the MFA. It was the limited use of social media during the Arab Spring that led diplomats to regard digital platforms as an important source of information (A. Lutyens, personal communication, July 10, 2018). By monitoring conversations and debates on digital platforms, diplomats could gain unique insight into the issues dominating societal conversations, the attitude of citizens toward their governments, and the events and issues shaping public opinion. Monitoring online conversations was thus a means of assessing the national temperament and the stability of foreign governments and regimes. Soon diplomats were analyzing public conversation on social media platforms, news websites popular blogs, and even the messaging application WhatsApp, where messages can be sent to vast numbers of users (G. Lampe, personal communication, June 26, 2018). Social media sites also offered insight into how one nation was perceived by the population of another. The Lithuanian embassy in London could, for instance, analyze the comments posted in response to its tweets as well as their sentiment to identify which Lithuanian policies are viewed as contentious by the British public. Such information could then be sent to the Lithuanian MFA to be integrated into the policy formulation process. Nowadays, Israeli, Polish, New Zealand, and U.S. embassies routinely integrate information gathered from digital platforms into their reporting to the MFA (A. Lutyens, personal communication, July 10, 2018; Israel MFA, 2017; Manor, 2016).

The migration of power back to embassies and ambassadors is intrinsically linked to their newfound ability to gather valuable information online. As Wichowski states, information is the force that powers decision-making. It enables the identification of threats, the mapping of allies and foes, and the coordination of joint ventures. Information is thus a government's most valuable foreign policy asset (Wichowski, 2015, p. 59).

Studies have, however, shown that an embassy's use of digital platforms is often reliant on the ambassador's attitude toward digitalization. Embassies headed by ambassadors who regard digital platforms as an asset are more likely to utilize digital platforms in public diplomacy activities. Such embassies are also more likely to use digital technologies in innovative ways (Manor, 2016). Conversely, embassies headed by ambassadors who regard digital platforms as a liability are likely to be inactive online. Thus, ambassadors now serve as digital gatekeepers. For this reason, MFAs often offer special digital training to their ambassadors. In the Finnish MFA, for example, each ambassador receives one-on-one digital training before being sent abroad, while in the Israeli MFA, ambassadors are collectively trained during the weeks leading up to their assignments (ibid.). Even the Lithuanian MFA, which has yet to create a structured training program, offers digital training to ambassadors appointed to prominent capitals (R. Paulauskas, personal communication, July 25, 2018).

Yet ambassadors can also use digital tools themselves to obtain public diplomacy goals. By establishing a digital presence, ambassadors can interact with the citizens of a foreign nation, influence the image of their own nations, and create digital ties with opinion makers including journalists, bloggers, and citizen journalists. Even more importantly, ambassadors can use digital tools to help their followers' make sense of the world around them. As foreign policy experts, ambassadors can interpret world events for their followers, explain how local and global processes impact one another, and narrate the actions of global actors. Ambassadors can also curate information for their followers thus helping them sift through the digital wasteland of Too Much Information (TMI). Lastly, ambassadors can expose digital publics to their nation's culture, values, and norms, thus building bridges between two nations.

Despite digitalization's impact on the role of ambassadors, few studies to date have investigated how ambassadors utilize digital technologies toward public diplomacy goals. Moreover, few studies have examined if ambassadors attract digital publics and help extend the digital reach of their embassies. Lastly, no studies to date have examined if and how ambassadors leverage digital tools to establish an authentic digital presence. This chapter aims to address these three gaps. To do so, it first evaluates the extent to which ambassadors contribute to the digital reach of their embassies. Next, the chapter presents three case studies that illustrate how ambassadors use digital platforms toward public diplomacy goals. Finally, the chapter explores how ambassadors can create a distinct brand that can attract digital publics. The following section offers a quantitative analysis of the digital reach of ambassadors.

THE APPEAL OF AMBASSADORS

The digital appeal of ambassadors may stem both from their rank and their craft. Even though ambassadors are no longer as extraordinary and plenipotentiary as they once were, their occupation is still accompanied by a certain degree of prestige. Ambassadors remain the sole representatives of their nation in a foreign land, they have the authority to speak on behalf of their government, they are granted access to the highest echelons of power both at home and in their capital of posting, they have a seat at the table of international negotiations, they are regularly exposed to secret and confidential information, and their title is still affixed as her or his "excellency." Moreover, while they are embroiled in the machinery of governments, they are not politicians, but rather civil servants who have successfully climbed the ladder of international diplomacy while serving at posts all over the world. Ambassadors are thus not spin doctors, but rather, are dedicated professionals whose role is still shrouded in an aura of credibility and legitimacy as they are the caretakers of global peace. People hoping to learn about the world may thus turn to these professionals.

The appeal of ambassadors also stems from their craft. Ambassadors are experts who can explain complex foreign policy issues in layman's terms. As such, they can offer digital publics a compelling analysis of world events. Ambassadors are also accustomed to viewing the world as a global chessboard, in which an action on one part of the board leads to an immediate reaction in another (Slaughter, 2017). Ambassadors can thus help digital publics understand the workings of a globally interconnected world in which the policies of one nation immediately impact the policies and priorities of another. Such sense-making is in great demand given that the global world is a liquid one in which new modalities of power constantly emerge. For instance, superpowers such as the USA still exist, yet they cannot fully exercise their superpower as they must consider the actions of new dominant nations. Moreover, regional conflicts now have global repercussions and vice versa, as was evident during the Crimean crisis, which morphed into a global crisis between the USA and Russia. Lastly, new and old powers constantly attempt to assert their influence over regional affairs, leading to a cobweb of conflicting interests. The Syrian Civil War, for instance, saw Syrian, Russian, and Iranian armies fight rebels backed by the USA and Saudi Arabia. In such a liquid and interconnected world, ambassadors can serve as a digital hitchhiker's guide to the universe (Bauman & Lyon, 2016).

Notably, ambassadors have seats at international summits and negotiations. As such, they can offer publics a "behind the scenes look" at the inner workings of diplomacy. Ambassadors also have in-depth knowledge of specific diplomatic domains. An ambassador to the World Trade Organization will be intimately familiar with the challenges facing global financial corporations, while ambassadors to the United Nations (UN) Human Rights Council will have insight into the workings of NGOs and UN agencies. CEOs of companies or directors of NGOs may thus follow ambassadors on digital platforms to obtain knowledge that is crucial to their organization's success. Finally, ambassadors can bring their own style and flair to digital platforms, thus speaking with unique and authentic voices. This may be more appealing to digital publics than an embassy account operated by an unknown and invisible digital team that is overburdened with official protocol.

The rank and craft of ambassadors may thus enable them to attract diverse digital publics, ranging from citizens looking to make sense of the world around them to journalists, politicians, other members of the diplomatic community, civil society organizations, NGOs, and business leaders. By doing so, ambassadors can increase the digital reach of their embassy and even diversify the audiences with which the embassy interacts. While diasporas may flock to embassy digital profiles, journalists may prefer to interact with ambassadors. To examine the extent to which ambassadors contribute to their embassies' digital reach, this chapter calculated the number of Twitter followers that embassies and their ambassadors attract. The decision to focus on Twitter rather than other digital platforms stemmed from the finding that MFAs view Twitter as a tool for information gathering, while Facebook is a tool for relationship management (Bjola, 2018). Given the assumption that ambassadors' digital appeal rests on the information they share and the analyses they offer, Twitter was more relevant to this analysis than Facebook or other digital platforms such as LinkedIn and Instagram.

Four samples were used to calculate the contributions of ambassadors to their embassies' digital reach. The Twitter accounts of all embassies and ambassadors were accessed and analyzed during June of 2018. The first of these consisted of the Twitter accounts of 33 London-based embassies and their ambassadors. London was selected given the high penetration of Twitter in the UK, as well as the fact that the diplomatic community in London has warmly embraced digital platforms. Most London-based embassies maintain a digital presence, and many are active on Twitter (Manor, 2017). The embassies and ambassadors included in the London sample were selected based on a desire to create a diverse sample in terms of world region and diffusion of digital technology (Van Dijck, 2017). The results of London's analysis may be seen in Table 9.1.

As seen in Table 9.1, most ambassadors in the London sample contribute substantially to the digital reach of their embassy. There are only eight ambassadors whose contribution to their embassies' digital reach is smaller than 10% (Austria, Denmark, Estonia, Finland, Greece, Ireland, Japan, and Slovenia). By comparison, there are ten ambassadors whose contribution to their embassy's reach is greater than 50% (Afghanistan, Bolivia, Cyrus, Gabon, Georgia, Iran, Latvia, Lebanon, Namibia, and Slovakia). These ambassadors thus attract more Twitter followers than their embassies. There are also three ambassadors whose contribution to their embassy's reach is greater than 80% (Afghanistan, Cyprus, and Iran). The average contribution of a London-based ambassador to his embassy's overall digital reach is 36%. It should, however, be noted that the average number of Twitter followers that ambassadors attract is significantly lower than that of their embassies. In conclusion, the results of the London sample suggest that ambassadors can substantially increase the digital reach of their embassy.

To further test ambassadors' possible contributions to their embassies' digital reach, an additional sample of 30 Washington-based embassies was analyzed. As was the case with the UK, Washington was selected due to the high penetration of Twitter in the USA and its adoption by embassies and diplomats. Moreover, embassies to Washington, D.C. tend to have large staffs given the importance of the USA to global diplomacy. This translates into more staffers who can help manage the digital

Table 9.1 The contributions of London-based ambassadors to their embassies' digital reach

Country	Number of followers—ambassador[a]	Number of followers—embassy	Ambassador's contribution to digital reach (%)[a]
Afghanistan	32,455	5659	85
Argentina	1425	3878	27
Australia	7640	9451	45
Austria	146	3155	4
Bolivia	489	296	62
Canada	3128	15,705	17
Cyprus	14,924	936	94
Denmark	668	7117	9
Estonia	182	2697	6
Finland	344	7096	5
Gabon	469	357	57
Georgia	2050	1018	67
Germany	2509	11,060	18
Greece	461	9781	5
Iran	8013	228	97
Ireland	2402	26,282	8
Israel	16,538	58,040	22
Japan	1040	13,413	7
Jordan	508	561	48
Latvia	1539	1468	51
Lebanon	283	140	67
Lithuania	2154	2515	46
Malawi	1398	2139	40
Namibia	761	536	59
Netherlands	1659	9533	15
Norway	1610	4067	28
Qatar	8423	22,197	28
Russia	23,310	81,337	22
Rwanda	1643	5929	22
Slovakia	2179	2100	51
Slovenia	197	2823	67
Sweden	4125	6831	38
USA	25,149	57,384	30
Average	5146	11,386	36

[a]As a percentage of the number of followers of both the ambassador and the embassy. The analysis did not identify users who may follow both the ambassador and the embassy

presence of ambassadors. As activity breeds digital followers, it was expected that the Washington sample would offer even more conclusive findings than the London sample. The results of the Washington analysis may be seen in Table 9.2.

Table 9.2 The contributions of Washington-based ambassadors to their embassies' digital reach

Country	Number of followers—ambassador	Number of followers—embassy	Ambassador's contribution to digital reach (%)[a]
Afghanistan	53,050	55,352	49
Australia	188,628	16,254	92
Austria	2853	4607	38
Canada	6150	9450	39
Cuba	11,891	6683	64
Denmark	4907	21,773	18
Finland	1728	9072	16
France	43,489	37,215	54
Georgia	3007	5635	35
Germany	9693	38,027	20
Iceland	1174	4029	23
Indonesia	581	16,903	3
Ireland	17,411	22,816	43
Israel	71,161	186,416	28
Jordan	6963	55,893	11
Latvia	1457	2675	35
Libya	1498	692	68
Lithuania	1339	1339	50
Mexico	7017	16,115	30
Netherlands	2503	37,942	6
New Zealand	3529	390	90
Norway	4562	11,922	28
Qatar	34,736	17,134	67
Rwanda	10,350	6844	60
Saudi Arabia	282,292	99,309	74
Slovakia	688	1586	30
Sweden	2156	20,838	9
Switzerland	3863	5860	40
Turkey	26,117	13,529	66
UK	10,064	58,154	15
Average	27,162	26,148	40

[a]As a percentage of the number of followers of both the ambassador and the embassy. The analysis did not identify users who may follow both the ambassador and the embassy

As was assumed, the Washington sample is even more demonstrative of ambassadors' substantial contributions to their embassies' digital reach. There are only three ambassadors whose contributions to their embassy's reach is smaller than 10% (Indonesia, the Netherlands, and Sweden), while one-third of the ambassadors in the Washington sample increase their embassy's reach by more than 50% (Australia, Cuba, France, Libya, Lithuania, New Zealand, Qatar, Rwanda, Saudi Arabia, and Turkey). As such, one-third of ambassadors in the Washington sample attract more Twitter followers than their embassies. The average contribution of a London-based ambassador to his embassy's overall digital reach is 40%. Notably, the average ambassador's digital reach was greater than that of the average embassy.

The results of the London and Washington samples both demonstrate that ambassadors can increase the reach and contribute to the digital presence of their embassy. Moreover, both the London and Washington samples attest to ambassadors' digital appeal. However, it is possible that the results of these analyses cannot be generalized to other countries given the high penetration of Twitter and its adoption by the diplomatic communities in the UK and the USA. As such, this chapter compared the Twitter reach of embassies and ambassadors in two MFAs—Denmark and the Netherlands. These samples enabled a cross-national comparison that moved beyond a single capital.

The decision to focus on the Danish and Dutch MFAs stemmed from the fact that both have recently taken measures to further facilitate their process of digitalization. In the case of the Danish MFA, this has included the appointment of a tech ambassador tasked with managing relationships with the tech industry (Danish MFA, 2017). With offices in the UK, USA (California) and China, the tech ambassador is also responsible for creating networks and partnerships with tech companies with the hopes of finding innovative solutions to complex challenges. The Dutch MFA recently launched a central social media unit titled "The Newsroom", tasked with monitoring and analyzing information on digital platforms and using such information to inform policy-making (Newsroom, 2015). In 2018, the Dutch MFA also held a digital diplomacy camp, which brought together hundreds of diplomats, media professionals and academics, for a two-day discussion on the future of public diplomacy and digitalization. It was thus assumed that both MFAs place an emphasis on digital activities and would thus motivate their ambassadors to be active on digital platforms.

Second, this chapter focused on the Dutch and Danish MFAs as few studies to date have examined their digital activities, even though both have long since begun their processes of digitalization. The Dutch MFA established its digital presence in 2009, while Denmark was utilizing digital technologies in 2013. Lastly, both MFAs were selected given their limited resources when compared with MFAs of wealthier and larger countries. Limited resources may further motivate embassies and ambassadors to utilize digital platforms as a means of augmenting their public diplomacy activities. Tables 9.3 and 9.4 include the results of the Dutch and Danish samples.

Table 9.3 The contributions of Dutch ambassadors to their embassies' digital reach

Country	Number of followers—ambassador	Number of followers—embassy	Ambassador's contribution to digital reach (%)[a]
Bulgaria	2624	2439	52
Cuba	1203	409	75
Hong Kong	1896	1889	50
Hungary	2007	646	76
Indonesia	2423	6854	26
Israel	367	1360	21
Kenya	5730	2820	67
Libya	7159	2630	73
Macedonia	3692	5673	39
Mexico	1734	2429	42
Munich	1085	533	67
Palestine	440	371	54
Philippines	658	674	49
Serbia	2307	2606	47
Singapore	1973	2193	47
South Africa	3353	10,678	24
Sweden	835	756	52
Uganda	1853	3587	34
United Kingdom	1695	9553	15
United Nations in New York	23,221	2998	89
USA	2503	37,942	6
Average	3274	4716	48

[a]As a percentage of the number of followers of both the ambassador and the embassy. The analysis did not identify users who may follow both the ambassador and the embassy

Table 9.4   The contributions of Danish ambassadors to their embassies' digital reach

Country	Number of followers—ambassador	Number of followers—embassy	Ambassador's contribution to digital reach (%)[a]
Australia	701	511	58
Croatia	402	737	35
Egypt	762	1890	29
EU	310	3573	8
France	979	1180	45
Geneva	2612	4596	36
Germany	1166	988	54
India	3724	1695	69
Ireland	1083	791	58
Japan	1958	46,358	4
Netherlands	820	94	90
Poland	791	803	50
Saudi Arabia	1418	78	95
UK	667	7117	9
United Nations in New York	3361	18,525	15
USA	4907	21,772	18
Average	1604	6919	42

[a]As a percentage of the number of followers of both the ambassador and the embassy. The analysis did not identify users who may follow both the ambassador and the embassy

When compiling the Dutch sample, it was discovered that only 21 Dutch ambassadors are active on Twitter in addition to their embassy. In most capitals, the Dutch digital presence is limited either to an ambassador's Twitter channel or an embassy's channel. Yet, the average Dutch ambassador included in the sample extends the digital reach of his embassy by 48%. There is only one ambassador in the sample whose contribution to his embassy's digital reach is less than 10% (the USA), while there are 9 ambassadors whose contributions are greater than 50% (Bulgaria, Cuba, Hong Kong, Hungary, Kenya, Libya, Munich, Palestine, and the United Nations in New York). The Dutch sample therefore also suggests that ambassadors can substantially extend the reach of their embassy on digital platforms, even in countries where Twitter penetration is relatively lower (Israel and Palestine) or where Internet penetration is relatively lower (Kenya, Libya, and Uganda).

The results of the Danish sample were equally conclusive, as the average Danish ambassador extends the digital reach of his embassy by 42%. Indeed, in six of the 16 embassies evaluated, the Danish ambassador's contribution is greater than 50%. However, as was the case with the Dutch MFA, it was discovered that only 16 Danish ambassadors are active on Twitter in addition to their embassy, a surprisingly low figure.

In summary, the results presented in this section demonstrate that ambassadors can substantially increase the digital reach of their embassies and contribute to their public diplomacy activities. Yet ambassadors can also use digital platforms to foster their own ties with digital publics and offer such publics added values: insight, analysis, information, curation and a "behind the scenes" look at international diplomacy. The following section includes three case studies that demonstrate how ambassadors can leverage digital technologies to create their own digital following.

The Disappearing Backstage of Diplomacy

For most of the twentieth-century, diplomacy was practiced behind an iron curtain. While diplomats would often pose for collective photographs, these were taken either before or after diplomatic deliberations. Diplomacy itself still took place within the inner sanctums of great palaces and hotels or behind the closed doors of historic halls. It was thus possible to distinguish between the stage of diplomacy (or the area in which diplomacy was portrayed), and the backstage of diplomacy (or the area in which diplomacy was practiced) (Shimazu, 2014). The invasion of communication technologies into the backstage of diplomacy began in the 1960s. It was in this decade that television cameras first enabled viewers to witness diplomatic deliberations in near-real time. Such was the case with the televised broadcast of the diplomatic duel between the American ambassador to the UN, Adlai Stevenson, and his Russian counterpart, Valeiran Zorin, during the Cuban Missile Crisis. Stevenson's revelation of Soviet ballistic missiles in Cuba stunned both the diplomats seated at the UN and the viewers of the evening news.

While the media's intrusion into diplomacy's backstage continued during the 1970s and into the 1990s, it could still be manipulated by diplomats. If diplomats believed that the presence of cameras might aid their diplomatic efforts, then journalists were allowed behind closed doors. If diplomats thought that cameras might curtail diplomatic efforts, they were left outside. As such, the media became a tool for applying diplomatic pressure. Such was the case during the 1990 peace negotiations when a frustrated U.S. Secretary of State James Baker berated the Israeli delegation for their negative approach (Friedman, 1990) and stated: "If that's going to be the approach, and that's going to be the attitude, there won't be any dialogue. And there won't be any peace...And so, it's gonna take some really good faith, and affirmative effort on part of our good friends from Israel. And if we don't get it, and if we can't get it quickly, I have to tell you Mr. Levin that everybody over there [in Israel] should know that the telephone number [of the State Department] is 1-202-456-1414. When you're serious about peace call us." Baker's rebuke was deliberately targeted at the cameras knowing full well that it would dominate the evening news cycle and portray Israel as the obstacle to peace in the Middle East.

Two events at the turn of the century increased the pressure on diplomats to allow cameras into the backstage of diplomacy. The first was the advent of CNN and the 24-hour news cycle, which necessitated a constant stream of news stories, images, and revelations. To meet the media's hunger for news, diplomats allowed cameras a supposed glimpse into the backstage of diplomacy. Such was the case with photographs that depicted Israeli Prime Minister Ehud Barak and Syrian Foreign Minister Farouk Ashara conferring with President Bill Clinton during a 1999 peace summit. Yet the intimacy captured by the cameras was not authentic. It was a well-orchestrated moment meant to offer the media voyeur a "behind the scenes" look at the inner workings of diplomacy and meet the demand for constant news.

The second event that infringed on the backstage of diplomacy was the emergence of the digital society. As was elaborated in Chapter 2, the values and norms of the digital society dictate the behavior that is demanded of digital society members. The norms celebrated by the digital society are those of openness and authenticity. Additionally, secrets are not allowed in the digital society as everything once done in private must now be done in public (Bauman & Lyon, 2016). This demand stems from the financial logic of the digital society and the need to provide a steady stream of information that can be analyzed by algorithms and monetized by tech companies. Every post, comment, and share is a bit of information that can be used to generate knowledge on digital users. It is knowledge that enables companies to tailor individuals' online experiences, to sell them products, and to tailor advertisements to individuals' life interests. As part of the process of digitalization, diplomats and diplomatic institutions have also made public that which was once private. For if diplomats wish to attract digital publics, build relationships with these publics, and shape how they view the world, then diplomats must also lift the veil of secrecy from diplomacy. For this reason, ambassadors now use digital platforms to offer online publics a look at the backstage of diplomacy.

Causey and Howard (2013) have stated that digital media have complicated diplomacy as they facilitate the exposure of diplomacy's backstage. Yet as the case studies reviewed in this chapter will show, diplomats can still limit the extent to which the backstage of diplomacy is exposed. One early example of transparent diplomacy was the Geneva 2 conference, held in January of 2014. The Geneva conference, co-sponsored by Russia and the USA, aimed to resolve the Syrian Civil War through direct negotiations between the Syrian government and Syrian rebels. Twitter users following the hashtag #Geneva2 were given direct access to the backstage of diplomacy as diplomats within the room were live-tweeting the deliberations. For instance, diplomats from both the UK and Russia tweeted images of the various delegations assembled in the conference room, thus informing Twitter users of who had been granted a seat at the negotiating table (Fig. 9.1).

Next, diplomats tweeted the position of each delegation. One tweet by the UN Relief and Aid Work Agency for Palestine quoted UN Secretary-General Ban Ki-moon as saying "All Syrians are looking to you gathered here to end the unspeakable human suffering." A tweet by the U.S. embassy to Syria quoted Secretary of State John Kerry as saying that President Bashar Assad and "those who have supported him can no longer hold an entire nation and a region hostage." The Qatari MFA quoted its Minister's conclusion that "Our duty compels us not to deceive the people and not to cave in at movements of despair." Twitter followers thus knew who was represented in the negotiating room, what their positions were, and what solutions were being discussed (Manor, 2014). Followers also had a visual glimpse into the backchannel negotiations taking place within the negotiating room, as is evident in the tweet in Fig. 9.2. So it was that the backstage of diplomacy grew even smaller.

The Geneva case study is important for two reasons. First, it demonstrates that the increased transparency of diplomacy is not a new phenomenon. The impact of digitalization on the working routines and communicative norms of diplomats were already taking shape in 2014.

Fig. 9.1 Delegations assembled at 2014 Geneva 2 conference (*Source* https://twitter.com/mfa_russia/status/425913644925210624?ref_src=twsrc%5Etfw%7Ctwcamp%5Etweetembed%7Ctwterm%5E425913644925210624&ref_url=https%3A%2F%2Fdigdipblog.com%2F2014%2F04%2F02%2Fdigital-diplomacy-what-is-it-good-for%2F)

Yet most of the tweets emanating from Geneva were authored by MFAs, not ambassadors. As such, the Geneva case study also demonstrates that the process of digitalization of MFAs and of individual diplomats can progress at different paces.

Nowadays, ambassadors are more prone to offering their followers access to the backstage of diplomacy. One notable example is the British diplomat Karen Pierce, who became the UK's Permanent Representative to the United Nations in March of 2018. Pierce, who joined Twitter in May of 2015, routinely publishes tweets from within the inner corridors of multilateral diplomacy. An analysis of Pierce's Twitter activities since assuming her new positions suggests that she publishes four

Fig. 9.2 Backchannel negotiations at Geneva 2 conference (*Source* https://twitter.com/StateDept/status/425996642504818688?ref_ src=twsrc%5Etfw%7Ctwcamp%5Etweetembed%7Ctwter- m%5E425996642504818688&ref_url=https%3A%2F%2Fdigdipblog. com%2F2014%2F04%2F02%2Fdigital-diplomacy-what-is-it-good-for%2F)

types of tweets. The first includes brief updates on deliberations at the UN Security Council alongside images from these deliberations. Such tweets offer digital publics real-time access into one of the world's most prestigious diplomatic forums. One such tweet, published on July 13, 2018, stated: "We do not advance peace by ignoring atrocities. Today's @UNSC-led [UN Security Council] #UNSC resolution is designed to protect the people of #South Sudan" by "limiting the flow of weapons that fuel the conflict" and "imposing sanctions against 2 individuals who have caused immeasurable suffering." The tweet included an image of Pierce and other UN permanent representatives voting in favor of a

Security Council resolution on South Sudan. A similar tweet, published on the 15th of May, decried the loss of Palestinian lives following violent clashes between Palestinian protestors and Israeli Defense Forces along the Gaza border. The ambassador's adamant condemnation of Israeli violence was accompanied by an image of the UN Security Council observing a moment of silence in memory of those who perished (Fig. 9.3).

Karen Pierce ✓
@KarenPierceUN

`Following`   ⌄

We are appalled by the loss of life in Gaza.

It is concerning that the peaceful protests have been exploited by extremists elements.

We urge restraint in the use of live fire.

Any further escalation is in no-one's interest.

UK remains committed to a two-state solution.

6:01 PM - 15 May 2018

Fig. 9.3 Karen Pierce tweets from within the Security Council chamber (*Source* https://twitter.com/KarenPierceUN/status/996405221369753600)

Another type of tweet published by Pierce focuses on UN Security Council visits to conflict areas. For instance, in May of 2018, the Permanent Representative published several tweets from the Security Council's visit to Burma, where it assessed the humanitarian plight of the Rohingya forced to flee their homes earlier that year. One tweet included a video taken from a helicopter flying over northern Burma and was accompanied by the words "More today, the #UNSC visited northern #Rakhine in #Burma. Flying overhead, the scale of devastation becomes clear. #Rohingya crisis." The video, viewed by more than 18,000 Twitter users, not only offered digital publics insight into the workings of the Security Council and its missions abroad, but also offered a prism or frame through which digital publics could interpret the situation unfolding on the ground in Burma: that of a humanitarian disaster. Later that same day, Pierce published a tweet that included two images: one from the Security Council's meeting with Burmese officials and another from a meeting with military personnel. The text of the tweet stated that the Security Council pressured Burma to create the conditions necessary for the Rohingya to return home and to thoroughly investigate the violence against them. Digital publics were thus granted real-time access into diplomatic deliberations.

A third type of tweet includes press statements issued by Security Council members. One such tweet from April 22, 2018 stated that the Security Council had discussed the situation in Syria and agreed that there was a need to reinvigorate attempts to find a political solution to the crisis and address the possible use of chemical weapons in Syria. The tweet was accompanied by a brief press statement that was captured with a digital device's camera. Digital followers of the Permanent Representative were thus directly privy to information that would normally be disseminated to the media first and after that to the public. These tweets, which offer digital publics direct access to diplomatic agreements, demonstrate how digitalization has changed the traditional relationship between the media, diplomats, and global citizens. Diplomats can now bypass the media and communicate news and frames directly to global publics.

Lastly, Pierce often publishes tweets that capture the human element of diplomacy. Such tweets usually consist of images of the Permanent Representative conferring with her peers, laughing with colleagues, or taking a break from multilateral diplomacy to congratulate peers appointed to new roles. It is these tweets that serve to offer a "behind the scenes" look at diplomacy that can satisfy the voyeurs of the digital society. Causey and Howard (2013) argued that authenticity is key to digital outreach, with authenticity defined as a balance between formal and informal communication. Pierce seems to strike that balance quite brilliantly.

CURATING INFORMATION

As was explored in Chapter 2, the digital society is one in which individuals face a daily barrage of TMI (Miller & Horst, 2017). Digital society members cannot hope to read all the status updates posted by their friends or all the articles recommended by social media platforms, nor can they view all videos published by celebrities or trending GIFs circulating the Twitterverse. From the perspective of the societal prism, it is possible that digital society members are drowned by design. The daily tidal wave of TMI may be an instrument to increase adoration of and trust in algorithms, for it is algorithms that tailor individuals' digital experiences and filter the information that reaches them. As such, algorithms guarantee that individuals see and access only that which is relevant or of interest to them.

Ambassadors can also help digital society members navigate their way across the high seas of TMI. Given their expertise and knowledge of international affairs, ambassadors can identify credible sources of information for their followers, recommend specific publications and media outlets, share insightful analysis, highlight important news stories or policy briefs, and separate fact from fiction. By curating information, ambassadors can also help their followers make sense of the world around them and, importantly, help stem the flow of disinformation and alternative facts.

One ambassador who routinely curates information for his followers is the EU's ambassador to the USA, David O'Sullivan. The ambassador joined Twitter in October of 2014 and has amassed more than 8,000 followers as of August 2018. An analysis of tweets published by the EU ambassador between April and August of 2018 suggests that O'Sullivan practices information curation on a nearly daily basis. Throughout the period of April to August, O'Sullivan published a host of tweets titled "Today's Must Read" or "Today's Must Watch." These tweets referred his followers to statements by EU officials regarding future trade relations between the EU and the USA, a joint statement by the EU and NATO on how to increase security on both sides of the Atlantic, opinion articles in the *Washington Post* dealing with trade tariffs imposed by the USA on imports from the EU, and a *New York Times* article that offers "a clear explanation of the economic realities behind deficits and surplus." Other "Must Reads" included opinion pieces written by EU officials or EU ambassadors, both in the USA and abroad.

While the ambassadors' tweets offered followers a daily recommendation of relevant and important news stories, they tended to focus on the issue of U.S.-EU trade. One tweet, published on August 3, 2018, referred followers to a statement by the EU Foreign Secretary. The tweet also quoted the EU Foreign Secretary as saying, "In a world that is terribly unpredictable and un-strategic, you can count on us [i.e., the EU] as a predictable and reliable partner." This tweet demonstrates that the ambassador curates information to help his followers make sense of the world around them. In an unpredictable world, Twitter users should regard the EU as a credible partner.

Notably, while in 2018 O'Sullivan focused on trade issues, in 2015, his information-curating activities focused on the EU's measures to stabilize the Greek economy (Manor, 2015). As such, the ambassador seems to utilize digital platforms to identify the issues that are of greatest importance to the EU and to set the agenda for his Twitter followers. Presently, the ambassador also recommends specific journalists. For instance, on April 2, 2018, O'Sullivan referred his followers to an op-ed published by Tom Wheeler, chairman of the U.S. Federal Communications Commission, dealing with EU attempts to regulate privacy on social media sites. This tweet not only identified a credible source of information, but also portrayed the EU as a leading force in the struggle to ensure the privacy of social media users in the post-Cambridge Analytica age. These kinds of tweets therefore create a positive frame, or prism, through which the EU may be viewed by the ambassador's followers.

Finally, the ambassador often published tweets that invoked the words "truth" and "facts." One such tweet, published on July 17, 2018 and shown in Fig. 9.4, included "useful facts" on how the EU automotive industry benefits the American economy. Another tweet from the 10th of June stated, "Truth on tariffs? The USA currently imposes individual tariffs rates of more than 15% on 330 separate manufactured EU goods. Yet when US companies sell their products to the EU, they encounter only 45 such tariff peaks." Similarly, another recommendation about a

David O'Sullivan ✓
@EUAmbUS

(Follow) ⌄

Today's useful facts and figures on EU car manufacturing in the United States 🔽
Learn more: trade.ec.europa.eu/doclib/press/i
...

EU Automotive Investments in the US lead to:
Jobs, Jobs, Jobs

120,000
directly employed by
EU car plants across the
US.

420,000
jobs generated by
EU car production in
the US.

5:33 PM - 17 Jul 2018

20 Retweets **13** Likes

🗨   ↻ 20   ♡ 13   ✉

Fig. 9.4 EU ambassador curating information for Twitter followers (*Source* https://twitter.com/EUAmbUS/status/1019228571120828416)

newspaper story began with the words "Facts show that Europe is the best trading partner of the U.S."

The rhetoric of facts and truth is not coincidental. Rather, it serves to separate the ambassador and the content he recommends from "fake" or false news stories and alternative facts that make their way across digital platforms. By making claims to truth and facts, the ambassador lends his prestige and rank to the information that he curates for his followers. This may increase followers' willingness to engage meaningfully with the sources of information that O'Sullivan identifies. Notably, by employing the rhetoric of facts and truth, the ambassador may also be able to create a positive association between the EU and truth, thus once again managing the image of the EU in the USA.

David O'Sullivan's digital activities are important given the political entity he represents. The digitalization of the EU's public diplomacy may represent an anomaly when compared with other MFAs. This is because the EU's foreign ministry, the External Action Service, was only established in 2010. Thus, unlike other MFAs, EU public diplomacy has always been practiced in the digital age. The External Action Service may thus have been spared some of the growing pains associated with the process of digitalization, including the need to transition from broadcast to communicative paradigms, the adopting of risk-tolerant communicative practices, the creation of new working routines, and the establishment of new departments. Yet EU digital activities also face challenges that are not common among other MFAs. As was stated at a recent conference at Oxford University, EU diplomatic communiques must be approved or represent the positions of all 28 member states. This prevents the EU's digital team from commenting on events as they unfold and practicing real-time diplomacy. Moreover, the digital team may only deal with issues that have obtained consensus among member states. This substantially limits the diversity of issues that may be addressed online and prevents the digital team from addressing contentious issues that are being debated by digital publics. Recent rifts within the EU, such as the rise of authoritarian regimes in Eastern Europe, may further hamper EU digital communications exactly at a time when digital publics may be in greater need of clarity and analysis.

However, it is through digital platforms that the vision of the EU as a political actor may be brought to life. By using a single Twitter account bearing the insignia of the EU, the 28 member states can speak with one voice, promote a single and coherent foreign policy, and offer a single perspective on global events and actors. It is thus on digital platforms that the EU can become like any other nation state. While digital activities may be hampered at the ministry level, it is at the ambassadorial level that the benefits of digitalization can be fully leveraged. As O'Sullivan's case study demonstrates, EU ambassadors can utilize digital platforms to promote a coherent foreign policy and identify the issues that are of greatest importance to the EU, thus bringing the dream of the EU to life.

A DISTINCT iBRAND

On June 6, 2015, columnist Maureen Dowd penned an article titled "From Paris, with Tough Love" in the *New York Times*. The article dealt with the tweets of the French ambassador to the USA, Gérard

Arnaud. With more than 43,000 followers on Twitter as of August 2018, Arnaud is one of the most popular ambassadors in the USA. His popularity does not stem from the issues he addresses or the insight he provides, but from the tone that he has adopted on Twitter. Chapter 2 of this book discussed the emergence of iBrands. It argued that within the digital society, all members are but brands that compete with one another over the attention of digital publics. To do so, individuals develop an authentic digital presence complete with a distinct appearance, tone, vernacular, and interests.

Arnaud is a branding genius. As Dowd herself wrote in the *New York Times* article, "More striking, he has invented a new form of digital diplomacy for our cacophonous, hyperconnected age, a zesty undiplomatic diplomacy that has shaken up this staid marble capital." The new form of diplomacy that Arnaud has invented is one characterized by frankness, bluntness, and directness. The French ambassador does not mince words, nor does he feel bound by the burdens of protocol, diplomatic etiquette, and double entendres. Perhaps the most obvious example is a tweet published by the ambassador in response to Donald Trump's assertion that France is the victim of terror attacks due to its lax gun regulations. "This message is repugnant in its lack of any human decency", tweeted the French ambassador, adding the word "vulture" in reference to Trump.

Yet the attack on Trump is by no means the only example of Arnaud's distinct tone on Twitter. On March 3, 2015, the ambassador addressed the negotiations between the Western powers and Iran pertaining to its nuclear weapons program. Much to the dismay of his American colleagues, Arnaud criticized the American negotiating position, tweeting: "Iran. We want a deal. They need a deal. The tactics and the result of the negotiation should reflect this asymmetry." In a tweet from 2014, he stated, "The invasion of Iraq in 2003 was an unmitigated disaster of which the Iraqis and the international community are still paying the price."

The Middle East is not the only policy area in which the French ambassador speaks his mind. In June of 2015, he published a tweet relating to the Greek financial crisis that stated "Nothing more unpleasant than the outpouring of hellenophobia in some circles. Greece needs our support and understanding." One day later, he commented on allegations that the USA was intercepting phone calls of European leaders and wrote "Fascinating that in the U.S. nobody cares that the NSA [National Security Agency] has been spying (on) ministers of allied countries. Spare us the high moral ground please." More recently, Arnaud has taken to commenting on newspaper and magazine articles. When in August of 2018 the magazine *Foreign Affairs* tweeted that the past seven decades have been marked by peace, the ambassador replied "Seven decades of peace? Wars of Indochina, Korea, Vietnam, Bangladesh, Afghanistan, Iraq/Iran, 4 Arab/Israeli wars and a lot of others. Millions of dead. This title is a bad joke."

Lastly, the French ambassador also tends to remind his followers of the underlying logic of the American financial system and its disastrous impact on the world. On August 8, 2018, Arnaud commented on the events that led to Britain's decision to exit the EU, and tweeted: "Let's not forget the economic consequences of neoliberal policies on blue-collar workers and the lower middle-class." A day later, the ambassador tweeted about a book he was reading titled *Crashed: How a Decade of Financial Crisis Changed the World*. Arnaud's summary of the book was "Impressive, throughout, technical but understandable. The consequences of unleashed greed." Greed, for lack of a better word, being viewed as good by Wall Street. Given that "America's Business is Business", Arnaud's tweets about neoliberalism are yet another example of his blunt and direct tone. When asked by the *New York Times* why he was so direct on Twitter, the ambassador answered that ambassadors no longer have access to the White House. The ambassador was thus using Twitter to get the attention of President Barack Obama, himself an aficionado of Twitter.

The *New York Times*' Maureen Dowd concluded that "Hierarchy and politesse be damned. Gérard Arnaud is the first great ambassador of the social media era. If Twitter is the digital French Revolution, full of raucous democracy and gleeful beheadings, then the French ambassador has defected to the 'Aux Barricades' camp." Dowd's conclusion is that the ambassador has joined the digital proletariat and subsequently has adopted their digital tone. He no longer tweets like a member of the elites, nor is he bound to their norms and decorum. Yet from the perspective of the technological prism, it may be argued that Arnaud has simply created a captivating iBrand. Any ambassador hoping to narrate his nation's policies, interact with digital publics, and shape their views of world events must first attract digital publics to his social media profiles. To do so, an ambassador must compete in the social media marketplace opposite all other iBrands ranging from heads of state to celebrities, YouTube stars, and social media personalities. Arnaud has been able to win such competitions not because of the content he shares, but because of the distinct tone and style he has adopted. Among a sea of ambassadors and diplomats he stands out; his brand eclipses all others. For someone so adamant in his rejection of neoliberal economics, his acceptance of the neoliberal logic of the digital society is striking.

Yet the question that must follow is, does the ambassador's iBrand contribute to French public diplomacy activities in the USA? There are two answers to this question. Arnaud's style has enabled him to attract followers from epistemic communities, or communities that are of great relevance to diplomacy. An analysis conducted for this chapter in July of 2018 examined the extent to which USA-based ambassadors attract global and local media outlets. The analysis included a sample of 538 news accounts on Twitter first compiled by Manor and Pamment (2019). The sample includes global news agencies (e.g., AFP), global news channels (e.g., CNN, Sky News), global newspapers (e.g., *New York Times*, *Le Monde*), magazines (e.g., *the Economist*, *Der Spiegel*), editors-in-chief of prominent newspapers, diplomatic correspondents of prominent newspapers, and Internet-based news publications in every world region. Graph 9.1 includes the number of news channels that follow 30 ambassadors to the USA.

As seen in Graph 9.1, the French ambassador attracts the largest number of news outlets and journalists on Twitter. While the average ambassador attracts 5 news outlets and journalists, Arnaud boasts 38 followers, including global news outlets (France 24, CNN), columnists from the *Washington Post* and *New York Times*, editors of the *Politico* online magazine, and writers from French publications such as *Le Monde*. By attracting the media, Arnaud may be able to influence the reporting of prominent newspapers as journalists adopt his narration of French policies. Thus, he may be able to create a receptive environment for his nation's foreign policy.

As Graph 9.2 shows, Arnaud is also one of the most popular ambassadors to the USA in terms of the overall followers on Twitter. Out of a sample of 28 ambassadors introduced earlier in this chapter, the French ambassador is ranked third, with more than 40,000 followers. A geolocation analysis of Arnaud's Twitter followers using the FollowerWonk application in August of 2018 revealed that he attracts a global digital audience. The French ambassador has large follower hubs in France, the UK, and the USA and medium-sized follower hubs in Afghanistan, Australia, Austria, Germany, Iran, Iraq, Israel, Italy, Japan, Morocco,

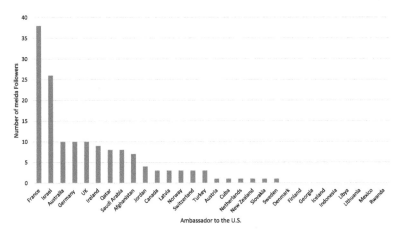

Graph 9.1 News outlets and journalists following ambassadors on Twitter

Poland, Romania, Spain, and Latin America. He also has smaller numbers of followers Russia, South Korea and North Africa.

Yet while Arnaud's iBrand is a popular one, it is not necessarily one that facilitates public diplomacy goals. The ambassador's open criticism of American values and policies, his label of the U.S. President as a "vulture", and his overall blunt demeanor may make for amusing reading, but not much else. Indeed, American digital publics may feel resentment toward Arnaud that would prevent them from engaging meaningfully with his messages, taking note of his narration of world events, being receptive to his nation's foreign policy objectives. Such was the case with a tweet that Arnaud published in May of 2015 that stated, "I know it is hard to say but: yes, invading Iraq was a mistake, yes, the French were right. Once you say it, you feel relieved." The comments on these tweets were quite negative. One user stated, "We were wrong to do anything to help France in 1917 & 1941." Another wrote "Please. I'm looking fwd [forward] to your twts [tweets] about France in ww2, Algeria, nuclear tests, sinking of ships. Let's hear yr [your] mea culpas." A third Twitter user suggested that France always felt relieved, even after its token resistance to the Nazis in World War II. It is thus possible that brand Arnaud is infringing on that of Brand France and even preventing France

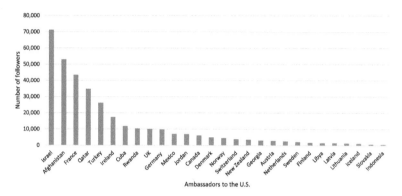

Graph 9.2   Number of Twitter users following ambassadors to the U.S.

from advancing its public diplomacy goals via digital means. In summary, like most digital society members Arnaud uses acrobatic fêtes to attract the gaze of digital publics. Like all members of the social media panopticon, he self-regulates his digital behavior so as to attract attention. Yet the question that follows is, when do acrobatic fêtes begin to jeopardize a nation's public diplomacy?

Conclusions

Technology has always impacted the role of ambassadors. Some advancements, such as the telegraph, reduced the agency of ambassadors as diplomatic decision-making migrated to the MFA. Other technologies, such as advancements in transportation, saw ambassadors move from the frontstage of diplomacy to the backstage. The digitalization of public diplomacy has seen ambassadors regain much of their lost agency as power has migrated back from the MFA to the embassy. It is embassies that are now tasked with tailoring public diplomacy messages to the unique attributes of foreign audiences and leveraging digital platforms as a tool for information gathering that may inform the policy formulation process. As power migrated to the embassy, it also migrated to the ambassador.

Yet ambassadors may also use digital technologies themselves to further their embassies' public diplomacy activities. As this chapter has demonstrated, ambassadors throughout the world contribute substantially to their embassies' digital reach. Be it in the UK or the USA or among the Dutch and Danish MFAs, ambassadors may be regarded as digital assets that increase and diversify an embassy's digital audience. For while diasporas and expats may follow an embassy's digital profile, ambassadors may be able to attract elites such as journalists, opinion makers and politicians. However, this chapter also found that in the Dutch and Danish MFAs, the number of ambassadors who tweet in addition to their embassy is relatively small. This may stem from limited digital resources or the belief that ambassadors will draw attention from the embassy and vice versa. Such an approach fails to build on the digital appeal and prestige of ambassadors, and thus limits an MFA's public diplomacy activities.

In 2013, Daryl Copeland envisioned the future diplomat as part activist, part analyst and part alchemist who is able to swim with comfort and ease, never flopping around "like a fish out of water, in the sea of people beyond the embassy wall. Unlike many serving envoys, this candidate prefers mixing with the population to mingling with colleagues" (Copeland, 2013, p. 62). The three ambassadors analyzed in this chapter demonstrate that the process of digitalization is steadily impacting the norms, values, and working routines of all diplomats, regardless of their age or seniority. Digitalization is not a process that is limited to digital natives who came of age in a digital world (Prensky, 2001). Digital immigrants, such as the ambassadors reviewed in this chapter, have also adopted digital technologies and integrated them into their daily activities. The three case studies do, however, demonstrate that ambassadors may use digital technologies toward different ends. The UK's Permanent Representative to the UN uses Twitter to further encroach on the backstage of diplomacy and offer digital voyeurs a "behind the scenes" look at the workings of multilateral diplomacy. The EU's ambassador to the USA curates information for his followers while bringing the dream of the EU to life as this ultra-national institution speaks with one voice and has one coherent foreign policy. Lastly, the French ambassador uses Twitter to attract attention from U.S. leaders. Yet all three also step out of their embassies' walls and offer followers a prism that contextualizes and illuminates the tasks of diplomats and their impact on world events.

Each ambassador also manifests a different aspect of the logic that governs the digital society. The UK's Permanent Representative has adopted the digital society's norms of transparency and openness. Deliberations in the world's most prestigious diplomatic forum, the UN Security Council, are made public while the Council's foreign activities are broadcast online in near-real time. Thus, everything done in secret is now done in public and the values of transparency and openness are further ingrained into the minds of all digital users. But the Permanent Representative also balances the logic of the digital society with diplomatic ends. As has been the case throughout the twentieth century, Karen Pierce offers followers a view into the Security Council, but not into the sensitive deliberations that take place between permanent representatives once the cameras leave the Council's room.

The EU's ambassador to the U.S. helps his followers navigate the treacherous sea of TMI. The ambassador curates information for his followers in the form of important news items, trusted media sources, and insightful analysis. Moreover, the ambassador employs the rhetoric of truth and facts to distinguish between real news and "fake" or false news, thereby helping digital publics sift through the wasteland of online news items. Lastly, the ambassador also offers digital publics real-time analyses of global affairs, thus meeting the digital society's demand to learn about events as they unfold. In 2015, the ambassador focused on the need to rescue the Greek economy; in 2018, he focused on the dangers of trade tariffs.

The French case study demonstrates that even ambassadors must develop an iBrand if they are to compete on the neoliberal social media marketplace. His brand is one that counters the notion of the traditional diplomat. On Twitter, the French ambassador is direct, blunt, and even offensive, thus ensuring that he is not sweetly ignored like the protagonists in Henry James' novel quoted at the beginning of this chapter. By negating digital publics' expectations of a senior diplomat, the ambassador can attract a sizable following, especially among journalists and media organizations. Yet his abrasive tone may also impede public diplomacy activities, given his frequent attacks on American values and history. The question that follows is, when does the iBrand become counterproductive to the goals of public diplomacy? Can an iBrand be successful in the social media marketplace, yet at the same time fail to create a receptive environment for a nation's foreign policy? The example of the French ambassador suggests that one must balance diplomatic decorum and social media fandom. As Causey and Howard (2013) have asserted, diplomats are now expected to be more open and transparent on the one hand, but still maintain a level of gravitas on the other.

It is, however, possible that Arnaud has his gaze fixed both on American Twitter users and audiences in France. As Sotiriu (2015) has argued, ambassadors now employ social media sites to communicate with digital audiences back home. Such activities demonstrate yet again that the digitalization of public diplomacy has given rise to domestic public diplomacy. Sotiriu also argued that ambassadors use social media sites to communicate with their peers, thus transporting the diplomatic community online. It is thus possible that Arnaud's iBrand is targeted at three different audiences.

Lastly, this chapter has demonstrated yet again that the logic of the digital society is influencing the self-narratives or metaphors through which diplomats conceptualize their craft. The self-narrative made evident in this chapter is that of real-time diplomacy. Digital publics now expect to learn about global events as they occur. They have become accustomed to this through the activities of online media organizations. The impetus for commenting on events as they unfold has also permeated into MFAs and has led to new values, norms, and working routines. In terms of working routines, ambassadors now share information with digital publics as they access it. Such is the case with the UK's Permanent Representative to the UN, who uses smartphone cameras to disseminate Security Council press releases or images from UN Security Council votes as they take place. Similarly, the EU's ambassador curates information on a daily basis while sharing analyses of EU institutions and officials as they are published online. From a normative perspective, diplomats' regard for information has also altered. Traditionally, diplomats safeguarded information, believing that information was power. Now diplomats share information so as to attract digital publics and influence their perceptions of world events and actors.

Unlike previous chapters, this one focused on diplomats rather than diplomatic institutions. It has thus demonstrated that digitalization is a process that is influencing the institutions and practitioners of public diplomacy. The next chapter includes a discussion of the insight and results shared throughout this book and glances into the future of the digitalization of public diplomacy.

References

Archetti, C. (2012). The impact of new media on diplomatic practice: An evolutionary model of change. *The Hague Journal of Diplomacy, 7*(2), 181–206.

Bauman, Z., & Lyon, D. (2016). *Liquid surveillance: A conversation.* Cambridge: Polity Press.

Bjola, C. (2013). Understanding enmity and friendship in world politics: The case for a diplomatic approach. *The Hague Journal of Diplomacy, 8*(1), 1–20.

Bjola, C. (2018). *Digital diplomacy and impression management.* Presentation. London: Canada House.

Causey, C., & Howard, P. N. (2013). Delivering digital public diplomacy. In R. S. Zaharna, A. Arsenault, & A. Fisher (Eds.), *Relational, networked and collaborative approaches to public diplomacy* (pp. 144–156). New York, NY: Taylor & Francis.

Copeland, D. (2013). Taking diplomacy public: Science, technology and foreign ministries in a heteropolar world. In R. S. Zaharna, A. Arsenault, & A. Fisher (Eds.), *Relational, networked and collaborative approaches to public diplomacy* (pp. 56–69). New York, NY: Taylor & Francis.

Dowd, M. (2015, June). From Paris, with tough love. *The New York Times.* Retrieved from https://www.nytimes.com/2015/06/07/opinion/sunday/maureen-dowd-from-paris-with-tough-love.html.

Friedman, T. (1990, June). Baker rebukes Israel on Peace Terms. *The New York Times.* Retrieved from https://www.nytimes.com/1990/06/14/world/baker-rebukes-israel-on-peace-terms.html.

Ish-Shalom, P. (2015). King diplomacy for perpetual crisis. *The Hague Journal of Diplomacy, 10*(1), 10–14.

Lampe, G. (2018). *Understanding US digital diplomacy* [In person].

Lutyens, A. (2018). *Investigating New Zealand's model of democratized public diplomacy* [In person].

Manor, I. (2014, April 2). *Digital diplomacy—What is it good for* [Blog]. Retrieved from https://digdipblog.com/2014/04/02/digital-diplomacy-what-is-it-good-for/.

Manor, I. (2015, August 9). *Developing best practices for ambassadors on Twitter* [Blog]. Retrieved from https://digdipblog.com/2015/08/09/developing-best-practices-for-ambassadors-on-twitter/.

Manor, I. (2016). Are we there yet: Have MFA s realized the potential of digital diplomacy? *Brill Research Perspectives in Diplomacy and Foreign Policy, 1*(2), 1–110.

Manor, I. (2017, March 23). *How embassies managed the London terror attack* [Blog]. Retrieved from https://digdipblog.com/2017/03/23/how-embassies-managed-the-london-terror-attack/.

Manor, I., & Pamment J. (2019). Towards prestige mobility? Diplomatic prestige and digital diplomacy. *Cambridge Review of International Affairs.*

Metzgar, E. T. (2012). Is it the medium or the message? Social media, American public diplomacy & Iran. *Global Media Journal, 12*(21), 1.

Miller, D., & Horst, H. A. (2017). The digital and the human: A prospectus for digital anthropology. In H. A. Horst & D. Miller (Eds.), *Digital anthropology* (pp. 3–38). London: Bloomsbury Academic.

Ministry of Foreign Affairs of Denmark. (2017). *Denmark names first ever tech ambassador.* Retrieved from http://um.dk/en/news/newsdisplaypage/?new sid=60eaf005-9f87-46f8-922a-1cf20c5b527a.

Newsroom [Lexis Nexis]. (2015, November 23). *141215 Newsroom presentative NL* [Video File]. Retrieved from https://www.youtube.com/watch?v=y4nESFy3FB4.

Paulauskas, R. (2018). *Understanding Lithuania's digital diplomacy model* [In person].

Prensky, M. (2001). Digital natives, digital immigrants part 1. *On the Horizon, 9*(5), 1–6.

Roberts, I. (2017). *Satow's diplomatic practice.* Oxford: Oxford University Press.

Seo, H. (2013). The "Virtual Last Three Feet": Understanding relationship perspectives in network-based public diplomacy. In R. S. Zaharna, A. Arsenault, & A. Fisher (Eds.), *Relational, networked and collaborative approaches to public diplomacy* (pp. 157–169). New York, NY: Taylor & Francis.

Shimazu, N. (2014). Diplomacy as theatre: Staging the Bandung conference of 1955. *Modern Asian Studies, 48*(1), 225–252.

Slaughter, A. M. (2017). *The chessboard and the web: Strategies of connection in a networked world.* New Haven: Yale University Press.

Sotiriu, S. (2015). Digital diplomacy: Between promises and reality. In C. Bjola & M. Holmes (Eds.), *Digital diplomacy theory and practice* (pp. 33–51). Oxon: Routledge.

Van Dijk, J. A. (2017). Digital divide: Impact of access. *The International Encyclopedia of Media Effects,* 1–11.

Wichowski, A. (2015). 'Secrecy is for losers': Why diplomats should embrace openness to protect national security. In C. Bjola & M. Holmes (Eds.), *Digital diplomacy theory and practice* (pp. 52–70). Oxon: Routledge.

CHAPTER 10

A Discussion of the Digitalization of Public Diplomacy

Hide your wives and daughters/Hide your groceries too/Great nations of Europe comin' through.

—Randy Newman

In September of 1814, the sovereigns of Europe descended upon Vienna to refashion their world. Deep within the halls of the Imperial Hofburg Palace and far from the prying eyes of their citizens, these sovereigns carved up a continent while in the background Ludwig van Beethoven gave voice to passion. This was the *World of Yesterday*, a world governed by secret negotiations and discrete diplomacy, and one that would come to an end in World War I. For it was in the wake of the secret alliances that sparked World War I that American president Woodrow Wilson formulated his new vision of "open covenants of diplomacy" (Bjola, 2014).

It is hard to imagine how the Congress of Vienna would have ended had all secret negotiations been leaked and made public. How could the Austrian Emperor face the Russian Tsar had the public learned that Austria regarded Russian cuisine as peasants' food? How could the King of Denmark dine with the King of Bavaria had the latter known that the former regarded him a buffoon? Would open diplomacy lead to the dissolution of the Congress? Or perhaps even to war? Would the world once again hear the Randy Newman's cry, "Hide your wives and daughters, hide your groceries too. Great nations of Europe comin' through?"

© The Author(s) 2019
I. Manor, *The Digitalization of Public Diplomacy*,
Palgrave Macmillan Series in Global Public Diplomacy,
https://doi.org/10.1007/978-3-030-04405-3_10

Despite the passage of nearly two hundred years since the Congress of Vienna and the increased transparency of diplomacy, in 2010 a shiver passed down the spine of the U.S. State Department when WikiLeaks released a quarter of a million internal American diplomatic cables (Causey & Howard, 2013). The publication of the cables, written between 1996 and 2010, included frank assessments by U.S. diplomats of world leaders and their governments. Hailed by some as an important step toward transparent governance, U.S. diplomats viewed it as a fiasco and a threat to American national security. Secretary of State Hillary Clinton stated, "It is an attack on the international community, the alliances and partnerships, the conversations and negotiations that safeguard global security and advance economic prosperity." Other lawmakers, such as former Senator Joe Lieberman, characterized the leak as "an attack on the national security of the United States and an outrageous, reckless, and despicable action that would leave those responsible with blood on their hands" (Harnden, 2010; Sheridan, 2010).

Beyond embarrassment, some diplomats wondered if they could continue practicing their craft in the digital age. The risk of publication meant that diplomats would need to censor their reports to MFAs, thus impairing their abilities to offer important analysis. Moreover, threat of publication would impair diplomats' ability to gather intelligence from sources within foreign governments. The digital age had already diminished diplomats' roles as representatives and channels of communications between governments (Archetti, 2012). Now it threatened to diminish their role as analysts.

Yet revisited from 2018, WikiLeaks may be viewed as a positive event that forced MFAs to embrace digital technologies and gave birth to a new form of public diplomacy. As Janice Gross Stein (2011) suggested, journalists, foreign commentators, academics, and foreign politicians were all surprised by the quality of analysis they read in the WikiLeaks cables. U.S. diplomats emerged as experts on their host nations, able to offer in-depth accounts of political and cultural transitions taking place around them. U.S. diplomats in Tunisia, for example, clearly stated that the ground was shifting under President Ben Ali. A year later, he fled his nation as part of the Arab Spring revolts.

From WikiLeaks emerged the model of a modern diplomat. While he or she may no longer hold a monopoly over communication and representation, diplomats remain foreign policy experts capable of providing decision makers with information, analysis, and forecasts that help them make sense of the world. At a time when crises are the norm, long-standing nations unravel into chaos, and alliances shift from region to region, such analysis is priceless. And while it is true that the British Prime Minister can simply call her French colleague, and that the British FCO (Foreign and Commonwealth Office) can monitor events in Syria through Sky News, leaders and MFAs remain dependent on the information and analysis provided by their diplomats. It is diplomats who are tasked with the unique assignment of interpreting world events through the national prism (Copeland, 2013). WikiLeaks therefore demonstrated that even in the twenty-first century, the diplomat is far from superfluous.

Causey and Howard (2013) have argued that in the wake of WikiLeaks, MFAs' already conservative culture grew even more conservative. The State Department, for instance, informed its diplomats that reading the WikiLeaks cables without proper security clearance would be a punishable offense. Yet from the perspective of 2018, a different picture emerges. As this book has demonstrated, the process of digitalization has seen MFAs increasingly adopt risk-tolerant approaches toward digital technologies. Fear of faux pas has been replaced by the expectation of blunders; the dread of trolls has made way for digital experimentation, and top-down command structures have adapted to a networked society. Since the WikiLeaks scandal of 2010, diplomats around the world have continued to perform a balancing act between the demands of the digital society, the affordance of digital technologies, and their public diplomacy goals. WikiLeaks did not halt the process of digitalization. Rather, WikiLeaks was a pivotal moment in its evolution. This was best exemplified in a statement made by Hugh Elliot, former head of the FCO's digital unit, that "The half-life of digital mistakes is very short. We now expect our diplomats to make mistakes, learn from them and move on" (Israel MFA, 2017).

Following WikiLeaks, elements within the State Department and other MFAs realized that information now wants to be free. As Alexis Wichowski (2015) argued, if information is quarantined, it will set itself free (with the possible help of a Swedish activist). This realization paved the way toward greater transparency in public diplomacy given MFAs' desire to control what information is made public, and when. While the motive of such transparency may still be an attempt to manage the flow of information, it can be regarded as an important step toward the Wilsonian vision of "open covenants of diplomacy." Indeed, since

2010 the State Department and other MFAs have dramatically altered their information-sharing practices. The deliberations of the Geneva 2 Conference on Syria were broadcast live to a global audience through Twitter, while the Iran nuclear accord was published online, where it could be criticized and debated by an empowered digital public. These examples demonstrate the leaps and bounds taken toward more open forms of diplomacy made possible by WikiLeaks and the accelerated digitalization of public diplomacy.

Finally, while WikiLeaks demonstrated the dangers of digitalization, it also illustrated some of its benefits. WikiLeaks was accompanied by a flurry of digital activity. Digital publics interested in the world around them and the governments who rule it debated the cables and their repercussions online. It was this heated, prolonged, and insightful debate that demonstrated to MFAs that digital publics have opinions on world affairs and that they wish to express these opinions. WikiLeaks may have thus facilitated a slow transition from monologue to dialogue-based public diplomacy.

Yet as this book has argued, to understand the digitalization of public diplomacy, one cannot fixate on an individual occurrence or an individual institution. Rather, one must first understand the logic of the digital society and realize that each MFA is amid its own unique process of digitalization. The book's main findings and conclusions are reviewed in the following section.

THREE MODEST GOALS

This book's first goal was to offer a new conceptual framework for understanding and researching the influence of digital technologies on the conduct of public diplomacy. This framework is rooted in the term "the digitalization of public diplomacy", which relates to a long-term process in which digital technologies impact the norms, values, and working routines of MFAs, as well as the metaphors or self-narratives that diplomats employ to conceptualize their craft. The digitalization of public diplomacy thus has normative, procedural and conceptual dimensions. This book's conceptual framework also asserts that each MFA is amid its own unique process of digitalization which is influenced by myriad organizational, national and global factors.

The book's second goal was to demonstrate that one cannot understand the "the digitalization of public diplomacy" without first characterizing the digital society. This is because public diplomacy is now practiced by social beings who belong to digital societies, or societies that have been fundamentally reshaped by digital technologies. Moreover, public diplomacy is now practiced opposite members of digital societies. It is through diplomats that the logic and culture of the digital society diffuse into MFAs. Analyzing contemporary public diplomacy therefore requires that one consider the values and norms of the digital society, as well as the expectations of digital society members.

The case studies reviewed in Chapters 3–5 have demonstrated that digitalization is in fact a long-term process and that MFAs do not exist in a binary state of being either digital or not digital. Rather, they are amid a process of fundamental change that challenges existing working routines, well-entrenched norms, and long held beliefs. These chapters narrated the process of public diplomacy's digitalization over a decade and illustrated how each act of digital interaction between diplomats and publics shaped the course of the process of digitalization. While in 2007 Swedish officials attempted to relinquish all control over their communication with digital publics and launch a virtual embassy, by 2018 MFAs transitioned to quarantined forms of engagement, which enabled diplomats to maintain some control over digital interactions. Such was the case with Twitter Q&A sessions. In this way, MFAs preformed a balancing act between the demands of digital publics for real-time interactions, MFAs risk-intolerant culture, and the goals of the "new" public diplomacy. Over time, and through a process of trial and error, diplomats began to create the conditions necessary for fostering relationships with digital publics by transitioning from monologue to quarantined dialogue. As digitalization is a process, quarantined engagement may soon be replaced by open dialogue.

Chapter 3 also analyzed the social media Q&A sessions of Israel's ambassador to the U.S. and the EU's ambassador to Israel. In both of these cases, the ambassadors in question remained on social media sites and engaged with digital publics despite being greeted by a windfall of profanities and accusations. These instances demonstrate a genuine desire of ambassadors to interact and/or engage with digital publics. The question that remains, however, is, what is the goal of such interactions? Did the ambassadors stay on social media to foster relationships with foreign populations, or were they hoping to influence the worldview of social media users? This book cannot offer a definitive answer to this question, as it did not interview the ambassadors in question. Yet the interviews conducted and the case studies analyzed in this book all suggest that there is a great conflict between diplomats' desires to interact with digital publics and foster relationships, and their well-entrenched norm of influencing the worldviews of foreign populations. Here again, this book finds that digitalization is a process, rather than a binary state, and that diplomats may be on a trajectory toward greater dialogue and engagement.

Lastly, Chapter 3 found that the digitalization of public diplomacy influences both diplomatic institutions and other societal institutions that orbit the world of diplomacy. This is especially true of the media. Early digital interactions between diplomats and digital publics were all labeled by media organizations as catastrophes and embarrassments simply because diplomats were rebuffed by social media users. These labels stemmed from the media's ignorance as journalists failed to appreciate the impact digital technologies were having on public diplomacy. Nowadays, tweets and posts are regarded by journalists as official government communiques, while interactions between diplomats and publics garner in-depth analysis.

Chapter 4 demonstrated that exogenous shocks also influence the process of digitalization. The Crimean crisis and Russia's use of digital platforms to contest the reality taking place in Crimea saw a shift from the "new" public diplomacy goal of relationship building to the traditional goal of influence. This chapter therefore segmented the digitalization of public diplomacy into two stages. One of the main differences between the two stages was the transition from targeted to tailored communication models. This transition is emblematic of the aforementioned conflict between diplomats' desires to create digital relationships and diplomats' well-entrenched goal of obtaining influence. This is because tailored messages are meant to meet the desires and needs of digital publics. Such messages are more influential as they correspond with publics' values, norms, histories and national narratives.

Chapter 4 also illustrated why the logic of the digital society should inform the research on contemporary public diplomacy. From the perspective of traditional public diplomacy, the Russian embassy's decision to publish the "Lame Duck Tweet" of President Obama makes little sense. Russian diplomats were surely aware that this message would not resonate with British publics, would not help foster ties between the embassy and the British population, and would not lead to changes in British foreign policy. As such, the tweet would not facilitate the acceptance of Russian foreign policy in the UK. Yet from the perspective of the digital society, this tweet was but one part of the iBrand adopted by the embassy, a brand characterized by fiery rhetoric, brazen language, and undiplomatic tones. Through this iBrand, the embassy sets itself apart from all others and attracts the attention of digital users and the media. The embassy's rhetoric is thus demonstrative of the acrobatic fêtes that all digital society members must employ to attract the gaze of post-panoptic surveillance (Manor & Soone, 2018).

The Russian embassy's brand is strategic as it aims to portray Russia as a nation that does not mince words or hide behind diplomatic jargon. Russia speaks plainly to the common person. This brand therefore echoes the sentiments of Brexit and the feeling that the UK has "had enough of experts." Finally, the tweet did garner mass media attention and appeared in news articles in ten different countries, as well as many British publications. It is thus emblematic of a "reverse CNN effect" in which diplomats, diplomatic institutions, and world leaders leverage digital platforms toward influencing the media's agenda rather than having the media dictate foreign policy priorities (Gilboa, 2005a, 2005b; Robinson, 1999). The Russian embassy and Donald Trump therefore employ similar logics and similar tactics.

The transition from argument- to narrative-based public diplomacy identified in Chapter 4 exemplifies how the logic of the digital society influences the working routines of MFAs. The digital society is one in which individuals must author an attractive self-narrative (Storr, 2018). This narrative is used to promote the individual on various digital profiles and toward different ends. While one's narrative on LinkedIn is used to seek employment, narratives on Facebook are used to obtain social validation. The logic of the narrative has been adopted by diplomatic institutions the world over. Reflecting on the Crimean crisis, Lawrence Freedman (2014) wrote, "In recent years, there has been much discussion of 'narrative' as an essential prerequisite of a successful strategy, a storyline that not only provides a justification for particular actions but also creates expectations for the future and so helps others, friends as well as opponents, adapt to a new situation. It is through words that crises are framed and their salient points identified."

Narratives are important because they offer structure and sense making. In a world that seems to be accelerating toward a state of perpetual crisis, diplomats' narratives can help digital publics make sense of world events and engender a sense of stability. Yet Chapter 4 also demonstrates that diplomats now engage in narrative competitions. During such competitions, truth and reality are contested, possibly increasing the senses of insecurity and uncertainty felt by many around the world. A world in which the Republic of Crimea both exists and does not exist, and in which Syria has been both liberated and bombarded into submission, is one that can no longer be fathomed.

In May of 2017, the U.S. Advisory Commission on Public Diplomacy published a report titled: "Can public diplomacy survive the Internet?" Chapter 4 poses a different question: Can the Internet survive public diplomacy? MFAs' use of digital platforms to create multiple realities and engage in narrative competitions fuel feelings of anxiety, and it is anxiety that leads the way toward societal friction, political extremity, and loss of faith in governments.

Chapter 5 examined how societal metaphors, narratives, and perceived threats can influence the process of digitalization in certain MFAs. As such, it offers a prime example of how norms, values, and metaphors diffuse into MFAs through diplomats. The view of social media echo chambers as the undoing of democracy, coupled with the fear of Russian Hybrid Warfare, led to new digital initiatives in MFAs. Many of these initiatives focused on strategic communications rather than relationship building. Yet this chapter also demonstrated that different MFAs contend with threats in different ways. While the British FCO leveraged its blogosphere to narrate the Syrian Civil War and limit the impact of Russian disinformation, the Israeli MFA sought to develop its algorithmic capabilities. This chapter therefore illustrated that digitalization is a unique process that evolves in different directions, and at different paces in different MFAs.

This chapter also analyzed diplomats' utilization of diverse digital technologies and did not focus solely on social media sites. Presently, the research corpus that examines digital technologies' impacts on public diplomacy is mostly fixated on diplomats' use of Twitter, Facebook, and other such sites (Hocking & Melissen, 2015; Melissen & de Keulenaar, 2017). Yet diplomats have adopted a host of digital technologies, ranging from the WhatsApp messaging application to Wikis. This book expands the current research by analyzing diplomats' employment of web-based platforms, smartphone applications, algorithms, and blogospheres. It is the diversity of digital technologies that diplomats employ which exhibits the innovative, agile, and inventive nature of MFAs. Over the course of a decade, diplomats launched the world's first virtual embassy, conducted shared social media campaigns, created personalized smartphone applications, and authored their own algorithms. These examples negate the common view of MFAs as outdated relics whose affinity for antiquated, top-down command structures prevents them from being instrumental in twenty-first-century diplomacy (Copeland, 2013).

Importantly, some MFAs seem to regard digital publics as naïve audiences who are easily manipulated by disinformation and who fall under the spell of Russian propaganda as children marching to the tune of the magic flute (Pamment, Nothhaft, Agardh-Twetman, & Fjallhed, 2018; Tucker et al., 2018). These views may not only limit diplomats' willingness to interact with digital publics, they are also misguided. Digital publics are intelligent, well-informed, and guided by a desire to understand events and actors shaping their world. To do so, they adopt healthy and diverse news diets, visit websites that negate their political affiliation and challenge government spokespersons online. Diplomats will only be able to leverage digital technologies toward relational goals if they come to value digital publics and appreciate their opinions. This is because trust and respect are the foundations of any relationship, whether online or offline.

Chapter 5 illustrated that analyzing the digitalization of public diplomacy can best be achieved by employing both the technological and societal prisms. The FCO's use of its own blogosphere and the prestige of ambassadors to narrate Russia's involvement in the Syrian Civil War are demonstrative of the societal prism in which social actors leverage digital technologies to obtain their goals. The technological prism best explains Israel's decision to burst filter bubbles through digital assets as technological design determined the MFA's public diplomacy activities.

Lastly, Chapter 5 examined different approaches to combating digital disinformation and propaganda. Some MFAs and governments have decided to invest in media literacy programs that teach citizens how to access accurate information and spot "fake" or false news on digital platforms. These capabilities may serve as another form of public diplomacy resources. Nations can share their digital expertise and media literacy programs with other nations as a means of strengthening ties and deepening relationships with foreign populations. At the moment, the UK government seems to have adopted this approach by offering digital aid to Baltic MFAs and governments.

Chapters 3 through 5 showed how the values and norms of the digital society influence diplomats and their institutions. By becoming

Twitter celebrities, the State Department's Alec Ross and Jared Cohen hammered the logic of the digital society into the minds of American diplomats. Their statement that open is good while closed is bad, and their belief that authenticity is key (Lichtenstein, 2010), epitomize the values that define the digital society—those of openness, authenticity and neo-liberalism. In the digital society, all once done in private must be done in the open so that information is readily available to algorithms, including public diplomacy (Bauman & Lyon, 2016). The Hamas terror movement's Q&A session elucidates that in the digital society, all actors must fashion an authentic and unique iBrand. It is the authenticity of the iBrand that sets one digital user apart from the other, that can separate Hamas from Daesh. Tailored public diplomacy is demonstrative of MFAs' need to offer digital publics an online experience that meets their unique interests, desires, and patterns of use of digital platforms. This is because digital publics have become accustomed to living in a society where their entertainment, news, and access to information are all algorithmically tailored to their heart's delight. Lastly, Israel's peer-to-peer diplomacy (Attias, 2012) demonstrates an adoration for algorithms that can now help map digital bridges, or social media users who can burst filter bubbles of anti-Semitism. Algorithms are thus not the undoing of diplomacy, but rather its weapon du jour.

Chapter 6 transitioned from narrating and charting the process of public diplomacy's digitalization to analyzing its possible outcomes. It was in Chapter 6 that this book's third goal of diversifying the public diplomacy research corpus was most visible. Moreover, this chapter sought to introduce a new model for measuring dialogic engagement between diplomats and digital publics. The analysis of five African MFAs and four Lithuanian embassies found that dialogic engagement between diplomats and digital publics remains a rare occurrence. This finding is in line with a host of studies conducted between 2011 and 2018 (Bjola & Jiang, 2015; Bjola & Manor, 2018; Clarke, 2015; Comor & Bean, 2012; Hocking & Melissen, 2015; Kampf, Manor, & Segev, 2015; Manor & Crilley, 2018; Metzgar, 2012).

Yet Chapter 6 did find that African MFAs offer their followers a unique national prism through which events in Africa and the world may be understood. Moreover, digital publics now have access to a breadth of information on African nations' diplomatic goals, initiatives, and achievements. New Zealand's unique vision of democratized public diplomacy may thus be advancing, albeit at a slow pace. In addition, a quantitative analysis found that African MFAs can set the agenda for discussions with digital publics by identifying issues that are of concern to diplomats. These activities may in time lead to two-way conversations on issues of mutual concern. Lastly, this chapter found that the Facebook profiles of Lithuanian embassies are used to answer diaspora questions and provide information on community events. These findings all suggest that dialogic engagement between diplomats and digital publics may also be progressing at a slow pace.

Notably, both Lithuania and African nations share a common challenge: a large and globally-dispersed diaspora. While the Lithuanian MFA views the diaspora as a diplomatic asset, African nations are financially reliant on diasporas. The analysis of four Lithuanian embassies suggests that these have become central to organizing diaspora events and strengthening the emotional bond between diasporas and their countries of origin. Facebook is used by embassies to invite diasporas to celebrate national achievements such as joining the OECD, commemorating cultural achievements, and celebrating Lithuanian independence. Digital technologies have thus had a re-territorializing effect as the boundaries of Lithuania extend to foreign realms, while the concept of citizenship is decoupled from one's physical location. Space is therefore manipulated by diplomats and borders become irrelevant.

The analysis of the five African MFAs suggests that they rarely deal with diaspora issues or deliberately target their diasporas, a surprising finding given diasporas' contributions to the financial stability of many countries in Africa. Yet it is possible that African MFAs are wary of interacting with their diasporas, as digital platforms can be used to condemn one's country of origin, disrupt its digital activities, and prevent it from obtaining diplomatic goals. Such was the case with the Eritrean diaspora (Bernal, 2014). In the case of African MFAs, digital technologies have had a de-territorializing effect in which the demarcation line between the nation and its diaspora is clearly marked. The conflicting results between the Lithuanian and African MFAs demonstrate yet again that the process of digitalization of public diplomacy is not uniform across all diplomatic institutions.

Chapter 7 dealt with MFAs' attempts to overcome the limitations of traditional diplomacy through the utilization of digital technologies. The theoretical prism employed in this chapter demonstrated that the digital society's desire to annihilate time and space leads to new diplomatic practices, such as diplomacy at a distance. The case studies of the virtual embassies of Sweden, the U.S., Israel, and Palestine suggest that distance may limit diplomats' relational abilities. Like drone operators who feel morally responsible only for that which is in their sight, so diplomats may only to be able to interact with digital publics that are in their sight. Thus, Palestinian diplomats can interact digitally with their Israeli neighbors, unlike American diplomats who fail to interact with distant Iranians. This chapter also examined diplomats' attempts to disseminate global narratives or frames. The analysis of the Turkish MFA lay bare that the digital society waits for no one. Those who fail to frame events in real-time and meet the expectations of digital publics forfeit the right to impact digital publics' understanding of world events. This chapter therefore finds that time and space remain omnipotent even in the digital age, for while distance can prevent digital engagement, time cannot be turned back.

Palestine's virtual embassy is unique as it represents an attempt to practice public diplomacy amid an active conflict. Unlike the USA and Iran, who have no diplomatic ties but are not in a state of war, Israel and Palestine are engrossed in an intractable conflict. This may be one reason why the Palestinian embassy did not address issues that Israeli publics view as especially contentious, ranging from payments to families of terrorists to alleged incitement against Jews in Palestinian schools. Addressing these issues could drive a wedge between the embassy and its followers, and lead to followers abandoning the embassy's profile. Rather than focus on negative or contentious issues, the embassy presents Israelis with credible and positive visions of the future. The embassy's attempts to portray a positive future is a sophisticated use of digital technologies in public diplomacy, as before peace can be negotiated, it must be imagined in the minds of conflicted communities. That is exactly what the Oslo Peace Accords achieved for a brief time, and what Palestine's virtual embassy may be achieving on Facebook.

Chapter 8 analyzed the selfie diplomacy activities of the USA and Poland. The chapter's main theoretical argument is that the use of digital platforms for image management individualizes the nation-state as it acquires the traits of a digital self. It has a profile page, profile picture, likes, ˙nd dislikes and can even interact with digital publics. Digital branding ˙ts thus facilitate the presentation of the nation-state in everyday life ˙row the distance between citizens and their nations. The analysis ˙s selfie in the age of Trump found that the State Department ˙˙a as the world's CEO. Seated within its fortress of solitude, America adopts the rhetoric of sanctions, the art of the deal and the policy of deregulation. While this selfie matches that of President Trump, it negates 60 years of American public diplomacy, as this nation morphs from the world's moral compass to its chairman of the board. Its motto is no longer "give me your tired, your poor" but instead, "show me the money."

While the State Department manages America's present-day selfie, the Polish MFA manages the nation's historic selfie. Poland's historical approach suggests that in an age in which images rule supreme, a nation's past is as important as its present. If Poland remains associated with the Holocaust, it may be unable to achieve its present-day foreign policy goals, as morality breeds legitimacy on the world stage (Mor, 2012; Quelch & Jocz, 2009; Van Ham, 2013). But if Poland distances itself from the Holocaust, it can re-associate itself with positive values such as multiculturalism and democracy. Thus, like individual selfies, national ones are a tool used to demonstrate conformity with desired norms, rather than exhibiting originality and individuality (Manor & Soone, 2018; Natarajan, 2014).

Poland's historic selfie is also emblematic of the digital society's desire to annihilate time. According to Manuel Castells (2013), the annihilation of time is obtained by de-sequencing life events. Such is the case with 20-year-old tech CEOs who manage 50-year-old employees or the view of retirement as a second adolescence. The Polish MFA de-sequences time by summoning the past to the present and using the past to shape Poland's present-day image. An important component of this de-sequencing of time is the use of historic photographs and maps. As Susan Sontag (1990) argued, photographs play an evidentiary purpose in modern societies. They are used in courts of law to establish that certain events did in fact take place. By using photographs to narrate its past, the Polish MFA lends credibility to its arguments.

The Polish MFA, however, is not the only one to produce images, photographs, and videos. Rather, the digitalization of public diplomacy has transformed MFAs into visual narrators. This process may also be explained through the logic of the digital society. First, visuals convey large quantities of information in a relatively short time. Thus, they are an effective way of disseminating information among digital publics who are flooded by a daily barrage of Too Much Infromation (TMI) comprised of blogs, vlogs, and status updates (Miller & Horst, 2017). Second, visuals lead to influence given that in modern societies, "seeing is believing." Tweets demonstrating the scale of destruction in Aleppo may have helped the UK rally domestic and foreign support for its diplomatic brawls with Russia, while Russian images of aid convoys making their way to a besieged Crimea may have helped spread its narrative of hate crimes against Russian minorities. Lastly, images increase the virality of digital content and thus enable diplomats to interact with larger audiences. This is important, for without attracting the public, diplomats cannot practice public diplomacy.

The analysis of the Polish selfie also found that the digitalization of public diplomacy has given rise to domestic public diplomacy. The Polish MFA operates Polish language Twitter accounts that help it create a domestic constituency by demonstrating the MFA's contribution to obtaining Polish national goals. Yet the Polish MFA is not the only one to develop a domestic constituency. In the globalized world, MFAs lose their monopoly over managing a nation's external affairs as numerous government ministries face the world and collaborate with their peers. MFAs' loss of territory within their governments necessitated that they adopt a new strategy of facing both the world and their citizenry, thus developing domestic constituencies. While some MFAs, such as Global Affairs Canada, focus on the delivery of digital consular aid, others, such as India, offer citizens direct access to MFA policy briefs and summaries of state visits. What emerges is that the digitalization of public diplomacy has given way to glocalized public diplomacy. While MFAs may target their citizens, these citizens also flock voluntarily to their MFAs' Twitter profiles, hoping to learn about world events through their nations' unique prism.

Chapter 8 included a discussion of the limitations of selfie diplomacy. One of these is the selfie's need to relate to the media's depiction of a nation. A nation labeled by the media as warmongering will find it difficult to promote a selfie of peaceful coexistence, while a nation torn by civil war may be unable to promote a selfie that attracts investments. There is thus a *credibility gap* between a nation's self-depiction and that of the media. The greater the gap, the less credible the selfie becomes. Selfies may also be influenced by the narratives of foreign countries. Russia, for instance, depicts Lithuania as a failed state that cannot exist without the support of Western Europe and NATO (R. Paulauskas, personal communication, July 25, 2018). Lithuania's selfie must contend with this depiction, for if it does not, it may also face a credibility gap. Selfie diplomacy is thus much more than mere nation branding. It is the authoring of a national self-image that is proactively managed, which comments on events in real-time and which adapts to the narration of other actors, be they the media or foreign governments.

Lastly, Chapter 9 examined the digitalization of ambassadors. This chapter found that the digitalization of public diplomacy is not limited to younger diplomats or those who were born into digital societies. The adoption of digital technologies has influenced the norms, values and working routines of the highest echelons of MFAs, as has the logic of the digital society. Notably, this chapter found that ambassadors can substantially contribute to the digital reach of their embassies due to their status and prestige, as well as their ability to explain complex foreign policy issues. Each ambassador represented in this chapter manifested a different value or norm of the digital society. The UK's Permanent Representative to the UN manifested the values of openness and transparency, the EU's ambassador to the U.S. manifested the norm of real-time access to information, and the French ambassador has created an iBrand that sets him apart from all his peers. Lastly, ambassadors' use of digital platforms to infringe on the "backstage" of diplomacy is representative of diplomats' needs to meet the demands of the digital society. Diplomats who do not lift the veil of secrecy from diplomacy will fail to attract digital publics.

One theme that was evident across this book's many chapters was the notion of "listening" to digital publics. It is the concept of listening that sets public diplomacy apart from other diplomatic practices, for listening gives voice to publics and foreign populations and thus facilitates interactions, engagement, and relationship building. However, listening can take different forms. One form of listening identified in this book is tied to New Zealand's unique vision of democratized public diplomacy (A. Lutyens, personal communication, July 10, 2018). In this instance, "listening" relates to taking digital publics' opinions and attitudes into account when formulating foreign policies. In the Lithuanian MFA, "listening" is the use of social media sites to monitor conversations in other nations and predict changes in these nations' foreign policies (R. Paulauskas, personal communication, July 25, 2018). In the case of the Obama administration's digital campaign to sell the Iran Deal, "listening" was the use of follower feedback to "tweak" campaign messages and identify messages that did not resonate well with intended audiences (Bjola & Manor, 2018). This book therefore finds that listening is also invariably influenced by intent. At times, listening relates to a process of two-way interactions, while other times it relates to crafting more influential messages. Here again, the conflict between the goals of the "new" public diplomacy and those of traditional public diplomacy is made apparent.

Another recurring theme evident across this book was that the digitalization of public diplomacy has led to public-centric diplomacy. Whether the intent is relationship building or influence, it is the "public" that now occupies MFAs and diplomats practicing public diplomacy. At times this public is valued, as is the case with digital natives managing embassy social media accounts (Manor & Kampf, 2019). These rely on public feedback to craft more engaging content. At other times, this public is viewed as naïve and highly susceptible to manipulation, as is the case with strategic communications initiatives. Moreover, in some instances this public is visible, be it in the form of Facebook profiles or Second Life avatars. Other times this public can only be imagined, as is the case with Israeli diplomats tweeting at citizens of Gulf countries. Yet in all these instances, the public takes center stage in public diplomacy, in addition to elites: the traditional target audiences of public diplomacy.

The third theme identified throughout this book is the mediatization of diplomats and MFAs. As James Pamment (2014), and Manor and Crilley (2019) have argued, MFAs and diplomats have adopted the logic and working routines of media institutions. Like media institutions, MFAs presently narrate issues, events, actors, and policies in near-real time. Moreover, as is the case with news framing, morality plays a crucial role in MFA narration as morality breeds legitimacy on the world stage and among digital publics. The U.S. State Department, for instance, used social media to argue that the Supreme Court's ruling on same-sex marriage exemplified America's commitment to equality and human rights. Similarly, the Turkish MFA framed the 2016 failed coup attempt as an attack on democracy and its core values rather than an attack on the Erdogan government. MFAs now also monitor the narratives spread by other diplomatic actors or news agencies and attempt to counter these. Indeed, the Turkish MFA's social media blitz was meant to counter the media's depiction of the Turkish government's crackdown as "Erdogan's Revenge." MFAs have adopted these media practices to both compete with media organizations over the attention of digital publics and challenge the media's role as information gatekeepers (Manor, 2016). By creating and disseminating their own frames, MFAs become less reliant on the media to shape the worldviews of foreign populations.

A fourth and final theme that was identified in this book was the association between digital activities and the obtainment of offline public diplomacy goals. This is an important association that is often overlooked. Many digital diplomacy studies, for instance, treat the digital realm as being distinct from the offline one. Yet this book has shown that diplomats, embassies, and MFAs employ digital technologies to obtain offline goals. The Israeli ambassador to Washington hoped to rally American support for Israel's 2014 War in Gaza through a Twitter Q&A. The UK FCO employs Twitter survey questions to better inform the British public on its activities to counter Daesh propaganda. Lithuanian embassies use Facebook to strengthen ties with diasporas and reverse a "brain drain", while the French ambassador to the USA has adopted a cynical tone to attract attention from U.S. leaders. Future studies should adopt a similar prism, for without it, one is unable to unearth the true relationship between diplomats, technology, and public diplomacy. The following section ties this book's conclusions together while identifying avenues of future research. For instance, comparative studies may investigate how certain factors lead to different processes of digitalization in different MFAs.

New Directions

The case studies reviewed in this book enable it to identify a host of factors that influence the digitalization of public diplomacy in a given MFA. These can be seen in Table 10.1.

Scholars hoping to further research the digitalization of public diplomacy may rely on Table 10.1 to conduct comparative studies. For instance, scholars may compare two government-wide approaches to technology and investigate how these different approaches influence the process of digitalization in MFAs. Similarly, comparative studies may analyze how different domestic agendas place the digitalization of public diplomacy on different trajectories. Scholars may also examine how the professional background of directors of digital units at MFAs influence the utilization of digital technologies by diplomats. Such comparative studies are important as they acknowledge that one cannot treat all MFAs as a monolithic unit. Rather, one must recognize that each MFA is on its own voyage of digitalization, which is impacted by a myriad of national and global factors, as well as organizational cultures.

Table 10.1 Examples of factors that influence the digitalization of public diplomacy in MFAs

Factor	Chapters	MFAs	Examples
MFA appointments	2	U.S. State Department	Alec Ross, Jared Cohen, and Anne-Marie Slaughter lead a digital zeitgeist of openness and engagement
Changes in administrations	6 and 7	Canada, U.S. State Department	Trudeau government relinquishes control over diplomats' digital communications, State Department rebrands America in accordance with Trump administration priorities
External shocks (top-down change)	3 and 5	Germany, New Zealand	Crimean crisis leads to restructuring of strategic communication unit in German MFA, Arab Spring leads to use of digital platforms for listening and reporting in New Zealand MFA
Digital experiments (bottom-up change)	3	UK, Canada	U.S. and UK diplomats share Daesh-related Tweets and thus become central to online conversations, consular crisis leads to Canadian tactics that "hack" algorithms
Government-wide adoption of digital technologies	2 and 5	US State Department, New Zealand	Obama administration's open government initiative, migration of New Zealand ministries to digital platforms
Government's domestic agenda	1 and 7	Poland, Norway	Polish legislation banning association between Poland and Holocaust leads to selfie diplomacy, rising water levels lead Norway MFA to networks with relevant NGOs
Willingness of foreign ministers to experiment with digital technologies	2 and 6	U.S. State Department, Sweden	Secretary of State Hillary Clinton embraces twenty-first-century statecraft, Foreign Minister Carl Bildt opens blog
Diaspora policies	3 and 5	Lithuanian, Ethiopia, India	Lithuanian attempts to reverse "brain drain" and foster ties with diasporas turn Facebook pages into diaspora bulletin boards, Ethiopian MFA publishes digital magazine for diaspora community, Indiann MEA launches "Know India" web-based platforms for second-generation diasporas

(continued)

Table 10.1 (continued)

Factor	Chapters	MFAs	Examples
Geographic location	5	New Zealand	Distance from Europe and Russia means New Zealand MFA does not focus on strategic communication
Digital migration of allies	5	New Zealand	New Zealand MFA migrates to digital platforms following UK and USA
Heads of digital units at MFAs	6 and 7	Palestine, Poland	Polish unit headed by former journalists and public relations specialists who may focus more on branding activities than relationship building, Palestine virtual embassy more dialogic as it is operated by committee for interaction with Israeli society
Age of diplomats managing embassy social media profiles	5	Canada, New Zealand, India	Digital natives that manage embassy social media profiles more likely to tailor content to follower feedback, value follower comments, and integrate follower sentiments into their reporting to the MFA
New foreign policies	3	Iran	Iran uses social media during UN General Assembly to present new vision for relationship with the West, Iran uses social media campaigns to rebrand itself as leading World Against Violence and Extremism
Participating in diplomatic conferences	3	Israel, Netherlands	In 2016 and 2018, Israel held two international conferences focusing on MFAs as service providers and algorithmic diplomacy, Dutch MFA held Digital Camp in 2018
Narratives spread by other actors	5	Lithuania	Russia's use of digital platforms to depict Lithuania as failed state motivates Lithuanian MFA to migrate online

Notably, this book's main argument has been that the digitalization of public diplomacy relates to the way digital technologies impact an MFA's working routines, norms, and values as well as the self-narratives or metaphors diplomats employ to conceptualize their craft. However, this book finds that the relationship between digital technologies and the working routines of MFAs is not always a direct one. At times, a government's public diplomacy initiative impacts the process of digitalization. For instance, the U.S. State Department's Public Diplomacy 2.0 initiative led to the creation of the Digital Outreach Team, which visited Arab language websites to converse with Muslim Internet users. The initiative thus led to a new working routine: reaching out to digital publics. The norm that followed was that of listening to digital publics. This initiative centered on the metaphor of the conversation in which diplomats speak *with* rather than *at* digital publics (Hayden, 2012).

Other times, the utilization of digital technologies by one MFA or government leads to fundamental changes in another MFA. For instance, Russia's use of digital platforms to spread narratives that contested the nature of events taking place in Crimea led several MFAs to adopt a narrative approach to public diplomacy. New working routines included the creation of digital campaigns, which used narratives to interpret world events and nations' foreign policies. The norm that followed was the view of narratives as a prism through which world events could be explained to digital publics, and through which various diplomatic initiatives could be linked to project a coherent foreign policy. Such was the case with the UK narrative, which portrayed Russia as a consistent violator of international law and a morally questionable nation that allowed the Assad regime to use chemical weapons with impunity. The metaphor that diplomats soon adopted was that of tailoring, as campaign messages could be "tweaked" based on follower feedback. Other examples of narrative-based public diplomacy include the Iranian President and UK Prime Minister's use of Twitter to outline their new foreign policy visions at the 2016 UN General Assembly.

The affordance of digital technologies can, however, lead to direct change in MFAs, whether through the design of digital technologies or the societal metaphors that they elicit. Canada's realization that algorithms prevent diplomats from reaching citizens in need of consular aid led directly to a new norm (such as experimenting with digital tactics to overcome algorithmic confines) and new working routines (such as employing trending hashtags in MFA tweets). Subsequently, Canadian diplomats conceptualized twenty-first-century public diplomacy through algorithmic communication models and not the linear communication models employed during the twentieth century.

In the cases of both the UK's FCO and Israel's MFA, new working routines were employed following the adoption of new metaphors in society at large. Recent years have seen the increased use of the terms "echo chambers" and "filter bubbles" to reference the negative consequences of algorithmic filtering on social media sites. The metaphor of the echo chamber led the FCO to pull publics onto its own blogosphere, where algorithmic filtering did not play an instrumental role. The echo chamber metaphor also led to a new norm in which diplomats regarded digital platforms as tools of mass deception. In the Israeli MFA, the societal metaphor of the filter bubble led to new working routines, such as employing network analysis to identify digital bridges or users who can help burst filter bubbles by introducing contradictory information. Israeli diplomats have in turn adopted the metaphor of algorithmic diplomacy. These examples illustrate yet again how societal conventions, metaphors, and norms diffuse into MFAs through diplomats.

Digital technologies also lead to new working routines by empowering other societal actors. Digital platforms, for instance, enable citizen journalists, bloggers, and new media organizations to frame world events and disseminate these frames to a globally connected public sphere (Clarke, 2015). As such, these actors can influence digital publics' understanding of the world around them. This has led diplomats to conceptualize digital platforms as competitive framing arenas in which they monitor the framing of events by media organizations and negate these frames. Diplomats' need to compete with media actors has also led to the publication of information in near-real time. Some ambassadors, for instance, have taken to publishing information as they access it, while relinquishing partial control over their most prized possession: information. The metaphor that diplomats and ambassadors have subsequently adopted is that of real-time diplomacy.

Lastly, a government's domestic agenda can also lead to changes in MFA norms and routines. The Polish government's attempts to distance Poland from the atrocities of World War II have led to selfie diplomacy activities and the norm of domestic public diplomacy. Table 10.2 identifies the various factors that can influence the norms, values, working routines, and metaphors of diplomats. Each of these warrants further attention from public diplomacy scholars. For instance, scholars may evaluate how societal metaphors diffuse into MFAs through diplomats and lead to new working routines and metaphors. Conversely, scholars may examine how the digital activities of one government or MFA result in normative and functional changes in another. This is an especially exciting avenue of research given findings that MFAs closely monitor one another on social media sites and learn from one another's utilization of digital technologies (Manor, 2016).

While societal metaphors, public diplomacy initiatives, and the affordance of digital technologies all impact MFAs, this book has argued that the demands and logic of the digital society also shape public diplomacy activities. For instance, the digital society is one in which things are done at a distance. This logic has given way to diplomacy at a distance in which virtual embassies are used to overcome spatial limitations and enable diplomats to interact with distant populations instantaneously. The digital society is also one that relentlessly aims to annihilate time and space. Subsequently, diplomats use Twitter to launch global social media campaigns that relegate the entire planet to a single constituency.

Table 10.3 summarizes the examples provided in each chapter pertaining to the digital society's influence on the working routines, norms, and metaphors of MFAs. Table 10.3 demonstrates that the process of digitalization of public diplomacy has normative, conceptual and procedural dimensions. Each dimension, which is influenced by the logic and demands of the digital society, is worthy of scholarly attention. While some scholars may seek to uncover the norms and values that the digital society elicits in diplomats, others may assess how the demands of the digital society shape diplomats' working routines. This book has merely taken a first step in this new direction.

This book has also underscored that digital technologies challenge diplomats' established working routines and norms. Yet scholars may also wish to pay attention to the way digital technologies facilitate the public diplomacy activities of MFAs. Some institutions now operate their own Wikis to crowdsource solutions to pressing problems, while in other MFAs, WhatsApp groups are used to coordinate consular action on a global scale and in real-time. The digitalization of public diplomacy thus also relates to the process by which digital technologies augment the abilities of MFAs and their embassies.

In summary, this book has demonstrated that the "digitalization of public diplomacy" can serve as a new conceptual framework for researching and understanding the influence of digital technologies on the conduct of public diplomacy. The last section of this chapter examines how this book answered challenges posed by four leading scholars.

Table 10.2 Factors that lead to changes in MFA working routines, norms, values and diplomats' self-narrative

Chapters	MFAs	Influencing factor	Changes in working routines	New norms or values	Self-narratives or metaphors employed by diplomats
2	USA	Public diplomacy 2.0 initiative and use of digital platforms to interact with the Muslim world	Establishment of State Department's Digital Outreach Team	Reaching out and listening to digital publics	Conversation
3 and 4	UK, Israel, Iran	Russia's use of digital platforms to spread narratives that contest events in Crimea, depict Eastern European countries as failed states	Creating digital campaigns that promote narratives, pre-authoring content, and adjusting campaign messages to audience feedback	Regarding narratives as prisms through which world events may be narrated and explained	Tailoring
3	Canada	Affordance of algorithms	Using trending hashtags, regarding citizens as boundary spanners that increase digital reach	Experimenting with tactics to "hack" algorithms	Algorithmic communication models
4	UK	Algorithmic filtering and societal metaphor of echo chambers	Pulling publics to FCO platforms, relying on testimonies of ambassadors/high-ranking diplomats	Viewing digital platforms as tools of mass deception	Echo chamber
4	Israel	Algorithmic filtering and societal metaphor of filter bubbles	Using network analysis to identify digital bridges	Relying on peer-to-peer diplomacy	Algorithmic diplomacy

(continued)

Table 10.2 (continued)

Chapters	MFAs	Influencing factor	Changes in working routines	New norms or values	Self-narratives or metaphors employed by diplomats
5	Lithuania	Using big data analysis to inform policy making	Creation of horizontal "listening" teams to monitor digital conversations in foreign countries	Regarding social media content as diplomatic reporting that should inform policy formulation process	Listening
6	Israel	Digital platforms enable multiple actors to frame world events	Monitoring framing of other actors, using media to negate other actors' frames	Challenging diplomats' traditional relationships with the media	Framing competitions
7	Poland	Government's domestic agenda	Monitoring publications and newspapers while demanding retractions, managing that nation's historic image to influence its present-day image	Communicating with national citizenry as a form of domestic public diplomacy	State as a brand
8	UK, EU	Old and new media actors use digital platforms to narrate events as they unfold	Ambassadors share information as they access it	Information-sharing as opposed to information-keeping	Real-time diplomacy

So Long, Farewell, Auf Wiedersehen, Good Night

Responding to a call by James Pamment, this book focused its analysis on the activities of diplomats and diplomatic institutions rather than "new" public diplomacy actors (e.g., connected publics, civil society organizations). While these actors have also been fundamentally impacted by digitalization, this book focused on diplomatic institutions given the scarce attention paid to MFAs thus far. Moreover, in line with Pamment's critique that scholars should map processes of change in MFAs rather than analyze their numbers of followers and the number of journalists they attract on social media sites, this book employed traditional methodologies. These included in-depth interviews, content analysis, framing analysis, and thematic analysis. These methodologies were necessary as this book sought to answer fundamental questions which have yet to be adequately addressed by scholars: How do MFAs define the term "engagement"? What type of content do MFAs publish on Facebook? How do embassies conceptualize the term "listening"? And how have new norms influenced the communicative culture of MFAs? Here again, this book takes but a preliminary first step, which hopefully other scholars will follow.

Building on the works of Jan Melissen, this book situated the study of public diplomacy at the intersection of digital sociology and anthropology. This is because diplomats are social beings, and MFAs are social institutions. It was thus through the lens of the digital society that this book sought to understand how digital technologies influence diplomatic institutions.

Relying on the works of Philip Seib, this book sought to illustrate how the practice of real-time diplomacy has come about and how it shapes the conduct of public diplomacy. This book finds that real-time diplomacy is one domain that elegantly ties together technological affordance, the logic of the digital society, and the norms and working routines of MFAs. The digital society is the real-time society, as digital technologies are used to annihilate space. In turn, digital society members demand to learn about world events as they occur. As media organizations began to meet this demand, so did diplomats, which led to a host of changes in MFAs ranging from the establishment of digital units to the view of social media sites as competitive framing arenas.

Finally, responding to a call by Corneliu Bjola, this book did not fall into the pit of cyber-pessimism. Rather, it sought to offer a frank

Table 10.3 How the logic of the digital society shapes the digitalization of public diplomacy

Chapter	Logic/demands of digital society	Normative (norms and values)	Procedural (working routines)	Conceptual (metaphors, self-narratives)
2	Annihilation of space	Seeking a global constituency	Reaching out to publics assembled on online platforms (e.g., DOT seeks interaction with "Muslim World")	Engagement
3	Competing over attention of digital publics by crafting distinct and authentic iBrand	Obtaining online virality	Adopting unique online tone (e.g., Russian embassy's Lame Duck tweet)	Digital tactics
4	Networks replace hierarchies as organizing structure of society	Networking with digital publics not digital elites	Forming networks with connected individuals (e.g., Israel's networks that burst filter bubbles)	Network diplomacy
5	Everything done in secret must be done in the open	Listening to digital publics, sharing policy initiatives	Collaborative policy formulation (e.g., New Zealand's unique vision)	Democratized public diplomacy
6	Society at a distance	Overcoming limitations of traditional diplomacy	Bypassing critical media landscapes, conversing with populations of enemy states (e.g., Israel's virtual embassy to the Gulf)	Virtual diplomacy
7	Rendering time meaningless	Using a nation's past to make sense of its present	Managing depictions of a nation's past in the media (e.g., Poland's historic selfie)	The state as a brand
8	Too much information, drowning digital publics by design	Sense making	Curating information for followers (e.g., EU ambassador to the USA)	Real-time diplomacy

evaluation of digital technologies' influence on the conduct of public diplomacy. At times, digital technologies have positive outcomes, such as facilitating public diplomacy activities that are truly public-centric. Other times, digital technologies are used to warp the public agenda through disinformation. In addition, this book responded to Bjola's call to examine the relationship between online and offline diplomacy and not treat them as distinct spheres.

As such, this book relied on the works and insights of the aforementioned four scholars and hopefully provided them with as much food for thought as they have provided the author. As stated in the introduction, this book had three goals. Whether it has achieved them can now be determined by the readers, who are invited to turn the page and begin their own study of the digitalization of public diplomacy.

REFERENCES

Archetti, C. (2012). The impact of new media on diplomatic practice: An evolutionary model of change. *The Hague Journal of Diplomacy, 7*(2), 181–206.

Attias, S. (2012). Israel's new peer-to-peer diplomacy. *The Hague Journal of Diplomacy, 7*(4), 473–482.

Bauman, Z., & Lyon, D. (2016). *Liquid surveillance: A conversation.* Cambridge: Polity Press.

Bernal, V. (2014). *Nation as network: Diaspora, cyberspace, and citizenship.* Chicago, USA: University of Chicago Press.

Bjola, C. (2014). The ethics of secret diplomacy: A contextual approach. *Journal of Global Ethics, 10*(1), 85–100.

Bjola, C., & Jiang, L. (2015). Social media and public diplomacy: A comparative analysis of the digital diplomatic strategies of the EU, US and Japan in China. In C. Bjola & M. Holmes (Eds.), *Digital diplomacy theory and practice* (pp. 71–88). Oxon: Routledge.

Bjola, C., & Manor, I. (2018). Revisiting Putnam's two-level game theory in the digital age: Domestic digital diplomacy and the Iran nuclear deal. *Cambridge Review of International Affairs, 31*(1), 1–30.

Castells, M. (2013). *Communication power.* Oxford: Oxford University Press.

Causey, C., & Howard, P. N. (2013). Delivering digital public diplomacy. In R. S. Zaharna, A. Arsenault, & A. Fisher (Eds.), *Relational, networked and collaborative approaches to public diplomacy* (pp. 144–156). New York, NY: Taylor & Francis.

Clarke, A. (2015). Business as usual? An evolution of British and Canadian digital diplomacy as policy change. In C. Bjola & M. Holmes (Eds.), *Digital diplomacy theory and practice* (pp. 111–126). Oxon: Routledge.

Comor, E., & Bean, H. (2012). America's 'engagement' delusion: Critiquing a public diplomacy consensus. *International Communication Gazette, 74*(3), 203–220.

Copeland, D. (2013). Taking diplomacy public: Science, technology and foreign ministries in a heteropolar world. In R. S. Zaharna, A. Arsenault, & A. Fisher (Eds.), *Relational, networked and collaborative approaches to public diplomacy* (pp. 56–69). New York, NY: Taylor & Francis.

Freedman, L. (2014). Ukraine and the art of crisis management. *Survival, 56*(3), 7–42.

Gilboa, E. (2005a). The CNN effect: The search for a communication theory of international relations. *Political Communication, 22*(1), 27–44.

Gilboa, E. (2005b). Global television news and foreign policy: Debating the CNN effect. *International Studies Perspectives, 6*(3), 325–341.

Harnden, T. (2010, November). WikiLeaks: Hillary Clinton states WikiLeaks release is "an attack". *The Telegraph.* Retrieved from https://www.telegraph.co.uk/news/worldnews/northamerica/usa/8169040/WikiLeaks-Hillary-Clinton-states-WikiLeaks-release-is-an-attack.html.

Hayden, C. (2012). Social media at state: Power, practice, and conceptual limits for US public diplomacy. *Global Media Journal, 11*(21), 1–21.

Hocking, B., & Melissen, J. (2015). *Diplomacy in the digital age.* Clingendael: Netherlands Institute of International Relations.

Israeli Ministry of Foreign Affairs. (2017). *Digital diplomacy conference summary* (pp. 6–19). Retrieved from https://www.state.gov/documents/organization/271028.pdf.

Kampf, R., Manor, I., & Segev, E. (2015). Digital diplomacy 2.0? A cross-national comparison of public engagement in Facebook and Twitter. *The Hague Journal of Diplomacy, 10*(4), 331–362.

Lichtenstein, J. (2010, July). Digital diplomacy. *The New York Times.* Retrieved from https://www.nytimes.com/2010/07/18/magazine/18web2-0-t.html.

Lutyens, A. (2018). *Investigating New Zealand's model of democratized public diplomacy* [In person].

Manor, I. (2016). Are we there yet: Have MFA s realized the potential of digital diplomacy? *Brill Research Perspectives in Diplomacy and Foreign Policy, 1*(2), 1–110.

Manor, I., & Crilley, R. (2018). The aesthetics of violent extremist and counter violent extremist communication. In C. Bjola & J. Pamment (Eds.), *Countering online propaganda and extremism: The dark side of digital diplomacy.* Oxon: Routledge.

Manor, I., & Crilley, R. (2019). The mediatization of MFAs: Diplomacy in the new media ecology. *The Hague Journal of Diplomacy.*

Manor, I. & Kampf, R. (2019). Digital nativity and digital engagement: Implications for the practice of dialogic digital diplomacy.

Manor, I., & Soone, L. (2018, January). The digital industries: Transparency as mass deception. *Global Policy*. Retrieved from https://www.globalpolicyjournal.com/articles/science-and-technology/digital-industries-transparency-mass-deception.

Melissen, J. (2005). The new public diplomacy: Between theory and practice. In J. Melissen (Ed.), *The new public diplomacy: Soft power in international relations* (pp. 3–27). New York: Palgrave Macmillan.

Melissen, J., & de Keulenaar, E. V. (2017). Critical digital diplomacy as a global challenge: The South Korean experience. *Global Policy, 8*(3), 294–302.

Metzgar, E. T. (2012). Is it the medium or the message? Social media, American public diplomacy & Iran. *Global Media Journal, 12*(21), 1.

Miller, D., & Horst, H. A. (2017). The digital and the human: A prospectus for digital anthropology. In H. A. Horst & D. Miller (Eds.), *Digital anthropology* (pp. 3–38). London: Bloomsbury Academic.

Mor, B. D. (2012). Credibility talk in public diplomacy. *Review of International Studies, 38*(2), 393–422.

Natarajan, K. (2014). Digital public diplomacy and a strategic narrative for India. *Strategic Analysis, 38*(1), 91–106.

Pamment, J. (2014). The mediatization of diplomacy. *The Hague Journal of Diplomacy, 9*(3), 253–280.

Pamment, J., Nothhaft, H., Agardh-Twetman, H., & Fjallhed, A. (2018). *Countering information influence activities: The state of the art.* Lund University.

Paulauskas, R. (2018). *Understanding Lithuania's digital diplomacy model* [In person].

Quelch, J. A., & Jocz, K. E. (2009). Can brand Obama rescue brand America? *The Brown Journal of World Affairs, 16*(1), 163–178.

Robinson, P. (1999). The CNN effect: Can the news media drive foreign policy? *Review of International Studies, 25*(2), 301–309.

Seib, P. (2012). *Real-time diplomacy: Politics and power in the social media era.* New York, NY: Palgrave Macmillan.

Sheridan, M. B. (2010, November). Hillary Clinton: WikiLeaks release an 'attack on international community'. *The Washington Post*. Retrieved from http://www.washingtonpost.com/wp-dyn/content/article/2010/11/29/AR2010112903231.html.

Sontag, S. (1990). *On photography.* London, UK: Penguin Books.

Stein, J. G. (2011). Diplomacy in the digital age. In J. G. Stein (Ed.), *Diplomacy in the digital age: Essays in honour of Ambassador Allan Gotlieb* (pp. 1–9). Ontario: Signal.

Storr, W. (2018). Book six: The digital self. In W. Storr (Ed.), *Selfie: How the West became self-obsessed* (pp. 243–303). London: Picador.

Tucker, J., Guess, A., Barberá, P., Vaccari, C., Siegel, A., Sanovich, S., ..., Nyhan, B. (2018). *Social media, political polarization, and political disinformation: A review of the scientific literature*. Hewlett Foundation.

United States Advisory Commission on Public Diplomacy. (2017). *Can public diplomacy survive the internet? Bots, echo chambers, and disinformation* (pp. 2–91). Retrieved from https://www.state.gov/documents/organization/271028.pdf.

Van Ham, P. (2013). Social power in public diplomacy. In R. S. Zaharna, A. Arsenault, & A. Fisher (Eds.), *Relational, networked and collaborative approaches to public diplomacy* (pp. 17–28). New York, NY: Taylor & Francis.

Wichowski, A. (2015). 'Secrecy is for losers': Why diplomats should embrace openness to protect national security. In C. Bjola & M. Holmes (Eds.), *Digital diplomacy theory and practice* (pp. 52–70). Oxon: Routledge.

Index

CPSIA information can be obtained
at www.ICGtesting.com
Printed in the USA
LVHW071259180920
666086LV00035B/388